HIP-HOP&RAP

COMPLETE LYRICS FOR 175 SONGS

HAL•LEONARD®

ISBN 0-634-04964-X

Visit Hal Leonard Online at
www.halleonard.com

It is a commonly held misconception that rap and hip-hop are one and the same. What most people are unaware of is that one is actually a component of the other. In theory, hip-hop is a culture, and like all cultures it is made up of several tenets: art (graffiti), dance (breaking), and music (turntablism and rap).

Few would refute the musicality of rap. When stripped to its core it is essentially nothing more than an incredibly raw form of poetry, one having roots that can be traced back to the storytelling practices of the West African griots on up through traditional Negro spirituals, gospel, and the blues. Rap is also, to quote Chuck D. from Public Enemy, "the black man's CNN." This is to say that it is a way for the denizens of the urban ghetto to express themselves verbally, spinning gritty street slang into captivating stories, socio-political commentary, and good time rhymes.

Just as with other forms of poetry, rap itself cannot be defined by a single style. Its purveyors run the gamut, evoking and capturing a wide variety of emotions and viewpoints through the use of carefully chosen vernacular. Artists like Public Enemy and Boogie Down Productions have canons of work that are largely focused on politically charged messages. Meanwhile, A Tribe Called Quest, Queen Latifah, and the Jungle Brothers, among others, preside over Afrocentric or culture-based rhymes. And then, of course, there is hardcore, a misleading term in and of itself. Acts like Run-DMC embodied the essence of hardcore, due to the brash delivery style of their rhymes coupled with the stark, rock-oriented backbeats. However, artists like Ice-T and N.W.A. (generally referred to as gangsta rap) are also considered hardcore thanks to the vitriolic, gang-tinged violence of their lyrics. But rap is not all politics and violence. As everyone knows, life needs to have a lighthearted balance, and to that end there has been no shortage of good time party

Run-DMC

Hayley Madden/Redferns Music Picture Library

rhymes within the medium. Rappers like Tone Loc, Young MC, and DJ Jazzy Jeff and the Fresh Prince (a.k.a. Will Smith) have upheld the tradition of fun, lighthearted, escapist fare. Naturally, newer artists such as Eminem, Master P., Jay-Z, and 50 Cent have managed to coalesce bits and pieces of these earlier subgenres into their own unique hybrids that mix storytelling, bling-bling materialism, and street savvy scenarios into captivating rhyme patterns.

Eminem

While poetry is the undeniable root of rap, the genre as music is equally important and has undergone a wide range of stylistic convergences. As with the more established popular art forms of rock 'n' roll and jazz, rap has been broken down into innumerable subgenres, each with its own unique take on the medium. While the lyrical aspect of rap carries on the age-old tradition of the spoken word, the musical influences careen from reggae to soul, R&B, and jazz. Without surprise it is a transplanted Jamaican who is generally regarded as the father of rap's musical side. DJ Kool Herc was there presiding over his Herculean sound system at the inception of the infamous New York block parties where DJs spun the records while neighborhood MCs freestyled verse over the beats in the 1970s. From those origins, seminal originators like Afrika Bambaata, Grandmaster Flash and the Furious Five, The Funky Four Plus One More, The Cold Crush Brothers, and The Sugarhill Gang manifested the Old School of rap, and were among the first bona fide rap groups to elevate the medium, taking it up from the streets of NYC into the clubs and onto the radio.

The Old School flourished predominantly on the East Coast from the late '70s through the early '80s, with hit records by Grandmaster Flash and The Sugarhill Gang making the all too infrequent trip outside the five boroughs to impact the rest of the world. But with the emergence of Run-DMC in the mid '80s, the genre shifted from the Old to the New School, a period in which a younger breed of MC proved hell-bent on taking the medium to newer, higher levels. The music of their predecessors had laid the groundwork, yet the progenitors of the New School spearheaded the movement of rap into America's musical mainstream via platinum selling albums and hitherto unheard of stadium tours.

The New School also presented the first wave of subgenre classification, usually a sign that a particular style of music is here to stay. Acts such as Boogie Down Productions, Public Enemy, and The Poor Righteous Teachers emerged waving the banner of militantly charged political and social commentary, the latter two outfits spicing up their verbiage with Nation of Islam intonations. Others, like A Tribe Called Quest, The Jungle Brothers, and Queen Latifah mined the more upbeat avenues of cultural diversity, labeling themselves The Native Tongues posse. The likes of LL Cool J and Big Daddy Kane dropped impassioned battle rhymes as well as slick love jams,

Ryan Murphy

Beastie Boys

while artists like The Ultramagnetic MCs kept the idiosyncratic nature of the genre alive and well via offbeat, stream-of-consciousness flows. And of course there was always room for party-oriented, upbeat rap that was as much about having a good time as anything else. Acts like Kid 'N Play, Biz Markie, and the early Beastie Boys provided listeners with the lighter side of rap, comical excursions that played well against the more serious nature of some of their counterparts. New York was a vibrant hot bed of rap during the late '80s and into the early '90s as influential outfits like The Juice Crew, the aforementioned Native Tongues, The Flavor Unit, and others dominated the streets, clubs, and charts.

Conversely, at the same time all of this was popping off, other pockets outside of New York—the undisputed Mecca and birthplace of rap—began emerging as future hotbeds of rap: Philly, Oakland, L.A., Miami, each metropolis having their own,

distinct take on the medium. While the pimp stylings of Too $hort may have captivated the San Francisco Bay area and the thundering BOOM! of Miami Bass had folks down in the Sunshine State giggling in the clubs, it was, without a doubt, the emergence of five men from Compton, California that truly provided rap with its next major movement.

When N.W.A. burst onto the scene in 1987 the face of rap quite literally was changed forever. By exposing a new, incendiary, in-your-face brand

Lynn Goldsmith/Corbis

N.W.A.

of rap, which was quickly labeled "Gangsta," N.W.A. put L.A. on the rap map and turned the world on its musical ears. Guns, drugs, and anti-police rhetoric became the flavor of the day, a stylistic viewpoint that still persists to this day and has helped to elevate (though some might disagree with this term) rap into the pop music stratosphere, causing it to be one of the most influential musical genres since rock 'n' roll.

As influential and controversial as Gangsta Rap was (and to a certain extent still is) there was a backlash of sorts within the rap community, and a new subgenre, The True School, was born as a result. Rising out of the small L.A. venue called The Good Life, the True School returned rap to its spoken word origins and Old School aesthetics, favoring deft wordplay over images of violence and misogyny. Acts like The Freestyle Fellowship, The Pharcyde, and others embraced the historical roots of rap and as a result helped push the medium into new and exciting arenas. Simultaneously, up north, crews like The Souls of Mischief and Digital Underground were doing the same thing, The Souls mining what would eventually become labeled "Backpacker" rap while Digital revealed themselves as the "Sons of the P" (paying homage to George Clinton's seminal Parliament funk entourage).

In the wake of the new millennium, all manner of tags are tossed around when trying to describe the current state of rap music. In Northern California artists like E-40 preside over "Mob" styled beats and attitude, while down in the southern states crews like the Cash Money Millionaires are the undisputed kings of the "Dirty South." Artists like E-LP, Mos Def, and J-Zone continue to keep NYC on the cutting edge of the medium, while savvy impresarios like P. Diddy keep the party going strong within the mainstream via hip fashion and hook-filled pop anthems. And rap continues to emerge from the most unlikely places. The Rhymesayers have Minneapolis locked down thanks to the deft turntable skills of Mr. Dibbs and

P. Diddy

the undisputed rhyme creativity of Atmosphere's Slug. Boston, Seattle, Atlanta, Chicago—the list goes on and on of cities hosting vibrant and influential rap scenes.

All the while mainstream chart toppers like Eminem, Jay-Z, Nas, 50 Cent, and Ja Rule continue to blur the lines between intricate lyrical poetry and gangsta exuberance. Furthermore, the continued relationship between rap and modern R&B in the form of collaborations continues to show the tight-knit unity that exists between these two urban musical forms.

Nas

These days it's almost impossible to categorize much of the rap saturating the airwaves, filling the shelves at the record stores, and finding its way onto the Internet, as it has become an amalgamation of all the styles that preceded it. If one thing is true, the artists of today are incredibly tuned into the history of their art form, no doubt a direct result of both the communal nature of the spoken word tradition as well as the ransacking nature of sampling.

Ja Rule

Yet for all of the diverse musical stylings attached to rap today, as well as the vibrant, often times over-the-top player imagery supplied via videos and the various subgenre labels that still persist—gangsta, hardcore, pop, etc.—rap is still ultimately all about the spoken word and the unique ways in which the modern day MCs choose to deliver it. The lyrics included in this book are not meant to be a means to an end in terms of understanding rap. Rather they should serve as a colorful introduction to the poetic variety that is inherent to the genre.

Spence D.
San Francisco, February 2003

ARTIST INDEX

ARTIST INDEX BY GENRE

GANGSTA RAP

Black Rob

Bone Thugs-N-Harmony

C-Murder

Cypress Hill

DMX

Dove Shack

Dr. Dre

E-40

50 Cent

Ice Cube

Ice-T

Ja Rule

Junior M.A.F.I.A.

Luniz

Mack 10

Mobb Deep

JT Money

Mystikal

N.W.A.

Nate Dogg

Notorious B.I.G.

St. Lunatics

Silkk the Shocker

Snoop Dogg

Sylk-E Fyne

Trick Daddy

Tru

2Pac

Warren G

NEW SCHOOL

Arrested Development

Black Star

Boogie Down Productions

Busta Rhymes

City High

Common

Das EFX

De La Soul

Digable Planets

EPMD

Missy "Misdemeanor" Elliot

Eric B. and Rakim

Fabolous

Fat Joe

Fu-Schnickens

Gang Starr

Guru

Jay-Z

Jurassic 5

Lost Boyz

Monie Love

MC Lyte

Method Man

Nas

Ol' Dirty Bastard

Onyx

OutKast

Redman

The Roots

Solé

Sporty Thievz

3rd Bass

A Tribe Called Quest

US3

Wu-Tang Clan

OLD SCHOOL HIP-HOP

DJ Jazzy Jeff & The Fresh Prince

Heavy D & The Boyz

KRS-One

LL Cool J

Public Enemy

Run-DMC

Salt N Pepa

Sugarhill Gang

POP RAP

Foxy Brown

Coolio

Da Brat

Eminem

Freak Nasty

Wyclef Jean

K.P. & Envyi

Kris Kross

Lil' Kim

Lil' Romeo

Ludacris

MC Hammer

Craig Mack

Mase

Pras Michel

Naughty By Nature

Nelly

Paper Boy

Philly's Most Wanted

Puff Daddy/P. Diddy

Will Smith

Tone Loc

Wreckx-N-Effect

Young MC

CONTENTS

Words and Music by
Jermaine Dupri and Super Cat

ALRIGHT
RECORDED BY KRIS KROSS

Just kick a little somethin' for them cars that be bumpin';
Somethin' real smooth you can just ride to.
Tell me how you feel—here we go.

The day seems nice and bright and everything feels alright.
Went to school without a fool tryin' to pick a fight.
I was loced-out, Kris Kross shirts and khakis,
Lookin' and feelin' like nothin' but a mack.
See, the bell rang and I got my dash.
Feelin' good cause it was the last day of school and I passed.
No moms trippin', so me and my mom went dippin'
To celebrate the fact that I wasn't slippin'.
The downtown scene was packed.
People screamin' from they ride to my ride and to the mack.
I says, "What I am is what I am is who I be."
And y'all should have seen how they was tryin' to get to me.
Cool, cause dissin' and no pay,
They're the reason why we are who we are to this very day.
And all that love keeps me and Chris tight.
Long as we give some love back everything's alright.

Now everything feels alright when I'm rollin' through my 'hood
And I see the one that used to do the dirt, then turned good.
Little kids try to be like me with the braids, the shades, some pants
And some Nikes, G, and yet more letters and the letters sayin',
"I'm your number one fan, could you write me back, man?"
Yes, I try to pass 'em my autograph—I try to do as many as I can.

Now it feels good when I'm rollin' through my 'hood.
Ain't nobody dissin' and a nigga thinks he's too good
'Cause I'm down like four flat tires, just a nappy kid from the proj,
Showin' I can do right and not do wrong.
Rappers and the Bee Gees comin' up strong.
And we ain't got no love for the side.
We only love those who love us back, right?

Now people seem to think what I do is a blast
'Cause I'm always on the road and I'm makin' some cash.
But they don't know, really know, the pressure it is
For some kids tryin' to make it in this here biz.
Early mornin' interviews, then we step to school.
Step from school back to interviews then it's on to other dues.
So, warm it up, Chris; I said, "Warm it up, Chris."
That's what I was born to do.
Now throw your hands in the air and wave from side to side,
If the feelin' that ya feelin' is the feelin' of pride.
See, I ain't come out wack, I come out right
Unlike those 'mose who tried to pass the mic.
It's the Daddy Mac, big thing, everything is real
But you wanna diss 'cause a nigga sold a couple mil'.
Look here, ya can't say nothin' if ya last in a line.
So, when you diss it, just lets me know I'm on your mind.
And it's alright.

Words and Music by Christopher Bridges,
Phalon Alexander, Nathaniel Hale and Billy Nichols

AREA CODES
RECORDED BY LUDACRIS, FEATURING NATE DOGG

CHORUS:
[NATE DOGG]
I've got hoes,
I've got hoes in different area codes,
(Area, area codes, codes,)
Hoes, hoes, in different area codes.
(Area, area codes, codes.)

[LUDACRIS]
Now, you thought I was just 7–7–0 and 4–0–4,
I'm worldwide, bitch, act like y'all don't know.
It's the abominable O-Man,
Globe trot international postman, neighbor dick dope man.
7–1–8s, 2–0–2s.
I send small cities and states I.O.U.s.
9–0–1, matter fact, 3–0–5.
I'll jump off the d-4, we can meet outside.
So control your hormones and keep your drawers on
'Til I close the door, and I'm jumpin' your bone.
3–1–2, 3–1–3,
2–1–5, 8–0–3.
Read your horoscope and eat some hors d'oeuvres,
Then I pump, one these hoes is self-serve.
7–5–7, 4–1–0,
My cell phone says "overload."

CHORUS

[LUDACRIS]
Now, every day is a holiday,
So, stop the violence and the 4–4 away; keeps you to hold today.
5–0–4, 9–7–2,
7–1–3, whatcha gon' do?

You checkin' up the scene, I'm checkin' a hoe tonight
With perpendicular, vehicular homicide.
3–1–4, 2–0–1,
Too much green, too much fun.
I bang cock in Bangkok, can't stop.
I turn and hit the same spot, think not.
I'm the thrilla in Manila, Schlong in Hong Kong.
Pimp 'em like vision, magic Don Juan
Man, after Henry with a coke and a smile
I just pick up the muthafuckin' phone and dial.
I got my condoms in a big-ass sack.
I'm slaggin' this dick like a New Jack, bitch.

[NATE DOGG]

Is it 'cause they like my gangsta walk?
Is it 'cause they like my gangsta talk?
Is it 'cause they like my handsome face?
Is it 'cause they like my gangsta ways?
Whatever it is, they love it and they just won't let me be.
I handle my biz—don't rush me, just relax and let me be free.
Whenever I call, come runnin', 2–1–2 or 2–1–3.
You know that I ball, stop frontin' 'fore I call a substitute freak.

CHORUS

[LUDACRIS]

9–1–6, 4–1–5, 7–0–4.
Shout out to the 2–0–6.
Everybody in the 8–0–8,
2–1–6, 7–0–2, 4–1–4,
3–1–7, 2–1–4, 2–8–1,
3–3–4, 2–0–5, I see ya.
3–1–8, 6–0–1, 2–0–3,
8–0–4, 4–0–2, 3–0–1,
9–0–4, 4–0–7, 8–5–0,
7–0–8, 5–0–2,
Hoes in different area codes…

Words and Music by Priest Brooks, Chan Gaines,
Kevin Gilliam, Kola Marion, Kim Proby and LaToya Williams

BABY IF YOU READY
RECORDED BY SNOOP DOGG

CHORUS:

Baby, if you're ready,
I can give you what you lookin' for.
I guarantee once you stay with me,
You'll want no more.
And baby, if you want it,
You can get it once we close the door, oh.

You know it's somethin' 'bout rollin' wit' a G like you.
Khakis, French braids wrapped up, all keepin' it true.
In the G, yes, when you see us
We won't dub any B–S that wanna see us get domed up.
A-team's on the hang like you bang for years.
Main bitch and I ain't switch, bring 'em to tears.
High pitch, like Eddie Kendricks, when you hit an appendix,
His and her's semis regulate the problem we finish.
Taught me how to grind, separate my nickels from dubs.
G wit' it when you winnin', so I'm showin' you love.
Had to check a broad yesterday for grillin' you down.
Shut it down quick cause me still wanna see these rounds.
Any beef you got, trust we gon' eat it together,
Hold it down in the 'hood while I get this cheddar.
Whether it's all grits or gravy, are we ready to tangle?
It's all G-heavenly, so you labeling me your angel.

CHORUS

You know you chose the best when you singled me out.
I got these cats at close range, I'm contagious to these lames.
We broke game, it's time to kill game, I feel your pain.
They wanna stretch you for some change.
Never worry, boo, I'm not gon' change.
It's gon' still feel the same;
Besides, you said you done with them games.

It ain't no love lost,
I holla that you know you're in, let's lead a new cause.
Boss bitch, and I can put that on the cross.
I'm-a bang for you and we gon' pull through.
So when I release you from them balls
We gon' look up at the stars, notice those stars.
They movin' inside us, to get us, it's gotta meant war.
And as for them broads, you know the rules.
It ain't a chicken alive that can walk in my shoes.
I paid dues; they see the Bentley pull up, brand new.
What the fuck, they better get on the bus.
Remember the dream about the house up on the hill,
Spinnin' the bottle, quarter mil', want a meal.

CHORUS

I got a fetish for thugs, rugged with mean mugs.
When he lonely, he phone me to please 'em.
Jeans saggin', buy size twelve, like, oh damn,
As he unclothed, my mind froze like, oh man.
Underestimated, but for one, she's just a-faded.
Call it how I see it, shoot the game, I'm tryin' to play it.
(So into you and your Davison House shoes.)
To flip a "yay" and choppin' bricks (it figures beyond six)
And he got incarcerated, departed, and used to hate.
He couldn't wait 'til you hit the gates to get activists ready.
Your type is what I'm diggin', gossip heard obsolete.
Plans occurred on the sneak, swing superb and unique.
Keep your pimpin' in tight, addicted, like, all night,
Like, eight inches, six-pack, dig that, it's alright.
Dead G over, burn like opium.
He's a straight trophy, and grip tight, I'm holdin' on.

CHORUS

Here's another one:
Yeah, Doggy's Angels.
And this is a Dogg House production.
My dogs, Battlecat, yeah.
It's how we do it, y'all.
Woof! Ha, ha.
Bow-wow, bow-wow, bow-wow.

Words and Music by Kurtis Walker, William Waring,
Mark Morales, Ronald Miller, Damon Yul Wimbley,
Vincent Lamont Mason and Kelvin Mercer

BABY PHAT
RECORDED BY DE LA SOUL

Phat, phat, uh.
Ain't nothin' wrong with big broads.
Phat, phat.

[POSDNUOS]
It's a sure bet
When I stare into your dark browns, I get
Overwhelmed, overjoyed, overstep
My bounds, on your touch subject:
Your weight, your shape's not what I date.
It's you; my crew don't mind it thick. (Uh-uh.)
Every woman ain't a video chick (Nah.)
Or runway model, anorexic.
I love what I can hold and grab on.
So if you burn it off then keep the flab on.
We gonna stay gettin' our collab' on. (Ow!)
Girl, we gonna stay gettin' our collab' on. (Ooh, ooh.)
We gonna stay gettin' our collab' on.

CHORUS:
[DEVIN THE DUDE]
Don't stuck on things they say, now, you know it's a nasty world.
Tryin' to get with ya anyway, 'cause I know you're a nasty girl.
We ain't never gon' discriminate; so let me compliment your size.
Ooh, ooh, ooh, ooh.

[E. YUMMY BINGHAM]
Yeah, it's nothin' but a little baby phat, phat.
It's nothin' but a little baby phat, phat.
It's nothin' but a little baby phat, phat.
It's nothin' but a little baby phat, phat.
Yeah, it's nothin' but a little baby phat, phat.

[POSDNUOS]

Claim you outta shape, you not outta place. (Uh-uh.)
You keep it natural with no powdered face.
Without exercise, you got the eye
Starin' you down, make me wonder why.
You women wanna frown at them stick figures
On them little-ass girls when a clique of niggaz
Run up and try to hurl game for real;
Your frame holds appeal
In the everyday world, and conceal it is not the way to go.
I'm tellin' you, I had to let ya know,
Ya need to let it all hang.

[DOVE]

Don't be scared to show a little of that thang, thang.
No matter how you weigh it, girl, it's feminine.
Kinda body everybody wanna know. (Yeah, yeah.)
Be the private dancer in my Luke show. (C'mon, girl.)
Skip the salad, girl, bring us both a menu,
Eat the whole box of chocolates I send you. (Heh.)
See, girl, ya more than just an apple in my eye.
I confess, I wanna get up in ya thighs.
The rest'll tell you all the things…

CHORUS

I love it when y'all broads wear it skin-tight. (Skin-tight.)
Make the big panties look like little panties. (Heh.)
Tryin' to lose that bottom, girl, you been right.
I saw who makes ya cookies, I should go and thank ya granny. (Uh-huh.)
Don't mind you bein' conscious of ya calories,
If gettin' paper was fat, man, you'd be salaries.
You ain't in this alone, I got a tummy, too.
Just lemme watch the weight, don't let it trouble you. (C'mere, girl.)
Nine, ten specimen, up in ya jeans.
You buy the size seven and just make it fit.
Slim Fast, lipo, and body creams,
I pray you won't endorse, I got a candle lit.

CHORUS (TWO TIMES)

Words and Music by
Bobby Ervin and Dedrick D'Mon Rolison

BACKYARD BOOGIE
RECORDED BY MACK 10

Yeah, yeah, yeah!

Saturday morning at the crack of sunrise,
Thank the men upstairs for lettin' me open my eyes.
It's a whole new game for me, like T-Lee.
It's nine-seven now, and I'm-a stay sucka free.
Thinkin' about all my homeboys behind bars
As I crease up my khakis and lace up my stars.
And everythang is straight—I'm in the full zone,
Gettin' paper every day; it's all I'm trippin' on.
'Cause ain't nothin' like a ride in Californ–I–A
With the top back, rollin' on a hot, sunny day.
It's one-oh, fo' sho', and I'm clownin' all the rookies
With a pocketful of cookies
And mashin' to the backyard boogie.

Get yo' boogie on, get yo' boogie on, get yo' boogie on,
And then we comin' wit' that.

CHORUS:
Backyard boogie, oogie, oogie, (Yeah,)
Backyard boogie, oogie, oogie. (It's all about that.)
Backyard boogie, oogie, oogie, (Unh,)
Backyard boogie, oogie, oogie. (It's the backyard boogie.)

CHORUS (2 TIMES)

Backyard boogie, oogie, oogie.
Backyard boogie, oogie, oogie.

Now, just throw yo' hands up high in the sky,
Representin' where you from, 'cause it's West 'til I die.
Put it down anywhere, take thangs for what they worth.
Been a rider since birth, and the earth is my turf.
So, I bails in the party, everythang is cool.
It's niggaz in the 'hood I ain't seen since high school
And everybody gots stripes 'cause we all paid dues.
Crimps, Damus, and other clicks and crews
Just gettin' they boogie on, hoochie bitches gettin' loose.
It kinda remind me of the truce in nine-deuce.
I'm even kickin' back, and I'm usually chicken-hawkin'.
The Bloods shootin' dice and the Crips are C-walkin'.
Now the party is jumpin' and the crowd's gettin' bigger—
Looked up and saw four hoes to every nigga.
And it's off the hook, got ya grindin' and humpin'
'Cause the backyard boogie be bumpin'.

(Unh, straight from Inglewood, and you know that it's all good.
You can put that on yo' 'hood, everyday,
And we comin' with that.)

CHORUS (3 TIMES)

Now it's out of control, and everywhere you look
Ain't nothin' but real niggaz; the bustas got shook.
And everybody left with the whole hustla bang,
And Daisy Dukes and khakis do seem to be the thang.
You choose or you lose while you conversatin'
Enough cock to go around, so ain't no playa hatin'.
I want homegirl over there in red
'Cause "Baby got back" like Mix-A-Lot said.
When I keep my composure, kick back like a pro
'Cause Mack 1–0 just refuse to save a hoe.
But it's a done deal, locked up, throw away the key
'Cause she gonna lead a backyard boogie with me.

(Get yo' boogie on, yeah,
Get yo' boogie on, Inglewood.
Get yo' boogie on, Inglewood, pause
Get yo' backyard boogie on.)

CHORUS (3 TIMES)

Straight from Inglewood, and you know that it's all good.
You can put that on yo' 'hood, everyday.
Mackness, mackness, unh!
Get yo' boogie on, get yo' boogie on.
Get yo' boogie on, nigga, get yo boogie on.
Get yo' boogie on, get yo' boogie on, baby, pause,
Get yo' backyard boogie on.
Gangstas don't dance—we boogie.
Niggaz run out and get yo' cookies.
Gangstas don't dance—we boogie.
Mack 10 ain't no motherfucker rookie.

Backyard boogie, oogie, oogie.
Backyard boogie, oogie, oogie.
Backyard boogie, oogie, oogie.
Backyard boogie, oogie, oogie.
Backyard boogie, oogie, oogie.
Backyard boogie, oogie, oogie.
Backyard boogie, oogie, oogie.
Backyard boogie, oogie, oogie.

BEEN AROUND THE WORLD

Words and Music by David Bowie,
Andy Morris, Lisa Stansfield, Ian Devaney,
Notorious B.I.G., Mason Betha,
Sean "Puffy" Combs, Ron Lawrence
and Deric Angelettie

RECORDED BY PUFF DADDY, FEATURING MASE AND NOTORIOUS B.I.G.

INTRO:

[MASE]

Yo, yo, this is Mase, you know what I'm sayin'?
You got niggaz that don't like me for whatever reason.
You got niggaz that don't wanna see my rich,
You got niggaz that's mad 'cause I'm always with they bitch.
Then you got niggaz that just don't like me, you know,
Those P–H–D niggaz; but you know I pop a lot of shit but I back it up though.
See, it's a difference, a lot of niggaz pop shit,
But a lot of niggaz don't make hits, but it's like this whole Bad Boy shit.
We come to bring it to y'all, niggaz: B.I., Puff, Lox, whoever, Black Rob.
If you wanna dance, we dance.

[MASE]

Now trick what? Lace who? That ain't what Mase do.
Got a lot of girls that'd love to replace you.
Tell you to your face, boo, not behind your back.
Niggaz talk shit, we never mind that.
Funny, never find that, puff a dime stack,
Write hot shit and make a nigga say, "Rewind that."
Niggaz know we go against the Harlem gigolo.
Getcha hoe, lick her low, make the bitch, hit the do'.
I represent honies with money—fly guys with gems.
Drive with the tints that be thirty-five percent.
Hoes hope I lay, so I look both ways.
Cop says, "Okay," my tint smoke gray.
Now way nigga leave without handin' me my shit,
Got plans to get my land and my six.
Niggaz outta pen'll understand this shit.
Pop champagne like I won a championship.

CHORUS:
[NOTORIOUS B.I.G. AND PUFF DADDY]
Been around the world and I, I, I,
And we been playa-hated. (Say what?)
I don't know and I don't know why,
Why they want us faded. (Ahehe.)
I don't know why they hate us. (Yeah.)
Is it our ladies? (Uh-huh.)
Or our drop Mercedes? (Uhh, uhh.)
Baby, baby!

[PUFF DADDY]
I was in one bedroom, dreamin' of a million, (Yeah.)
Now I'm in beach houses, cream to the ceiling. (That's right.)
I was a gentleman, livin' in tenements,
Now I'm swimmin' in all the women that be tens. (Hoo.)
Went from Bad Boys to the Crushed Linen Men,
Now my dividends be the new Benjamins. (Uh-huh.)
Hoes of all complexions—I like cinnamon.
Mase, you got some hoes; well nigga, send 'em in. (C'mon.)
What you waitin' for? Let the freak show begin.
How they came? In a truck?

[MASE]
Nah, Puff, that's a Mercedes.

[PUFF DADDY]
C'mere, baby, you don't like the way it's hot and hazy?
Never shady? You must be crazy.
It's ridiculous, how you put your lips on this.
Don't kiss right there, girlfriend, I'm ticklish, (Heheh.)
And I be switchin' fees with a wrist full of Gs.
Nigga, please, I'm the macaroni with the cheese.

CHORUS

[PUFF DADDY AND MASE]
Now Puff rule the world, even though I'm young.
I make it my biz to see that all ladies come. (Yeah.)
Get 'em all strung from the tip of my tongue,
Lick 'em places niggaz wouldn't dare put they faces. (C'mon.)

Before I die, hope I, remake a flow by
In the brand new treasure on a old try.
Now, when my third dry, even when the smoke lie,
Eat the mammy's chocha and drive her loca.
We never ride far, packed five in a car.
Save money for the drinks; I'm about to buy the bar. (Yeah.)
And everywhere I drive, I'm a star,
Little kids all on the corner scream, "That's my car!"

It was days couldn't be fly, now I'm in a T.I.
Come in clubs with B.I., now a nigga V.I. (Uh-huh.)
Rock tons of gold, 'nuff money I fold,
Roll the way you wanna roll, break a hundred out the toe.

CHORUS (2 TIMES)

[PUFF DADDY]
You know, sometimes I gotta ask myself,
Why's there so much jealousy in the world?
Don't look at mine, get yours.

BIG DADDY
RECORDED BY
HEAVY D & THE BOYZ

Words and Music by Dwight Myers,
Tony Dofat and Herbert Brown

What's the deal?
I wanna know, is this love for real?
Or could it be lust that I feel?
You got it going on and on, like a real fly sex appeal,
Extra ill, sun sweet, dress to kill.
You got me open like a token, hot and smokin'
Jacuzzi bubble bath, laughin', jokin',
Candlelight, talking about how you and your ex-man fight.
Tropical sight, beach sand white, listen,
Seafood dishes, wine cooler, champagne wishes
Waterbed head, fine do with some riches.
Our loveable, huggable, I love the cute
As long as I'm around and down, nothin' could ever trouble you.

CHORUS:
I want your body, the way you touch me
Rather be in your Caddie,
You could be my Big Daddy.
Take it slowly, heaven hold me
Rather be in your Caddie,
You could be my Big Daddy.

I spend quality time.
Cute face, haircut like the Halle design.
Keep my day laced up with fly gear and makeup,
But you should see her when she wake up;
Never could we break up.
Shop 'til you drop 'cause the cream don't stop.
Buy you a bunch of outfits; you're sexy, you're hot.
So she could look good for her Hef D
Overweight, loving MC rub you gently.
You know it's C, big CEO sex-o-pee,
Mac game similar next to gold and flex.

You might feel me creeping to your room late at night
It's hell—a waterbed—so get it right.
You be like that, it's that big man, we all up tonight.
Game ear tight, why you caught up in the hype?
That's right, that's miggie, miggie, biggie.
Baby, you're ready for Big Daddy.

CHORUS

You on my mind, like, all the time.
You genuine and you fine,
Missing you like dollar sign.
Boo, be all that and then some,
Job all that mad income,
Hand New Yorkers wish you represent from.
Twenty-four/seven, you the one that I be sweating.
You and time, that's no question,
Couldn't be nothin' less than
Sexually the best, next to me, I confess.
You got me hooked on like phonics, or weed heads on chronic.
Now sit, you're ready, you give me Moore like Demi,
Good and plenty.
Nothin' could compare to you, Boo, I swear to you.
I feel for you, for real for you.
All I wanna do is be with you.
Might even steal for you.
You walk like, talk like sexy
When you kiss me, you bless me,
Undress me, caress me.
On my mind, like, all the time.
You genuine and you fine,
Missing you like dollar sign.

CHORUS

Words and Music by Shawn Carter,
Tim Mosley and Joshua Kyambo

BIG PIMPIN

RECORDED BY JAY-Z, FEATURING BUN B AND PIMP C

[JAY-Z]

Uhh, uh, uh, uh.
It's big pimpin', baby...
It's big pimpin', spendin' Gs.
Feel me, uh-huh uhh, uh-huh.
Ge-ge-geyeah, geyeah.
Ge-ge-geyeah, geyeah.

You know I thug 'em, fuck 'em, love 'em, leave 'em
'Cause I don't fuckin' need 'em.
Take 'em out the 'hood, keep 'em lookin' good.
But I don't fuckin' feed 'em,
First time they fuss, I'm breezin',
Talkin' 'bout, "What's the reasons?"
I'm a pimp in every sense of the word, bitch.
Better trust than believe 'em,
In the cut where I keep 'em
'Til I need a nut, 'til I need to beat the guts,
Then it's "beep, beep," and I'm pickin' 'em up.
Let 'em play with the dick in the truck.
Many chicks wanna put Jigga fist in cuffs,
Divorce him and split his bucks.

Just because you got good head, I'm-a break bread
So you can be livin' it up?
Shit, I parts with nothin', y'all be frontin'.
Me give my heart to a woman?
Not for nothin', never happen.
I'll be forever mackin'.
Heart cold as assassins, I got no passion,
I got no patience, and I hate waitin',
Hoe, get yo' ass in
And let's RI – I – I – I – I – I – IDE, check 'em out now.
RI – I – I – I – I – I – IDE, yeah,
And let's RI – I – I – I – I – I – IDE, check 'em out now.
RI – I – I – I – I – I – IDE, yeah.

CHORUS 1:
[JAY-Z]
We doin' big pimpin', we spendin' cheese.
Check 'em out now,
Big pimpin' on B.L.A.D.s
We doin' big pimpin' up in N.Y.C.
It's just that Jigga Man, Pimp C, and B–U–N B.
Yo, yo, yo, big pimpin', spendin' cheese
We doin' big pimpin', on B.L.A.D.s
We doin' big pimpin' up in N.Y.C.
It's just that Jigga Man, Pimp C, and B–U–N B.

[BUN B]
Nigga, it's the big Southern rap impresario
Comin' straight up out the black barrio.
Makes a mill' up off a sorry hoe
Then sit back and peep my scenario.
Oops, my bad, that's my scenario.
No, I can't fuck a scary hoe.
Now every time, every place, everywhere we go,
Hoes start pointin', they say, "There he go!"
Now these motherfuckers know we carry mo' heat than a little bit.
We don't pull it out over little shit,
And if you catch a lick when I split, then it won't be a little hit.

Go read a book, you illiterate son of a bitch
And step up yo' vocab.
Don't be surprised if yo' hoe stab
Out with me and you see us comin' down on yo' slab,
Livin' ghetto-fabulous, so mad,
You just can't take it.
But, nigga, if you hatin' I, then you wait while I get yo' bitch butt-naked.
Just break it,
You gotta pay like you weigh wet wit' two pairs of clothes on.
Now get yo' ass to the back as I'm flyin' to the track,
Timbaland let me spit my pro's on
Pump it up in the pro-zone.
That's the track that we breakin' these hoes on.
Ain't the track that we flow's on,
But when shit get hot, then the glock start poppin' like ozone.
We keep hoes crunk like Trigger-man,
Fo' real, it don't get no bigger, man.
Don't trip, let's flip, gettin' throwed on the flip,
Gettin' blowed with the motherfuckin' Jigga Man, fool.

CHORUS 2:

[BUN B]

We be big pimpin', spendin' cheese.
We be big pimpin' on B.L.A.D.s.
We be big pimpin' down in P.A.T.
It's just that Jigga Man, Pimp C, and B–U–N B.
'Cause we be big pimpin', spendin' cheese.
And we be big pimpin' on B.L.A.D.s.
'Cause we be big pimpin' in P.A.T.
It's just that Jigga Man, Pimp C, and B–U–N–B, nigga.

[PIMP C]

Uhh…smokin' out, throwin' up, keepin' lean up in my cup.
All my car got leather and wood, in my 'hood we call it "buck."
Everybody wanna ball, holla at broads at the mall.
If he up, watch him fall, nigga, I can't fuck wit' ch'all.
If I wasn't rappin', baby, I would still be ridin' Mercedes,
Chromin', shinin', sippin' daily; no rest until whitey pay me.
Uhh…now what y'all know 'bout them Texas boys
Comin' down in candied toys, smokin' weed and talkin' noise?

CHORUS 2

Words and Music by Notorious B.I.G.

BIG POPPA
RECORDED BY
NOTORIOUS B.I.G.

To all the ladies in the place with style and grace,
Allow me to lace these lyrical douches in your bushes.
Who rock grooves and make moves with all the mommies?
The back of the club, sippin' Moet, is where you'll find me.
The back of the club, mackin' hoes, my crew's behind me.
Mad question askin', blunt passin', music blastin',
But I just can't quit
'Cause one of these honeys, Biggie gots ta creep with,
Sleep with, keep the EP a secret, why not?
Why blow up my spot 'cause we both got hot?
Now check it, I got more mack than Craig and in the bed,
Believe me, sweetie, I got enough to feed the needy; no need to be greedy.
I got mad friends with Benzes
C-notes by the layers—true fuckin' players.
Jump in the Rover and come over,
Tell your friends, "Jump in the GS3," I got the chronic by the tree.

CHORUS:
(I love it when you call me big poppa.)
Throw your hands in the air, if youse a true player.
(I love it when you call me big poppa.)
To the honeys gettin' money, playin' niggaz like dummies.
(I love it when you call me big poppa.)
If you got a gun up in your waist, please don't shoot up the place
'Cause I see some ladies tonight who should be havin' my baby,
Baby.

Straight up, honey, really I'm askin'
Most of these niggaz think they be mackin', but they be actin'.
Who they attractin' with that line, "What's you name? What's your sign?"
Soon as he buy that wine, I just creep up from behind
And ask what your interests are, who you be with,
Things to make you smile, what numbers to dial.

You gon' be here for a while? I'm gon' go call my crew.
You go call your crew,
We can rendezvous at the bar around two.
Plans to leave, throw the keys to Lil' Caese.
Pull the truck up, front, and roll up the next blunt
So we can steam on the way to the telly, go fill my belly
A t-bone steak, cheese eggs, and Welch's grape jelly.
Conversate for a few, 'cause in a few we gon' do
What we came to do, ain't that right, boo? (True.)
Forget the telly, we just go to the crib
And watch a movie in the Jacuzzi, smoke Ls while you do me.

CHORUS

(How ya livin' Biggie Smallz?)
In mansion and Benzes,
Givin' ends to my friends and it feels stupendous.
Tremendous cream, fuck a dollar and a dream.
Still tote gatts strapped with infrared beams.
Choppin' o's, smokin' lye and Optimos.
Money hoes and clothes, all a nigga knows.
A foolish pleasure, whatever.
I had to find the buried treasure, so grams, I had to measure.
However, living better now, Gucci sweater now,
Drop-top BMs, I'm the man, girlfriend.

(Honey, check it.
Tell your friends to get with my friends
And we can be friends,
Shit, we can do this every weekend.
Alright? Is that alright with you?
Yeah, keep bangin'.)

CHORUS

BREAKADAWN
RECORDED BY DE LA SOUL

Words and Music by Stevie Wonder,
Susaye Greene-Brown, William Robinson Jr.,
Rose Ella Jones, Kelvin Mercer,
Vincent Lamont Mason and David J. Jolicoeur

Ah one, two; ah one, two.
Ah one, two; ah one, two.

CHORUS:
Breakadawn…breakadawn.
Ah one, two; ah one, two.
Breakadawn…breakadawn.
Ah one, two; ah one, two.

CHORUS (2 TIMES)

[POSDNUOS]
I was born in the Boogie Down CAT scan
Where my building fell down on the rats and
People sorta super-wanna trip to the penile (Penile.)
While I settle off the shores of the Long Isle.
My father's clean, not mean; my mind is clear when I transmit.
I am the man-ner of the family 'cause the pants fit.
I want to let forensics prove that I can mends,
Groove wit' the thread from needle outta hay; wanna say
Salutations to the nation of the Nubians.
We 'bout to place you in that "3 Feet" of stew again.
I got the frequency to shatter Missus Jones's perm.
I gotta "Hey Love" all the honies 'cause they're short-term.
Tallyin' the score, I'm for the shottie in the jacket.
For the brotha, he's a nigga when he packs it.
So get your butt out the sling; I stung Muhammad, float a note.
That means I'm def, so like the autographs you sign until the—

CHORUS (2 TIMES)

[DOVE]

Aiyyo! Groove with the mayor, hazard on the sayer,
Wave the eighteen mil', eat a still.
Sack or bag of troubles, make the single double.
Loop the coin and join the minimum wage.
I had a plan: if I was the man, I'd throw the J.
Lay it low, and late night I get 'sessed.
Uncondition my ways of the everyday sunset.
Wagin' my days to the one bet
'Cause your breaks'll have the carrot of cakes.
Whether mine, out of line, I breeze into the early mornin',
Freak the W–I–C call and get a tap on my shoulder
'Cause the days of the breaks be just about over.
The arts of the six won't play my bag of tricks.
I got the sevens in my pocket somewhere.
Reasons for the Cheer All-Temperature, here.
I keep it to the rear, and then I'm EXPLODING.

[POSDNUOS]

I be the fab, I be the fabulous; but see, unlike the Chi,
I got the flea up in the name, "ah one, two; ah one, two."
Can't no one bend my cousin' from the Peter Piper like the others
Latchin' onto when I caught the fame "ah one, two; ah one, two."
Pass the task to ask me 'bout the Native Tongue again, my friend.
I tell you Jungle Brothers, "On The Run," "ah one, two; ah one, two."
I'm shakin' hands with many devils in the industry.
Believe the Genesis life fill with stills mean that I'm def.
So like the autographs you sign until the—

CHORUS (2 TIMES)

[DOVE]

We in the morning', at the end, but in the end, I be the is
'Cause in the mix, man, it's alright.
Mama got the rhythm to my daylight.
My pops gots enough, so best to leave or sail the waves
To the Long—I laid the anchor in the 'Ville.
And how I relate, the same side of my gates,
Paper days, mess up my mind, ground zero degrees.
And the weather feels fine.
You opened my eyes, man; thought I had a man,
But how could I eyescan? I wasn't around.
I see the states and played the dates in the far-far,
Gathered the new from the zoas around,
Grew up with Mikey Rodes and played the codes.
Sometimes I don't budge without my cous' Fuzz/Fuzz.
A simple, "How ya do?" Ah, check it from my friends and my crew
Makes it definitely special.

[POSDNUOS]

Now there's no "Shiny, Happy People" in the crew; we play the rough.
I got the huff and puff to blow the house low.
You know, the never-ending factor while I'm over, tell a squid.
"I know an Enterprising brother, so report to the bridge."
I bounce a ball with my left, a squid with my right.
('Cause a squid is just a punk.)
Yo, he deserved to lose the fight.
I might meander 'cross your dream, travelin' up the stream.
Plug the "Wonder, wonder why you're lonesome tonight."
We see the girls scream as if we're shocked by the live shell.
Let's round 'em up and get 'em back to the hotel,
Motel, Holiday Inn-fact!
I'm gonna let you know, once again, that De La Soul
Is sure to show you we will hit the charter harder
Than the normal rappin' fool, "ah one, two; a one, two."

Words and Music by
Marvin Young and Matt Dike

BUST A MOVE
RECORDED BY YOUNG MC

This here's a tale for all the fellas
Try to do what those ladies tell us.
Get shot down 'cause you're over zealous,
Play hard to get and females get jealous.
Okay, smarty, go to a party,
Girls are standin', the crowd is showin' body.
A chick walks by, you wish you could sex her,
But you're standin' on the wall like you was Poindexter.
Next day's function, high-class luncheon.
Food is served and you're stone cold munchin'.
Music comes on, people start to dance,
But then you ate so much you nearly split your pants.
A girl starts walkin', guys start gawkin',
Sits down next to you and starts talkin'.
Says she wanna dance 'cause she likes the groove.
So come on, fatso, and just bust a move!

You're on a mission and you're wishin'
Someone could cure your lonely condition.
You're lookin' for love in all the wrong places—
Not fine girls, just ugly faces.
From frustration, first inclination
Is to become a monk and leave the situation.
But every dark tunnel has a lighter hope,
So don't hang yourself with a celibate rope.
New movie's showin', so you're goin'.
Could care less about the five you're blowin'.
Theater gets dark just to start the show
When you spot a fine woman sittin' in the front row.
She's dressed in yellow, she says, "Hello,
Come sit next to me, you fine fellow."
You run over there without a second to lose;
And what comes next? Hey, bust a move!

If you want it, baby, you've got it.
If you want it, baby, you've got it.
Just bust a move!

In the city, ladies look pretty.
Guys tell jokes so they can seem witty.
Try to tell a joke just to get some play,
Then you try to make a move, and she says, "No way."
Girls a-fakin', goodness-sakin'.
They want a man who brings home the bacon.
Got no money and you got no car,
Then you got no woman and there you are.
Some girls are sophistic, materialistic.
Lookin' for a man makes them opportunistic.
They're lyin' on the beach perpetratin' a tan
So that a brother with money can be their man.
So, on the beach your strollin', real high rollin'.
Everything you have is yours and not stolen.
A girl runs up with somethin' to prove
So don't just stand there, bust a move!

Your best friend Harry has a brother Larry.
In five days from now, he's gonna marry.
He's hopin' you can make it there, if you can,
'Cause in the ceremony you'll be the best man.
You say, "Neat-o," check your libido
And roll to the church in your new tuxedo.
The bride walks down just to start the wedding
And there's one more girl you won't be getting.
So you start thinkin', then you start blinkin'.
A bridesmaid looks and thinks you're winkin'.
She thinks you're kinda cute so she winks back,
And now you're feelin' really fine 'cause the girl is stacked.
Reception's jumpin', bass is pumpin'.
Look at the girl and your heart starts thumpin'.
Says she wants to dance to a different groove.
Now you know what to do, go bust a move!

Words and Music by Gary Grice, Clifford Smith,
Cory Woods, Dennis Coles, Jason Hunter,
Lamont Hawkins, Robert F. Diggs Jr.,
Russell Jones, Isaac Hayes and David Porter

C.R.E.A.M. (CASH RULES EVERYTHING AROUND ME)

RECORDED BY WU-TANG CLAN

INTRO:
[RAEKWON THE CHEF AND METHOD MAN]

What that nigga want, God?

Word up, look out for the cops.

(Wu-Tang five finger shit.)

(Cash rules.)

Word up, two for fives over here, baby.

Word up, two for fives, them niggaz got garbage down the way.

Word up, know what I'm sayin'?

(Cash rules everything around me, C.R.E.A.M. Get…)

Yeah, check this ol' fly shit out.

Word up.

(Cash rules everything around me.)

Take you on a natural joint.

(C.R.E.A.M., get the money.)

Here we, here we go.

(Dollar, dollar bill, y'all.)

Check this shit, yo!

[RAEKWON THE CHEF]

I grew up on the crime side, the *New York Times* side,

Stayin' alive was no jive.

At the second hands, moms bounced on old men,

So then we moved to Shao-Lin land.

A young youth, yo, rockin' the gold tooth, 'Lo goose.

Only way I begin to get off was drug loot.

And let's start it like this son, rollin' with this one and that one,

Pullin' out gatts for fun.

But it was just a dream for the teen who was a fiend.

Started smokin' woolies at sixteen.

And runnin' up in gates and doin' hits for high stakes,
Makin' my way on fire escapes.
No question I would speed for cracks and weed.
The combination made my eyes bleed.
No question I would flow off and try to get the dough
All stickin' up white boys in ball courts.
My life got no better, same damn 'Lo sweater.
Times is rough and tough like leather.
Figured out I went the wrong route
So I got with a sick-ass click and went all out,
Catchin' keys from across seas, rollin' MPVs,
Every week we made forty Gs.
Yo, nigga, respect mine
Or anger the Tec-9.
Ch-chick-POW!
Move from the gate now.

CHORUS:

[METHOD MAN]

Cash rules everything around me.
C.R.E.A.M.
Get the money
Dollar, dollar bill, y'all.

[INSPECTOR DICK]

It's been twenty-two long, hard years of still strugglin',
Survival got me buggin', but I'm alive on arrival.
I peep at the shape of the streets
And stay awake to the ways of the world 'cause shit is deep.
A man with a dream, with plans to make cream
Which failed—I went to jail at the age of fifteen.
A young buck sellin' drugs and such, who never had much,
Tryin' to get a clutch at what I could not, could not…
The court played me short, now I face incarceration.
Pacin', goin' up-state's my destination.
Handcuffed in back of a bus, forty of us.
Life as a shorty shouldn't be so rough.

But as the world turns, I learned life is hell.
Livin' in the world no different from a cell.
Everyday I escape from Jakes givin' chase, sellin' base,
Smokin' bones in the staircase.
Though I don't know why I chose to smoke sess,
I guess that's the time when I'm not depressed.
But I'm still depressed, and I ask, "What's it worth?"
Ready to give up, so to speak, the Old Earth.
Who explained, "Workin' hard may help you maintain
To learn to overcome the heartaches and pain?"
We got stick-up kids, corrupt cops, and crack rocks
And stray shots, all on the block that stays hot.
Leave it up to me while I be livin' proof
To kick the truth to the young black youth.
But shorty's runnin' wild, smokin' sess, drinkin' beer
And ain't tryin' to hear what I'm kickin' in his ear.
Neglected, but now, but yo, it gots to be accepted:
That what? That life is hectic.

CHORUS (4 TIMES)

Niggaz gots to do what they gotta do to get a bill,
Ya know what I'm sayin'?
'Cause we can't just get by no more.
Word up, we gotta get over, straight up and down.

CHORUS (4 TIMES)

Words and Music by Larry Troutman,
Roger Troutman, Woody Cunningham,
Norman Durham, Ronnie Hudson
and Mikel Hooks

CALIFORNIA LOVE (REMIX)

RECORDED BY 2PAC, FEATURING ROGER TROUTMAN AND DR. DRE

CHORUS 1:
[ROGER TROUTMAN]
California knows how to party.
California knows how to party.
In the cit-ay of L.A,
In the cit-ay of good, ol' Watts,
In the cit-ay, the city of Compton,
We keep it rockin'!
We keep it rockin'!

[DR. DRE]
Now, let me welcome everybody to the wild, wild, west:
A state that's untouchable like Elliot Ness.
The track hits ya eardrum like a slug to ya chest.
Pack a vest for your Jimmy in the city of sex.
We in that Sunshine State with a bomb-ass hemp beat,
The state where ya never find a dance floor empty
And pimps be on a mission for them greens.
Lean, mean, money-makin' machines servin' fiends.
I been in the game for ten years, makin' rap tunes,
Ever since honeys was wearin' Sassoon.
Now it's '95 and they clock me and watch me,
Diamonds shinin', lookin' like I robbed Liberace.
It's all good from Diego to tha Bay,
Your city is tha bomb if your city makin' pay.
Throw up a finger if ya feel the same way.
Dre puttin' it down for Californ–I–A.

CHORUS 1

[DR. DRE]
Yeah, now make it shake! Come on!

CHORUS 2:

[ROGER TROUTMAN]
Shake, shake it, baby.
Shake, shake it, shake it, baby.
Shake, shake it, shake it, Cali.
(Shake it, Cali.)
Shake, shake it, baby.
Shake, shake it.
Shake, shake it, mama.
Shake it, Cali.

[2PAC]
Out on bail, fresh outta jail,
California dreamin'.
Soon as I stepped on the scene I'm hearin' hoochies screamin',
Fiendin' for money and alcohol;
The life of a West Side playa, where cowards die, it's our ball.
Only in Cali, where we riot, now rallies
Are live and die in L.A., we wearin' chucks, not Ballies.
(Yeah, that's right.)
Dressed in Locs and khaki suits and ride is what we do.
Flossin', but havin' caution, we can lie with other crews.
Famous because we program
Worldwide, let 'em recognize from Long Beach to Rose Grands.
Bumpin' and grindin' like a slow jam.
It's West Side, so you know the row won't bow down to no man.
Say what you say, but give me that bomb beat from Dre.
Let me serenade the streets of L.A.,
From Oakland to Sacktown, the Bay area in bag down.
Cali is where they put they mack down.
Give me love!

CHORUS 1

[DR. DRE]
Yeah, yeah, now make it shake…uhh.

CHORUS 2 (2 TIMES)

[DR. DRE AND 2PAC]
Uh, yeah, uh, uh, Long Beach in tha house, uh, yeah.
Oaktown, Oakland defiantly in tha house. (Ha, ha, ha.)
Frisco, Frisco.
Hey, you know L.A. up in this Pasadena, where you at?
Yeah, Inglewood, Inglewood always up to no good.
Even Hollywood tryin' to get a piece, baby.
Sacramento, Sacramento, where you at?
Yeah.

[2PAC]
Throw it up y'all, throw it up, throw it up!
I can't see ya! (California love!)
Let's show these fools how we do it on this West Side
'Cause you and I know it's tha best side.

[DR. DRE]
Yeah, that's right.
West Coast, West Coast,
Uh, California love.
California love.
Yeah.

CHORUS 1

OUTRO:
[ROGER TROUTMAN]
Just come on,
Shake, shake it, baby, baby, baby.
Shake it, mama, shake it, mama, shake it, mama.
The Richter scale,
Talkin' about an earthquake on the Richter scale.
In the city of Compton, city of Compton,
Where tha girls shake their booties.
Shake it, mama, shake it, baby, shake, shake it, baby.
Shake, shake it...

Words and Music by Shawn Carter,
Irving Lorenzo, Jeffrey Atkins and Rob Mays

CAN I GET A...
RECORDED BY JAY-Z,
FEATURING AMIL AND JA RULE

[JAY-Z]
What? Well, fuck you, bitch.

Bounce wit' me, wit' me, wit' me, wit' me.
Can you bounce wit' me, bounce wit' me, wit' me, wit' me?
Can you bounce wit' me, bounce wit' me, ge-gi-gi-gi-gi-gi?
Can you bounce wit' me, bounce wit' me, ye-ye-yeah?
Uh-huh, uh-huh, bounce wit' me, bounce wit' me.
Can ya, can ya, can ya bounce wit' me, bounce wit' me?
Ya-yah-yah, ya-ya-yah-yeah, bounce wit' me, bounce wit' me.
Ge-gi, ge-gi-gi-gi-geyeah, bounce wit' me, bounce wit' me.
Get it!

Can I hit in the morning
Without givin' you half my dough?
And even worse, if I was broke, would you want me?
If couldn't get you finer things,
Like all of them diamond rings bitches kill for,
Would you still roll?
If we couldn't see the sun risin' off the shore of Thailand,
Would you ride then, if I wasn't droppin'?
If I wasn't a eight-figure nigga by the name of Jigga,
Would you come around me or would you clown me?
If I couldn't flow futuristic,
Would ya put your two lips on my wood and kiss it?
Could ya see yourself with a nigga workin' harder than nine-to-five,
Content with six, two jobs to survive?
Or do you need a balla, so you can shop and tear the mall up,
Brag, tell your friends what I bought ya?
If you couldn't see yourself with a nigga when his dough is low,
Baby girl, if this is so, yo—

CHORUS 1:
[JAY-Z AND AMIL]

Can I get a, "fuck you"
To all these bitches from all of my niggaz
Who don't love hoes, they get no dough?
Can I get a, "woop, woop"
To all these niggaz from all of my bitches
Who don't got love for niggaz without thugs?
Now you can bounce wit' me, uhh.
Bounce wit' me, bounce wit' me.
Can ya, can ya, can ya bounce wit' me, bounce wit' me?
Uh-uh, Major Coins, Amil-lion.
Bounce wit' me, bounce wit' me.
Uhh, yo, bounce wit' me.
Can ya, can ya, can ya bounce wit' me, bounce wit' me?
Yeah, uh-uh, uh-uh.

[AMIL]

You ain't gotta be rich, but fuck that.
How we gonna get around on your bus pass?
'Fo' I put this pussy on your mustache,
Can you afford me, my niggaz, breadwinners?
Never corny, ambition makes so horny.
Not the fussin' and the frontin',
If you got nuttin', baby boy, you betta
Git up, git out, and get somethin', shit!
I like a lot of P—rada, Alize and vodka,
Late nights, candlelight, then I tear the cock up.
Get it up, I put it down every time it pop up, huh.
I got to snap 'em, let it loose, then I knock ya.
Feel the juice, then I got ya, when you produce a rocka.
I let you meet Momma and introduce you to Poppa,
My coochie remains in a Gucci name.
Never test my patience, nigga, I'm high maintenance,
High class; if you ain't rollin', bypass.
If you ain't holdin', I dash yo.

CHORUS 2:
[JAY-Z]

Now can you bounce for me, bounce for me?
Uhh, can ya, can ya, can ya bounce wit' me, bounce wit' me?
Uhh! Gi-gi-gi-geyeah-geyeah.
Can you bounce wit' me, bounce wit' me?
Uhh! Gi-gi-gi-gi, can you bounce wit' me, bounce wit' me?
Uhh! Yeah!

[JA RULE]

It ain't even a question how my dough flows,
I'm good to these bad hoes.
Like my bush wet and un-dry, like damp clothes.
What y'all niggaz don't know, it's easy to pimp a hoe.
Bitches betta have my money fo' sho'
Before they go runnin' they mouth, promotin' half.
I be dickin', they back out, go 'head, let it out.
I fucks with my gatt out, bounce and leave a hundred,
Makin' 'em feel slutted even if they don't want it.
It's been so long
Since I met a chick ain't on my tips, but then I'm dead wrong,
When I tell 'em, "Be gone."
So hold on to the feelin' of flossin' and platinum
'Cause from now on you can witness Ja the I-con
With hoodies and timbs on, 'cause I thugs my bitches,
VeVe, studs my bitches, then we rob bitch niggaz.
I'm talkin' 'bout straight figures,
If you here, you wit' us.
If not, boo, you know what?
I still fucked you.

CHORUS 3:
[JAY-Z]

Now can ya bounce wit' me, bounce wit' me?
Ge-gi, ge-gi-gi-gi, bounce wit' me, bounce wit' me.
Wit' me, wit' me, wit' me, bounce wit' me, bounce wit' me.
Bounce, bitch, bounce, wit' me, wit' me, wit' me, wit' me.
Can ya bounce wit' me, wit' me?
Ge-gi, uh-huh, uh-huh, uh-huh, uh-huh.
Uh-huh, uh-huh, uh-huh, uh-huh, uh-huh, uh-huh, uh.
Can ya bounce wit' me, bounce wit' me?
Geyeah!

Words and Music by C. Chase, E. Fletcher,
Greg Prestopino, Mashion Myriak,
Mason Betha, Matthew Wilder,
S. Robinson, Steve Jordan,
M. Glover and Sean Combs

CAN'T NOBODY HOLD ME DOWN
RECORDED BY PUFF DADDY, FEATURING MASE

[PUFF DADDY]
Bad Boy, we ain't gon' stop.

[MASE]
Now, with Sean on the hot track, melt like it's hot wax.
Put it out, all the stores, bet you could shop that. (That's right.)
Leave a nigga with a hot hat, frontin' like
Bad Boy ain't got tracks. (Nigga, stop that!)
There's no guy slicker than this young, fly nigga,
Nickel-nine nigga, floss, you die quicker. (Uh-huh.)
This fed time, outta town pie flipper
Turn Cristal into a crooked-I sipper.
Everybody want to be fast, see the cash,
Fuck around they weak staff, get a heat rash.
Anything in Bad Boy way, we smash. (We smash.)
Hundred-G stash, push a bulletproof E-class. (Ehehe.)
I'm through with bein' a player and a baller,
Just want me one bad bitch so I can spoil her.
Mase wanna be the one you respect, even when you're vexed.
Rock Versace silks over spilled brunette.
Got green never seen, so you suck my jewels.
Clutch my ooze, anything I touch, you bruise.
Puff make his own laws, nigga, fuck your rules. (That's right.)
Goodfellas, you know you can't touch us dudes.

[PUFF]
Don't push us 'cause we're close to the edge.
We're tryin' not to lose our heads.
A-hah, hah, hah, hah.

[MASE]
Broken glass everywhere, glass shatters.
If it ain't about the money, Puff, I just don't care. (That's right.)
I'm that Goodfella fly guy, sometimes wiseguys
Spend time in H–A–W–A–I–I.
(Mase, can you please stop smokin' lah-lah?)
Puff, why try? I'm a thug, I'm-a die high.
I be out in Jersey, puffin' Hershey,
Brothers ain't worthy to rock my derby.
Though I'm never drugged, I'm the venom in the club G.
Though I know the thug be wantin' to slug me. (Uh-huh.)
Could it be I move as smoove as Bugsy? (Yeah.)
Or be at the bar with too much bubbly? (C'mon.)
Yo, I think it must be the girls want to lust me,
Or is it simply the girls just love me?
Brothers wanna rock the Rolls, rock my clothes,
Rock my ice, pull out Glocks, stop my life. (Uhh.)
I'm like, "Damn, how these niggaz got they trust?
Used to be my man, how you gonna plot on my wife?"
Do you think you snake me 'cause they hate me?
Or he got his P–H–D: Player Hater's Degree? (Ahaha!)

CHORUS:
[MASE AND PUFF DADDY]
Can't nobody take my pride.
Uh-uh, uh-uh.
Can't nobody hold me down, oh no.
I got to keep on movin'.

[MASE]

Quit that! (Uh-huh.)

You a big cat? (Yeah.)

Where your chicks at? (Yeah.)

Where your whips at? (Where dey at?)

Wherever you get stacks, I'm fix that.

Everything that's big dreams, I did that. (That's right.)

Don't knock me 'cause you're boring.

I'm record sales soaring, straight touring.

Simply a lot of men be wantin' to hear me

'Cause their words just don't offend me. (Uh-uh, uh-uh.)

We spend cheese in the West Indies,

Then come home to plenty cream Bentleys. (Ahehe.)

You name it, I could claim it.

Young, black, and famous with money hangin' out the anus.

And when you need a hit, who you go and get? (Who?)

Bet against us? (Not a sure bet.)

We make hits that'll rearrange your whole set, (That's right.)

And got a Benz that I ain't even drove yet.

Don't push us, 'cause we're close to the edge.

We're tryin' not to lose our heads.

A-hah-hah-hah-hah.

I get the feeling, sometime, that make me wonder

Why you wanna take us under.

[PUFF]

Why you wanna take us under?

CHORUS

CANTALOOP (FLIP FANTASIA)
RECORDED BY US3

Words and Music by Mel Simpson,
Geoff Wilkinson, Rahsaan Kelly
and Herbie Hancock

Ladies and Gentlemen,
As you know, we have something special for you
At Birdland this evening:
A recording for Blue Note Records.

What's that? Yeah, yeah, yeah.
Funky, funky, how
'Bout a big hand now?
Wait, wait a minute.

Groovy, groovy,
Jazzy, funky, pounce, bounce, dance as we
Dip in the melodic sea.
The rhythm keeps flowin', it drips to MC.
Sweet sugar pop
Sugar pop rocks, it pops ya, don't stop
'Til the sweet beat drops.
I show and prove
As a stick in move.
Hear the poems recited on top of the groove.
Smooth mind,
Floating like a butterfly.
Notes start to float subtle like a lullaby.
Brace yourself as the beat hits ya.
Dip, trip, flip fantasia.

(Ah, ah, ah, what's that?
Biggity, biggity, bop.)

Feel the beat drop,
Jazz and hip-hop
Drippin' in the dome, and mix is on the lock.
Funk and fusion,
A fly illusion
Keeps ya coastin' on the river we cruisin'.

Up, down, 'round, and 'round,
'Round the found
But nevertheless, ya gots to get down.
Finesse the freak
Through the beat so unique,
Ya move your feet, the sweat from the heat.

Back to the fact,
I'm the mack
And I know that
The way I kick the rhymes some would call me poet.
Funky flowin' goin'
On with the sweet sound
Caught in the groove, in Fantasia I'm found.
Trip the tour upon the rhymes they soar
To an infinite height, to the realm of the hardcore.
Here we go, off I take ya.
Dip, trip, flip fantasia.

Jump to the jam
Boogie-woogie jam slam.
Bust the dialect, I'm the man in command.
Come flow with the sounds of the mighty mic masta,
When I rhyme on the mic, I bring a sucka disasta.
Beaucoup bucks and I still rock Nike
With the razzle-dazzle star I might be.
Scribble-scrabble
On the microphone I babble
As I flip the funky words into a puzzle.
Yes, yes, yes,
On and on as I flex.
Get with the flow, words manifest.
Feel the vibe from here to Asia.
Dip, trip, flip fantasia.

I've found it at last.
Put it on.

Words and Music by Jerry Duplessis,
Robby Pardlo, Ryan Toby, Giscard Xavier,
Chuck Young, Ahmir K. Thompson,
Leonard Hubbard, Tarik Collins and Scott Storch

CARAMEL

RECORDED BY CITY HIGH

You can say I'm plain Jane, but it's not the same.
I ain't into big names, but I like nice things.
I watch boxing matches and tha football games.
I wouldn't mind being an actress, but I love to sing.
I like goin' out, takin' walks and stuff,
I don't run with many girls 'cause they talk too much.
I enjoy quiet nights at home, curl up next to ya.
Know I ain't a virgin, that don't mean I'm havin' sex with ya.

CHORUS:

Anywhere I go I'm spotted
And every thing I want, I got it.
Five-five with brown eyes,
Smile like the sunrise.

CHORUS

Baby, look me in my eyes
And tell me if I'm the kinda girl you like.
I'm feeling you cause, baby, you're my kinda guy.
Think about it, you just might
Wanna run with this all night long.
And if you want me, we can keep this going.
Let me tell you, I'm the type that's strong.
And I don't trust a lot of men, I'm independent,
I ain't like some other women.

CHORUS (2 TIMES)

Ven aqui, ven aqui, mama.
Baby girl, don't you know you're a star?
See, we could take a little trip to mi casa,
Spend the night popping Cris' in the hot tub.
See, I ain't never seen no girl like you.
Every sexy, little thing you do.
Five-five, brown eyes, with your thick thighs,
Every time I see your smile, it's got me hypnotized.

Mira, (So, can I get your number?)
Mi amor, me ama bien.
Te encantara si quisieras lo tendras.
(I don't know what you said, but I like it.)
Dondequiera, soy notada
Lo que que me hayo me consigo
Y morena, ojos negros
Y sonrisa soleada.

CHORUS

Five-five with brown eyes,
Smile like the sunrise.
Five-five with brown eyes,
Smile like the sunrise.

Words and Music by Christopher Bridges,
Arbie Wilson and Bobbie Sandmanie

CATCH UP
RECORDED BY LUDACRIS, FEATURING INFAMOUS 2-0 AND F.A.T.E.

CHORUS:

All this drinkin' gon' catch up
And all this smokin' gon' catch up.
But some niggaz just really don't give a fuck.
But some niggaz just really don't give a fuck.
All this drinkin' gon' catch up
And all this smokin' gon' catch up.
But some bitches just really don't give a fuck.
But some bitches just really don't give a fuck.

[LUDACRIS]

Now let me be quite frank 'cause I'm that crazy nigga Luda,
Always got a drink and I'm steady smokin' buddha.
I do the evil that'll bend you, when I get you I'm-a sit you down,
Then take it to the mental and essential and clown.
Every chance I get, bitch, I'm hit.
Not by no bullet or no pellet, but the smoke from the can a beer shit.
I might just be too high,
Then put my middle finger up when I'm ridin' by,
And say, "hi" to plenty liquors, and I know it's a sin,
And if ya tell me, "stop drinkin'" I'll just do it again.
So when I get old, I'm-a rock, roll, shake, and shiver
With some blacked-out lungs and a fucked-up liver.

CHORUS

[INFAMOUS 2-0]

Ey yo, I do this for bluntheads and winos, Steward Avenue homes,
Niggaz from G-Row committed to slanging blo,
Doublin' dough twenty-four-seven.
Fuck po-po's, I'm blowin', dro' out the Ac' Legend,

Runnin' wit' two-strike felons
And I pack four-fours like Hank Aaron.
Then'll smoke a L, bust shells,
And dare ya to tell.
Walk up in the club, pretty thug, fucked-up off-head shots,
Sippin' Courvousier, watchin' hoes drop it like it's hot,
Shakin' tits and twats, placing big-face twenties and cock.
Loading clips and glocks,
Knowin' we got the haters hot, the ballin' don't stop.
Just drop more Gs on drink and drugs, live it up, young nigga,
'Cause it's gon' catch up.

CHORUS

[F.A.T.E.]
Now wit' the help of Henn and Coke,
I grab my pen and pad and wrote
Somethin' that I knew was dope and represent the kinfolk.
Pimp a hoe until she broke wit' mo' lines than chopped coke.
Ey yo, it's 2–0, I'm Eastside's King, but I'm a writer with a twist of Amaretto,
My shit even come out better, grab a blunt and put it together.
What a nigga really need, run up in the club and blow a motherfucker 'til he bleed.
Could it be an Icehouse put his lights out, or the club get closed out?
If it's hoes out, I show out, call Tyheed, get Dro'd out.
There's no doubt I love my life, love the light,
Love to write, love the mic.
So take a drag, grab a bag and match up.
Hennessey and bad weed—believe me, it catch up.

CHORUS

[F.A.T.E.]
Git it right.
Ludacris, F.A.T.E., Fullster, Infamous 2–0, ATL.
We are the dirty south's dirtiest, disturbing the peace.

[WHITE GUY]
Hey, bring on the bitches!

CHECK THE RHYME

Words and Music by Leon Ware, Minnie Riperton, Richard Rudolf, Kamal Ibn Fareed, Malik Taylore, Muhammad Ali, Owen McIntyre, Roger Ball, Alan Gorrie, James Stuart, Stephen Ferrone and Malcolm Duncan

RECORDED BY
A TRIBE CALLED QUEST

[Q]
Back in the days on the boulevard on Linden,
We used to kick routines and presence was fittin'.
It was I, the Abstract

[P]
And me, the five-footer,
I kicks the mad style, so step off the frankfurter.

[Q]
Yo, Phife, you remember that routine
That we used to make spiffy, like Mister Clean?

[P]
Um, um, a tidbit; um, a smidgen.
I don't get the message, so you gots to run the pigeon.

[Q] You on point, Phife?
[P] All the time, Tip.
[Q] You on point, Phife?
[P] All the time, Tip.
[Q] You on point, Phife?
[P] All the time, Tip.
[Q] Well, then grab the microphone and let your words rip.

[PHIFE DAWG]
Now here's a funky introduction of how nice I am—
Tell your mother, tell your father, send a telegram—
I'm like an energizer, 'cause, you see, I last long.
My crew is never, ever wack because we stand strong.
Now, if you say my style is wack, that's where you're dead wrong.
I slayed that body in El Segundo, then "Push It Along."

You'd be a fool to reply that Phife is not the man
'Cause you know and I know that you know who I am.
A special shot of peace goes out to all my pals, you see,
And a middle finger goes for all you punk MCs
'Cause I love it when you wack; MCs despise me.
They get vexed; I roll next—can't none contest me.
I'm just a fly MC who's five-foot-three and very brave.
On job remaining, no, I'm chaining 'cause I misbehave.
I come correct in full effect, have all my hoes in check,
And before I get the butt, the jim must be erect.
You see, my aura's positive—I don't promote no junk.
See, I'm far from a bully and I ain't a punk.
Extremity in rhythm—yeah, that's what you heard.
So just clean out your ears and just check the word.

[Q]
Check the rhyme, y'all.
Check the rhyme, y'all.
Check the rhyme, y'all.
Check the rhyme, y'all.
Check the rhyme, y'all.
Check the rhyme, y'all.
Check it out,
Check it out.
Check the rhyme, y'all.
Check the rhyme, y'all.
Check the rhyme, y'all.
Play tapes, y'all.
Check the rhyme, y'all.
Check the rhyme, y'all.
Check it out,
Check it out.

[P]
Back in the days on the boulevard on Linden,
We used to kick routines and presence was fittin'.
It was I, the Phifer.

[Q]
And me, the Abstract
The rhymes were so rumpin' that the brothas rode the 'zack.

[P]
Yo, Tip, you recall when we used to rock
Those fly routines on your cousin's block?

[Q]
Um, let me see—damn, I can't remember.
I receive the message, and you will play the sender.

[P] You on point, Tip?
[Q] All the time, Phife.
[P] You on point, Tip?
[Q] Yeah, all the time, Phife.
[P] You on point, Tip?
[Q] Yo, all the time, Phife.
[P] So play the resurrector and give the dead some life.

[Q-TIP]
Okay, if knowledge is the key, then just show me the lock.
Got the scrawny legs, but I move just like Lou Brock—
With speed; I'm agile, plus I'm worth your while.
One-hundred-percent intelligent black child.
My optic presentation sizzles the retina.
How far must I go to gain respect? Um.
Well, it's kind of simple—just remain your own
Or you'll be crazy, sad, and alone.
Industry rule number four-thousand-and-eighty:
Record company people are shady.
So, kids, watch your back, 'cause I think they smoke crack.
I don't doubt it—look how they act.
Off to better things, like a hip-hop forum.
Pass me the rock and I'll storm the crew and proper.
What you say, Hammer? Proper.
Rap is not pop—if you call it that, then stop.

N.C., y'all, check the rhyme, y'all.
S.C., y'all, check it out, y'all.
Virginia, check the rhyme, y'all.
Check it out, out.
In London, check the rhyme, y'all.

Words and Music by Calvin Broadus,
Andre Young, O'Shea Jackson,
Lorenzo Patterson, Melvin Bradford
and Ricardo Brown

CHIN CHECK
RECORDED BY N.W.A., FEATURING SNOOP DOGG

[911 DISPATCH] 911, forty, reporting.

[WOMAN] Hello, 911? Help me! Help me!

[911] What is your emergency?

[WOMAN] There's someone in my house! There's someone in my house!

[911] Can you please run by your address for me?

[WOMAN] 1–5–1 Shenandoah, Shenandoah.

[911] Ma'am, where inside the house are you?

[WOMAN] (Oh my God!)

[911] Ma'am, where inside the house are you?

[WOMAN] In my room, they're in my room.

[911] Ma'am, calm down. Deputies are on the way. Is the door locked?

[WOMAN] *(Shriek)*

[911] Ma'am?

N–N, dup-dup-dup-double-U, A–A, A–A.

N–N, dup-dup-dup-double-U, A–A, A–A.

[ICE CUBE]

(N–N, dup-dup-dup-double-U, A–A, A–A.)

What the fuck's up, Dre?

[DR. DRE]

You tell me, you talk to Ren?

[MC REN]

I'm right here, nigga.

(N–N, dup-dup-dup-double-U, A–A, A–A.)

Release the hound.

[SNOOP DOGG]

Bow, wow, wow.

Wha, wha, wha, what, what, what.

[ICE CUBE]

I'm a Nigga Wit' an Attitude, thanks to y'all,
And I don't give a fuck, I keep it gangsta y'all.
I'm-a ride for my side in the CPT.
God bless the memory of Eazy-E.
If it wadn't for me, where the fuck you'd be?
Rappin' like the Treacherous Three, fuckin' cowards.
I'd have seen Dre rockin' parties for hours,
And I'd have seen Ren fuckin' bitches from Howard,
And I'd have seen Snoop give away Eddie Bauer's.
So fuck Jerry Heller and the white superpowers.

[MC REN]

This the shit niggaz kill for.
They hear the villain niggaz spittin' with them nigga flows.
Fuck you hoes, fuck you bitch-ass niggaz, too.
Got somethin' for you, broke these niggaz wearin' skirts like the Pope.
Who them niggaz that you love to get? (Us.)
Who them niggaz that you fuckin' wit'? (Us.)
Love the girl, that weed and shit. (What?)
The saga continues with the world's most dangerous group,
Four-deep in the coup. (I'm-a spill it.)

CHORUS:

I'm-a smoke where I wanna smoke. (Fuck that.)
I'm-a choke who I wanna choke. (Fuck that.)
I'm-a ride where I wanna ride. (Fuck that.)
'Cause I'm a nigga for life, so I'm a nigga 'til I dizzy.

(N–N, dup-dup-dup-double-U, A–A, A–A.)
I'm-a smoke where I wanna smoke. (Fuck that.)
I'm-a choke who I wanna choke. (Fuck that.)
(N–N, dup-dup-dup-double-U, A–A, A–A.)
I'm-a ride where I wanna ride. (Fuck that.)
'Cause I'm a nigga for life, so I'm a nigga 'til I dizzy.

[DR. DRE]

A pencil, a pen, or a glock,
I'm the original, subliminal, subterranium, titanium,
Criminal-minded, swift
D–R–E with that fuck-a-bitch shit. (Fuck a bitch.)
A couple o' notes and get you hog-tied in rope.
Dope like tons of coke, cutthroat.
You don't want the pistols to whistle, candy-paint Impala.
I make hoes pop collars.

[SNOOP DOGG]

Goddamn hoes, here we go again.
Fuckin' with Ren, playin' to win.
(He got the) coke in hand, (I got the) juice and gin:
Same shit you was fuckin' wit' way back then.
We keep it crackin' from the actin' to the jackin'.
G'ed up, C'ed up motherfucker, blaze the weed up.
We all on deck, fool, so put your heat up.
I stay on deck, so me don't get wet.

[ICE CUBE]

Look, my nigga, we can scatter like buckshots.
Let's get together, make a record, why the fuck not?

[MC REN]

Why the fuck not?

[DR. DRE]

Why the fuck not?

[SNOOP DOGG]

Why the fuck not?

[ICE CUBE]

'Cause I'm tight as the night
I had to wipe activator off the mic
In nineteen eighty-five.

[SNOOP DOGG]

(N–N, dup-dup-dup-double-U, A–A, A–A.)
Real niggaz, bitch, ya know, ha-hah.

[ICE CUBE]

We cause tragedy erratically,
Systematically, in your house without a key.
How fucked up that'd be.
Gatt'll be near your anatomy, my form of flattery.

[DR. DRE]

Assault and battery, 'cause we comin' with that street mentality.
Straight West Coast rider academy.
Concrete, nigga, that's my reality.

[SNOOP DOGG]

We tend to bus' on the niggaz that get mat at me.

[DR. DRE]

Was it a bitch in the mix?

[SNOOP DOGG]

Well, it had to be.

[DR. DRE]

Lying tricks told them dicks I had a key.
Hoes make the world harder than it have to be.
(Yeah, that's right.)

CHORUS (2 TIMES)

N–N, dup-dup-dup-double-U, A–A, A–A.
N–N, dup-dup-dup-double-U, A–A, A–A.
N–N, dup-dup-dup-double-U, A–A, A–A.
N–N, dup-dup-dup-double-U, A–A, A–A.
N–N, dup-dup-dup-double-U, A–A, A–A.
N–N, dup-dup-dup-double-U, A–A, A–A.

Words and Music by MC Lyte, Rashad Smith,
Nile Rodgers and Bernard Edwards

COLD ROCK A PARTY

RECORDED BY MC LYTE, FEATURING PUFF DADDY

INTRO:
[PUFF DADDY]
I thought I told you that we won't stop.
I rock the party that rocks your body.
I'll rock the party that rocks your body.
Let's go!

CHORUS:
[MC LYTE]
I rock the party that rocks the body.
You rock the party that rocks the body.
I rock the party that rocks the body.
You rock the party that rocks the body.

[MC LYTE]
So what's your status?
I be the baddest "B" to hit the scene since the gangsta lean.
I'm all ears, so what you got to say?
I hope you bubblin' it, baby,
Now bubblin' it my way, let it rain.
Ain't no sword up in the game, still want you the same.
Ain't a thing changed.

Instead of knocking boots we be kicking down Gore-Tex,
Except it ain't raw sex.
Roughnecks throw your hands in the air,
Lemme hear you say, "Oh yeah!"
Trust you me, I blow up shop
About to blow the roof right off of hip-hop.

CHORUS

[MC LYTE]

I'm scorching hot, burn the roof off the jam.
Got a lot, but I'm cramming to understand
How I got it like this.
See, I'm gifted and blessed,
But I'm never lifted off of any kind of stress.
I stress that I'm a witness to this jam,
Lyte the MC is who I am.
I cold rock a party in the B-girl stance.
I rock on the floor, make the fellas wanna dance.
Now I be the uh and it's all good.
And if you understood:
Trust you me, I blow up shop
I ain't nuttin' but real hip-hop.

CHORUS

[MC LYTE]

MC Lyte, some say I'm shady. (That's right.)
That's me: complicated rap star, meet Lyte the MC.
You see, I'm on to you, baby, and your mechanism,
How you hit it when you're in it so hot you keep it fizzling.
No, ooh, ah, she, ooh, and all of that, too.
Keep me wetter than the waters of Kalamazoo.
Nigga, who you come here wit'?
Where your posse at? Uh, leave your boys alone.
Tell her you won't be back, I got the cheese, baby.
My cheddar's better, I got that milk for that Amaretto.
Trust you me, I blow up shop.
Had a little nig' callin' the cops.
Watch me!

CHORUS (2 TIMES)

I rock the party that rocks the body.
You rock the party that rocks the body.

[PUFF DADDY]
Upside down you turning me, turning me.
Round and round you turning me, turning me.

CHORUS

[PUFF DADDY]
Upside down you turning me, turning me.
Round and round you turning me, turning me.
Upside down you turning me, turning me.
Round, round, round, round, round.
Turning me, turning.

Words and Music by
Ice-T and Afrika Islam

COLORS
RECORDED BY ICE-T

Yo, Ease, let's do this.

I am a nightmare-walking, psychopath-talking
King of my jungle, just a gangster stalking,
Living life like a firecracker, quick is my fuse.
Then dead as a death pack, the color I choose.
Red or blue 'cause a blood, it just don't matter.

Sucker die for your life with my shotgun scatters.
We gangs of L.A. will never die, just multiply.

You see they hit us, then we hit them,
Then we hit them and they hit us, man.
It's like a war, ya know what I'm sayin'?
People don't even understand, they don't even know what they dealing with.
You wanna get rid o' the gangs, it's gonna take a lot of work.
But people don't understand the size of this.
This is no joke, man, this is for real.

You don't know me, fool.
You disown me, cool.
I don't need your assistance, social persistence.
And problems I got, I just put my fist in.

My life is violent, but violent is life.
Peace is a dream, reality is a knife.
My colors, my honor, my colors, my all,
With my colors upon me, one soldier stands tall.
Tell me, what have you left me? What have I got?
Last night in cold blood my young brother got shot.
My home got jacked, my mother's on crack,
My sister can't work 'cause her arms show tracks.

Madness, insanity, live in profanity,
Then some punk claimin' they understandin' me.
Give me a break, what world do you live in?
Death is my sect, guess my religion.

Yo, my brother was a gangbanger
And all my homeboys bang.
I don't know why I do it, man, I just do it.
I never had much of nuffin', man.
Look at you, man, you've got everything goin' for yourself
And I ain't got nuffin', man, I've got nuffin'.
I'm living in the ghetto, man.
Just look at me, man, look at me.

My pants are saggin', braided hair,
Suckers stare, but I don't care.
My game ain't knowledge, my game's fear.
I've no remorse, so squares beware.

But my true mission is just revenge.
You ain't in my sect, you ain't my friend.
Wear the wrong color, your life could end.
Homicide's my favorite venge.

Listen to me, man,
No matter whatcha do, don't ever join a gang.
You don't wanna be in it, man.
You're just gonna end up in a mix of dead friends and time in jail.
I know.
If I had a chance like you,
I would never be in a gang, man.
But I didn't have a chance.
You know, I wish I did.

I'll just walk like a giant, police defiant.
You'll say to stop but I'll say that I can't.
My gang's my family, it's all that I have.
I'm a star, on the walls is my autograph.

You don't like it, so you know where you can go.
'Cause the streets are my stage and terror's my show.
Psychoanalyze, tried diagnosing me wise.
It was a joke, brother, the brutality died.

But it was mine, so let me define
My territory; don't cross the line.
Don't try to act crazy 'cause the bitch don't thank me,
You can be read like a punk,
It wouldn't o' made me.
'Cause my color's death, though we all want peace.
But our war won't end, they'll always see.

See, the wars of the street gangs will always get to me, man.
But I don't wanna be down with this situation, man.
But I'm in here, if I had something betta to do,
I think I'd do it.
But right now I'm just down here, boy.
I'm tryin' to get money 'cause I'm smart.
I'm gonna get paid while I'm out here.
I'm gonna get that paper, ya know what I'm sayin'?
If I had a chance like you, maybe I would be in school.
But I'm not; I'm out here living day to day, surviving,
And I'm willing to die for my colors.

Y'all please stop, 'cause I want y'all to live.
This is Ice-T.
Peace.

Words and Music by Sean "Puffy" Combs,
Mark Curry, Robert Plant,
John Bonham and Jimmy Page

COME WITH ME
RECORDED BY PUFF DADDY

Uh-huh, yeah…

Hear my cries; hear my call.
Lend me your ears; see my fall.
See my error; know my faults.
Time halts; see my loss.
Know I'm lacking, back-tracking.
Where I met you, pistol packing.
Itchy finger, trigger-happy,
Tryin' to trap me, pay a rap.
Wire tap, backstab me,
Break the faith, fall from grace.
Tell me lies; time flies.
Close your eyes; come with me.

Come with me.
Yeah, come with me.
Uh-huh, yeah.

You said to trust you; you never hurt me.
Now I'm disgusted, since then, adjusted.
Certainly you fool me, ridicule me,
Left me hangin', now shit's boomerangin'
Right back atcha—think long-range,
Narrow-minded, left me blinded; I co-signed it.
Shit backfired but I'm bouncin' back.
I grind it—not many would bear the pressure.
You comprehend me; you want to end me.
You offend me; it's drama.
Come with me, feel the trauma.

Come with me, yeah.
Yeah, come with me.
I close my eyes and I see you standing there.
I cry tears of sorrow; I die.
Uh-huh, yeah.

I fought my enemies, fought my foes.
Damn these hoes—you're steppin' on my toes.
Back up off me, take your hands off me,
Gimme room to breathe.
I'm not hearin' it; I'm not fearin' it.
I'm up to my ears in it—bullshit, I'm destructive.
Some women find that seductive,
Some say it's lunacy.
But luckily, I've been movin' on.
I ignore you.
Sorry if I bore you; I neglect you.
Don't mean to disrespect you.
Can't you see?

I love you dearly and that's sincerely,
But you annoy me; you can't avoid me.
I'm here to stay forever and
Ever and a day that's never.
I can't let you go.
I can't forget it, why you did it.
I won't permit it; I won't acquit it.
I wanna fight you; I'll fuckin' bite you.
Can't stand nobody like you.
You can't run; you can't hide.
No surprise, close your eyes.
Come with me.

Yeah, Come with me.
Come with me.

Yeah, I like this.
Come on, yeah.
Turn me up.
I need you to turn me up.

Yeah, yeah, yeah, come on now, yeah.

Hear my cries; hear my call.
Lend me your ears.
Uh-huh, you ready now?
Come on, check this out.
Hear my cries; hear my call.
Lend me your ears.
Uh, wanna get this right.
I wanna get this right for you.

Hear my cries; hear my call.
Lend me your ears; see my fall.
See my error; know my faults.
Time halts; see my loss.
Know I'm lacking, back-tracking.
Where I met you, pistol packing.
Itchy finger, trigger-happy,
Tryin' to trap me, pay a rap.
Wire tap, backstab me,
Break the faith, fall from grace.
Tell me lies; time flies.
Close your eyes; come with me.

REPEAT EIGHT TIMES:

I'm-a take you with me.
I wanna bite you; I'll fuckin' bite you.
Can't stand nobody like you.

You can't run; you can't hide.
No surprise, close your eyes.
Come with me.
I'm-a take you with me.
I'm here to stay forever and
Ever and a day that's never.
Come with me.

Uh-huh, yeah...
Come with me.

Words and Music by Pharrell Williams,
Chad Hugo, Al'Baseer Holly and Joel Witherspoon

CROSS THE BORDER
RECORDED BY
PHILLY'S MOST WANTED

[BOOBONIC]

Yo, once the Mo' start drippin', hoes start tippin'.
Tell 'em my name Boo, you know, we all hittin'.
But look, mammy, I got three drinks in me, stuck
And I ain't tryin' 'a talk, I'm tryin' 'a fuck.
If the pussy gets wetter, chicks, I never sweat her.
I'm gettin' all the cheddar, bitch, read the letter.
I patterned the plan,
Get a dick-suck wit' a gatt in my hand.
Bitch, it's thug passion.
Chicks drive by in their whips, they be flashin'.
"Do you know 'Bonic and Lib?" they be askin.
If the bitch wanna ask me shit, I'm-a hit
Attitude just like Cancun, I'm-a trip.
Now nigga's pissed,
Know why? 'Cause I'm the shit.
If you cop a five, imagine what I'm gon' get.
Lights out.
Most Wanted bring the bikes out.
Ball out.
Bitches on the back, ass all out.
I got hoes wit' accents and I don't mean Hyundai's.
My hands touched more bricks than Quamay's.
Ice'll blind you,
For real, dog, believe me.
Only feel comfortable around Ray Charles and Stevie,
So I'm-a take it easy.

CHORUS:
[FEMALE VOICE]
So why don't you run across the border, man?
(I'll run 'cross the border, papa.)
And what will you bring me back, mama?
(You know what I'll bring you back, papa.)
So don't forget (I won't forget.)
To bring me back (To bring you back.)
What I need (What you need.)
Tonight. (Tonight.)
Will you run across the border, mama?
(I'll go 'cross the border, papa.)

[MR.]
I know the fuck you heard.
Give me head while I drive,
Bitch, I like to swerve.
I'll take you to the airport so you can cop them birds.
Now is you 'bout it, mammy?
Whoa, let me know.
Is it the dick, the car, the looks, or the dough?
She said, "Mostly the dough, playa, I don't lie."
I hit once, then hit her girlfriend.
Ask, "When can we all get together again?"
And I never love hoes,
What you talkin' about?
I party your wife, nigga,
You be eatin' her out
And I sat there and told you that I cum in her mouth
And my connect the only reason she be runnin' down south.
Bitches high for a ride, dependin' who key startin'.
So fuck a Jaguar,
Cop a Aston Martin, pardon,
No talkin', Mr., say sparkin'.
Niggaz can't understand,
They still walkin'.

CHORUS

[BOOBONIC]
Hot-ass whips is what they see Boo in.
We play down in C–A–N–C–U–N.
Uh, nice wit' the O-flex outta line.
Cut a bitch off like O.J.
Y'all ain't ready.
That's why all y'all niggaz look hurt
When y'all see me, more Franklin's than Kirk.
And I'm spendin' 'em up wit' GP.
Thick tube socks, I rock like I'm from D.C.
Cash Money as in Juvenile like B.G.

[MR.]
Top down on the Cadillac Allanté.
I get street stripes like Carlito Brigante.
Dog, I tax y'all 'cause it costs to live
And I still show no love like foster kids.
I rent out homes in the 'hood and live across the bridge.
My car's hotter than Negril.
While y'all walk, I wheel.
Oh, your Roley go tick and tock? It's not real.
And keep a piece around my neck, I know worth ya deal, nigga.

CHORUS

Words and Music by Roger Troutman,
David Gamson, Parris Smith and Eric Sermon

CROSSOVER
RECORDED BY EPMD

[ERICK SERMON (E-DUB)]

Erick Sermon's in the house!

Let's get up, let's get down.

Roll wit' the hardcore funk, the hardcore sound.

Let's get wit' this mackadocious funk material.

So simple when I rock wit' the instrumental.

Who am I? (E–D the Green-Eyed Bandit.)

Control my career so I can never get stranded.

But the rest are gettin' brand Nubian,

Changed up they style from jeans to suits and

Thinkin' about a pop record, somethin' made for the station.

For a whole, new relationship of a new type of scene,

To go platinum and clock-mad green.

A.k.a: a sellout, the rap definition.

Get off that, boy, change your mission.

Come back around the block,

Pump Color Me Badd to the, ah, tick-tock.

Let them know your logo, not a black thing,

My background sing, my background sing for the crossover.

The crossover.

[PMD]

The rap era's outta control, brother's sellin' their soul

To go gold; going, going, gone, another rapper sold

(To who?) To pop and R&B, not the M.D.

I'm strictly hip-hop, I'll stick to Kid Capri.

Funk mode, yeah kid, that's how the Squad rolls.

I know your head is bobbin' 'cause the neck knows.

(Not like other rappers.) Frontin' on they fans, the ill

Tryin' to chill, sayin', "Damn, it be great to sell a mill."

That's when the mind switch to the pop tip

(Kid, you're gonna be large.) Yeah, right, that's what the company kicks.

Forget the black crowds, you're wack now,
In a zoot suit, frontin' black, lookin' mad foul.
I speak for the hardcore (rough, rugged, and raw.)
I'm outta here, catch me chillin' on my next tour.
From the U.S. to the white cliffs of Dover,
Strictly underground funk—keep the crossover.
The crossover.

[ERICK SERMON (E-DUB)]

(So whatcha sayin'?) You wanna go pop goes the weasel?
You know you should be rockin' the fans wit' something diesel.
But you insist to piss me off, black,
So I flex the biceps so I can push 'em back.
So real hardcore hip-hop continue to wreck it
And all sucker MCs duck down and get the message.
So ban the crossover, yo, who's wit' me?
(Hit Squad), Yeah, P, hit me.

[PMD]

Another megablast, funky dope style from 'cross yonder.
(So, help me Rhonda, help, help me Rhonda.)
(Yo, from what?) The crossover, yeah crossing you over,
Outta here, gone, peace, nice to know ya. (See ya.)
What a way to go out, "no clout" is what the fans will shout
'Cause you got gassed and took the wrong route.
Came on the scene chillin', freakin' a funky dope line,
But when they finished wit' you: (beep) flatline.
Some say, "There's no business like show business,"
But if this the truth, please explain why is this:
Rappers been around long, makin' mad noise, you see,
Still I haven't seen one rapper livin' comfortably.
No time to pick and wish on a four-leaf clover.
I stick to underground—keep the crossover.
The crossover.

Words and Music by Eric Henry Thomas

DA' DIP
RECORDED BY FREAK NASTY

This goes out to all the women in the world, especially her.
You know it don't even matter your age, don't even matter your color.

You fellas, I ain't forget about y'all.
This is for everybody who like to dance.
Just listen to what I'm sayin'
And do it and take a chance.

CHORUS:

I put my hand upon your hip
When I dip, you dip, we dip.
You put your hand upon my hip
When you dip, I dip, we dip.
I put my hand upon your hip
When I dip, you dip, we dip.
You put yours and I put mine
And we can get down low and roll it 'round.

Get on the floor like I said before,
Y'all remember that down low.
Just put a little dip with it
Now put those hips with it.
Pop it, push it, rock it, roll it, can't control it?
I can hold it, it's all in fun so take a chance.
Just get on the floor and do that dance, y'all.
I know you like it, so don't try to fight it.

Turn around, baby, let me see it from the back, yeah,
I like it like that.
Get up now, roll those hips,
Drop down, double up on those dips.
Freak Nasty wanna see can y'all do this right like me.

CHORUS

Back again with the second verse,
It's all clean, so I'm not gonna curse.
Droppin' bass like a bad habit,
Love all women 'cause I gotta have it.
Comin' at y'all in stereo,
I'm ridin' that thing like a rodeo.
Hang on, baby, 'cause the ride is rough,
And don't stop 'til you get enough.

Have them girls in the front
Now or later just bumpin' that rump.
Raise it up, let me see that round,
Slap it, girl, make it jiggle 'round,
'Round and 'round that rump goes
Where it stop, yo, no one knows.
Freak Nasty wanna see if y'all do this right like me.

CHORUS

ANNOUNCER:
Well alright, y'all, if you ain't dippin',
You must be trippin'.
If you ain't doin' the down low,
You gots to go to the people that's movin' slow on the dance flo'.
Yo! DJ! Pump it up some more.

It's off to the show in the limo
Before the show gotta make that dough,
Pay them girls what they worth,
Slip that money under that skirt.

Take it off, baby, let me see
You might get a little more loot chi-chi.
String-havin, that's so much fun
Playin' that side, between them buns.
Shawty got it on like moms teasin'
And she know I'm starvin'.
Lick you up then like you down,
But I ain't finished, girl, turn around!
Lick you up and down your back
'Cause I'm that freak, I'm freaky like that.
Freak Nasty wanna see can y'all do this right like me.

CHORUS

Settin' it off to another level.
You diggin' Freak Nasty without a shovel?
This is my world; I'm just a squirrel
Tryin' to get a nut, so what's up?
Yo! DJ! When the party's getting slow
Throw on this jam on and watch them flow.
Takin' over like in ninety-four
When I had the world gettin' down low.
New Orleans born ATL-livin',
Freak Nasty's what I'm givin'.
My juice is sweet like Georgia peaches.
Women suck it up like leeches (uh-huh).
It feels so good, you must admit you like this.
Shhhhhhhhhh…
Yeah, y'all know the song,
So come on, won't you sing along?

CHORUS

Words and Music by Pharrell Williams,
Chad Hugo and Mike Tyler

DANGER (BEEN SO LONG)
RECORDED BY MYSTIKAL

You know what time it is, nigga,
And you know who the fuck this is:
Danger! Danger!
Get on the floor!
The nigga right, chea!
Sing it!

CHORUS:
Been so long (Sing it!)
Since he's been on.
So please (Get on the floor!)
Show me (The nigga right chea!)
What it is that you want to see.

Go tell the DJ to put my shit on.
I'm keepin' you niggaz and bitches in jump from the minute I get on.
Taking they shit off, showing they tattoos, screamin' and hollerin' and all.
Got the gift to come up with it, put it together, deliver it,
Make them feel it, bitch, I been on!
Sharp, like you pulled me out the pencil sharpener.
Bad, like that student in the principal's office.
Put rappers in coffins, they dive like dolphins.
I'm the lyrical marvel, officer, watch yourself,
Or fuck around and get beside yourself.
I know, go ahead, though,
Bounce them titties, shake ya ass, drop that pussy, stay in line, hoe.
Fucker think, 'cause you can can,
Cocked up, head down, pussy poppin on a handstand.
Leave that pussy smokin' if you gonna lose something,
Then bend over and bust that pussy open.

CHORUS (2 TIMES)

My fuckin' concert, line around the corner,
Parking cars, niggaz lookin' for they bitch, nothin' on her!
You lookin' good, mama, why? Pshh, what's up, homie?
Sirens, limousines, and the club owner.
Yeah bitch, you!
If you late, ain't no getting in this, bitch,
'Cause it's filling up inside from the floor to the ceiling up
The building ain't big enough!
I'm backstage bouncin', adrenalin building up.
The pussy cutter—did I stutter?
The heart flooder make your woman drawers melt like butter.
Down like Nelly, hype like Belly,
The rhyme seller, kick ass like Jim Kelly!
Stand up, round out, boot up and frown,
Tell a nigga if he wanna try it, then, bitch, come on down!
No sweat, no blood, no tears,
And if I tell you it's the shit then, bitch, that's what it is!

CHORUS (2 TIMES)

Danger! Talkin' 'bout danger!
Motherfucker, look!
Get on the floor!
The nigga right chea!
Danger! (Motherfucker!) Watch your back!
Danger! (Look, look!) Nigga, what? (Look, look!)
Get on the floor!
The nigga right chea!
Get 'em up!

CHORUS (2 TIMES)

Danger! Danger!
Get on the floor!
The nigga right chea!
Sing it!
Danger! Danger!
Get on the floor!
The nigga right chea!
Huh!
This is my motherfuckin' floor!

Words and Music by Trevor Smith, Henry Stone,
Freddy Stonewall, Rashad Smith and Larry Dermer

DANGEROUS

RECORDED BY
BUSTA RHYMES

INTRO:

Hey, another one of them Flipmode joints.
Busta Rhymes, y'all, word, mother, y'all, check it out.
Just swing to the left, swing to the right.
Make ya feel good, feel alright.
One time, feel good, yeah y'all.
Busta Rhymes in the place, y'all.
Makin' you feel real good, y'all.
Flipmode is the Squad in the place, y'all.

Buckwild to all of my niggaz who don't care.
Floss like a bunch of young, black millionaires.
Makin' ya run, me and my Dunn, stackin' my ones,
Floss a lil', invest up in a mutual fund.
Blowin' the horn, a sense of every day I was born.
Never dream I see a nigga landscaping my lawn.
Dangerous, my nigga shit be accurate.
Have to get the flow be so immaculate.

Aiyyo, Aiyyo, watchin' my dough, sippin' Moe',
Slippin' in slow, them pretty bitches sayin' "hello."
Anyway, go 'head and diss, play your Oil of Olay,
Little honey dip within a little cariola.
I don't mean to hold you up, but I got somethin' to say,
Swear to only give you hot shit everyday.
Afraid of us, you know this ain't no game to us.
You strange to us, that's when we gettin' dangerous,
Come on!

CHORUS:

This is serious.
We could make you delirious.
You should have a healthy fear of us
'Cause too much of us is dangerous.
So dangerous, we so dangerous.
My Flipmode Squad is dangerous.
So dangerous, so dangerous.
My whole entire unit is dangerous.

Hold your breath, we swingin' it from right to left.
Word to Wyclef: nigga shit be hot to death.
Stayin' alive, you know only the strongest survive,
Holdin' my heat, under my seat, whippin' my five.
Bassline for all of my people movin' around,
Give me a pound, all of my niggaz holdin' it down,
Cuttin' you up, the new shit, ruckin' you up,
Fuckin' you up, my black hole, suckin' you up.
Back in the days, a nigga used to be ass out.
Now a nigga holdin' several money market accounts.
Blaze the street, and then I would just like to announce,
Feelin' my groove, my jigga-jigga makin' you bounce.
Others is fair, me and my niggaz breakin' the bread,
Straight gettin' it, we got you niggaz holdin' your head.
Afraid of us, you know this ain't no game to us.
You strange to us, that's when we gettin' dangerous,
Come on!

CHORUS

One time, y'all,
Throw your hands real high, y'all.
Yeah, get down, y'all.
Let me see you all, y'all.
Busta Rhymes, Flipmode, y'all.
Nineteen ninety-eight, y'all.
Ha! Get down, y'all.
Let's have a ball, y'all.

Feelin' the heat up in the street, rockin' the beat.
Step up in the club, take me to my reserved seat.
Comin' around, all of my niggaz surround me.
So much bottles of liquor, y'all niggaz'll drown me.
Makin' ya drunk, feelin' the funk, blazin' the skunk,
Stay hittin' with the shit that blow a hole in ya trunk.
Afraid of us, you know this ain't no game to us.
You strange to us, that's when we gettin' dangerous,
Come on!

CHORUS

Words and Music by Larry Troutman,
Roger Troutman, Michael Johnson, Aaron Clarke,
John Fergeson and David Fergeson

DITTY
RECORDED BY PAPERBOY

Yo, this is how I'm comin' for the nine deuce.
Another fat, fat track, so Rhythm D, pour the orange juice
And let's relax while sippin' on yak because it's like that.
I'm claustrophobic, so Paperboy wears prophylactic,
I wear a jimmy for the skins 'cause it's a long trip.
Front row seats,
Aiyyo, I know she's on the nine-inch just to get a piece of the green.
But she's an undertaker.
Now you know the Paper is an around-the-world heartbreaker.
Me be singin' first, but yo, had to have a breakdown.
Playin' you fools, so now you know why my belly's round.
Takin' the rap back up and scoopin' up crowds just like a steel shovel.
Not from the ghetto, but yo, takin' it to another level.
Let the beat ride, but hold on to your women, G,
Cause now that I'm rich, so many women wanna do me,
It make a man say, "Damn."
I'm finally taxin' more play than homie Sam.
But let me speak to the weak, I mean the rookies.
My time is held up extremely for cookies.
Just let me clock this groove in ninety-two.
Hey, you don't bother me and I sure 'nough won't bother you.
And ah, you just watch a brother flowin' like Niagara.
Think before you step because these niggaz just might stag ya.
Although I'm labeled with the black fade,
It's gold Ds on my four, and gold Lex 'cause I got it made.
I broke the veto once again because I had to
And just like Jody Watley, baby girl, I can have you.
Just let me work this track, and yo, any way is okay.
Your place or mine, all night until the next day.
Unh.

Do the ditty if you want to
Because then I can see if I want you.
Just do the ditty-ditty if you want to
Because then I can see if I want you.

Now here we go from the top.
Second verse of the same song
With the conclusion, all should be happy with ding-dong.
It's just a mad park, a grip, G,
It's like every nickel-and-dime nigga be like,
"See, don't you remember me?"
A hustler and it's on with more hoes to le' go.
Keep 'em chunky like Prego so they can play with my eggo.
I have a tendency to flow, start off with my own groove,
Pick up the mic, and all of a sudden, I see high movin'.
Guess it's like magic, and Paperboy is the magician.
If I was a vacuum, I'd be suckin' up competition.
Let it ride again, and yo, believe I got my own thing.
Straight Bahama hoes so miss me with the chick from Soul Train
And I'm-a break my note just to show up tokin'.
Tote on his ass when I scoop him, 'cause we bud smokin.'
A black man tryin' to make it and that ain't no fair,
But just like BeBe and CeCe, "I'll take you there."
Huh.

Do the ditty if you want to
Because then I can see if I want you.
Just do the ditty-ditty if you want to
Because then I can see if I want you.

Now here we go.
Uh, let's take a trip to another land,
Park a grip, come back, and watch the hoes tan.
Jump in the Lex-o and roll out to my cabin.
Believe me, my brother, more hoes than you can imagine.
All on the ding-a-ling, just because the gold rings
But I'm like-a sayin', you ain't heard a damn thing.
Make sure you got the jim-hats strapped for protection
Because to me, my life is more than my erection.
And give me a hand, if you a fan, it ain't over yet
'Cause doin' the ditty with Paperboy makes the ocean sweat.
Leave you kinda startled, like the funk off of Fritos,
Make you man jealous while hoes cheese like Doritos.
It ain't my fault, I play the piper with concern.
And I ain't from Mount Vernon, but a brother's money-earnin'.
And for those disagree and then jack, that's a pity.
Just bob your head for Paperboy and the ditty.
Yeah.

Do the ditty if you want to
Because then I can see if I want you.
Just do the ditty-ditty if you want to
Because then I can see if I want you.

DO FOR LOVE
RECORDED BY 2PAC

Words and Music by Carsten Schack,
Kenneth Karlin, Bobby Caldwell,
Alfonse Kettner and Tupac Shakur

Turn it up loud.
Hahaha! Ahahaha, hey man!
You a little sucker for love, right?
Word up! Hahahahaha!

I shoulda seen you was trouble right from the start,
Taught so many lessons how not to mess with broken hearts;
So many questions.
When this began we was the perfect match,
Perhaps we had some problems but we workin' at it.
And now the arguments are gettin' loud.
I wanna stay but I can't help from walkin' out.
Just throw it away, just take my hand and understand,
If you could see I never planned to be a man.
It just wasn't me, but now I'm searchin' for commitment in other arms,
I wanna shelter you from harm; don't be alarmed.
Your attitude was the cause, you got me stressin'
Soon as I opened up the door with your jealous questions.
Like, "When can I be…", you're killin' me
With your jealousy; now my ambition's to be free.
I can't breathe 'cause soon as I leave, it's like a trap.
I hear you callin' me to come back.
I'm a sucka for love…that's right, sucka for love.

CHORUS:

What you won't do, do for love.
You tried everything, but you don't give up.
What you won't do, do for love.
You tried everything, but you don't give up.

Just when I thought I broke away and I'm feelin' happy,
You try to trap me, say you pregnant, and guess who the daddy?
Don't wanna fall for it, but in this case, what could I do?
So now I'm back to makin' promises to you, tryin' to keep it true.
What if I'm wrong? A trick to keep me on and on.
Tryin' to be strong and in the process, keep you goin'.

I'm 'bout to lose my composure, I'm gettin' close
To packin' up and leavin' notes, and gettin' ghost.
Tell me, who knows a peaceful place where I can go?
To clear my head, I'm feelin' low, losin' control.
My heart is sayin', "leave," oh, what a tangled web we weave
When we conspire to conceive.
And now you gettin' calls at the house, guess you cheatin'.
That's all I need to hear 'cause I'm leavin'.
I'm out the door, never no more will you see me.
This is the end cause now I know you've been cheatin'.
I'm a sucka for love.
Damn sucka for love, sucka for love, sucka for love.

CHORUS

Now he left you with scars, tears on your pillow and you still stay,
As you sit and pray, hoping the beatings'll go away.
It wasn't always a hit and run relationship;
It used to be love, happiness, and companionship.
Remember when I treated you good?
I moved you up to the hills, out the ills of the ghetto 'hood.
Me and you a happy home, when it was on.
I had a love to call me own.
I shoulda seen you was trouble, but I was lost, trapped in your eyes,
Preoccupied with gettin' tossed—no need to lie.
You had a man and I knew it,
You told me, "Don't worry 'bout it, we can do it."
Now I'm under pressure, make a decision 'cause I'm waitin'
When I'm alone I'm on the phone havin' secret conversations, huh.
I wanna take your misery,
Replace it with happiness, but I need your faith in me.
I'm a sucka for love, sucka for love.
Know you ain't right, G,
But yet, I'm a sucka for love.

CHORUS

I'm a sucka for love, sucka for love.
Sucka for love.

Words and Music by Keith Elam,
Chris Martin, Greg Mays and Daryl Barnes

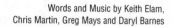

DWYCK
RECORDED BY GANG STARR, FEATURING GREG NICE AND SMOOTH B

INTRO:

[GREG NICE]

Ah yeah, here's another Gang Starr sure shot,
Featuring the one and only,
Uh heh, heh, heh, handily, handily boy, Nice and Smooth,
Hey, hey, hey, hey!

Gang Starr has got to be da sure shot.
Nice and Smooth has got to be da sure shot.
Gang Starr has got to be da sure shot.
Nice and Smooth has got to be da sure shot.

[GREG NICE]

Greg Nice! Greg N–I–C–E,
Droppin' dem basso, ah oui oui.
Rock for a fee, not for free.
Maybe I'll do it for charity.
Now my employer or my employee
Is makin' Greg N–I–C–E very M–A–D.
Don't ever think of jerkin' me.
I work hard for my royalty.

Put lead in ya ass and drink a cup of tea.
Peace to Red Alert and Kid Capri.
Ooh-la-la, ah oui-oui, I say Muhammad Ali,
Ya say Cassius Clay,
I say butter, you say Parkay.
It's alright if ya wanna make me sway.
I'm on the way uptown, took deuce to the tre.
I originate, they duplicate,
I praise the Lord and keep the faith.
It's alright, keep bitin' at da bait.
Ninety-two, uh! One year later,
Peace out Premier, take me out wit' da fader.

[GURU]

I chant eenie-meenie-minie-moe,
I wreck da mic like a pimp pimps hoes.
Here's how it goes: I am a genius, I mean this.
I shake this, you'll take this, I'm kinda fiendish.
You wish that you could come into my neighborhood;
Meaning my mental state.
Still, I'm five-foot-eight.
Crazy as I wanna be
Cause I make it orderly.
You could say I'm sorta da boss, so get lost.
Tha brotha dat will make you change opinions,
Dominions, I'm in them
When it's time to kick shit from the heart,
Plus I get a piece of the action,
I'm feelin' satisfaction from the street crowd reaction.
Chumps pull guns when they feel afraid,
Too late when they dip, in the kick they get sprayed.
Lemonade was a popular drink and still is.
I get more props den stunts den Bruce Willis.
A poet like Langston Hughes,
And can't lose when I cruise
Out on the expressway,
Leavin' the Bodega, I say, "suave."
Premier's got more beats den barns got hay.
Clips are inserted into my gun
So I can take the money, neva have ta run.

[SMOOTH B]
I left my Phillie at home,
Do you have another?
I wanna get blunted, my brother,
Now may I make a mark?
Then make a spark
Over this phat track, or should I say dope beat?
Subtract, delete.
All of the wick-wack that wanna be abstract,
But they lack the new knack
That's comin' from way, way back.
Hey, yo, Premier, please pass that buddha sack,
You hear, we quit?
Now way, bullshit.
I told ya before, we come back wit' more hits.
I provide bright flava, so you could sketch me.
Do me a favor: don't try and catch me.
Slightly ahead of the game, I'm not a lame.
Ask him, he'll tell you the same:
He knows my name.
Smooth, I drop jewels like paraphernalia.
I'm infallible; not into failure,
Like a rhinoceros, my speed is prosperous
And pure knowledge expands from my esophagus.
I write here tonight to bring truth to the light.
My dialogue is my own 'cause Smooth B will neva bite.

Words and Music by Marvin Gaye, David Ritz,
Odell Brown, Joseph Cartagena and Lashan Lewis

ENVY

RECORDED BY
FAT JOE

Yo! This is going out to all my peeps locked down:
Charlie Rock, L.D., all my peeps who passed away, yeah.

I remember when we used to chill on a hill,
When Forest Projects used to be Godsville.
Brothers was whyin, others was cool,
Some hit the island, some smoked fools.
Me, I chose the life of crime since day one.
Thirteen years old, already tryin' to cop a gun.
I never understood why my pops would beat me.
No matter what I did, yo, he'd still mistreat me.
That's why I never listened to a thing he said
And I wasn't just mad when I used to wish him dead.
Instead, me and Ma Dukes kept tight,
Promised that one day everything would be alright.
Fourteen years old, cutting mad classes,
Puffing on a bone, breaking car glasses.
Nothing but dreams of cream on my mind,
Shook motherfuckers on the block droppin' dime.
Everybody knew Joey Crack represented
And if I told them I'd take your life,
Hey yo, I meant it.
That's the way it goes when you deal
With the real fake jacks and get your cap peeled.

CHORUS:
Hey, Joey, let's just get this money.
Brothas, just be whylin.
Hey, Joey, you can't trust nobody.
Brothas, they be triflin'.

Yeah, Momma never said life would be so hard.
Sometimes I find myself alone, just praying to God,
Hoping that today won't be the last.
I mean, just the other day this kid I knew got blasted.
(Say word.) Word, it wasn't over no cash,
It was over some broad who liked to auction off the ass.
He was a cool kid, although we lost him big.
If he was a real nigga, then he wouldn't have got did.
Life's strife and then you die.
Nobody dies of old age, but in the hands of another guy.
That's why I keeps an alibi.
Guiliani wants to see a brother fry,
So I maintain to keep my mind peace focused,
Keep the gatt there in case a nigga wanna smoke this.
Times are difficult on the streets of New York.
It's kinda hard tryin' to hope for and not get caught.
Blue eyes is on my back with intentions of arresting me,
But they won't get the best of me 'cause riches are my destiny.

CHORUS

No one expected me to blow like this.
What was once hand-me-downs is now the best of Atanovich.
Yukon Jeeps creepin' through the streets,
Catchin' the eye of every big booty cheek freak.
Dayton rims so shiny you can see your reflection,
Green plush interior, under the seat, the heat for protection.
Momma, look at me now, got a house in Long Isle
For my spouse and my child.
D.E.L. condos for first-impression hoes,
No more holes in my gibros, strictly denim and clothes.
Airwaves blasting my latest single,
All up in the Mecca Club, making Lucci while I mingle,
Jingle jewels in the face of past enemies.
Eat your heart out, son, you never was a friend to me.

CHORUS

Big Joe, South Bronx,
Represeeeeeeeeeeeent.

Words and Music by Stephen Shockley,
Otis Stokes, Norman Beavers, Marvin Craig, Fred Lewis,
Tiemeyer McCain, Thomas Shelby, Fred Alexander,
Mark Wood, Artis Ivey and Brian Dobbs

FANTASTIC VOYAGE
RECORDED BY COOLIO

Come on, y'all, let's take a ride.
Don't you say "shit," just get inside.
It's time to take your ass on another kind of trip,
'Cause you can't have the hop if you don't have the hip.
Grab your gatt with the extra clip
And close your eyes and hit the switch.
We're going to a place where everybody kick it,
Kick it, kick it, yeah, that's the ticket.
Ain't no bloodin', ain't no crippin',
Ain't no punk-ass nigga's set trippin'.
Everybody's got a stack and it ain't no crack,
And it really don't matter if you're white or black,
I wanna take you there like the Staple Singers,
Put something in the tank and I know that I can bring ya.
If you can't take the heat, get yo' ass out the kitchen,
We're on a mission,

CHORUS:
Come along and ride on a fantastic voyage.
Slide, slide, slippity-slide
With the switches on the block in a sixty-five.
Come along and ride on a fantastic voyage.
Slide, slide, who ride?
Ain't no valley low enough or mountain high.

I'm tryin' to find a place where I can live my life
And maybe eat some steak with my beans and rice,
A place where my kids can play outside
Without livin' in fear of a drive-by.
And even if I get away from them drive-by killers,
I still got to worry about those snitch-ass niggaz.
I keep on searching and I keep on looking,
But niggaz are the same from Watts to Brooklyn.
I try to keep my faith in my people,
But sometimes my people be actin' like they evil.
You don't understand about runnin' with a gang
'Cause you don't gang bang
And you don't have to stand on the corner and slang
'Cause you got your own thang.
You can't help me if you can't help yourself.
You better make a left.

CHORUS:
Come along and ride on a fantastic voyage.
Slide, slide, slippity-slide,
I do what I do just to survive.
Come along and ride on a fantastic voyage.
Slide, slide, who ride?
That's why I pack my forty-five.

Life is a bitch and then you die,
Still tryin' to get a piece of the apple pie.
Every game ain't the same, 'cause the game still remains.
Don't it seem kinda strange ain't a damn thing change?
If you don't work, then you don't eat
And only down-ass niggaz can ride with me.
Hop, hop, hop your five quickly down the block.
Stay sucka-free and keep the bustas off your jock.

You gotta have heart, son, if you wanna go
Watch this sweet chariot swing low.
Ain't nobody cryin', ain't nobody dyin',
Ain't nobody worried, everybody tryin'.
Nothin' from nothin' leaves nothin'.
If you wanna have something, you better start frontin'.
What ya gonna do when the five rolls by?
You better be ready, so you can ride.

CHORUS:

Come along and ride on a fantastic voyage.
Slide, slide, slippity-slide
When you're living in a city, it's do or die.
Come along and ride on a fantastic voyage.
Slide, slide, who ride?
You better be ready when the five roll by.
Just roll along, that's what you do.
Just roll along, that's right.
Just roll along, that's what you do.
Just roll along, that's right.

Do you want to ride with me?

Words and Music by Kenyatta Blake, William Broady, Ryan Corwin,
Cameron Giles, Jeremy Graham, Albert Johnson, Keith Murray,
Reggie Noble, Lawrence Parker, Walter Reed and Joseph Simmons

5 BOROUGHS

RECORDED BY KRS-ONE, FEATURING VIGILANTE, BUCKSHOT, KEITH MURRAY, CAM'RON, KILLAH PRIEST, PRODIGY, REDMAN, AND REVEREND RUN

Yo, yo, brand new KRS, y'all, Maximum Strength.
Five boroughs of death, we rep to death.
Yo, Kris set it for the Bronx…

[KRS-ONE]
We hit 'em and get 'em, we stick 'em and jig 'em,
We pick 'em and kick 'em.
Flippin' them whip and I'm wing-clippin' them lip
'Cause I'm cold sick of them.
Much quicker than them,
Lyrically trickin' and my Tribe be on a Quest like Tip and them
On every avenue, puttin' the full clip in 'em.
Splittin' and strippin' 'em down while spittin' a round
Into them, sound clash, see winnin' them just beginnin' them.
Get rid of every bit of them with the negative idioms.
I don't even consider them,
In the new millennium, we killin' them.
Breeze Deep, Kenny, and Will and them, KRS-One, we thrillin' 'em.
Many battles, we been in them, now we rebuildin' them.
We blaze, fulfillin' them, Keith, Jesse, Jamil, and them.
We originate styles, other be stealin' them.

[VIGILANTE]
You got a good rise in your Rolodex—who flow is next?
Comin' out to fuck with the best, put it in your chest,
Inhale it and hold that, blow it out when I say let go.
Let's see if you can hold your breath by the time I flip to the next flow.

This sho' is real, this is the deal, guns I'm runnin'.
Gotta make it out of town to flip my shit and keep it comin'.
Then bring it back with another sack of raps to blow your back out.
How many of y'all wanna go for yours?
I keep my dogs in the crackhouse.

[BUCKSHOT]
Let's take a walk through Crown Heights,
Steppin' through the city at night, with the shit and two mics.
Form a little lynch mob and stomp through the five boroughs.
Head back to Brooklyn in the Expo.
Back on the block, I see the cops, everybody clockin'
Buckshot, when you see the rocks—me, I got you shocked.
Why not? You see the recipe.
Buckshot, I represent Brooklyn and my nigga, Biggie.

[KEITH MURRAY]
I'm from C–I, L–I, F–L–Y.
Where the niggaz and the bitches stay paid fly and high.
Where a slut'll get mad if you call her a bitch
And a rat'll get mad if you call her a snitch.
Where the rich emerge with the niggaz from the ditch
And it's a myth, they get niggaz from the suburbs, that's herbs.
Yo, this is for my niggaz on the block all day
Who don't give a fuck, waitin' for crime to pay.
Put your money on it, yo, we never fronted.
Long Island got some of the best niggaz that ever done it.
From Riverhead to C.I. to Brentwood to Wyndanch,
Niggaz comin' through will not stand a chance.
From Roosevelt to Freeport to Hempstead to Uniondale,
Comin' deep from the depths of hell.
I'm dead serious, even though you see my smilin'.
Rough enough to break New York from Long Island.

[CAM'RON]
We destroy niggaz, need advice cause I heard 'em sayin', "Jesus Christ."
You should see the sight: cookin' ox-tail, peas, and rice.
Makin' about a G a night, they can't read or write
But I got every creed and type—you need a dyke, baby girl, I see the light.

But sometime y'all get crimey-crimey, grimy-grimy.
But those with a tiny hiney, they get whiny-whiny.
So guard your girl, Harlem World, cock the gun, pop it, son.
Fila fam', illa players, Killa Cam is still the man.
Uptown massive, Uptown the borough.
Uptown let the Cali no sorrow.
Uptown trestle, Uptown, of course.
I grab you, they got me turn up to North.
And if dem turn up North, hurt no, tell de boss.
And if dem tell me off, dey are a bunch of ghosts.
And if dem gal are up, well den, dem know da gal are boss.
De rap dancehall, try on de Moschinos.
And if dem tie me off, dem can call me Cedro.
I put a rap to a sing-a-long in all de crew.
And if da gal a bitch, over the rainbow.

[KILLAH PRIEST]
Yo, hit you with the force of an iron horse.
Tear your face off the planet, leavin' one-third damaged
Wit'cha back cracked, the earth canvas, leavin' mountains slanted.
Rock the earth off the axle,
Crabs to polar bears beneath the sea gravel.
Thoughts be runnin' wild like the Lil' Rascals
Puttin' dinosaurs inside of figure-fours, rip you with nine-inch claws.
Chasin' muthafuckas through malls and clash in the halls.
Beatin' muthafuckas through walls, stompin' through floors
And jumpin' down elevator shafts,
Searchin' for they ass, stayin' low in the grass,
Wearin' a gas mask, wrappin' their hands up in plastic bags
Onstage like a savage goin' made.
What? Yeah, yeah, sooooo!

[PRODIGY]
Yeah, by all means, you know you gotta put Queens on it,
Put cream on it, Q.B., we rep often.
Take over your party, slam dance wit'cha 'hood.
Took your ladies back to the projects with us
Then sent her ass back on the Q-train home.
Satisfied, she learned the words to my thug song.

See, we one big borough of dons with firearms
And we never use those 'til the man act
Other than he's s'posed to, nigga—what I'm s'posed to do?
Shots whistle, damn near missed dat.
Shoes get pissed at.

[REDMAN]
From the tip of my Timbs, to my eyebrows,
The hostile English, Old E widemouth.
Get PCP fiends jumpin' off cliffs,
And if you had the balls, you'd be walkin' off stiff.
My paragraph alone is worth five mics (uh-huh),
A twelve-song LP—that's thirty-six mics (uh-huh).
And while you win on hype (uh-huh), I spit on your snipe
And tell you, "Fuck you," and that bitch on your bike.
Brick City!

[REVEREND RUN]
Aiyyo, now bust it.
Never try me crimey, I'm grimy, so don't deny me.
I be Little like your Rascals and Stymie to fly that hiney.
Buy me keys, to my Benz and my Coupe.
Like Jay and Run and D.M.C.'s—that's the name of my group.
(Now speed it up.)
Beat to the rhythm of the rhyme.
I'm givin' up a dime, there go another line you figured.
Never drivin' by nine, never givin' up a dime if you was never been that nigga.
If you really wanna test me, brother, don't stress me or you just be bowlin'.
It's Reverend like Jesse, brother, that's just me and that's just my colon.

The five boroughs of death, we rep to death.
Step aside, little niggaz, show time, yep.
It's goin' down the moment we inside the spot.
Let's rock 'n' roll, you know the M.O., it gets real
When the five boroughs of death, we rep to death.
Step aside, little niggaz, show time, yep.
It's goin' down the moment we inside the spot.
Let's rock 'n' roll, you know the M.O., it gets hot.

Words and Music by
Osten Harvey and Craig Mack

FLAVA IN YA EAR
RECORDED BY CRAIG MACK

Yo, Mack, I don't even understand
How they didn't understand you in that Mary joint.
Yeah, I know man.
Kick that ol' robotic, futuristic, George Jetson, crazy joint!

Just like uniblab, robotic kickin' flab.
My flavor be the badder chitter-chatter,
Madder than the Mad Hatter.
I bet you my shit come out fatter,
Got the data
To turn your body into antimatter. (Body into antimatter.)
And just like a piece of Sizzlean,
You'll fit inside my stomach
With the eggs and grits between. (Take em down, Mack.)
The king is what I mean.
I mean, my man get a cup
And put some change inside your hand. (Take 'em down, Mack.)
Now hold up,
Let's make this official. (Make it official.)
Everybody, let's agree that MCs need a tissue. (Wake 'em up.)
The funk's my only issue.
I bet your mama miss you
And I bet the Mack take off like an MX missile.
No more of your whinin'.
On the charts climbing
As I make the funk,
Kickin' out more harder than a diamond. (Harder than a diamond.)
And if you didn't know who's rhyming,
I guess I'm gonna say, "Craig Mack" with perfect timing.
You won't be around next year,

My rap's too severe, kickin' mad flava in ya ear.
(Kick it down.)

Here comes the brand new flava in ya ear.
(Brand new flava in ya ear,
Time for new flava in ya ear.)
I'm kickin' new flava in ya ear.
(Mack's the brand new flava in ya ear.)

Craig Mack, one-thousand degrees.
You'll be on your knees
And you'll be burnin', beggin', "please.
Brother, FREEEZE!" (Boy!)
Man's indisputed and deep-booted.
Funk smoke that leaves your brains booted.
This bad MC with stamina like Bruce Jenner,
The winner, tasting MCs for dinner.
You're crazy like that glue. (You're crazy like that glue.)
To think that you
Could out-do
My one-two
That's sick like the flu. (Shake 'em down, Mack.)
Boy, I flip, boy, all the time
'Cause, boy, the rhyme you're kickin' (Ha! Boy!)
Ain't worth a dime.
Seems like there's no competition
In this rap world expedition.
You come around,
I'll knock you out of position. (Knock 'em out!)
No flav' could ever dig a grave
For the Mack, the power pack in black,
Makin' cement crack. (Make it crack.)

And here comes the brand new flava in ya ear.
Mack's the brand new flava in ya ear.
Here comes the brand new flava in ya ear.
(Here comes the brand new flava,
Time for new flava in ya ear.)
In ya ear,
I'm kickin' new flava in ya ear.
(Boy! Mack's the brand new flava in ya ear.
Flavor down.)
Here comes the brand new flava in ya ear.

(Flavor, flavor, here comes the flavor.
Time for new flava in ya ear.)
I'm kickin' flava in ya ear.
(Mack's the brand new flava in ya ear,
Flavor in ya ear, boy.)

Ha! The Mack's dope
With more hope than your Pope,
But for MCs, more knots than rope.
I'd like to break it down,
Down-breakin',
Forsaken,
Lords of MCs shakin'
With this track that my man's makin'.
MCs will run like a bomb threat,
I bet. (What?)
Or better yet, (Huh?)
Make you sweat.
Gettin' hotter than the sun get. (Yup!)
Craig Mack is the flav' that romps from here to Tibet. (Boy!)
I break all rules with my action
That the Mack sends to MCs—stop relaxin'.
This brand new sheriff that's in town,
Gettin' down,
Leavin' bodies buried in the ground. (Rest in peace.)
I set up rhymes for a decoy
To off a bad boy. (Ooh!)
Watch the MCs I destroy and… (Boy!)

Here comes the brand new flava in ya year.
(Time for new flava, time for new flava in ya ear.
Fla-VOR!)
I'm kickin' new flava in ya ear.
(Time for the flav', Mack's the brand new flava in ya ear.
Boy, here comes the Mack.)
Here comes the brand new flava in ya ear.
(Ha! Time for new flava in ya ear,
Wakin' up with flavor!)
I'm kickin' brand new flava in ya ear.
(Mack's the brand new flava in ya ear.
Ha! Boy!)

Words and Music by
Joseph L. Kirkland and Joseph Cartagena

FLOW JOE
RECORDED BY FAT JOE

Ah, yeah!
Da fat gangsta!

CHORUS:
You gotta flow, Joe.
You gotta flow, Joe.
You gotta, gotta, gotta, gotta let 'em know, Joe.
You gotta flow, Joe.
You gotta flow, Joe.
You gotta, gotta, gotta, gotta let 'em know, Joe.

Bust it, check it, watch how I wreck it.
Niggaz watch your back, shit is gettin' hectic.
I catch vibes like Count Basie, sucker won't face me.
I'm so much flavor you can taste me.
I'm underground like a gutter,
You never catch me, stutter,
Everybody knows that I'm butter.
I'm not the man with sensitivity.
The name is Fat Joe, the label's Relativity, huh.
I chop a rapper like a meat cleaver.
I'm burnin' hot, people think I have a fever.
Check it, if niggaz wanna front, then come wit' it,
If you're havin' second thoughts, well then forget it.

See, I dig in my crates, I don't perpetrates.
I got shit sewn like Billy Bathgate.
Beware like Cocoa, yo, I'm not a slow boat.
Got so much dough I va-cate in Acapulco.
Crazy as they come, I'm not the one.
We can do this with the hands or take it to the guns.
You know I can flow, the name is Fat Joe.
I can flow, I can flow, I can flow.

CHORUS

Yeah, yeah, everybody knows Fat Joe's in town.
'Nuff respect for the Boogie Down.
I'm livin' in the Bronx on an ave called Trinity.
My name rings bells within the vicinity.
Peace to the money makers always plottin' mono.
Together we gettin' dough, just like Lucky Luciano.
People always tell me, "Yo, you're dope Joe,"
But I'm not a car, so I don't get gassed like Amoco.
Never ate the paint, no, I'm not a sucker.
Never liked him, so to hell with the fucker.
Always on my own, never sweatin' nobody.
Warm up a crowd like a bottle of Bacardi.
I can kick it this way, I can kick it that-a-way,
I kick a funky style from New York to Piscataway.
Suckers best scam now in ninety-three:
It's all about the Fat Man, peace to Finesse, Showbiz, and A.G.,
Gizmo, Little Hec', and Kool Micskit. (Say what?)
My crew from Uptown
And if you mess around then you'll catch a beat-down.
See, I got this in a smash,
If a rapper steps up, he'll get smoked like a blunt full of hash.
My style of rap is legendary.
Fuck with the man, then you'll end up in the cemetery.
And that's the word to Ma Duke.
I never fake moves, I'll go out like a troop.
So act like you know, the name is Fat Joe.
I can flow, I can flow, I can flow.

CHORUS

Yeah, see, I rip the mic if you put me to a test.
Troop, it gets so bad I make you wanna wear a vest
'Cause I'm too hot to handle,
Rockin' niggaz out like Livingston Bramble.
Rappers come heavy, but, yo, I weigh a ton.
I won't lose weight 'cause I'm not on the run.
I'm on point like a sniper, hyper than hyper.
On the D–L, overlooked by C-Cypher.

Never get caught, I'm on top with my game.
Flip a fat ride, there's no need for a train.
Rappers come close, but they just can't make it.
When it comes to the funk, you know I won't fake it.
Peace to Serge and my right-hand, Flex.
And when I grab the mic, nobody wants to rock next.
The name is Fat Joe, 'cause Joe is livin' phat.
Niggaz gettin' jealous 'cause I got a contract.
But I don't sweat it, I know the style is raw.
You can't compare me to a cornball.
And you know I kick game like a hottie.
Now in ninety-three they should free John Gotti.
If you step, battle, and I'm gonna mash your toes.
You know I got the flow.

CHORUS (3 TIMES)

Words and Music by Kandi L. Burruss, Christopher A. Stewart,
Tonya M. Johnston and Jeffrey Thompkins

4 5 6

RECORDED BY SOLÉ, FEATURING JT MONEY AND KANDI

[JT MONEY]
Yo, what's up?
What's up, baby?
Dis yo' nigga.

[SOLÉ]
Nigga, where da fuck you at?

[JT MONEY]
Mister Good Dick, what you say?

[SOLÉ]
I said, where da fuck you at?

[JT MONEY]
What, how you feel?
How you say you feel?

[SOLÉ]
I feel like you need to get home before yo' shit be outside.

[JT MONEY]
You say you daddy to come through and regulate?
What? Put his thang down, what?
It's all good.

[SOLÉ]
It could be four, five, or six,
You bet' not be nowhere laid up wit' no bitch.
You betta bring that home to momma, don't be playin' and shit.
If you get horny when you out, no need for eyein' them hoes.
Why eat a burger when you got steak and potatoes at home?
A short drive is all it takes, I'm just a phone call away.
Ain't no excuses, muthafucka, for you runnin' astray.
I give it to you when you want it, ain't no other like mine.
Yo' ex-bitch can't fuck with this, so don't be wastin' no time.
The Indian, the black mix, boy, like I told you before
And we can ay-yi-yi the fur rug on my living room floor.
And ain't none hoe gon' bring it like you know I'm-a bring it
And ain't none hoe gon' freak it like you know I'm-a freak it.
And ain't none hoe gon' shake it like you know I'm-a shake it,
And ain't none hoe gon' take it like you know I'm-a take it.
So don't make me come lookin' for you, pull you outta some mix,
Then turn around and bust you in yo' shit for four, five, or six.

CHORUS:
[KANDI]
I don't care if it's four, five, six, seven, eight in the morning,
Boy, you better call me when you think you gettin' horny.
I don't give a damn 'bout who you with
Just as long as you ain't givin' up my shit.
I don't care if it's four, five, six, seven, eight in the morning,
Boy, you better call me when you think you gettin' horny.
I don't give a damn 'bout who you with
Just as long as you ain't givin' up my shit.

[JT MONEY]
You know me as a player, your pipe layer, your all-night stayer.
All up in your sauce when you need your rocks off,
Knock your socks off, baby, off thee chain in this bitch.
Have you wide ass open while I'm slangin' this dick.
Got you lovin' this shit, suckin' and fuckin' this dick.
Wanna go and make some bucks for this dick.
Fightin' all in the club for this dick.

I'm that player that you chose.
Long as you satisfied, baby, fuck them other hoes.
Jus keep my pussy horny so you can put it on me.
Girl, you know I'm the only one who can satisfy your monkey.
Ain't nobody gon' do you like I do
When I put this love stick inside you.
Money-man guaranteed to satisfy you.
Have you open all night like a drive-through.
So bring yo' thang on, so I can get my bang on.
I hope you likes a good fuck because my game strong
And I ain't lyin', girl; you wouldn't if you could quit.
I signs my name on that pussy, Mister Good Dick.
That's my shit.

CHORUS

[SOLÉ]

Now nigga, what you gon' do?
Ugh, let me put this good lovin' on you.
We can do everything that you want to
'Cause I like it real freaky, nigga—don't you?
That's right, don't make no promises.
Can't find none better than momma's is.
Stay wet, stay tight, keep you comin' back.
Go all night, feelin' right, you be lovin' that.
Hell yeah, like wanna make enough moves,
Fuckin' you, boy, like I got somethin' to prove.
Runnin' loose, fuck it, nigga, gotta pay dues.
Make you wanna tell ya boys all about whose.
No talkin' now, come get the good shit.
Make you never wanna fuck another 'hood bitch.
Have ya breakin' off plans to come and lay me.
Muthafucka, don't ever try and play me.

CHORUS

Words and Music by Dante Givens, Courtenay Henderson, Lucas MacFadden,
Mark Ali Postic, Charles Stewart, Marc Stuart and Julius Brockington

FREEDOM
RECORDED BY JURASSIC 5

CHORUS:

Hold on to this feelin'—FREEDOM, FREEDOM!
Hold on to this feelin'—FREEDOM, FREEDOM!

[CHALI 2NA]

Yo! Seldom traveled by the multitude.
The devil's gavel has a couple fooled.
My culture's screwed
'Cause this word is misconstrued.
Small countries exempt from food
'Cause leaders have different views.
You choose.

[AKIL]

What mean the world to me is bein' free.
Live and let live and just let it be.
(Let it be.)
Love, peace, and harmony,
One universal family,
One god, one aim, and one destiny.

[MARC 7]

Oh, yeah?
Imagine life without a choice at all,
Given a vote without a voice at all.
These be the problems that we face:
I'm talkin' poverty and race.
But no matter what the case, we gotta—

CHORUS

[SOUP]

Yo! I'm the first candidate to hate.
Had to beat on the drum to communicate.
For what was to come to those who were hung?
They would decapitate the tongue
If you would mention the word
FREEDOM.

[CHALI 2NA]

Got people screamin', "Free Mumia Jamal!"
But two out of three of y'all will be at the mall.
I'm heated wit' y'all.
The defeated will fall,
Incomplete an' unsolved
When the word "freedom" 's involved.

[AKIL]

Yo! My forefathers hung in trees to be free.
(Rest in peace.)
Got rid of slavery, but kept the penitentiary.
And new freedom got a shotgun
And shells with your name.
Release the hot ones
And let freedom reign.

[SOUP]

I'm a former boat prisoner,
Hollywood visitor.
Dance for cats segregated on wax.
Cap Amos and Andy
For the freedom
They just won't hand me.

CHORUS

[MARC 7]
'Cause there's not a lot of time.
Your heart, body, soul, and your mind.
It's so true, it ain't been heard in so long.
That's the reason why we name this song—

CHORUS

[MARC 7]
'Cause there's not a lot of time.
Your heart, body, soul, and your mind.
It's so true, it ain't been heard in so long.
That's the reason why we name this song
FREEDOM.

Words and Music by Andre Young, Cordozar Broadus,
George Clinton Jr., Garry Shider and David Spradley

FUCK WIT DRE DAY (AND EVERYBODY'S CELEBRATIN)

RECORDED BY DR. DRE, FEATURING SNOOP DOGGY DOGG

Yeah, hell yeah.
Know what I'm sayin'?
Yeah.

[DR. DRE]
Mista Busta, where the fuck ya at?
Can't scrap a lick, so I know ya got your gatt.
Your dick on hard from fuckin' your road dogs.
The 'hood you threw up with, niggaz you grew up with
Don't even respect your ass.
That's why it's time for the Doctor to check your ass, nigga.
Used to be my homie, used to be my ace.
Now I wanna slap the taste out yo' mouth,
Make you bow down to the row.
Fuckin' me, now I'm fuckin' you, little hoe.
Oh, don't think I forgot, let you slide,
Let me ride, just another homicide.
Yeah, it's me, so I'm-a talk on.
Stompin' on the "Eazy"-est streets that you can walk on,
So strap on your Compton hat, your locs,
And watch your back 'cause you might get smoked, loc.
And pass the bud, stay low-key, B.G.,
'Cause you lost all your homie's love.
Now call it what you want to.
You fucked wit' me, now it's a must that I fuck wit' you.

[DR. DRE]

Yeah, that's what the fuck I'm talkin' about.

We have your motherfuckin' record company surrounded.

Put down the candy and let the little boy go.

You know what I'm sayin', punk motherfucker?

(We want Eazy, we want Eazy.)

[SNOOP DOGGY DOGG]

Bow, wow, wow, yippy yo, yippy yay.

Doggy Dogg's in the motherfuckin' house.

Bow, wow, wow, yippy yo, yippy yay.

Death Row's in the motherfuckin' house.

Bow, wow, wow, yippy yo, yippy yay.

The sounds of a dog brings me to another day.

Play with my bone, would ya, Timmy?

It seems like you're good for makin' jokes about your jimmy.

But here's a jimmy joke about your mama that you might not like:

I heard she was the "Frisco Dyke."

But fuck your mama, I'm talkin' about you and me,

Toe to toe, Tim M–U–T.

Your bark was loud, but your bite wasn't vicious

And the rhymes you were kickin' were quite bootylicious.

You get with Doggy Dogg, oh is he crazy?

With ya mama and your daddy hollerin', "Bay-bee."

So won't they let you know

That if you fuck with Dre, nigga, you're fuckin' with Death Row?

And I ain't even slangin' them thangs.

I'm hollerin', "1–8–7" with my dick in yo' mouth, bitch.

[DR. DRE]

Yeah, nigga,

Compton and Long Beach together on the motherfucker.

So you wanna pop that shit,

Get yo' motherfuckin' cranium cracked, nigga?

Step on up, now, we ain't no motherfuckin' joke,

So remember the name:

Mighty, mighty D–R, yeah, motherfucker!

[DRE AND SNOOP]

Now understand this, my nigga, Dre can't be touched.
Luke's bendin' over, so Luke's gettin' fucked, busta.
Musta, I thought I was sleazy
Or thought I was a mark 'cause I used to hang with Eazy.
Animosity made ya speak, but ya spoke.
Aiyyo, Dre, what up?
Check this nigga off, loc.
If it ain't another hoe that I gots ta fuck with,
Gap teeth in ya mouth so my dick's gots to fit
With my nuts on ya tonsils.
While ya onstage rappin' at your wack-ass concerts
And I'm-a snatch your ass from the backside
To show you how Death Row pull off that whore ride.
Now you might not understand me
'Cause I'm-a rob you in Compton and blast you in Miami.
Then we gon' creep to South Central
On a Street Knowledge mission, as I steps in the temple,
Spot him got him, as I pulls out my strap.
Got my chrome to the side of his White Sox hat.
You was tryin' to check my homie, you better check yo' self
'Cause when you diss Dre, you diss yourself, motherfucker.

Yeah, nine-deuce.
Dr. Dre droppin' chronic once again.
It don't stop, punishing punk motherfuckers real quick-like.
Doggy Dogg in the motherfuckin' house.
Long Beach in the motherfuckin' house.
Compton-style nigga, straight up, really doe.
Breakin' all you suckas off somethin' real proper-like.
You know what I'm sayin'?
All these sucka-ass niggaz can eat a fat dick.
Yeah, Eazy-E, Eazy-E, Eazy-E can eat a big, fat dick.
Tim Dog can eat a big, fat dick.
Luke can eat a fat dick.
Yeah.

Words and Music by
Christopher Martin and Keith Elam

FULL CLIP
RECORDED BY GANG STARR

Big L, rest in peace, rest in peace, rest in peace.
Oh…do you wanna mess with this?
Oh…one of the best yet.
We've got it; you can feel the realness in this business of rap.
Go ahead.

Fresh out the gate again,
Time to raise the stakes again,
Fatten my plate again.
You cats know we always play to win.
G and G, to the stars, son.
Haters took this shit too far, son.
So that's all for you, I'm wipin' out your whole team.
I'll splatter your dreams with lyrics to shatter your schemes.
The badder you seem, the more lies you tell.
The more lies you sell, nobody's surprised you fell
Into my death trap, right into my clutches,
Stupid, you know the Gur must bless every single mic he touches.
I've suffered just so I can return harder.
Wanna be a shit starter,
Fuck around, make you a martyr.
I make you famous,
Turn around and make you nameless
'Cause you never understood how vital to me this rap game is.
Save it and hold that, you catch a hot one.
Rhymes will chase a fake nigga down soon as I spot one.

CHORUS:
Full clip, do you wanna mess with this?
Gang Starr, one of the best yet.
I'm nice like that.
It's all good in this business of rap.
Full clip, do you wanna mess with this?
Gang Starr, one of the best yet.
I'm nice like that.
It's all good, so I suggest you take a rest.

So if you stand in my way,
I'm-a have to spray.
Learn that if you come against me, son, you're gonna have to pray.
Since back in the day, I held the weight and kept my head up.
They wanna see the guard catch and L—it's all a set-up.
I give no man or thing power over me.
Why these niggaz so jealous and lookin' sour over me?
I'm bolder, G, I'm like impossible to stop.
I'm like that nigga in the ring with you, impossible to drop.
I'm like two magazines fully loaded to your one,
Plus I ain't gonna quit spittin' 'til you're done,
Plus, more than ever,
I got my whole shit together,
More than a decade of hits that'll live forever.
Catch a rep off my name, you're bound to fry.
Know how many niggaz that I know that's down to die?
We never fail and we ain't never been frail.
You niggaz talk crime but you scared of jail.

CHORUS

Attackin' like a slick Apache,
Lyrics are tripper-happy,
Blowin' back just for the way you lookin' at me.
Cock back, Blau, I hit you right now.
I don't know why so many y'all wanna be thugs anyhow.
Face the consequence
Of your childish nonsense.
I can make your head explode just by my lyrical content.

Get ya in my scope and metaphorically snipe ya.
I never liked ya,
I gas that ass and then ignite ya.
The flamethrower
Make your peeps afraid to know ya.
How many times I told ya:
Play your position, small soldier.
My art is colder, makes me want to resort to violence.
Stop beatin' me in the head, son; nah, I'm not buyin' it.
I'm ready to blast,
Ready to surpass and harass.
I'm ready to flip, yeah, and ready to dip with all the cash.
I hold my chrome steady with a tight grip
So you're done already 'cause this one might hit.

CHORUS

FUNKDAFIED

Words and Music by Jermaine Dupri, Shawntae Harris,
O'Kelly Isley, Ronald Isley, Rudolph Isley, Ernie Isley,
Marvin Isley and Chris Jasper

RECORDED BY DA BRAT, FEATURING JERMAINE DUPRI

Hard times in the funk

INTRO:
[JERMAINE DUPRI]
Yeah, so funkdafied.
So let's take a ride with Da Brat,
Tat, tat, tat on that ass.

CHORUS:
[DA BRAT]
So, so, so funkdafied.
So, so, so funkdafied.
So, so, so funkdafied.

[DA BRAT]
Open up, open up and let the funk flow in
From this nigga named "J" and his newfound friend.
I'm hittin' switches like Erick on the solo creep
Fo' yo' jeep it's the B–R–A–T.
Puttin' the dip in your hip from right to left.
It's the Ghetto West bitch and I'm so def.
Nigga, that's my click,
Nigga, that's who I rolls with
And we kicks nothin' but the fat (sh, sh, hhh).

Them calls me the funkdafied, funkalistic,
Vocalistic with the real shit,
We got the shit you can't funk wit'. (Why?)
Because we so funkdafied. (Why?)
We make you move from side to side.
Well, it's da G–H, da E–T–T–O, nigga.
Brat and J.D. comin' like that big baby.
So lay back and listen as I catch up on my pimpin'
And freak this dest just like Ashford and Simpson.
'Cause I'm—

CHORUS

Puttin' it down (puttin' it down) ain't no thang to me,
And ain't too many hoes that can hang with me.
It's like that and as a matter of fact,
When it comes, Da Brat, tat, tat, tat,
I make your neck snap back.
Meaning I got the hit that-a getcha bent.
Tearing the roof off this mutha like Parliament.
I'm on a roll, in control like Janet, damn it!
Brat, you're the funk bandit and they can't handle it.
I know, that's why I keep hittin' 'em with this grammar,
Lettin' all y'all know that I'm the real mama jama.
Straight to the head like a chronic sack,
I pass the mic to Da Brat and, yo, I passed it back.

Well-a, sisters and fellas,
It's time to get your groove on.
I provide the funkdafied sounds that make yo' move homes.
Breaking these fools off proper-like,
It's so S–O–S–O–D–E–F, dynamite.
Hummin', hummin', comin' up atcha like Ralph K.,
And since this ain't no Honeymoon, I'm here to stay.
And the way we comin' atcha, baby, we can't miss.
There's a new tag team in town, nigga, whomp, there it is.

CHORUS (2 TIMES)

Words and Music by Matt Dike,
Marvin Young and Michael Ross

FUNKY COLD MEDINA
RECORDED BY TONE LOC

Cold cooling at a bar,
And I'm lookin' for some action.
But like Mick Jagger said,
"I can't get no satisfaction."
The girls are all around,
But none of them wanna get with me.
My threads are fresh and I'm lookin' def.
Yo! What's up with L–O–C?
The girls are all jockin'
At the other end of the bar,
Having drinks with some no-name chump
When they know that I'm the star.
So I got up and strolled over
To the other side of the cantina.
I asked the guy, "Why you so fly?"
He said, "Funky Cold Medina."

This brother told me a secret
On how to get more chicks:
Put a little Medina in your glass
And the girls'll come real quick.
It's better than any alcohol
Or aphrodisiac.
A couple of sips of this love potion
And she'll be on your lap.
So I gave some to my dog,
When he began to beg
Then he licked his bowl and he looked at me
And did the wild thing on my leg.
He used to scratch and bite me;
Before he was much meaner.
But now all the poodles run to my house
For the Funky Cold Medina.

You know what I'm sayin'?
I got every dog in my neighborhood breaking down my door.
I got Spuds McKenzie, Alex from Strohs.
They won't leave my dog alone with that Medina, pal.

I went up to this girl
She said, "Hi, my name's Sheena."
I thought she'd be good to go with
A little Funky Cold Medina.
She said, "I'd like a drink,"
I said, "Okay, I'll go get it."
Then a couple of sips, she cold-licked her lips
And I knew that she was with it.
So I took her to my crib
And everything went well as planned.
But when she got undressed, it was a big old mess—
Sheena was a man.
So I threw him out;
I don't fool around with no Oscar Meyer wiener.
You must be sure that the girl is pure
For the Funky Cold Medina.

You know, ain't no plans with a man,
This is the eighties and I'm down with the ladies.
Ya know?
Break it down.

Back in the saddle,
Looking for a little affection,
I took a shot as a contestant
On the Love Connection.
The audience voted
And, you know, they picked a winner.
I took my date to the Hilton
For Medina and some dinner.
She had a few drinks,
I'm thinkin' soon what I'll be gettin'.
Instead she started talkin' 'bout
Plans for our weddin'.
I said, "Wait, slow down, love, not so fast,
I'll be seein' ya."
That's why I found you don't play around
With the Funky Cold Medina.

Ya know what I'm sayin'?
That Medina's a monster, y'all.
Funky Cold Medina.

Words and Music by Cordozar C. Broadus,
Tracy La Marr Davis, Keiwan Dashawn Spillman
and Danny Elliott Means

G'D UP
RECORDED BY SNOOP DOGG, FEATURING TRAY-DEE, GOLDIE LOC, AND BUTCH CASSIDY

[TRAY-DEE]

I bang with the gang that don't need no intro.
We run from East Long Beach to West South Central.
Credentials to kick flows and rip shows,
Dip fours and pimp hoes while the Indo blow.
You know that West Coast low mentality,
Focused on reality but livin' in a whole 'nother galaxy.
We keep it straight, hard but guard the spot.
Bangers snatch chains in the parking lot.
Don't matter, there still be fine hoes to gather.
Pick about the thickest bitch and I gots to have 'er.
It's routine, the coupe clean, let's hit the show.
You know we all fuckin' once they glimpse the po,
Wit' the satin in my hand, pack the gatt on my lap
'Cause it's hatin' when you're skatin' and your pockets is fat.
Don't act for a minute like your ass surprised.
Just recognize the real way that gangstas ride.

[SNOOP DOGG]

If it ain't chronic, don't blaze it up.
And if it ain't a Chevy don't raise it up.
You know we keep it bangin', don't fake the funk
So all the real niggaz stay gangsta'd up.
We makin' paper only suckas claim to touch
By stickin' to the script and never changin' up.
You know we keep it bangin', don't fake the funk.
Keep it real, muthafucka, stay gangsta'd up.

[GOLDIE LOC]
It's goin' down, muthafuckas, like that.
Sounds like Battlecat been upstairs wit' Zapp.
And the knockin' don't stop,
I hope nobody don't call the cops.
It don't stop, the beat'll make your pop block.
No better yet, 'cause this shit'll keep your glock cocked.
You think I'm trippin'.
Fool, I ain't bullshittin',
You better read up on this shit to keep the latest nonfiction.
Watch out for the friction.
This West Coast on mine, and fuck anybody dissin'.
Nigga, listen Dogg House style 'cause I'm a gangsta crip.
C-walkin', holdin' on the extra clip.
Now you wanna be a friend
But you gonna make me unload and slap the other clip in reload.
You wanna go toe to toe.
Sit my pistol down on the ground on the pound,
Nigga, hell no.

[BUTCH CASSIDY]
I must stay gangsta'd up 'cause it just lives in me,
And when I seen enough,
I guess that's when I'll free somebody.
Once said from Willie C., "Nigga, don't speak on me,"
I won't stop, so let me be,
We are from the streets, somebody.

[SNOOP DOGG]
I'm a Long Beach, East Side, mad-ass lunatic,
Gang-bang, slap-a-bitch nigga out to get a grip
On the grind, gettin' mine,
Ask the homies on the nine-o, you know.
We still own niggaz who talk bitch shit.
Real niggaz feel this: let's get rich.
Under the sun with the young ones:
TLC and all the DPG's.
Down for whatever, whoever wanna see me now.
You lookin' like me, I guess you wanna be me now.
It take a whole lot to be Snoop D–O–dub.

You gotta put it down and always stay G'd up.
All-star shoes with the G apparel.
If I fall in the club, I might bust a pair of Stacy Adams.
You never catch me lookin' R&B.
I might be in a three-piece suit lookin' way O.G.,
Blazin' a ounce with the homie cat
Or Ruff Dogg 'cause I love puttin' hustlers on the map.
I keep it gangsta for sho-do-lo,
And I always got the motherfuckin' do-do smoke.
For all my locs and kin folks, this is for y'all,
Let me hit somethin', Dogg.
Beware of my clique.
We hopin' and droppin' nothin' but the gangsta shit.

Dogg House, somethin' for the nine-to-five plus four pennies.
Tray-Dee, Goldie Loc,
My nigga, Battlecat, on the beat, hustlers for life.
West Side, you can't spell the West without the E–S.
Ah yes, we connectin', y'all.
That's how we do it. (Do it to 'em, do it to 'em.)
And we out. (See ya, see ya.)

Words and Music by Stevie Wonder,
Doug Rasheed, Artis Ivey
and Larry Sanders

GANGSTA'S PARADISE
RECORDED BY COOLIO

As I walk through the valley of the shadow of death,
I take a look at my life and realize there's nothin' left
'Cause I've been blasting and laughing so long
That even my mama thinks that my mind's gone,
But I ain't never crossed a man that didn't deserve it.
Me be treated like a punk, you know, that's unheard of.
You better watch how you're talking and where you're walking
Or you and your homies might be lined in chalk.
I really hate the trip but I gotta loc.
As they croak, I see myself in the pistol smoke.
Fool! I'm the kinda G that little homes wanna be like,
On my knees in the night sayin' prayers in the street light.

CHORUS:
Been spending most of our lives living in the gangsta's paradise.
Been spending most of our lives living in the gangsta's paradise.
Keep spending most of our lives living in the gangsta's paradise.
Keep spending most of our lives living in the gangsta's paradise.

Look at the situation they got me facin';
I can't live a normal life; I was raised by the state.
So I gotta be down with the 'hood team.
Too much television watching got me chasing dreams.
I'm a educated fool with money on my mind.
Got my ten in my hand and a gleam in my eye.

I'm a loc'd-out gangsta, set-trippin' banger
And my homies is down so don't arouse my anger.
Fool! Death ain't nothin' but a heartbeat away.
I'm living life, do or die, what can I say?
I'm twenty-three now, but will I live to see twenty-four?
The way things is goin', I don't know.

Tell me, why are we so blind to see
That the ones we hurt are you and me?

CHORUS

Power in the money, money in the power.
Minute after minute, hour after hour,
Everybody's runnin' but half of them ain't lookin'
What's goin' on in the kitchen, but I don't know what's cookin'.
They say I gotta learn, but nobody's here to teach me.
If they can't understand it, how can they reach me?
I guess they can't, I guess they won't, I guess they front.
That's why I know my life is outta luck, fool!

CHORUS

Tell me, why are we so blind to see
That the ones we hurt are you and me?
Tell me, why are we so blind to see
That the ones we hurt are you and me?

Words and Music by Christopher Wallace,
Kimberly Jones, Roy Ayers, Sylvia Striplin
and B. Bedford

GET MONEY
RECORDED BY JUNIOR M.A.F.I.A.

CHORUS:
Fuckin' bitches…get money.
Fuckin' niggaz…get money.

You wanna sip Mo' on my living room floor,
Play Nintendo wit' Caese and Nino,
Pick up my phone, say "Poppa not home,"
Sex all night, mad damn in the morn,
Spend my vee, smoke all my weed.
Tattoo on tit sayin' B–I–G.
Now check it—
Picture life as my wife, jus' think,
Full-length minks, fat X and O link
Bracelets to match.
Conversation was all that,
Showed you the safe combination and all that.
Guess you could say you the one I trusted.
Who would ever think that you would spread like mustard?
Shit got hot, you sent feds to my spot,
Took me to court, tried to take all I got.
Another intricate plot
The bitch said I raped her.
Damn, why she wanna stick me for my paper?
My Moschino mother, Versace hottie
Come to find out, you was fucking everybody.
You knew about me wit fake I.D.,
Cases in Virginia, body in D.C.
Why always me?
That's what I get for trickin'.
Came out on bail, commence the ass-kickin'.

Lickin' the door, wavin' the four-four.
All you heard was "Poppa, don't hit me no more."
Disrespect my click—my shit's imperial,
Fuck around and make milk box material.
You feel me, suckin' dick, runnin' your lips,
'Cause of you, I'm on some real fuck-a-bitch shit.

CHORUS (4 TIMES)

Niggaz, better grab a seat,
Grab on ya dick as this bitch gets deep,
Deeper than a pussy of a bitch six feet.
Stiff dicks feel sweet in this little petite,
Young bitch from the streets guaranteed to stay down,
Used to bring work outta town on Greyhound.
Now I'm in *Billboard*, now niggaz pressed to hit it,
Play me like a chicken, thinkin' I'm pressed to get it.
Rather do the killin' than the stick-up jooks,
Rather count a million while you eat my pussy.
Push me to the limit, get my feelings in,
Get me open while I'm cummin' down your throat-in,
You wanna be my main squeeze, nigga, don'tcha?
You wanna lick between my knees, nigga, don'tcha?
Wanna see me wit Big and Three down the ave,
Blow up spots on bitches because I'm there.
Break up affairs, lick shots in the air,
You get vex and start swingin' everywhere.
Me, shifty? Now you wanna pistol-whip me?
Pull out your nine, while I cock on mine?
And, what, nigga? I ain't got time for this.
So what, nigga, I'm not to hear that shit.
Now you wanna buy me diamonds and Armani suits.
Age of the Adini and Chanel Nine boots.
Things to make up for all the games and lies:
Hallmark cards, sayin', "I apologize."
Is you wit' me? How could you ever deceive me?
But paybacks a bitch, motherfucker, believe me.
Naw, I ain't gay, this ain't no lesbo flow,
Jus' a lil' somethin' to let you motherfuckers know.

CHORUS

Words and Music by Nile Rodgers,
Bernard Edwards, Will Smith,
Samuel J. Barnes and J. Robinson

GETTIN' JIGGY WIT IT
RECORDED BY WILL SMITH

Bring it...woo...uh, uh, uh, uh.
Ha, ha, ha, ha!
What , what, what, what?
Ha, ha, ha, ha!

On your mark, ready, set, let's go.
Dance floor pro, I know you know.
I go psycho when my new joint hit.
Just can't sit.
Gotta get jiggy wit' it.
Ooh, that's it.
Now honey, honey, come ride.
DKNY all up in my eye.
You gotta Prada bag with a lotta stuff in it,
Give it to your friend, let's spin.
Everybody lookin' at me,
Glancin' at the kid,
Wishin' they was dancin' a jig
Here with this handsome kid.
Cigar-cigar right from Cuba-Cuba.
I just bite it.
It's for the look, I don't light it.
Ill-way to 'Ami on the ance-day oor-flay.
Yo, my cardio is infinite. (Ha, ha!)
Big Willie style's all in it.
Gettin' jiggy wit' it.

CHORUS:
Na, na, na...gettin' jiggy wit' it.
Na, na, na...gettin' jiggy wit' it.

What? You wanna ball with the kid?
Watch your step, you might fall tryin' to do what I did.
Mama, uh, mama, uh, mama come closer.

In the middle of the club with the rub-a-dub.
No love for the haters, the haters,
Mad 'cause I got floor seats at the Lakers.
See me on the fifty-yard line with the Raiders.
Met Ali, he told me, I'm the greatest.
I got the fever for the flavor of a crowd pleaser.
DJ play another from the prince of this.
Your highness, only mad chicks ride in my whips.
South to the west to the east to the north,
Bought my hits and watch 'em go off, a-go off.
Ah yes, yes y'all, ya don't stop,
In the winter or the (summertime),
I makes it hot.
Gettin' jiggy wit' 'em.

CHORUS

Eight-fifty I.S., if you need a lift.
Who's the kid in the drop?
Who else? Will Smith,
Living that life some consider a myth.
Rock from South Street to one two fifth,
Women used to tease me,
Give it to me now nice and easy,
Since I moved up like George and Weezy.
Dream to the maximum, I be askin' em,
"Would you like to bounce with the brother that's platinum?"
Never see Will attackin' 'em,
Rather play ball with Shaq and 'em,
Flatten 'em.
Psyche.
Kiddin'.
You thought I took a spill, but I didn't.
Trust the lady of my life, she's hittin',
Hit her with a drop top with the ribbon,
Crib for my mom on the outskirts of Philly.
You tryin' to flex on me?
Don't be silly.
Gettin' jiggy wit' it.

CHORUS (3 TIMES)

Words and Music by Peter Lord,
Sandra Kay St. Victor and Jeffrey Vernon Smith

GHETTO HEAVEN

RECORDED BY COMMON, FEATURING D'ANGELO

God bless...

[D'ANGELO]

Hmmm...doo...yeah.
Know I love my baby, my baby loves me.
Layin' in some heaven, need a little company.
Let's go into a heaven, time to get some Ghetto Heaven,
Ghetto...

[COMMON]

Searchin' for a love throughout the ghetto.
Young girls is thick, righteousness is narrow.
I got my third eye on the sparrow.
Want my peoples straight and rock sweet apparel.
The mother of my child, we not together.
Baby, it's your back, I got forever.
As the weather talks to us,
Him rockin' the Holy Spirit walks through us.
The blunted eyes of the youth search for a guide.
A thug is a lost man in disguise.
The rise and fall of a nation, even when the buildings tumble,

I still stand tall, I walk through the valley wit' a life preserver
Feelin' at times that I might just murder.
Yo, but that ain't what I was sent for.
I want folks to say, "His life, it meant more
Than any car, any rock, or any broad.
He found Ghetto Heaven in himself and God."

CHORUS:
[D'ANGELO]
Ghetto Heaven, standin' in some Ghetto Heaven.
Ghetto Heaven, standin' in some Ghetto Heaven.
Ghetto...

[COMMON]
Love, your happiness don't begin wit' a man.
Strong woman, why should you depend on a man?
I understand you want a man that's resourceful.
If he pay your bills, he feel like he bought you.
Talkin' to a friend about what love is,
Her man didn't love her 'cause he didn't love his.
Hugged her from afar, said what I felt.
You never find a man 'til you find yourself.
Time helps, mistakes you can learn from
'Cause one man fucked up, men you shouldn't turn from.
You want a certain type of guy, gotta reach a certain point, too.
At the destination a king will anoint you.
Goin' through the storm, many bodies stay warm.
That relationship died for you to be born.
You worth more than anything you could cop in a store.
For you to grow, he had to go, so what you stoppin' him for?
Not even I could ignore bein' alone, it's hard.
Find heaven in yourself and God.

[D'ANGELO]
I know I love my baby, my baby loves me.
I'm layin' in some heaven, need a little company, yeah.
It's twenty-four-seven, time to get some Ghetto Heaven,
Time to get some Ghetto Heaven,
Ghetto Heaven, Ghetto Heaven.
It's time to get some Ghetto Heaven,
Time to get some Ghetto Heaven.

[COMMON]
This music is so much bigger than me.
As far as happy, yo, it's like a trigger to me.
Dealin' with crab rappers and groupie broads,
Record execs, at times, it do be hard.
But to choose words and be heard across waters,
Doin' somethin' you like to support daughters,
Keepin' your guys who collectin' court orders,
Conveyin' messages that the ancestors brought us,
Thought of things to say, to become the end thing for the day,
Somehow that didn't seem the way for me to make it.
Music is a gift that is sacred.
I hope you didn't use it hopin' you could grow to it,
Whether servin' or a surgeon, you gon' go through it.
Can't imagine goin' through it, without soul music.
It's like Donnie Hath' helped me see Lonnie's path.
On my behalf, let's take whole steps to Imhotep
And show depth as we make people nod.
Find heaven in this music, and God.
Find heaven in this music, and God.
Find heaven in this music, and God.

[D'ANGELO]
Ghetto Heaven.
Ghetto Heaven.

Words and Music by
Albert Joseph Brown III and Kyle Albert West

GHETTO IS A STRUGGLE
RECORDED BY TRU, FEATURING PEACHES

CHORUS:

[PEACHES]

The ghetto is a struggle, but we've got to change our lives.
We've got to change our lives, oh, oh.
The ghetto is a struggle, but we've got to change our lives.
We've got to change our lives, oh, oh.

[MASTER P]

I've done seen it all in the bricks.
Somebody said he would never change.
The homies killin' up each other;
Shit, I guess that is the dope game
And if you look like a thug, then that mean trouble.
See my next-door neighbor knockin' on the window.
She wanna fuck.
And my water don't get hot; I got bleach in my holey socks,
And my mom started stressin' us, why I start sellin' rocks.
And this street got me crazy.
Momma said, "I can't lose my baby," (Damn.)
But see, these niggaz so shady. (Ha, bro?)
Fuck the world if they take me.

CHORUS

[C-MURDER]

The ghetto is a struggle to me.
Who can I be?
Will it bring trouble to me?
Before I rest in peace, I ask my auntie to look up in the sky and thank
Before she turn another trigger, take another drink.

I know it's hard,
Tryin' to survive and not die and stay alive.
But who you really foolin'?
'Cause we all live a lie.
It ain't the same, wishin' ya didn't have any,
Didn't want it and take it.
But if the situation right, then it's your pockets I'm breakin'.
I lost my conscience when I lost my big brother.
Ask my mother—I'm never changin' my ways,
Not even for *The Source* cover.
I puts it down like that on this track
To give back to the 'hood.
It's a struggle. (It's a struggle.)
It's all good. (It's all good.)

CHORUS

[SILKK THE SHOCKER]
The ghetto is a struggle, so I gots to make a change.
You know, it's hard on the streets, but I've gots to maintain.
Mom pullin' up on my sleeve, tellin' me, "Don't leave."
I'm like, "I gots to do what I gots to do,
Because, if I don't, I don't eat."
Grew up with the rats and the roaches.
Tryin' to stay focused. (Stay focused.)
Tryin' to survive in this world, but it's like I stay hopeless.
The world is a ghetto and I can't escape that. (Can't escape that.)
Every time I try to prove 'em wrong, y'all just prove 'em right.
Shit, and I hate that.
I know I've made some mistakes, black.
Deep in the ghetto, tryin' to find the queen,
Tryin' to avoid the 'hood rat.
We've got to make a change;
And in fact, we should.
Just because we in the ghetto,
We should still dream see past the 'hood.

CHORUS (2 TIMES)

Words and Music by Shawntae Harris,
Eldra DeBarge, Betty Wright,
Carlton Ridenhour and Hank Schocklee

GHETTO LOVE
RECORDED BY DA BRAT, FEATURING T-BOZ

I had some problems
That no one could seem to solve them.
But you had the answer:
You told me to take a chance
And learn the ways of love, my baby,
And all that it has to offer.
You told me your secret love won't let you down.
Oh, all my love, baby.

Hey nigga, ain't shit gonna ever change
Between you and your boo.
Put a hold on me ever since I held you.
What compelled you to be my nigga besides passion and love?
You ran up on a real bitch with understanding and trust.
Fuck the others, none of them compare to us.
And under covers, you my muthafucka nigga.
When you stickin' my stuff,
You laid pipe unlike any other plumber.
Took me shoppin' all day and at night you kept me cummin',
Made dinner—collard greens, candied yams, and steak—
Taught me how to measure grams, cook rocks, and chop weights.
Caught a case 'cause your boy ran his mouth too much
And it's a disgrace, how the pain felt to miss your touch.

But as the days keep passin', keep it actin' with stacks of letters.
Hit you so you don't forget us
When you'd rather not be livin' in the cellar.
Hella muthafuckas want your occupation
But they can keep pacin' 'cause I'm gonna be waitin' on my baby.

CHORUS:
[T-BOZ]
And all this love is waiting for you,
My baby, sweet darling.
And all this love is waiting for you.

[DA BRAT]
Don't worry 'bout a thing, nigga, stay down.
As long as you can hang, I'm-a be around.

Ran into your boy, had heard he'd spread the word
That you was soft, braggin' he collectin' your cheese
And pissing me the fuck off.
The first thought of committing a felony never left,
I missed the big breaths you took when we was puffin' an L.
Just the little things you do with the bigger ones I saw better
SL five-hundreds, colorful Gucci sweaters and leathers, diamond letters.
Girl you broke, I saved the sugar for you,
Keep the business runnin', droppin' off keys in Cancun.
Cash rules and you remain to be the king of my throne.
Position taken, flippin' calendar pages 'til you get home.

Wanna blast your boy for snatchin' up my happiness.
But I regret what'll happen to this dollar foundation
If I'm incarcerated, too.
You can make it through.
We bail on the jealous who tell us the opposite of that.
Forever you and Brat.
I tried to take the blame, but you preferred to handle my fame,
So I'm waitin' with open arms to rekindle the flame.

CHORUS (3 TIMES)

Words and Music by Barry Alan Gibb,
Maurice Ernest Gibb, Robin Hugh Gibb,
James Brown, Russell Jones, Ronald Lenhoff,
Samuel Michel, Nel Jean and Bobby Byrd

GHETTO SUPASTAR (THAT IS WHAT YOU ARE)
RECORDED BY PRAS MICHEL

Man, man, look at the sky.
All these stars, man.
The stars look beautiful tonight—look at 'em.

CHORUS:
Ghetto superstar, that is what you are.
Comin' from afar; reachin' for the stars.
Run away with me to another place.
We can rely on each other, uh-huh.
From one corner to another, uh-huh.

Some got hopes and dreams; we got ways and means.
The supreme dream team, always up with the schemes.
From hubcaps to sellin' raps, name your theme.
My rise to the top, floatin' on this cream.
Who the hell wanna stop me? I hated those who doubt me.
A million refugees with unlimited warrantees.

Black Caesar, dating top skeezers.
Diplomatic legalese, no time for a Visa.
They just begun, I'm-a shoot them one by one.
Got five sides to me—somethin' like a pentagon.
Strike with the forces of King Solomon,
Lettin' bygones be bygones, and so on, and so on.

I'm-a teach this cat how to live in the ghetto,
Keepin' it retrospective from the get-go.
Lay low, let my mind shine like a halo.
P-P-Politic with ghetto senators on the deal-o.

132

CHORUS

One, two, and you don't stop, yo.
My eyes is sore bein' a senator,
Behind closed doors, hittin' truth to the sea floor.
The rich go north, ignore the tug-of-war
While the kids are poor, open new and better drug stores.
So I became hardcore, couldn't take it no more.
I'm-a reveal everything, change the law.
I find myself walkin' the streets,
Tryin' to find what's really goin' on in the streets.

Now, every dog got his day, needless to say,
When the chief away, that's then them cats want to play.
I told you, mess around, you fools like Cassius Clay.
Stretch my heater, make you do a pot of beret.
Kick your balls like Pele, pick 'em doin' ballet.
Peak like Dante, broader than Broadway.
Get applause like a matador, cry, yellin', "Ole!"
Who the hell wanna save me?
From B.K. to Cali, come on.

CHORUS

Just when you thought it was safe in a common place,
Showcase your finest is losin' fast in the horse race.
Two-faced, gettin' defaced, out like Scarface.
Throw your roll money, let me put on my screwface.
Well, I'm paranoid at the things I said,
Wondrin' what's the penalty from day to day.
I'm hangin' out, partyin' with the girls that never die.
You see, I was pickin' on the small fries, my campaign tellin' lies.
Was just spreadin' my love, didn't know my love
Was the one holdin' the gun and the glove.
But it's all good as long as it's understood
It's all together now in the 'hood.

CHORUS (2 TIMES)

Words and Music by Harry Wayne Casey,
Richard Finch, Cordozar Broadus, Andre Young,
Steve Arrington, Steve Washington, Raymond Turner,
Daniel Webster and Mark Adams

GIN AND JUICE
RECORDED BY SNOOP DOGG, FEATURING DR. DRE

INTRO:

[DR. DRE]

Heah, hah, hah!

I'm serious, nigga; one of y'all niggaz got this ass muthafuckin' up.

Aiy baby, aiy baby, aiy baby, get some bubblegum in this muthafucka.

Steady, long, steady, long, nigga.

[SNOOP DOGG]

With so much drama in the L–B–C,

It's kinda hard bein' Snoop D–O–double G.

But I, somehow, some way,

Keep comin' up with funky-ass shit, like, every single day.

May I kick a little something for the Gs (Yeah.)

And make a few ends as (Yeah!) I breeze through.

Two in the mornin' and the party's still jumpin'

'Cause my mama ain't home.

I got bitches in the living room gettin' it on,

And they ain't leavin' 'til six in the mornin'. (Six in the mornin'.)

So what you wanna do, sweetie?

I got a pocket full of rubbers and my homeboys do, too.

So turn off the lights and close the doors.

But (But what?) we don't love them hoes, yeah!

So we gonna smoke an ounce to this.

Gs up, hoes down, while you muthafuckas bounce to this.

CHORUS:

Rollin' down the street, smokin' Indo,
Sippin' on gin and juice,
Laid back, with my mind on my money
And my money on my mind.
Rollin' down the street, smokin' Indo,
Sippin' on gin and juice,
Laid back, with my mind on my money
And my money on my mind.

Now that I got me some Seagram's gin
Everybody got they cups, but they ain't chipped in.
Now this types of shit happens all the time.
You got to get yours but, fool, I gotta get mine.
Everything is fine when you listenin' to the D–O–G.
I got the cultivating music that be captivating he who listens
To the words that I speak as I take me a drink to the middle of the street
And get to mackin' to this bitch named Sadie. (Sadie?)
She used to be the homeboy's lady. (Oh, that bitch.)
Eighty degrees, when I tell that bitch, "Please."
Raised up off these N–U–Ts, 'cause you gets none of these.
At ease, as I mob with the Dogg Pound, feel the breeze.
Bitch, I'm just—

CHORUS

Later on that day, my homie Dr. Dre
Came through with a gang of Tanqueray
And a fat-ass J of some bubonic chronic that made me choke.
Shit, this ain't no joke.
I had to back up off of it and sit my cup down.
Tanqueray and chronic, yeah, I'm fucked up now.
But it ain't no stoppin', I'm still poppin'.
Dre got some bitches from the city of Compton
To serve me—not with a cherry on top—
'Cause when I bust my nut, I'm raising up off the cot.
Don't get upset, girl, that's just how it goes.
I don't love you hoes, I'm out the do'.
And I'll be—

CHORUS (2 TIMES)

Words and Music by Hugh Montenegro,
Buddy Kaye, Williard C. Smith and Jeffrey Townes

GIRLS AIN'T NOTHING BUT TROUBLE

RECORDED BY DJ JAZZY JEFF & THE FRESH PRINCE

Listen homeboys, don't mean to bust your bubble,
But girls of the world ain't nothin' but trouble.
So next time a girl gives you the play,
Just remember my rhyme and get the hell away.

Just last week when I was walkin' down the street,
I observed this lovely lady that I wanted to meet.
I walked up to her and I said, "Hello."
She said, "You're kind of cute."
I said, "Yes, I know.
But by the way, sweetheart, what's your name?"
She said, "My friends like to call me Exotic Elaine."
I said, "My name is the Prince," and she said, "Why?"
I said, "Well, I don't know; I'm just a hell of a guy!
But enough about me, yo, let's talk about you
And all the wonderful things that you and I can do."
I popped some cash and in a little bit of time,
I showed some cash and the girl was mine.

I took her all over town, I wined her and dined her.
She ask me, did I like her; I said, "Well, kinda."
All of a sudden she jumped out of her seat,
Snatched me up by my wrist and took me out to the street.
She started grabbin' all over me, kissing and hugging,
So I shoved her away, I said, "You better stop buggin'."
She got mad and looked me dead in my face,
Threw her hands in the air and yelled out, "Rape!"
I got scared when she started to yell,
So I handed her my wallet and ran like hell.
I was duckin' through alleys right and left,
But when the cops caught up they almost beat me to death.
I was arrested, charged with aggravated assault.
(Yo, Clancy, we got him!) But it wasn't my fault.

Nevertheless, don't mean to bust your bubble,
But girls of the world ain't nothin' but trouble.
So next time a girl gives you the play,
Just remember my rhyme and get the hell away.

I was in a bar one Friday night,
Coolin', watchin' a Mike Tyson fight.
I was maxin' and relaxin', sippin' on Tequila
When this girl walked up, she said, "Hi, my name is Sheila."
I responded by saying, "Hello."
She paid for my drink and then said, "Let's go."
Twenty minutes later, things were starting to cook
As we pulled up into her house, I said, "I'm with you, toots."
The music was soft and there was wine in the glasses.
She started winking and making little passes
At me, she pat me close, that's when she got bold:
She started feeling up my back, I said, "Oh, you're hands are cold."
We went to her bedroom thinking of one thing,
Took the phone off the hook to avoid the annoying ring.
I caressed her body and I kissed her cheek
And that's when I observed those satin bedsheets.
I felt that it was time for me to make my move.
I thought I better hurry up before I busted a groove.
I leaned down to kiss her, but then out of the blue
A door slammed and a voice said, "Baby, where are you?"

Her boyfriend busted in, he grinned an evil grin,
And said, "Boy, I'm-a tear your butt limb from limb."
I was scared as hell, where was I supposed to go?
I just yelled, "Geronimo," and jumped out the window.
Just my luck, we were in a snowstorm
And all I had was my underwear on to keep me warm.
And to top the night off, I had to break in my place
Because my keys were on pants back on Sheila's bookcase.
I was done sneezing and coughing,
I hope this doesn't happen often.

But nevertheless, don't mean to bust your bubble,
But girls of the world ain't nothin' but trouble.
So next time a girl gives you the play,
Just remember my rhymes and get the hell away.

[DJ JAZZY JEFF]
Yo man, you think they see your point?

[FRESH PRINCE]
I don't know; I don't think they really do.

[DJ JAZZY JEFF]
I think you should give 'em another example.

[FRESH PRINCE]
Alright, give me a scratch; let's make it funky right here.

I got a ring on my phone, May fifth last year,
It was my girlfriend Betty, I said, "Hello, dear.
I was just about to call you, I got a couple tickets to the Run-DMC concert."
("I'm wit' it.")
"It's six o'clock now, at eight will you be ready?"
("Yeah.")
"Alright, fine, see you then, Betty."
I combed my hair, washed, and brushed my teeth,
Got funky-fresh dressed in my La Coq Sportif.
Got to Betty's at eight, I was ready to jet
Until Betty's mom said, "Betty's not ready yet."

I sat there for at least an hour,
It was ten after nine before she got in the shower.
Nine thirty-five, she comes downstairs
And said, "I need a little longer to finish my hair."
At ten o'clock we had then missed the show.
She comes downstairs and says, "Let's go."
"Go where? Go to sleep, I'm gone."
I was steamin' like a demon as I drove home.

But it just goes to show, not tryin' to burst your bubble,
But girls of the world ain't nothin' but trouble.
So next time a girl gives you the play,
Just remember my rhyme and get the hell away.

[DJ JAZZY JEFF]
Man, first your parents just don't understand,
Then you having these crazy nightmares.

[FRESH PRINCE]
I know—why me, man, why me?

[DJ JAZZY JEFF]
What's next?

[FRESH PRINCE]
Now these girls, man, you know how it is.
Can't live wit' 'em, can't live wit'out 'em.

Words and Music by
Jermaine Dupri and Chris Kelly

GIVE IT 2 YA
RECORDED BY DA BRAT

Give it to ya.
One for da money,
Two for da bass,
Three to get ya goin'
'Cause Da Brat in da place!

It's me, da O.G. funk bandit. (Who's dat?)
Da B–2, da R–A–T and in fact
If you ain't heard of me
Take a seat, lay back and listen
As I bust for yo' ass on dis funkdafied mission.
(Just kick off your shoes and relax your feet.
Party on down wit' Da Brat and her beat.)
Now it goes like dis and dat how it goes.
I'm-a give it to all you niggaz and hoes.
So listen up, make sure you listen up well,
And don't miss shit 'cause this bitch be bad as hell.
(True of matter is I splatta it.) Talk shit
and in a gangsta's way dat's how dem fools get dealt wit'.
So what you wanna do, bitch? Don't even trip,
(Step up, step up.) And I'm-a bust your lip
'Cause I know dat you know dat I know you don't want me to.
But keep on trippin' and I'm-a give it to you.

(Da Brat is da fantastic, romantic, single-handed bandit, and damn it!)
Don't get no betta, betta it don't get.
No mo' than da flow dat I flow for you niggaz and hoes.
Devastatin', captivatin', elevatin' am I operatin',
And I love to get high.
(Well nigga, fire up, nigga, fire it up.)
At your request, I guess it's time for me to get fucked up.

It goes (One puff, two puff, three puff, four.)
From the bottom to the top, top to the bottom I go.
So now you know what I ain't and what I is.
It's da baddest new bitch in da hip-hop biz.
O.G. is what I am,
A brat is what I be.
Blunts are what I smoke,
And you can't see me.
So let it go, 'cause my shit is tight.
Take it how I give it and enjoy da night.

For da nine fuckin' four, it's Da Brat, and you don't know.
You betta ask some muthafuckin' body.
Loddy-doddy, I came to the party, bitch!

Word up, hey; word up, hey; word up, hey.
For real, doe.
Shit!

GOING BACK TO CALI

Words and Music by Christopher Wallace,
Osten Harvey and Roger Troutman

RECORDED BY NOTORIOUS B.I.G., FEATURING PUFF DADDY

[BIGGIE] Yo!

[PUFF DADDY] Yo, Big, wake up, wake up, baby.

[B] Mmm, yo…

[P] Yo, Big, wake yo' ass up, c'mon.

[B] I'm up, I'm up! I'm up, I'm up.

[P] Big, wake up!

[B] I'm up, baby, what the fuck, man? What's up?

[P] C'mon now, it's a quarter to six; we got the seven-thirty flight.

[B] Mmm…yeah.

[P] Yo, Big, Big, Big.

[B] Yeah, I hear you dog, I hear you, all right, seven-thirty.

[P] Yo, take down this information.

[B] Ain't no pen.

[P] Tell your girl then to remember it or somethin'.

[B] Alright, honey, yeah, right this down.

[P] Alright, flight five-oh-four.

[B] Five-oh-four.

[P] Leaving Kennedy…

[B] Kennedy…

[P] On the L–A–X.

[B] Oh! Cali?

[P] No doubt, baby. You know we gotta get this paper.

[B] Ah, no doubt, alright.

[P] You alright?

[B] I'm up, I'm up.

[P] Yo, Big.

[B] I'm UP, man.

[P] Flight five-oh-four.

[B] Alright, seven-thirty I'm-a meet you at the airport.

[P] California.

[B] Yeah.

[NOTORIOUS B.I.G.]

When the la-la hits ya,
Lyrics just splits ya.
Head so hard that ya hat can't fit ya.
Either I'm wit'cha or against ya.
Format venture, back through the maze I sent ya.
Talkin' to the rap investor,
Nigga wit' the game tight,
Bic that flame right,
Spell my name right:
B–I, double G, I–E.
Iced out, lights out, me and Caese-a-lio
Gettin' head from some chicks he know.
See, it's all about the cheddar,
Nobody do it better.
Goin' back to Cali, strictly for the weather,
Women, and the weed—sticky green.
No seeds, bitch, please.
Poppa ain't soft,
Dead up in the 'hood, ain't no love lost.
Got me mixed up,
You drunk them licks up.
Mad 'cause I got my dick sucked
And my balls licked, forfeit, the game is mine.
I'm-a spell my name one more time, check it:
It's the N–O, T–O, R–I, O
U–S, you just lay down, slow.
Recognize a real don when you see Juan,
Sippin' on booze in the House of Blues.

CHORUS:

I'm goin', goin' back, back to Cali.
I'm goin', goin' back, back to Cali.
I'm goin', goin' back, back to Cali.
I'm goin', goin' back, back to Cali.

If I got to choose a coast, I got to choose the East.
I live out there, so don't go there.
But that don't mean a nigga can't rest in the West,
See some nice breasts in the West.
Smoke some nice sess in the West,
Y'all niggaz is a mess.

Thinkin' I'm gon' stop,
Givin' L.A. props.
All I got is beef with those that violates me.
I shall annihilate thee.
Case closed,
Suitcase filled with clothes.
Linens and things, I begin things.
People start to flash eight-eighteens and two-thirteens,
Three-thirteens, B–I–G.
Frequently floss hoes at Roscoe's.
If I wanna squirt her,
Take her to Fatburger.
Spend about a week on Venice Beach
Sippin' Crist'o with some freaks from Frisco.

CHORUS

Cali got gunplay,
Models on the runway,
Screamin', "Biggie, Biggie gimme one more chance."
I be whippin' in the freeway,
The N–Y–C way.
On the celly-celly with my homeboy Lance,
Pass hash from left to right,
Only got five blunts left to light.
I'm set tonight.
Paid a visit to Versace stores.
Bet she suck until I ain't got no more,
Only in L.A.
Bust on the bitches belly,
Rub it in they tummy,
Lick it, say it's yummy,
Then fuck yo' man,
Fuck your plan,
Is it rock the Tri-State?
Almost gold, five Gs at show gate
Or do you wanna see about seven digits?
Fuck hoes exquisite?
Cali, great place to visit.

CHORUS (3 TIMES)

Words and Music by Wyclef Jean

GONE TILL NOVEMBER
RECORDED BY WYCLEF JEAN

INTRO:

I dedicate this record, "The Carnival," to all you brothers
Takin' long trips down south: Virginia, Baltimore,
All around the world.
And your girl gets this message that you ain't comin' back.
She's sittin' back in the room, the lights are off, she's cryin',
And then my voice comes in—POW—in the middle of the night,
And this is what I told her for you:

CHORUS:

Every time I make a run, girl, you turn around and cry.
I ask myself, "Why, oh why?
See, you must understand, I can't work a nine-to-five,
So I'll be gone 'til November."
 Said, "I'll be gone 'til November,
  I'll be gone 'til November."
   Yo, tell my girl, "Yo, I'll be gone 'til November,
    I'll be gone 'til November,
     I'll be gone 'til November."
      Yo, tell my girl, "Yo, I'll be gone 'til November.
       January, February, March, April, May,
        I see you cryin' but, girl, I can't stay.
         I'll be gone 'til November,
          I'll be gone 'til November,
           And give a kiss to my mother."

When I come back there'll be no need to clock,
I'll have enough money to buy out blocks.
Tell my brother, "Go to school in September,"
So he won't mess up in summer school in the summer.
Tell my cousin Jerry, wear his condom.
If you don't wear condom, you'll see a red lump.
Whoa-oh-oh-oh, you sucker MCs, you got no flow.
I heard your style, you're so-so.

CHORUS

I had to flip nuttin' and turn it into somethin'.
Hip-hop turns to the future rock when I smash a punk. (Bing!)
Commit treason, then I'll have a reason
To hunt you down, it's only right, it's rappin' season.
Yeah, you with the loud voice, posin' like you're top-choice,
You're voice, I'll make a hearse out of your Rolls Royce.
Besides, I got my girl to remember
And I'll commit that I'll be back in November.

CHORUS

I know the hustle's hard,
But we gotta enterprise the carnival.

Words and Music by Dwight Myers,
Luther Vandross and Peter Phillips

GOT ME WAITING
RECORDED BY HEAVY D & THE BOYZ

CHORUS:

Got me waiting, anticipating.
You got me thinking I want your love.
I'm try'n to show you I really, really want to know you.
You got me thinking I want your love.

I got a funny feelin', honey, that you're kinda diggin' me,
But every time you see me, word is bone—you been ignorin' me.
I know your name; yes I do, because your girls told me.
I know where you live, you wanna bet, because your girls showed me.

But I'll parlay and stay out of your way,
Figurin' I won't be ignorant; I'll catch you the next day.
When I'm in focus I notice you only move with a chosen few.
Irreplaceable, what's up with insatiable you?

I never figured you for the quiet type,
On the down low, the low-profile type.
I always thought you was a rah-rah mama,
Servin' up crazy confusion, causin' drama.

What's the matter, huh? Cat got your tongue,
Or some mack got you strung, or maybe I ain't the one?
I wanna know 'cause if I don't, it's gonna haunt me.
Yo, word up, you got me thinkin' you want me.

CHORUS

I'm steady pickin' my brain tryin' to figure your game.
What's your angle? Tell me where you're comin' from.
The whole picture is strange, so I'm diggin' the frame
Because I like what I see and I want some.

So tell me, what's your plot? What's your plan?
You're lookin' for a brother to get got: I'm your man.
But believe in me; you wanna be with me
But you won't even talk to me to tell me what it is you see in me.

I gotta hear it from your girls uptown.
But word got around from my crew in Brooklyn and in the boogie-down.
Said you had a thing for me,
And what would it take for a date and wait, swing with me.

I got your cards—you're playin' hard to get.
I'm long and I'm strong and if it's on I keep it soft and wet.
Let me know 'cause if you don't it's gonna haunt me.
Yo, word up, you got me thinkin' you want me.

CHORUS

Look at all the cuties swingin' in the party.
Look at all the cuties swingin' in the party.

I never stumble 'cause I'm humble and I'm ready to rap.
You got me feelin' like I'm sleepin' and it's keepin' me trapped.
But still in all, you want to stall and have a fellow on lay-away,
Frontin' for nothin' like it's somethin' for me to stay away.

Emotional trips; get a grip because I'm losin' it.
Ideas were clear, had it in gear, now you're confusin' it.
I had the thought that you were caught and you were goin' steady.
Wasn't checkin' for me 'cause you had a friend already.

But I'm gonna put it all aside 'cause God is on my side.
Swallow my pride, strive, and follow my guide.
Let me know 'cause if you don't it's gonna haunt me.
Yo, word up, you got me thinkin' you want me.

CHORUS

GOT YOUR MONEY

Words and Music by
Pharrell Williams, Chad Hugo
and Russell Jones

RECORDED BY OL' DIRTY BASTARD

Oh, Baby...
I dedicate this to all the pretty girls,
To all the pretty girls,
To, oh, all the pretty girls in the world;
And the ugly girls, too,
'Cause to me you're pretty anyway, baby.

You give me your number; I call you up.
You act like your pussy don't interrupt.
I don't have no problem with you fuckin' me,
But I have a little problem with you not fuckin' me.
Baby, you know I'm-a take care of you
'Cause you say you got my baby and I know it ain't true.
Is it a good thing?
No, it's bad, bitch; for good or worse, makes you switch.
So I walk on over with my Cristal.
Bitches, niggaz, put away your pistols.
Dirty won't be havin' that in this house
'Cause, bitch, I'll cripple your style.
Now that you heard my calm voice,
Couldn't get another nigga, coochie won't get moi.

CHORUS:

If you wanna look good and not be bummy,
Girl, you'd better gimme that money.
Hoo! Hey, Dirty baby, I got your money,
Don't you worry, I said, hey baby, I got your money.
If you wanna look good and not be bummy,
Girl, you'd better gimme that money.
Hoo! Hey, Dirty baby, I got your money,
Don't you worry, I said, hey baby, I got your money.

Yo, I glanced at the girl; girl glanced at me.
I whispered in her ear, "You wanna be with me?"
You wanna look pretty though, in my video.
Ol' Dirty on the hat and I let you all know.
Just dance, if you're caught up in the Holy Ghost trance.
If you stop, I'm-a put the killer ants in your pants.

I'm the O–D–B, as you can see.
F.B.I., don't you be watchin' me.
I don't want no problems, or I'll put you down
In the ground where you cannot be found.
I'm just Dirt Dog, tryin' to make some money,
So give me my streets and gimme my honey.
Radios play this all day, every day.
Recognize I'm a fool and you lovin' me.
None of you now better look at me funny,
Now you know my name, now gimme my money.

Just sing it, girls.
Just shake it right now!
Just sing it, girls.
Just shake it right now!

If Dirty wants to sing, I think y'all should let him.
I think y'all should give him his money.
That's how I like it, girl.
Sexy, sexy, sexy,
Sexy, sexy, sexy,
Sexy, sexy, sexy,
Sexy, sexy, sexy.

Yo, yo, niggaz playin' in the club like this all night.
Bitches, put your ass out and let me hold it tight.
You're lookin' at my wrist sayin' it's so nice!
The price fits the diamonds shining in disco lights.
You'd better help me solve my problem
Or I'm-a get this money and rob them.
Lucky dog when I won the lotto,
Ran up my card for carrying raw loads.
Now you can call me Dirty
And then lift up your skirt.
And if you want some of this,
God, make Ol' Dirty Dirt bust your ass.
Stop annoying me; yeah, I play my music loud.
Take the Bastard Ol' Dirty to move the crowd.
They say he had his dick in his mouth.
Eddie Murphy taught me that back at the house.
Now gimme my money.

Words and Music by Clifford Smith, Robert Mays,
Masir Jones, Lorenzo Patterson, Andre Young,
Earl Simmons and Irving Lorenzo

GRAND FINALE
RECORDED BY DMX, FEATURING METHOD MAN, NAS, AND JA RULE

[DMX]

I ain't goin' back to jail next time the County or the State see me.
It's gonna be in a bag, uhh!
This is it, baby, end of the road, ha hah!
When you a dog, you a dog for life!
You don't hear me though; you don't hear me though,
You don't hear me though, c'mon, c'mon!

[METHOD MAN]

Watch them young guns that take none,
Nobody safe from the Friday the Thirteenth.
Ghetto Jason, itchy trigger-finger achin'
Snatch yo' ass, bloodbath, take your first step down a thug path.
Ain't no love here, just slugs here.
Kids know the half: you get plugged here.
That's just impossible for the weak to last,
Now behold the unstoppable.
Third eye watchin' you, watchin' me
Throwin' rocks from the penalty box.
Cop a plea, Young G, we was born to die.
Don't cry for me, just keep the heat closely and ride for me
'Cause we family, for better or worse,
You and I from the dirt, you snatch purse.

So hard it hurt to be here, and each year,
I'm pourin' out more beer for deceased peers.
Holdin' fort, police line, "Do Not Cross,"
They found his corpse in the loft with the head cut off,
And butt naked; homicide the crime method,
Add another killer verse to the murder record,
The grand finale.

[NAS]
Hot corners, cops with warrants, every block is boring.
Friday night, getting bent, lick a poem.
My dog, not even home a month yet, and blaze a girl in the stomach.
He robbin' niggaz who pumpin'.
Lil' Blood got popped by the Group Home cat.
Everybody nervous in the 'hood, pullin' they gatts.
Fiend yellin' out, "Who got those?"
Go and see shorty snot-nosed,
He don't floss, but he got dough, thug faces,
Fugitives runnin' from court cases.
Slugs shootin' past for the love of drug paper,
Queens cap peelers, soldiers, drug dealers.
And God'll throw a beam of lightning down 'cause he feel us.
Max the next one strike me down if I'm not the realest.
The Mayor wanna call the SWAT team to come and kill us,
But dogs are friends,
If one see the morgue, one'll live to get revenge.
And we ride to the end; brave hearts blow the lye with Henn,
And still rise, took alive with live men.
My man got three six-to-eighteens,
And only five in the belly of the beast.
Didn't wanna hear the shit, I tried to tell him on the streets,
It's irrelevant, the beast love to eat black meat,
And got us niggaz from the 'hood hangin' off his teeth.
We slangin' to eat, bringin' the heat,
Bullet holes, razor scars in the pain in the street, huh.

CHORUS:

[JA RULE]

When you a dog, you a dog for life. (Ride or die.)
My dogs feel pain from love. (See eye to eye.)
Give us one shot at life. (Let us fly.)
Come on, niggaz! (We dogs for life.)
When you a dog, you a dog for life. (Ride or die.)
My dogs feel pain from love. (See eye to eye.)
Give us one shot at life. (Let us fly.)
Come on, niggaz! (We dogs for life.)

[METHOD MAN]

There's a mad money out here, dog, mad money out here.
What, you tryin' to get it? (Word up.)
You gonna bust your gun to get it? (Tsh, whatever, yo!)
I hear you, I hear you.

[DMX]

Uhh, I've lost my grip on reality, or so it would seem.
Pinch myself to wake up 'cause I know it's a dream.
Niggaz that don't know me see me and think I'm-a rob 'em,
Niggaz that know me well see me and think I'm a problem.
I'm just a nigga that's misunderstood,
But, word to God, I turn your last name to Underwood,
'Cause if I see it, I'm-a take it and run with it, that's me.
What type of bullshit is this nigga on? That's D,
The dog come and getcha outside.
The more blood flows when I plug holes with the snub-nose.
Gun blows, bullets whistle, wouldn't miss you.
Hit you all up in your mouth like it tried to kiss you.
Drama, it's right here, how much you need?
Beat you down with gatt, see how much you bleed.
How much you plead for your life, you was a killer
And all the bitches comin' up out that ass you feelin' gettin' realer.
Now beg for your life one more time, one more crime, one more nine.
C'mon, cry nigga, it's over!
This is the shit that hits hard.
You either the last one standin' or the last one to fall.

CHORUS

Words by Shawn Carter, Mark James and Martin Charnin
Music by Shawn Carter, Mark James and Charles Strouse

HARD KNOCK LIFE (GHETTO ANTHEM)
RECORDED BY JAY-Z

Check the bass line out, uh-huh.
Jigga (bounce wit' it), uh-huh, uh-huh, uh-huh, yeah.
Let it bump, though.

CHORUS:
[*Annie* sample]
It's the hard-knock life for us.
It's the hard-knock life for us!
'Stead-a treated, we get tricked,
'Stead-a kisses, we get kicked.
It's the hard-knock life!

From standin' on the corners boppin',
To drivin' some of the hottest cars New York has ever seen,
For droppin' some of the hottest verses rap has ever heard,
From the dope spot, with the smoke glock,
Fleein' the murder scene, you know me well.
From nightmares of a lonely cell, my only hell.
But since when y'all niggaz know me to fail?
Fuck naw, where all my niggaz with the rubber grips, bust shots?
And if you with me, mom, I rub on your tits and whatnot.
I'm from the school of hard knocks; we must not
Let outsiders violate our blocks and my plot.
Let's stick up the world and split it fifty-fifty, uh-huh.
Let's take the dough and stay real jiggy, uh-huh,
And sip the Cris' and get pissy-pissy,
Flow infinitely like the memory of my nigga, Biggie, baby!
You know it's hell when I come through
The life and times of Shawn Carter,
Nigga: Volume Two, y'all niggaz get ready.

CHORUS

I flow for those dro'ed out,
All my niggaz locked down in the ten by fo', controllin' the house,
We live in hard knocks, we don't take or borrow blocks.
Burn 'em down and you can have it back, Daddy, I'd rather that.
I flow for chicks wishin' they ain't have to strip to pay tuition.
I see you vision, mama, I put my money on the long shots,
All my balers that's born to clock.
Now I'm-a be on top whether I perform or not.
I went from lukewarm to hot, sleepin' on futons and cots
To king-size dream machines, the green fives,
I've seen pies, let the thing between my eyes analyze
Life's ills, then I put it down, type Braille.
I'm tight grill with the phony rappers, y'all might feel we homies.
I'm like, still, y'all don't know me, shit!
I'm tight grill when my situation ain't improvin'.
I'm tryin' to murder everything movin', feel me?!

CHORUS (2 TIMES)

I don't know how to sleep, I gotta eat, stay on my toes.
Got a lot of beef, so logically, I prey on my foes.
Hustling's still inside of me, and as far as progress,
You'd be hard-pressed to find another rapper hot as me.
I gave you prophecy on my first joint, and y'all lamed out.
Didn't really appreciate it 'til the second one came out.
So I stretched the game out, x'd your name out,
Put Jigga on top and drop albums non-stop for ya, nigga!

CHORUS (2 TIMES)

It's the hard-knock life!
It's the hard-knock life!

Words and Music by
Eugene Record and Barbara Acklin
Additional Lyrics by MC Hammer

HAVE YOU SEEN HER
RECORDED BY MC HAMMER

Ah, yeah, I'm glad I put this tape in.
I'm just gon' cruise down the road,
Look at the stars in the sky,
And drift off into the sweet memories that I have
Of a love that my heart has been searching for
For so long, and I know somewhere,
If I keep searching, that love I'll find.
The picture grows clearer and clearer,
From the back to the front of my mind,
And like love, a love I know I'll have,
The girl that I want—she'll be mine.
And she'll be fly, and it'll last.

I see her face and I can't let go.
She's in my dreams and my heart, so let me know:
(Have you seen her?)
Have you seen her?
(Tell me, have you seen her?)

I'm looking for that love.
She's a thought and a vision in my memory.
I haven't met her, but tell me, where could she be?
(Have you seen her?)
Have you seen her?
(Tell me, have you seen her?)

I'm looking for that special love.
(Love, oh love, love is a feeling that I need.)
Love is a feeling that the Hammer definitely needs.
(Please be mine.)
Baby, be mine.
(I need your love to make it.)
I need your love to make it,
So why don't you be mine?

The search is going on from coast to coast.
A woman for a man who's propping the most.
(Have you seen her?)
Have you seen her?
(Tell me, have you seen her?)

My heart is beating strong,
This love cannot be wrong.
I need her and I want her, so come on to my home.
(Have you seen her?)
Have you seen her?
(Tell me, have you seen her?)

I'm-a keep looking—
At the movies, in my car, on my stereo,
At a game, or on a "Different World" or the "Cosby Show."
(Have you seen her?)
Have you seen her?
(Tell me, have you seen her?)

Yo, veo, tell me, what's up?
At the track, at the club, or out buying dub,
If you've seen her, then I'll have her, 'cause I'm in love.
(Have you seen her?)
Have you seen her?
(Tell me, have you seen her?)

My heart is hurting so bad,
(Love, oh love, love is a feeling that I need.)
Love is a feeling that I know I need.
(Please be mine.)
Be mine, baby.
(I need your love to make it.)
I need your love to make it,
Why don't you be mine?
(Baby, be mine.)
Where could she be?

At the store around the corner,
Or wondering at night,
Or chilling with another brother holding the mic.
(Have you seen her?)
Have you seen her?
(Tell me, have you seen her?)

Hammer, you know I'm looking,
Calling all my friends all around the place:
Guy, Lavrette, or my homie, Rob Base.
(Have you seen her?)
Have you seen her?
(Tell me, have you seen her?)

If you've peeped her out, tell me,
Yo, veo on the phone,
Ted, Dre, or Ed Lover,
Fab Five, homies—won't you help a young brother?
(Have you seen her?)
Have you seen her?
(Tell me, have you seen her?)

I got a picture in my mind.
The thought is so clear of the love I need here,
Like D–B Magic, and why don't you appear?
(Have you seen her?)
Oh baby, why don't you appear?
(Tell me, have you seen her?)

I can see yo' face.
I'm seeing her face, again and again.
Come knocking at my door, and you know I'll let you in.
(Have you seen her?)
Have you seen her?
(Tell me, have you seen her?)

Oh, my sweet love.
Searching 'round the world, what more can I say?
The girl is hard to see, like an unseen VeeJay.

(Have you seen her?)
(Tell me, have you seen her?)

158

Words and Music by Mohandas, Robert Hill, Kevin Keaton,
Reggie Noble, Lawrence Parker and B. Robinson

HEARTBEAT
RECORDED BY KRS-ONE, FEATURING REDMAN AND ANGIE MARTINEZ

[REDMAN]

Alright, everybody move back from the ropes.
If you don't move back, we're gonna turn this music off
And that's my word, move back!
Word is bond, let's get this shit goin'.
Word up, it's the Funk Doc in the house.
Say, "Hell, yeah!" "HELL YEAH!"
Say, "Fuck, yeah!" "FUCK YEAH!"
Word up, it's the Funk Doc Spock, you don't stop.
It's my man, KRS, you don't stop.
It's the girl, Angie, you don't stop.
With the hah, ha-ha, ha, ha-ha, hah!

[ANGIE MARTINEZ]
It's the Butter Pecan Rican speakin', deletin'
Other radio jocks that think they competin'.
They pre-sweetened like candy; I'm hot like pepper.
Big up to Sandy, but my name is Angie
Martinez, what a true microphone fiend is,
Steppin' up, lovely, with "My Adidas,"
Through your speakers, representin' boriquas
And all hip-hop rhyme seekers.
You may think I'm crazy-right, but I'm crazy-hype.
Slay this nice, y'all, every time Angie grab the mic,
I jams it right tonight, not the hardest,
But peep the style of this Puerto Rican goddess.

[REDMAN]
Aiyyo, yo, yo, yo, stop the music!
Aiyyo, back up off the ropes, man, word up!
Yo, get from this, off the ropes.
Now Aiyyo, yo, yo, KRS-One, come again, the selector.

[KRS-ONE]
It's been a long time, but we made it, you waited.
You gettin' frustrated cause these MCs in trainin'.
Skills on the mic for a royalty, save it.
Pullin' down rap so that others can't make it.
They can't fake it in front of KRS, they naked.
That same old MC trend, I'm here to break it.
The highly conceptional, multidirectional,
Hot in ninety-seven, so I guess I'm flexible.
Rap relieve stress, so yes, I guess it's medical.
All your wrecking and rapping is still theoretical.
Redman, you know you must understand. (What up?)
Redman, you know you gots to understand. (Hah! What up, love?)
Angie, rockin' with the one B–D–P (Ha, ha, ha!)
Representin' right now at Hit Factory.

[REDMAN]
One, two, hah, and you don't quit.
It's Kris and Angie with the ultimate.
On, two, hah, and you don't quack.
It's Funk Doc, smoke weed and don't smoke crack.
Ha, ha, ha, hah, and you don't quit.
Hoohah, hahah, and you don't quit.
I rocks jams like Samsonites with mics,
Stage two boomin' system and flood the lights.
The lyrical fo'-fo's lettin' off like suppose,
Reggie Reg is rockin' on the ra-di-o!
Hah, huh, the ooh-child, too chill.
Caps peeled, someone in my bed like Dru Hill.
Raise 'em up 'cause I feel my spot can't be touched.
No time for the Pauline jack, hit the clutch.
Shotgun what? It's the high exalted
Ruler of the buddha, the cash make my pockets
Stick out like a tumor; for the consumers,
I get busy with La Pluma, detonate the bomb
To make you hibernate sooner, certified Luna-
Tic my click run deeper than Charlie Tuna,
Kahunas, raw for the able, key movers,
All over the 'hood like them crooked-I coolers.
Bang maneuvers from Jerz to Vancouver,
Back in the Bronx with heartbeats ample looped up.
I blast like Kris, funk abyss,
Like a phone chauvinist with a Roley on the wrist.
Psych! I can afford it, less I slaughtered.
Three platinum, niggaz, and none of 'em prerecorded.
KRS-One need to be runnin' for office,
So Butter Pecan Rican, tell them to get off his.

HEY LUV (ANYTHING)
RECORDED BY MOBB DEEP, FEATURING 112

Words and Music by Kejuan Muchita,
Albert Johnson, Jonathan Williams, Marvin Scandrick,
Quinnes Parker, Daron Jones and Michael Keith

To let it ride...

[PRODIGY]
Tssh, shorty, come here (112).
Listen, listen, listen, I know, I know. (Ooh.)
(Love you.) Goddamn.
(Need you.) Hear me out, though.
(Let's ride.) Yo. (Let's ride.)

Hey love, I wanna hold you and talk to you,
Put my arms around ya shoulder and walk wit'chu.
Be the one that'll serve you, my word to you.
I know that nigga don't be doin' what he 's'posed to do.
I got much more to give than homie do,
And you so fine, I just wanna roll wit'chu.
You a queen bitch and you need a king close to you.
You need a nigga like P to just flow wit'chu,
And I gotta try, 'cause anything's possible.
And you just might see things the way I do.
I just wanna get next to you, friends wit'chu,
Burn hundreds, wake up in the bed wit'chu.
I love when you walk, how that body move.
Pardon my mouth, I'm just being honest, boo.
I will pay for airtime just to vibe wit'chu.
Kisses and hugs until the next time you swing through.

CHORUS:

[112]

So many things that I wanna do:
Wanna kiss, wanna touch, wanna taste, never teasing you.
Ooh, baby, 'cause I only wanna be with you.
Girl, you know, anything that you need, I got it.
Million dollar shoppin' spree, I got it.
Anything that you want, I got it.
You know, I got it, ask me, I got it.

[HAVOC]

Ma, I want you in the worst way, and I ain't thirsty or nothin',
But when I see somethin', boo, I go hard for the one,
Hit my cell, I'm-a take you out to eat
And kill any misconception that you got of Mobb Deep.
Throw that bug in ya ear, and it's about time
'Cause a nigga like me been wantin' you for years.
Bumped heads here and there, but never got the chance.
Best to those who wait, once I get up in them pants.
Ain't no one-minute man.
'Posed to be with him? Better change those plans.
Anything you gots ta do, lotta screw,
Must be out his monkey-ass mind.
How the hell he gettin' tired of you?
Lemme light that fire that ya body desire,
Get you back to being sexy, single, "Free," like Mya
'Cause I treats 'em right, you know how I rock it.
Wherever you at, girl, I'm on the next flight.

CHORUS

[PRODIGY]

Sit back, I got this, baby, girl, you straight?
For sure, rest assure you in the arms of strength.
Baby, I'll die for my loved ones, make no mistake.
I'm not that man, I keep my gun on bait.

[HAVOC]
And it's a cold world, ya man don't understand ya pain.
And I know you gettin' tired of the same ol' same.
He expect to keep you locked with that five-karat ring?
Let's cop that old real while 112 sing.

[112]
Anything you want, and anything you need,
Just pick up the phone and call me.
Ooh, anything, anything you want, (Anything you need.)
And anything you need,
Ooh, I'll come running.

CHORUS (2 TIMES)

Yeah, 112,
Mobb Deep, (Let's rock this.)
Let's go. (Prodigy.)
Da-da-da-da-da. (Havoc.)
Oh, let's go.
Let's ride. (That's right.)

Words and Music by
Ice-T and Afrika Islam

HIGH ROLLERS
RECORDED BY ICE-T

Speed of life, fast; it's like walkin' barefoot over broken glass.
It's like jumpin' rope on a razor blade.
All lightning-quick decisions are made.
Lifestyle plush, females rush.
This high-profile personality who earns his pay illegally,
Professional liar, schoolboys admire,
Young girls desire, very few live to retire.
Cash flow extreme, dress code supreme, vocabulary obscene,
Definition street player, you know what I mean.

The high rollers.
The high rollers.

People of the city, stop foolin' yourself.
Crime rules the streets, who the hell else?
All the police have gone out to play
Because, for enough cold cash, they'll look the other way.
Just look at the cars as they go by:
Benz, Ferraris, trucks up high,
Beepers connecting players to big-time deals
With all of this technology, who needs to steal?
Just live a life of leisure every night and day
And you're livin' proof that crime does pay.

Your life is dangerous and reckless.
You eat fly guys and girls for breakfast.
You're a titan of the nuclear age.
Your muscles flex with a Uzi or twelve-gauge.
And you love the game, that's why you boast,
Because you're high-priced, high-speed, high-post.

You're a high roller.
High rollers.
When I say, "High roller," I mean the best.
Forget the half-steppers, eject the rest,
Because these high-ranked officials of our city streets
Make millions all triggered by electric beeps.
They dress in diamonds and rope chains,
They got the blood of Scarface runnin' through their veins.
Silk shirts, leather suits,

Hair always fresh, eel-skin boots,
Large hearts, though their sizes vary,
Bankrolls that take two pockets to carry.
Cruisin' in their 500 Benz Sedan
With their systems peaked out, rockin' "Pusher Man."
Yes, their fashion's high and hard to beat,
They buy their Gucci from Gucci's, not the swap meet.
Eat very well, much clientele,
And whatever you need, they probably sell.

The high rollers.
The high rollers.

Oh yes, I'm here to tell you females also roll,
Drive the same cars, sometimes wear more gold.
Cold as an igloo, or hot as a flame,
They'll shake ya, break ya, and you won't know their name.
Gangstas to the max, all marks will be taxed,
These girls drive Ferraris, not Cadillacs.
Respect is demanded, most men don't understand it
'Til they peep the huge bank that these girls have landed.
They're junkies for fun, love life on the run,
And if things get hot, they will pull a gun.
Prey on the lame, no shame to the game,
And they all seek power, fuck the fame.

The high rollers.
The high rollers.

Now radio stations probably won't play
This record because of the things I say.
They'll say I'm glamorizin' the hustlin' 'hood,
And a record like this can do no good.
But I'm not here to tell ya right or wrong,
I don't know which side of the law you belong.
Yes, the game has flash, but sometimes hurts.
Behind any mistake, hard times lurks
And jail's not your only problem, though it may seem
You just may die by a barrage from an M-16.
But to each his own, choose the mobile phone,
The tailored suit, the luxury home.
You'll never get caught 'cause you got nerves of ice,
And you're much smarter than those crooks on "Miami Vice."

Right, you wanna be a high roller.
High roller.

Words and Music by Jeffrey Atkins,
Taiwan Green and Irving Lorenzo

HOLLA HOLLA
RECORDED BY JA RULE

CHORUS:

(Holla, holla.)
All my niggaz that's ready to get (dollaz, dollaz).
Bitches know who can get 'em a little (hotta, hotta).
Come on, if you rollin' wit' me, (follow, follow).
It's murder...

Think you fuckin' wit' Ja? Nada.
Whatcha wanna go, dolla for dolla? (Holla, holla.)
My niggaz is (hotta, hotta).
Fucks plenty bitches, and dug ditches for petty niggaz.
You look in me eyes and tell me they style ain't ridiculous.
(Bitches, bitches) pop da pussy and bounce like (hit it, hit it).
Sure, if your favorite is long (get it, get it), baby, baby,
Don't you wanna leave tonight and fuck wit' me?
'Cause we really need to be freakin' off at any cost.
It's on me, if you married, then get a divorce.
When I hits it, some women get twisted.
Have 'em twitchin', like "Damn, look what the dick did."
I just wanna hit it the worst way, right after a long day,
And put the puss on lay-away, heard me?
I'm that dirty nigga that get you hot, and heat it,
Baby girl, if you want it as bad as you need it.

CHORUS (2 TIMES)

Let me holla at my true thugs.
If niggaz want war, bust slugs.
Nigga, what? I'm hotta, hotta and just can't be touched,
Plus, anybody that fucks wit' me gonna get felt.
How many want it? Determines how the slugs get dealt,
'Cause I (spit 'em, spit 'em),
Choke them niggaz like roaches and then (clip 'em, clip 'em).
Long as I'm alive, I'm-a (hit 'em, hit 'em).
Respect mines, to the day of my demise.
Don't fuck wit' me, 'cause the flow's (killa, killa).
Whoever, ever, who wants it?
It's yours, now your gonna (get it, get it).
(Feel a, feel a) nigga full of holes.
Treat 'em like hoes and show no love to them homo thugs.
It's us you wanna fuck wit'
As soon as them slugs skip from body to body,
Go from grave to bit.
I don't respect it, plus niggaz committed treason.
Who want it wit' Ja? Who ready to die breathing?

CHORUS (2 TIMES)

Ja baby, one of the many, many niggaz who sip Henney
With the, the two-seaters, sittin' on twenties,
I, I be wit' runnin' in, runnin' out.
Then, thou bestow hit 'em up, gun 'em down.
Niggaz ain't ready for Ja, anyway, anyhow.
I give it, give it to the niggaz claimin' that they live it.
Real (niggaz, niggaz) brandish the iron and flash
Like (hold this, hold this) when you got nothin' to live for.
Notice, niggaz be hot and more explosive.
Focus, ready rip 'em up with the dope, this
My life, niggaz is frontin' and stuntin' for nothin'.
Better act right, 'fore I spark and dim your lights.
I'm a hazard to niggaz, a bastard to bitches,
When in doubt, go for stealth and clap the finish.
Anything movin', rightfully hit for wrongdoin'.
I'm-a follow and encourage all my niggaz to what?

CHORUS

Words and Music by Pharrell L. Williams,
Cornelius Haynes and Charles L. Brown

HOT IN HERRE
RECORDED BY NELLY

Hot in…
So hot in herre…
So hot in…

I was like, good gracious, ass is bodacious,
Flirtatacious, tryin' to show faces.
Lookin' for the right time to shoot my stream. (You know.)
Lookin' for the right time to flash them keys.
Then, um, I'm leavin', please believin', (Oh!)
Me and the rest of my heathens.
Check it, got it locked at the top of the four seasons
Penthouse, rooftop, birds I feedin'.
No deceivin', nothin' up my sleeve, no teasin'.
I need you to get up, up on the dance floor,
Give that man what he askin' for
'Cause I feel like bustin' loose and I feel like touchin' you, (Uh-uh.)
And can't nobody stop the juice so, baby, tell me what's the use?

CHORUS 1:

(I said,)
It's gettin' hot in herre. (So hot.)
So take off all your clothes.

I am gettin' so hot, I wanna take my clothes off.

Why you at the bar if you ain't poppin' the bottles?
What good is all the fame if you ain't fuckin' the models?
I see you drivin' sportscar, ain't hittin' the throttle,
And I be down and do a hundred, top down, and goggles.
Get off the freeway, Exit 106 and parked it.
Ashtray, flip gate, time to spark it.
Gucci collar for dollar, got out and walked it,
I spit game 'cause, baby, I can't talk it.

Warm, sweatin', it's hot up in this joint.
Vocal, tank top, all on at this point.
You're with a winner so, baby, you can't lose,
I got secrets, can't leave Cancun.
So take it off like you're home alone
You know, dance in front your mirror while you're on the phone,
Checkin' your reflection and tellin' your best friend,
Like, "Girl, I think my butt gettin' big."

CHORUS 1 (2 TIMES)

CHORUS 2:
(Nelly hang all out.)
Mix a little bit, ah, ah, ah,
With a little bit ah, ah, ah.
(Nelly just fall out.)
Give a little bit, ah, ah, ah,
With a little bit, ah, ah, ah.
(Nelly hang all out.)
With a little bit, ah, ah, ah,
And sprinkle a that, ah, ah, ah.
(Nelly just fall out.)
I like it when ya ah, ah.
Girl, baby make it, ah, ah.

Stop pacin', time wastin'.
I got a friend with a fold in the basement. (What?)
I'm just kiddin', like Jason, (Oh.)
Unless you gon' do it.
Extra, extra, eh, spread the news.
Shaq and Nelly took a trip from the Luna to Neptunes,
Came back with somethin' thicker than fittin' in Sassoons.
Say she like to think about cuttin' in restrooms.

CHORUS 1 (4 TIMES)

CHORUS 2

Words and Music by Cornell Haynes and Jason Epperson

HOT SHIT (COUNTRY GRAMMAR HOT SHIT)

RECORDED BY NELLY

CHORUS:

I'm goin' down, down, baby, yo' street in a Range Rover,
(C'mon,)
Street sweeper, baby, cocked ready to let it go.
(Hot shit!)
Shimmy, shimmy cocoa what? Listen to it pound.
Light it up and take a puff, pass it to me now.

CHORUS

Mmm, you can find me in Saint Louis, rollin' on dubs,
Smokin' in clubs, blowin' up like Cocoa Puffs,
Sippin' on Bud, gettin' perved and gettin' dubbed.
Daps and hugs mean mugs and shoulder shrugs
And it's all because 'ccumulated enough stretch just to navigate it,
Wood decorated on chrome, and it's candy-painted,
Fans fainted while I'm entertainin'.
Wild, ain't it? How me and money end up hangin'
I hang with Hannibal Lector (Hot shit!) so feel me when I bring it.
Sing it loud (What?), I'm from the Lou' and I'm proud.
Run a mile for the cause, I'm righteous, above the law.
Playa, my style's raw, I'm born to mack like Todd Shaw.
Forget the fame and the glamour,
Give me Ds wit' a rubber hammer.
My grammar be's Ebonics, gin tonic and chronic,
Fuck, bionic, it's ironic, slammin' niggaz like Onyx.
Lunatics 'til the day I die,
I run more game than the Bulls and Sonics.

CHORUS (2 TIMES)

Who says pretty boys can't be wild niggaz?
Loud niggaz, O.K. Corral niggaz?
Foul niggaz, run-in-the-club-and-bust-in-the-crowd niggaz?
How nigga? Ask me again and it's goin' down, nigga.
Now, nigga, come to the circus and watch me clown, nigga,
Pound niggaz, what you be givin' when I'm around, nigga?
Frown niggaz, talkin' shit when I leave the town, nigga.
Say now, can you hoes come out to play now?
Hey, I'm ready to cut you up any day now.
Play by my rules, boo, and you gon' stay high.
May I answer yo' Third Question like A.I.?
Say "hi" to my niggaz left in the slamma
From Saint Louis to Memphis,
From Texas back up to Indiana,
Chi-town, K.C., Motown to Alabama,
L.A., New York Yankee niggaz to Hotlanta,
'Ouisiana, all my niggaz wit' Country grammar,
Smokin' blunts in Savannah, blow thirty mill' like I'm Hammer.

CHORUS (2 TIMES)

Let's show these cats how to make these milli-ons
So you niggaz quit actin' silly, mon,
Kid quicker than Billy, mon,
Talkin' really and I need it, mon,
Foes, I kick 'em freely, mon, 'specially off Remi, mon.
Keys to my Beemer, mon, holla at Beenie Mon.
See me, mon, chiefin', rollin' deeper than any mon
Through Jennings, mon, through U-City back up to Kingsland
Wit' nice niggaz, shiest niggaz who snatch yo' life, niggaz.
Trife niggaz who produce and sell the same beat twice, nigga.
Ice niggaz all over, close to never sober
From broke to havin' dough 'cause my price Range is Rover.
Now I'm knockin' like Jehovah: let me in now, let me in now.
Bill Gates, Donald Trump, let me in now.
Spin now, I got money to lend my friends now.
We in now, candy Benz, Kenwood and tens now.
I win now (Whoo!) fuckin' lesbian twins now.
Seein', now, through the pen, I make my ends now.

CHORUS (2 TIMES)

Words and Music by Bruce Fisher, Leon Ware, Stanley Richardson,
Quincy Jones, Tupac Shakur and Johnny Jackson

HOW DO U WANT IT
RECORDED BY 2PAC,
FEATURING K-CI AND JOJO OF JODECI

CHORUS:
[K-CI AND JOJO]
How do you want it?
How do you feel?
Comin' up as a nigga in the cash game,
Livin' in the fast lane—I'm for real.
How do you want it?
How do you feel?
Comin' up as a nigga in the cash game,
Livin' in the fast lane—I'm for real.

[2PAC]
Love the way you activate your hips
    And push your ass out.
        Gotta nigga wantin' it so bad,
          I'm about to pass out.
            Wanna dig you
               And I can't even lie about it.
                  Baby, just alleviate your clothes,
                    Time to fly up out it.
                      Catch you at the club,
                  Oh shit, you got me fiendin'.
              Body talkin' shit to me,
            But I can't comprehend the meanin'.
        Now if you wanna roll with me,
    Then here's ya chance.
    Doin' eighty on the freeway,
Wait, police catch me if they can.

Forgive me, I'm a rider,
Still, I'm just a simple man.
All I want is money,
Fuck the fame, I'm a simple man.
Mister International,
Playa with the passport,
Just like a ladder, bitch,
Get you anything you ask for.
It's either him or me.
Champagne or Hennessy,
A favorite of my homies
When we floss on our enemies,
Witness as we creep to a low speed.
Peep what a hoe need,
Puff some more weed,
Funk, ya don't need.
Approachin' hoochies with a passion,
Been a long day,
But I've been drivin' by attraction
In a strong way.
Your body is bangin'.
Baby, I love it when ya flaunt it.
Time to give it to daddy nigga.
Now tell me how you want it.

CHORUS

Tell me, is it cool to fuck?
You think I come to talk?
Am I a fool or what?
Positions on the floor,
It's like erotic.
Ironic,
'Cause I'm somewhat psychotic.

I'm hittin' switches on bitches
Like I been fixed with hydraulics.
Up and down like a roller coaster,
Come up beside ya,
I ain't quittin' 'til the show is over
'Cause I'm a rider,
In and out just like a robbery.
I'll probably be a freak
And let you get on top of me.
Get her rockin' these
Nights full of Alizé.
A livin' legend,
You ain't heard about these niggaz played in Cali days.
Delores Tucker, you's a muthafucker.
Instead of tryin' to help a nigga,
You destroy a brother worse than the others.
Bill Clinton, Mister Bob Dole,
You too old to understand the way the game is told.
You're lame, so I gotta hit you with the high facts.
Won't someone listen?
Makin' millions.
Niggaz top that; they wanna censor me.
They rather see me in a cell,
Livin' in hell
With only a few of us to live to tell.
Now everybody talkin' about us,
I could give a fuck.
I'd be the first one to bomb and cuss.
Nigga, tell me how you want it.

CHORUS

Raised as a youth, tell the truth.
I got the scoop on how to get a bulletproof,
'Cause I jump on the roof.
Before I was a teenager,
  Mobile phone, SkyPager,
    Game rules, I'm livin' major.
      My adversaries is lookin' worried.
        They paranoid of gettin' buried,
          One of us gonna see the cemetery.
            My only hope is "survive,"
              If I wish to stay alive.
                Gettin' high, see the demons in my eyes.
              Before I die,
            I wanna live my life and ball,
          Make a couple million
        And then I'm chillin.
Fade 'em all, these taxes for me
Crossed up with people tryin' to sue me.
Media is in my business
And they actin' like they know me.
But I'm-a mash out, peel out.
I'm murder quick,
That's with the whip 'n' fuckin' steel out.
Yeah, nigga, it's some new shit,
So better get up on it.
When ya see me,
Tell a nigga how ya want it.
How do you want it?

CHORUS (4 TIMES)

Words and Music by Reggie Noble,
Erick Sermon and Clifford Smith

HOW HIGH
RECORDED BY METHOD MAN AND REDMAN

INTRO:

Takin' it from the top?
Tippy? Tippy?
How high?
The ultimate high.

[METHOD MAN]

'Scuse me as I kiss the sky.
Sing a song of six pence, a pocket full of rye.
Who the fuck wanna die for their culture?
Stalk the dead body like a vulture?
Tical get, hmm.
Blacker than your blackest stallion.
Hit your house 'n' projects.
I represent the Shao-Lin, my nigga.
Hell yes, Apocalypse now, the gun blow,
It be goin' down, diggy-diggy down, diggy down, down.

[REDMAN]

While the planets and the stars and the moons collapse,
When I raise my trigger-finger all y'all niggaz hit the decks!
'Cause ain't no need for that, hustlers and hardcores,
Raw to the floor like Reservoir Dogs.
The Green-Eyed Bandit can't stand it,
With more Fruitier Loops than that Toucan Sam, bitch.
Plus the bombazee got me wild.
(Fuckin' with us) is a straight suicide.

[METHOD MAN]

10–9–8–7–6–5–4–3–2 murder, one, lyric at your door.
Tical bring it to that ass raw.
Breakin' all the rules like glass jaws.
Nigga, you got to get mine to get yours.
Fucka, we don't need no rap tour;
I'd rather kick the facts and catch you with the rap-ture.
More than you bargained for,
Tical that stays open like an all-night store.
For real, I keeps it ill like a piece of blue steel
Pointed at your temple with the intent to kill
And end your existence, M–E–T.
Ain't no use for resistance, H–O–D.

[REDMAN]

I be's the ultimate rush to any nigga on dust,
The Egyptian musk, used to have me pull mad sluts.
I shift like a clutch with the Ruck,
Examine my nuts, I don't stop 'til I get enough.
Your shit broke down, light your flare,
Since the dark side tears you into Hollywood squares.
Six million ways to die, so I chose.
Made it six million and one with your eyes closed.
The blindfold cold, so you can feel the rap
And shatter the glass and second-half on your monkey ass.
And yo, my man (Tical), hit me now.
Bitches use to play me, now they can't forget me now.
Forget me not, I rock the spot, check glock.
Empty off a lickin' off a hip-hop.
Fuck the *Billboard*, I'm a bullet on my block.
How you dope when you paid for your *Billboard* spot?

CHORUS:

Look up in the sky, it's a bird, it's a plane,
It's the Funk Doctor Spock smokin' buddha on a train.
How high? So high that I can kiss the sky.
How sick? So sick that you can suck my dick.
Look up in the sky, it's a bird, it's a plane.
Recognize Johnny Blaze, ain't a damn thing changed.
How high? So high that I can kiss the sky.
How Sick? So sick that you can suck my dick.

[METHOD MAN]
'Til my man, Raider Ruckus, come home,
It ain't really on 'til the Ruckus get home.
Puff a meth bone, now I'm off to the red zone.
We don't need your dirt weed, we got a fuckin' "O."
Check it, I brings havoc with my hectic,
Bring the pain, lyrics screamin' for antiseptic.
Movin' on your left, kid, and I'm methed out my fuckin' dome piece,
Plus I got no love for the beast.
Hailin' from the big East Coast
Where niggaz pack toast,
Home of the drug kingpins and cutthroats.
(Hey boy, you's the rude boy on the block.
You try and stop the bum rush, you will get popped.)
As I run around with a racist,
My style was born in the fifty staircases.
Dig it, "F" a rap critic;
He talk about it while I live it.
If Red got the blunt, I'm the second one to hit it.

[REDMAN]
I got the verbs, nouns, and glocks in ya.
Enter the center, lyrics bang like Ricochet Rabbit.
I brings havoc with an AK-matic.
Rollin' blunts, an all-day habit,
I get it on like Smif 'n' Wess.
Punks take a sip and test,
Who split your vest?

The funk phenomenon,
I'm bombin' you like Lebanon.
Blow canals of Panama
Just off stamina.
Style's not to be fucked with, or played with,
Fuck the pretty hoes, I love those Section-A bitches.
Hittin' switches,
Twistin' wigs with fat mathematical-type scriptures.
I dig up in your planets like Diga, boo.
Scared you, blew you
To smithereens, fuck the Marines, I got machines
To light the spliff and read *Mad* magazine.
I fly more heads than Continental,
Wreck ya five times like U.S. Air off an instrumental.
Look, I'm not a halfway crook with bad looks,
But I may murder your case like your name was Cal Brooks.
I breaks 'em up proper—
Ask Biggie Smalls, "Who shot ya?"
Funk Doctor, with the twelve-gauge Mossberg.
Look, I got the tools like Rickle
To make your mind tickle
For the nine nickel. (Yo Red, yo Red!)
Punk-ass, pussy-ass.
(You ain't gotta say no more, man, that's it.)
Word up, Tical, we out.
(It's over.)

HYPNOTIZE

Words and Music by Sean "Puffy" Combs, Notorious B.I.G.,
Deric Angelettie, Ronald Anthony Lawrence,
Ron Badazz and Andy Armer

RECORDED BY NOTORIOUS B.I.G.

Uhh, uhh, uhh, c'mon.

Hah, sicker than your average Poppa,
Twist cabbage off instinct, niggaz don't think shit stink.
Pink gators, my Detroit players,
Timbs for my hooligans in Brooklyn.
Dead right, if they head right, Biggie there Air Nike.
Poppa been smooth since days of Underoos.
Never lose, never choose to, bruise crews who
Do something to us, talk go through us,
Girls walk to us, wanna do us?
Screw us? Who us?
Yeah, Poppa and Puff (Ehehe.)
Close like Starsky and Hutch, stick the clutch,
Dare I squeeze three at your cherry M3?
(Take that, take that, take that, ha, ha!)
Bang every MC easily, busily.
Recently, niggaz frontin', ain't sayin' nuttin'. (Nope.)
So I just speak my piece (c'mon), keep my piece.
Cubans with the Jesus piece (Thank you, God),
With my peeps packin', askin' who want it,
You got it, nigga, flaunt it.
That Brooklyn bullshit, we on it.

CHORUS:
Biggie, Biggie, Biggie, can't you see?
Sometimes your words just hypnotize me,
And I just love your flashy ways.
Guess that's why they broke and you're so paid. (Uh.)
Biggie, Biggie, Biggie (uh-huh), can't you see?
Sometimes your words just hypnotize me, (Hypnotize.)
And I just love your flashy ways. (Uh-huh.)
Guess that's why they broke and you're so paid. (Hah!)

I put hoes in N–Y in DKNY. (Uh-huh.)
Miami, D.C., prefer Versace. (That's right.)
All Philly hoes, dough and Moschino. (C'mon.)
Every cutie wit' a booty bought a Coogi. (Hah!)
Now, who's the real dookie, meanin' who's really the shit?
Them niggaz ride dicks, Frank White push the sticks
On Lexus LX, four and a-half,
Bulletproof glass, tints—if I want some ass.
Gon' blast, squeeze first, ask questions last.
That's how most of these so-called gangstas pass.
At last, a nigga rappin' 'bout blunts and broads,
Tits and bras, ménage-trois, sex in expensive cars.
I still leave you on the pavement,
Condo paid for, no car payment.
At my arraignment, note for the plaintiff,
Your daughter's tied up in a Brooklyn basement. (Shh.)
Face it, not guilty, that's how I stay filthy (not guilty)
Richer than Richie, 'til you niggaz come and get me.

CHORUS

I can fill ya wit' real millionaire shit; (I can fill ya.)
Escargot, my car go one-sixty swiftly.
Wreck it, buy a new one.
Your crew on the run, run, run, your crew run, run.
I know you sick of this name-brand nigga wit'
Flows; girls say he's sweet like licorice.
So get with this nigga, it's easy,
Girlfriend, here's a pen, call me 'round ten.
Come through, have sex on rugs that's Persian. (That's right.)
Come up to your job, hit you while you workin'. (Uh.)
For certain, Poppa freakin', not speakin'.
Leave that ass leakin' like rapper demo tell them,
Hoe, take they clothes off slowly,
Hit 'em wit' the force like Obi,
Dick black like Toby. (Obi…Toby.)
Watch me roam like Gobi, lucky they don't own me.
Where the safe? Show me, homie. (Say what, homie?)

CHORUS (2 TIMES)

Words and Music by Jeffrey Atkins,
Kenneth Gamble, Irving Lorenzo,
Cynthia Loving and Robert Mays

I CRY
RECORDED BY JA RULE, FEATURING LIL' MO

CHORUS:
[LIL' MO]
When I cry, you cry, we cry together.
Said, I cry, you cry, we cry together.
Said, I cry, you cry, we cry together.
Said, I cry, you cry, we cry together.

I love my life, I love my wife.
Bad time to prevail, it overwhelmed me.
I'm livin' in hell, but livin' wealthy
And know these hoes love me because I'm a star.
I can't even cop a drink at the bar,
Get me some bottles of that Remi Martin,
Let's get the party crackin' right here.
Fuck the V.I.P.
Now when my baby loves me,
Home wit' tears in her eyes
And when I get in, I hurt her more by tellin' her lies.
She ain't surprised at me, just surprised that we
Been together for this long, and I can be
The one to mistreat her, thought it last forever
'Cause if I cry, you cry, we cry together.

CHORUS

From what I recall, we was lil' niggaz,
Cuttin' school, gettin' high wit' da hottest bitches.
Livin' life so free, that we ain't fearin'
The ills of the world in the heat of drug dealin'.

You and I then made a killin'
And stuck together in this land of forbidden treasure.
Love is the only evil seed that could sever a tie this close,
Not the love between us, but your love for the dough.
You went O.T., started makin' M–O–N–E–Y.
All my good niggaz gotta die,
But shit could last forever.
I wish shaft was pleasure
'Cause when you die I cried, we cried together.

CHORUS

Wash away your tears (my love),
You ain't gotta cry no more (my love).
I'm puttin' on everything out (my love).
And my pain, it's my love.
And I want this world to smile for me,
Don't shed a tear 'cause the nigga died happily.
My momma warned me life was a muthafucka,
But I ignored the warning and kept on hustlin'.
And every night, she just look at me wit'
Tears in her eyes and they be sayin' shit
Like, "I don't want my baby to die."
Brought so much pain into a life,
Gotta make it better 'cause when ma cried, I cried,
We cried together.

CHORUS

[LIL' MO]

Ooh, you cry, then I cry, then we cry.
When he cries, I cry together, together.
When I cry, then you cry,
Then we'll cry together.
Baby, 'cause when Ja cries, Mo cries,
We'll cry, together.
If he cries, I'll cry,
Then we'll cry together.

I GET AROUND
RECORDED BY 2PAC

Words and Music by Roger Troutman,
Larry Troutman, Shirley Murdock, Ron Brooks,
Tupac Shakur and Gregory Jacobs

(I get around.)
Aw, yeah.
('Round and 'round, 'round it go.)
I get around,
Still clown with the underground
When we come around.
('Round and 'round, 'round it go.)
Stronger than ever.

Back to get wreck,
All respect to those who break they neck
To keep they hoes in check,
'Cause, hoes, they sweat a brother majorly,
And I don't know why your girl keeps pagin' me.
She tell me that she needs me,
Cries when she leaves me,
And every time she sees me, she squeeze me,
Lady, take it easy…
Hate to sound sleazy, but tease me.
I don't want it if it's that easy.
Eh, yo, bus' it, baby got a problem sayin' "bye-bye."
Just another hazard of a fly guy.
You ask me, "Why?"
It don't matter, my pockets got fatter,
Now everybody's lookin' for the ladder.
And ain't no need in bein' greedy,
If you wanna see me,
Try a beeper number, baby, when you need me,
And I'll be there in a jiffy.
Don't be picky; just be happy with this quickie.
But when you learn you can't tie me down,
Baby doll, check it out:
I get around.

Whatcha mean, ya don't know?
('Round and 'round, 'round it go.)
I get around.
The underground just don't stop for hoes.
I get around
('Round and 'round, 'round it go.)
I get around.

Hey yo, Shock, let them hoes know—

Now you can tell from my everyday fits, I ain't rich,
So cease and desist with them tricks. (Tricks.)
I'm just another black man caught up in the mix, (Mix.)
Tryin' to make a dollar out of fifteen cents. (A dime and a nickel.)
Just 'cause I'm a freak
Don't mean that we could hit the sheets.
Baby, I can see that you don't recognize me.
I'm Shock-G, the one who put the satin on your panties,
Never knew a hooker that could sham me.
I get around.

What's up, love, how you doin'? (Alright.)
Well, I've been hangin', sangin', tryin' to do my thang.
Oh, you heard that I was bangin'
Your home girl you went to school with?
That's cool, but did she tell you about her sister and your cousin?
Thought I wasn't.
See, weekends were made for Michelob,
But it's a Monday, my day,
So just let me hit it, yo.
And don't mistake my statement for a clown.
We can keep in the down low, long as you know
I get around.

('Round and 'round, 'round it go.)
Tupac-alypse Now, don't stop for hoes.
I get around.
('Round and 'round…)
Why I ain't called you? (Hahaha…please.)

Fingertips on the hip as I dip.
Gotta get a tight grip, don't slip.
Loose lips sank ships, it's a trip.
I love the way she licks her lips.
See me jockin',
Put a little twist in her hips.
'Cause I'm watchin',
Conversations on the phone
'Til the break of dawn.
Now we all alone—why the lights on?
Turn 'em off, time to set it off,
Get you wet 'n' soft.
Something's on your mind, let it off.
You don't know me, you just met me,
You won't let me.
Well, if I couldn't have it (silly rabbit),
Why you sweatin' me?
It's a lot of real Gs doin' time
'Cause a groupie bit the trooper, told a lie.
You picked the wrong guy.
Baby, if you're too fly,
You need to hit the door, search for a new guy,
'Cause I only got one night in town,
Break down or be clowned.
Baby doll, are you down?
I get around.

('Round and 'round, 'round it go.)
('Round and 'round, 'round it go.)

Words and Music by Thomas Mc Elroy,
Denzil Foster, Jay King, Garrick Husband,
Jerold Ellis, Anthony Gilmour, Michael Marshall,
Ron Bell, Claydes Smith, Robert Mickens,
Donald Boyce, Richard Westfield,
Robert Bell and George Brown

I GOT FIVE ON IT
RECORDED BY LUNIZ

Creep on it, on it, on it, on it.
Whoo, see, I'm ridin' higher and higher, whoo!
Kinda broke, so ya know, all I got's five,
I got five.

[YUKMOUTH]
Player, give me some brew, and I might just chill,
But I'm the type that like to light another joint like Cypress Hill.
I'm-a steal doobies, spit loogies
When I puff on it,
But it ain't enough on it.
Go get the S–T, I–D–E–S, never less.
I'm mellow fresh,
Rollin' joints like a cigarette.
So pass it 'cross the table like ping-pong.
I'm gone, beatin' my chest like King Kong.
It's on, wrap my lips around a forty,
And when it comes to get another stogie,
Fools all kick in like Shinobi.
   No, me ain't my homie.
      To begin with it's too many heads
         To be poppin' at my friend,
            Hit it, unless you pull out the phat, crispy,
               Five-dollar bill on the real before it's history,
                  'Cause fools be havin' them vacuum lungs,
                     And if you let 'em hit it for free you holla,
                        "Dum-dum-dum-dum."
                           I come to school with the Taylor on my earlobe,
                              Avoidin' all the thick teasers, skeezers, an weirdos
                                 That be blowin' off the land like, "Where's the bomb at?"

Give me two bucks,
You take a puff and pass my bomb back.
Suck up the dank like a Slurpee,
The serious bomb will make a nigga go delirious like Eddie Murphy.
I got more growin' pains than Maggie,
'Cause homies nag me
To take the dank out of the baggie.

CHORUS:

I got five on it,
Grab your forty, let's get keyed.
I've got five on it,
Messin' wit' that Indo weed.
I've got five on it,
It's got me stuck and I'm tow back.
I've got five on it,
Partna, let's go half on a sack.

[KNUMSKULL]

I take sacks to the face, whenever I can.
Don't need no crutch,
I'm so keyed up 'til the joint be burnin' my hand.
Next time I roll it in a hampa,
To burn slow so the ashes won't be burnin' up my hand.
Bra hoochies can hit,
But they know they got to pitch in,
Then I roll a joint that's longer than your extension.
'Cause I'll be damned if you get high off me for free.
Hell naw, you better bring your own spliff, chief.
Wassup? Don't babysit that.
Better pass the joint, stop hittin' 'cause you know ya got asthma.
Crack a forty open, homie, and guzzle it
'Cause I know the weed in my system is gettin' lonely.
I gotta take a whiz test to my P-O.
I know I failed 'cause I done smoked major weed, bro.
And every time we with Kris, that fool rollin' up a fattie,
But the Tanqueray straight had me.

CHORUS

[KNUMSKULL]
Hey, make this right, mate,
Stop at the light, mate.
My yester-night thang got me hung off the night train.
You fade, I face,
So let's head to da East,
Hit the stroll to 9–0 so we can roll big hashish.
I wish I could fade the eighth, but I'm low budget,
Still rollin' a two-door Cutlass, same ol' bucket.
Foggy windows, smokin' Indo,
I'm in the land gettin' smoked wit' my kinfolk.

[YUKMOUTH]
Been smoked,
Yuk'll spray ya, lay ya down
Up in the Oak, the town.
Homies don't play around,
We down to blaze a pound.
Then ease up,
Speed up through the E.S.O.,
Drink the V.S.O.P. with a lemon squeeze up
And everybody's rolled up,
I'm da roller that's quick to fold a
Blunt out of a bunch of sticky dosia.
Hold up, suck up my weed is all you do,
Kick in feed, 'cause where I be's we need tab like a foo-foo.

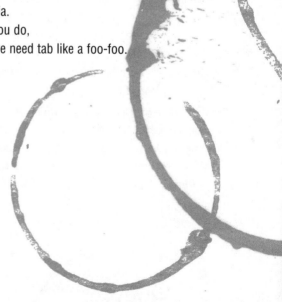

Words and Music by Sean Combs,
Michael Carlos Jones, Mario Winans,
Taurian Shropshire, Frankie Romano
and Chauncey Hawkins

I NEED A GIRL (PART TWO)
RECORDED BY P. DIDDY, FEATURING GINUWINE, MARIO WINANS, AND LOON

[GINUWINE]
Ooh, ooh, ooh!

[P. DIDDY]
Yeah, this that bounce right here.

[GINUWINE]
Come on, now!

[P. DIDDY]
Time to move on, time to be strong.
Don't stop now, straight to the top, now.

[GINUWINE AND MARIO WINANS]
Someone who truly understands how to treat a man,
This is what I need.

[P. DIDDY]
Girl, you made me believe again.
If you happy, then be with him.
Go 'head, mommy, breathe again.
Go 'head, mommy, make it hot now.
I need me a love that's gon' make my heart stop, now.
And what I need is simple:
Five-foot-five with dimples,
Potential wife credentials,
Know about the life I'm into, life I've been through,
And how I had a triflin' mental.

So ride with me, G Force, fly with me.
Times get hard—cry with me, die with me.
White beach sands—lie with me.
My advice is forget the limelight.
Let's make love while we listen to Frank White.
So tight, now I understand life.

CHORUS:
[GINUWINE, MARIO WINANS, AND P. DIDDY]
What I need, (Yeah, take that!)
Is a pretty woman next to me (A pretty woman, yeah, baby.)
To share the dreams that I believe. (Dream with me, believe in me.)
Maybe we could start a family. (Start a family, baby.)
Someone who truly understands how to treat a man.
This is what I need.

[LOON]
Listen to me now, what should I say, now?
Come on, ma, been a whole day, now I wanna lay 'round
And sip coladas, dipped in Prada.
I'm smooth as Erik Estrada, dipped in dollars.
We out in Vegas, Nevada, bubble bath in the champagne glass
'Bout the size of a campaign ad.
You don't know how you look to me,
But if love was a crime, you be a crook to me
'Cause mommy, I've done been around the world, seened a lot of places.
Been around your girl, believe I read faces.
I can tell she don't want me prevail,
But I learn my lesson watchin' Sean bless it.
So why listen to her and start guessin'?
Mommy, you ain't ready to ride, to start dressin'.
I need a girl receive my mom's blessin'.
Confession: my love no contestin',
I need affection.

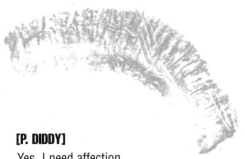

[P. DIDDY]
Yes, I need affection.
Let's go, Mario!

[MARIO WINANS]
Girl, what the hell is on your mind?
I could be dumb, but I'm not blind.
There's somethin' leakin' in your mind.
Don't look too good for you and me; always did agree
That ain't what I need, baby!

CHORUS:

[G & M] What I need is a pretty woman next to me
[MARIO] Oh, please, baby.
[G & M] To share the dreams that I believe.
[MARIO] I need a girl in my life.
[G & M] Maybe we could start a family.
[G] Start a family, baby.
[G & M] Someone who truly understands how to treat a man,
This is what I need.

[P. DIDDY]
Ay, yo, the sun don't shine forever,
But as long as we're here, then we might as well shine together.
Never mind the weather,
Go somewhere and get our minds together,
Build a love that-a last forever.
So let's stop the pain, stop the rain,
Put stress to rest, girl, stop the games.
Name the spot, mommy, I got the plane,
Roll through rough, I got the range.

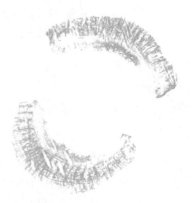

Ma, I got some thangs, knowed to put rocks in rings,
Push a hundred-foot yachts and thangs.
Your man don't play, have you ever been to St. Tropez?
Or seen a brother play Amando Lay?
Girl, I wanna just look in your eyes and watch the sunrise.
No more lies, no more tears to cry,
No more reasons for leavin'; do I believe in?
Love you 'til the day I stop breathin'.
I love you, girl.

CHORUS:

[G & M] What I need is a pretty woman next to me
[G] Standin' next to me, girl.
[G & M] To share the dreams that I believe.
[G] When I wake up in the morning...
[G & M] Maybe we could start a family.
[G] I wanna see your pretty face, yeah.
[G & M] Someone who truly understands how to treat a man,
This is what I need.

[FEMALE] Is that all you want?
[G & M] Is a pretty woman next to me...
　[FEMALE] Made the sacrifice...
　　[G & M] To share the dreams that I believe.
　　[FEMALE] And maybe, maybe we...
　　　[G & M] Maybe we could start a family.
　　　Someone who truly understands how to treat a man,
　　　This is what I need, is a pretty woman next to me
　　　To share the dreams that I believe.
　　　Maybe we could start a family.
　　　　Someone who truly understands how to treat a man.
　　　　This is what I need.

Words and Music by Bob Marley

I SHOT THE SHERIFF
RECORDED BY WARREN G

I shot the sheriff.

I had to shoot the sheriff, it was justifiable.
He mistaked me for somebody who was liable
For all the many murders, L.A. and war fields.
We keep makin' war shields.
Streets keep souls,
Young brothers lose control.
I seem to maintain through this,
Watch where ya kick it, they'll put you in a twist.
And it ain't nobody like my down-ass homie
And the police always tryin' to pin some bullshit on me.
I keep away from fools,
They do crime and it attracts cops.
Cops got guns and cuffs
And cells to stuff you in.

I shot the sheriff.

They tryin' to stick with some bullshit that I did not do.
You know who—the boys in blue.
There they go with they assumptions,
Slavery's over; let us have somethin'.
Why you wanna pull me over?
'Cause I'm bumpin'?
I just made a new song.
My profession is music.
Your profession is protection with gatts,
Then use it on him when he's tryin' to take my life away.
I'm just tryin' to live my life today,
So I keep away from fools,
They do crime, it attract cops.
Cops got guns and cuffs
And cells to stuff you in.

I shot the sheriff.

I shot the sheriff.
I did not shoot the deputy—I didn't have to
'Cause in this game, they always tryin' to blast you
and leave it to the cops to find out who did the murder.
They harass the wrong clan and arrest the wrong man:
The homie day-dog got strapped, but that's okay
'Cause I'm gonna work for life
So he can see another day.
A homie's a homie,
A fake is a snake.
Straight game from the pen from the homie, Jake.
So I keep away from fools,
They do crime, it attract cops.
Cops got guns and cuffs
And cells to stuff you in.

Words and Music by Osten S. Harvey,
Carlton D. Ridenhour and Keith M. Shocklee

I STAND ACCUSED
RECORDED BY PUBLIC ENEMY

I see I'm peeking out, ready to rumble.
So now I'm speaking out against those
That flip the way the story goes.
One never knows
Who be flippin' the script.
Whatever the traitor's name,
May aim is dunk 'em like I'm Chris Webber.

So many phone, smilin' faces,
Traces of slander.
Got em comin' outta funny places.
I had it and hear 'em talkin' loud behind my back.
What was good for the 'hood is what they say is wack.
I take the stabbin' and grin, when I'm hit
'Cause I know the suckas smile
When I leave 'em, what I'm comin' wit'.

I can't complain about the money,
Although the suckas in the back,
They talkin' shit and laughin' like it's somethin' funny.
I aim to make changes
And never change unless it's for the better
'Cause I always been a go-getter,
Clean hustler.
Rhyme instead of muscle, yeah.
Born when ya thinkin' I'm gone.
The terror era is on.

I stand accused.
To the crews I paid my dues.
I stand accused.
I refuse to stand and lose.
I stand accused.
To the news I kick da blues.
I stand accused.
I refuse.

I hear 'em talkin' and walkin'.
Behind my back, I'm attacked.
Fuck the knife in the back
'Cause it feels like they got an axe.
Yeah, I can dig it wit' a shovel.
I never dig dirt wit' the devil.
Instead I'm on that other level,
But I took time to reach down
To help the black and brown.
I never stood around,
I hear 'em talkin' behind my mind.
In an ocean of sharks
And a back full of hack marks.

They say I'm fallin' off.
Yeah, they better call it off
And get muscle and find another hustle quick.
Sick and tired of critics,
But I can take a hit.
I'm all man,
Alley-oopin' the vocal on the jams.
But they don't know it,
They can blow it and take a puff of this joint.
I see I'm kissin' it off the cuff.
Behind the back I'm pullin' axes and blades
Out of the arms and the legs.
Still, my fellas get paid.
The terror era is on.

Fuck a critic, fuck, fuck a critic.
All the fuckin' critics can get the did dit.
All a fuckin' critic does is draw a fuckin' line.
Cross a line and diss my rhyme
And then they ass is mine.
If you find a critic dead,
Remember what I said.
Who killed a critic?
Guess the crew did it.

Say paybacks a crazy-ass message
Sent to the writers who criticize.
They're fuckin wit' a freedom fighter
Who raises flags
And dragged the Klan in body bags.
I hung 'em up in Mississippi and bum fuck.
This is Chuck, so what the hell.
You think I did it for
To open doors from Carolina to Arkansas
And lemme let 'em, I met 'em.
I told my boys, "Forget 'em."
And what they did got rid of me—negative.
But ninety-four got stunts and blunts in da mix.
I hear the crowd fallin' vic'
To old ghetto tricks,
But if I wasn't your cousin,
We'd leave 'em in the dozens
Of sellin' out and bailin' out.
Half-pint, forty-ounce,
Announce to the rest we had a fall-out.

I never took a drink,
Never took a hit or bribe,
Or got spread by what a silly rumor said.
Never sang or gang-banged,
Sold out or rented hip-hip
'Cause I know when to stop.

Words and Music by Eldra P. DeBarge,
William Randall DeBarge, Etterlene Jordan,
Dedrick D'Mon Rolison and Warren Griffin III

I WANT IT ALL
RECORDED BY WARREN G, FEATURING MACK 10

[WARREN G]
What's up Negros and negrettes?
It's your boy, Warren G, you know what I'm sayin'?
Chillin' with the homeboy, Mack 10,
And we gon' lay a lil' sumpin' down for y'all;
Let y'all know what time it is;
Show you how we keepin' it real wit' it.
You know, 'cause this world is built on material thangs
But we ain't trippin' off that.
We want y'all to know this, check it:

CHORUS:
[WARREN G]
I want it all: money, fast cars,
Diamond rings, gold chains, and champagne.
Shit, every damn thing.
I want it all: houses, expenses, my own business,
A truck, hmm, and a couple o' Benzes.
I want it all: brand new socks and drawls
And I'm ballin' every time I stop and talk to y'all.
I want it all, all, all, all.
I want it all, all, all, all, all.

[WARREN G]
They say, "There go Warren G with that envious stare."
I love this game too much, I wish these haters wasn't here.
It's a shame, we came too far to turn back.
It's a cold world, it gets so hard, you learned that
From fallin', tryin' to walk from crawl,
Tryin' to hustle up from broke to ballin'.

And yeah, y'all, in effect, that's all me:
The jiggy G–Z, all my niggaz that keep it real and do it easy.
Believe me, young nigga, fat meat is greasy
And shit stank, so if you plot a lick and hit a bank
And get away, or get gaffed the very next day,
Don't cry, hold your head up high.
And remember what you told yourself, nigga.
I said, remember what you told yourself, nigga.
I said, remember what you told yourself, nigga.
I said, remember what you told yourself, nigga.

CHORUS

[MACK 10]
I want it all, so I got to wake up and ball,
And thanks to y'all, I got plaques on the wall.
Mack 10 laced with the know-how to paper chase.
Crushed ice, throw my rollie face in the platinum fan base.
From networkin' and hustlin', no doubt, I got clout
And live the lifestyle that Robin Leach talkin' about.
Slow down, player, don't hate 'cause you can't relate
The Bentley Coupes and kickin' gears on Harleys with the straights.
I got more limelight than Vegas on cable.
Will it enable to shoot C-note yo's at the crap table?
And while you can't get off the ground, I'm gettin' high.
A nigga fly and fly with the desire to build an empire.
I strapped up and took flight like a missile.
Told them loud and clear as a whistle,
"Hoo-bangin'" is official.
Handin' out gold medallions at roll call.
I'm-a ball and never fall 'cause Mack 10 want it all.
What?

CHORUS

[WARREN G]
Me and 10 get paid, escapade to the spot.
We hot like rocks served on hot blocks.
I notice money make the world circulate,
So we gon' stack and stack and take a sip and percolate.
Bump, let the woofers sub. (Sub.)
Show the homies love. (Love.)
Warrant to the G, (G.)
And Little G-Dub. (Dub.)
Surface on the low, slide or don't slide at all.
Ride or don't ride at all.

[MACK 10]
Warren, I couldn't be more serious about my 'fetti.
I stay tight on the mic and keep the pen movin' steady.
I want it all, dog, and it might be greed.
I hate to trip, but I got two little mouths to feed.
They don't know nuttin' about no excuses and disrespect
Or somebody bein' jank with they daddy's royalty check.
And at that point, I'm through talkin', dog, enough said.
So, if you owe Mack money, then I suggest you break bread.
I want it all.

CHORUS (3 TIMES)

[WARREN G AND MACK 10]
Mack 10, what up?
I know the paper's out there, ha, ha, yeah.
Warren G, what up?
You know the paper's out there, ha, ha, yeah.
G-Funk, what up?
You know the paper's out there, ha, ha, that's right.
What? Hoo-bangin'? What up?
We know the paper's out there, ha, ha, that's right.
What? The whole world,
Paper's out there, speak on it, ha, ha.
Wrong: all the 'hood.
Right: all the 'hood rats.
What up?
You know all the paper's out there.

Words and Music by Rene Moore,
Angela Winbush, Sean Carter
and Inga Marchand

I'LL BE
RECORDED BY FOXY BROWN,
FEATURING JAY-Z

[JAY-Z]
That's right, papa, that's right.
How we do, yeah, Ill nana.
Uh-huh, uh, come on.

[FOXY BROWN]
What up, pop?
Brace yourself as I ride on top.
Close your eyes as you ride right out your socks.
Double, lose his mind as he grind in the tunnel.
Wanna gimme the cash he made off his last bundle.
Nasty girl, don't pass me the world.
I push to be not the backseat girl.
Don't deep-throat the C-note she float.
Murder, she wrote, and keeps the heat close.
Firm nigga, we 'posed to be the illest on three coasts.
Familiar, bigger than Icos.
Y'all, Danny DeVitos, small niggaz,
All I see is the penny heaters, that's all niggaz.
No shark in this year raise it bigger,
Fifteen percent make the whole world sit up
And take notice, nana take over.
Y'all take quotas to hit papa.

CHORUS:

[JAY-Z]

Straight out the gate, y'all, we drop hits.
Now tell me, how nasty can you get?
All the way from the 'hood to your neck of the woods,
It's ripped, one thing for sure—
I'll be good.
Straight out the gate, y'all, we drop hits.
Now tell me, how nasty can you get?
All the way from the 'hood to your neck of the woods,
It's ripped, one thing for sure—
I'll be good.

[FOXY BROWN]

I'm 2 Live, Nasty As I Wanna Be.

[JAY-Z]

Don't shake your sassy ass in front of me
'Fore I take you there, and tear your back out.

[FOXY BROWN]

That shit ain't happened since the Mack was out.

[FOXY BROWN]

Uhh, rollin' for Lana, dipped in Gabbana,
Nineties-style, you find a style.
Right away, it's the fit, wanna taste the shit.
Put me on a bass and throw your face in it, fucker.
Na-na, y'all can't touch her.
My sex drive all night like a trucker.
Let alone the skills I possess
And y'all gon' see by these mil's I possess.

Never settle for less, I'm in excess,
Not inexpensive D.V.S.
To the two, that's just the way I'm built.
Nasty—what?
Classy, still.

CHORUS

[JAY-Z]
Well, you can hoe what I got, roll with the rock.
The fella Capo in the candy-apple drop.
Will tears fall to your eyes if I don't stop?
Can ya throw it like a quarterback, third in the lot?

[FOXY BROWN]
Dig me, I get you locked like Biggie, wit' Irv in the spot.
Word, middie, the cop, 'n' biddie.
Uhh, I'm the bomb-digi, punana,
Sexy, brown thing, uh, Madon' y'all.
Make 'em turn over from the full-court pressure
To undress ya and shit all over your asses.
I ain't playin' knockin'- out at the Williams,
I'm sayin', what's the sense in delayin'?
I'm tryin' to run G from the P to the A.M.
I saw your little thing, now I'm swayin', okayin'.
(Ah, shit, uh, uh.)

CHORUS

Words and Music by Clifford Smith,
Robert F. Diggs Jr., Valerie Simpson
and Nickolas Ashford

I'LL BE THERE FOR YOU/YOU'RE ALL I NEED TO GET BY

RECORDED BY METHOD MAN, FEATURING MARY J. BLIGE AND NOTORIOUS B.I.G.

[METHOD MAN]
Rugged style, it's enough to make a hard rock smile.
Ha, ha, ha, cheeba-cheeba, y'all.
Cheeba-cheeba, y'all, and you don't stop.
Yeah, yeah, cootie in the chair.
Cheeba-cheeba, y'all, and you don't stop.
Yeah, yeah, cootie in the—check Tical.

CHORUS:
[MARY J. BLIGE WITH NOTORIOUS B.I.G. SAMPLE]
You're all I need.
(Lie together, cry together,
I swear to God, I hope we fuckin' die together.)
You're all I need...
(Lie together, cry together,
I swear to God, I hope we fuckin' die together.)
To get by, ahh.

[METHOD MAN]
Shorty, I'm there for you anytime you need me.
For real, girl, it's me in your world; believe me.
Nuttin' make a man feel better than a woman,
Queen with a crown that be down for whatever.
There are few things that's forever, my lady.
We can make war or make babies.

Back when I was nothin',
You made a brother feel like he was somethin'.
That's why I'm with you to this day, boo; no frontin'.
Even when the skies were gray,
You would rub me on my back and say, "Baby, it'll be okay."
Now that's real to a brother like me, baby.
Never, ever give my cootie away, and keep it tight, aight?
And I'm-a walk these dogs so we can live
In a fat-ass crib with thousands of kids.
Word, life, you don't need a ring to be my wife.
Just be there for me and I'm-a make sure we
Be livin' in the f'n lap of luxury.
I'm realizing that you didn't have to funk wit' me,
But you did; now I'm going all out, kid.
And I got mad love to give you, my nigga.

CHORUS (2 TIMES)

[MARY J. BLIGE]
Like sweet morning dew,
I took one look at you
And it was plain to see,
You were my destiny.
With you I'll spend my time.
I'll dedicate my life,
I'll sacrifice for you,
Dedicate my life for you.

[METHOD MAN]
I got a Love Jones for your body and your skin tone.
Five minutes alone, I'm already on the bone.
Plus, I love the fact you got a mind of your own.
No need to shop around; you got the good stuff at home,

Even if I'm locked up North, you in the world.
Wrapped in three-fourths of cloth, never showin' your stuff off, boo.
It be true: me for you, that's how it is.
I be your Noah, you be my Wiz.
I'm your Mister, you my Missus, with hugs and kisses.
Valentine cards and birthday wishes? Please,
Be on another level of planning, of understanding
The bond between man and woman and child;
The highest elevation, 'cause we above
All that romance crap; just show your love.

CHORUS

I'm sick of police.
Ha, ha, ha, cheeba-cheeba, y'all.
And you don't stop.
Yeah, yeah, cootie in the—Tical!
Cheeba-cheeba, y'all, and you don't stop.
Yeah, yeah, cootie in the chair, Tical!
Cheeba-cheeba, y'all, and you don't stop.
Yeah, yeah, cootie in the chair, Tical!
Mary J. raw, and Meth-Tical.
(Like sweet morning dew.) Yeah, yeah.
(I took one look at you.) Cootie in the chair, Tical.
(And it was plain to see.) Cheeba-cheeba, y'all.
(You were my destiny.) Cheeba-cheeba, y'all.
Cheeba-cheeba, y'all, bring it on, yeah.
What's that shit that they be smokin'?

No romance without finance, for now.
Baby, please, ninety-five.
Ticallion Stallion, ha, ha, ha, ha.
Man, woman, and child, yeah.

(Anything you need; anything you need.)

I'M A THUG
RECORDED BY TRICK DADDY

Words and Music by Rafe VanHoy,
Maurice Young and Adam Duggins

CHORUS:

I don't know what this world's gonna bring
But I know one thing: this is the life for me.
Baby, 'cause I'm a thug,
All day, every day.
Baby, 'cause I'm a thug,
Wouldn't change for the world.
Uh-huh, 'cause I'm a thug,
That's right, you heard.
Baby, 'cause I'm a thug.
Uh-huh, oh yeah.

Check it out—
Could it be my baggy jeans or my gold teeth
That make me different from y'all?
Ain't trippin', dog,
But listen, dog,
I've been raised a little different, dog.
I'm just doin' my thang,
These are my ghetto slangs
And I'm representin' thug shit.
This is who I roll with.
Watch them niggaz that's gonna love this,
Niggaz who out on bond,
On the run, got ten years on parole.
Since you can't say it, dog, I'm-a say it for y'all.
Motherfuck the po-pos,
Fuck the judge and the CEOs.
Fuck the DA and the Pos,
Fuck the family of the victim,
Witness that's snitchin' ass hoes, nigga.

CHORUS

See, I'm so tight, niggaz be like,
"That nigga got so many hoes

and I know he got clout.
Look at his mouth,
That nigga got so many golds."
Niggaz be tellin' they hoes,
"There's somethin' up with that nigga.
Bitch, I've been watchin' you watchin' him.
You must wanna fuck this nigga."
My name alone been known
To break up happy homes.
No disrespect, dog,
But you ain't have no business answerin' her phone.
If your ass wasn't home,
Me an' her been get, get, gettin' it on
And you couldn't have been hittin' her right
'Cause every second night, she been hittin' the phones.
She want a thug.

CHORUS

Since y'all niggaz wanna smoke the blunts,
Tote the guns,
I'm-a show you how to thug it, dog.
Give me half a pill
And some Zephanyll
And I'm like, "Fuck it, dog,"
As long as my ecstacy got the best of me.
And none of you niggaz ain't stressin' me.
I got one request in this, bitch,
You can have the rest of this shit.
If a nigga drop some shit
And it's wack as hell,
And don't make no damn sense,
Take it back, talk about it.
And tell your dog, "Don't even buy that shit."
And I don't care who he is,
Or where he from,
I represent thug shit
And you ain't gotta give me my props
Or nominate me,
'Cause, damn it, I love this.

CHORUS (2 TIMES)

Words and Music by Dwayne Simon,
James Todd Smith and Steven Ettinger

I'M THAT TYPE OF GUY
RECORDED BY LL COOL J

You're the type of guy that can't control your girl.
You try to buy her love with diamonds and pearls.
I'm the type of guy that shows up on the scene
And gets the seven digits, you know the routine.
You're the type of guy that tells her, "Stay inside,"
While you're steady frontin' in your homeboy's ride.
I'm the type of guy that comes when you leave.
I'm doin' your girlfriend, that's somethin' you can't believe
'Cause I'm that type of guy.

You're the type of guy that gets suspicious.
I'm the type of guy that says, "The puddin' is delicious."
You're the type of guy that has no idea
That a sneaky, freaky brother's sneakin' in from the rear.
I'm the type of guy to eat it, when he won't
And look in the places that your boyfriend don't.
You're the type of guy to try to call me a punk,
Now knowin' that your main girl's bitin' my chunk.
I'm the type of guy that loves a dedicated lady.
Their boyfriend's are boring, and I can drive 'em crazy.
You're the type of guy to give her money to shop.
She gave me a sweater (kiss), thank you, sweetheart.
I'm that type of guy.

I'm the type of guy that picks her up from work early,
Takes her to breakfast, lunch, dinner, and breakfast.
You're the type of guy eatin' a TV dinner,
Talkin' about, "Goddamn it, I'm-a kill her."
I'm the type of guy to make her say, "Why you're illin', Bee?"
You're the type of guy to say, "My lower back is killin' me."
Catch my drift?
You're the type of guy that likes to drink Old English.
I'm the type of guy to cold put on a pamper.
You're the type of guy to say, "What you talkin' 'bout?"
I'm the type of guy to leave my drawers in your hamper.
I'm that type of guy.

I'm that type of guy.
You know what I mean?
Check it out.

T–Y–P–E–G–U–Y.
I'm that type of guy to give you a pound, and wink my eye
Like a bandit, caught me red-handed, took her for granted.
But when I screwed her, you couldn't understand it
'Cause you're the type of guy that don't know the time,
Swearin' up and down, "That girl's all mine."
I'm the type of guy to let you keep believin' it.
Go 'head to work while I defrost it and season it.
I'm that type of guy.

I'm that type of guy.
Know what I mean?
I'm that type of guy.
So ridiculous, so funny.
I don't know.
Come on down.
Yeah, like real cool, you know what I mean?
I like just goin' to your front door, ringin' bells
And just like, ha, leave.

THE INFLUENCE

RECORDED BY JURASSIC 5

Words and Music by Dante Givens,
Courtenay Henderson, Lucas Macfadden,
Mark Ali Potsic, Charles Stewart,
Marc Stuart and Martin Paich

[ZAAKIR]
Yo! I create off drum drops and ate away blacktops.
Grab the mic so you don't react.
The double-X Polo shirt with the hat to match.
In fact, we verbally vibrate your track.

[MARC 7]
Then crush your confidence like plastic condiments,
Build you up to break you down like forgotten monuments.
The question is this: will they return with the hot shit,
Or keep it on the low flow?

[CHALI 2NA]
Yo! And for you confused bastards, 2na the blues master.
Quick to grab the mic, crews fast and sound clashing.
Critical mass, pinnacle blast have been deflected,
Hypodermic vocals, I flash—get you infected.

[AKIL]
I don't sip on brew, so this Bud's for you.
Speak when spoken to whenever you come through.
My vibes fill you, Internal Revenue,
You rhyme prostitute for little or no loot.

[ALL]
'Cause a lotta these kids think that commercial
Is rocking fly suits and jewelry.
But we can rock shows with no rehearsal,
With the Rebels of Rhythm and Unity.

[ZAAKIR]
Yeah, 'cause I'm nice, smooth, hard as a bone.
Since I pick up the microphone, I'm hotter than brimstone.
The razor sharp, crossbow accurate.
We drop the multiverbal milligram supplement.

[AKIL]
Plus, in bed, theological word advance.
Been Too Legit To Quit before the Hammer pants.
The parents to the pen converts words to song.
Stay blacker than the New Year Harlem Renaissance.

[CHALI 2NA]
No comp—we paint a darker picture in your sector,
Perfect verbal architecture, sparking lectures.
Lyrics infectious, fuck your Lexus—
If you ain't giving God your praise, then it's useless.
Like when MCs try to make hits, and them shits flop,
Running races like they was Penelope Pitstop.
Develop these hits rock bottom; the disk jock's got 'em
Souped up, but this rhyme is beatin' his loops up.

CHORUS:
[ALL]
Like, dah dah. (Dah dah.)
Bah dee dee dee dah dah. (Dah dee dee dee dah dah.)
Bah dah dah dah dee dee dee dee dah dah.

[MARC 7]
I can see clearly now, top of the pile with my style.
Check profile, it shifts like sundial.
Crisp like young smiles, we rip and run wild.
Intent to rock crowds, some bit like Rott-wilds.

[AKIL]
Your game is disconnected, misdirected,
Disrespected—when we come in, expect some next shit.
The J–U–R–A, classic forte.
Get low-down and dirty like the inner moray.

[ZAKIR]
My heart pump the rhythm of the militant street life.
Soldier of composure up under the streetlight.
The coat style, prototype, professional.
Media light shine bright, now kill all the
Bullshit, cheap talk, and lip service,
Jealousy and envy and undertone cursed in your verses
Serve the purpose of a nigga living nervous,
Unsure and uncertain, but about to short-circuit.

CHORUS (2 TIMES)

[MARC 7]
Aiyyo! My gift of gab should be sold in bags.
Boost up the price tag, make a wack rapper mad.
Rely on my right side, securing our tape tight.
Tasty tangibles to your mandible and clavicle.

[CHALI 2NA]
Yo! Easily 2na be cleverly swelling my treasury.
Vocal pedigree for you critics who try to measure me.
But easily I'm about to run you down my resume.
Had a bundle of struggle from birth to my present day.

[AKIL]
Yo! Your love don't compute; perhaps you need a boost,
A magical flute, some nose candy to toot.
Before you get loose, express, and tear the roof,
You claim you got the juice, but you lame and out the loop.

[ZAAKIR]
So I associated myself with fossilized figures.
Crack the summer sizzler, hit the real live niggas.
My influence is gunshots and trauma units,
Street trends with material word friends.

CHORUS (2 TIMES)

Words and Music by Larry Muggerud,
Louis Mario Freese and Senen Reyes

INSANE IN THE BRAIN
RECORDED BY CYPRESS HILL

Who you tryin' to get crazy with, ese?
Don't you know I'm loco?

To da one on da flam,
Boy it's tough.
I just toss that ham on the fryin' pan like Spam,
It's done when I come in, slam.
Damn, I feel like the Son of Sam.
Don't make me wreck shit wit' an automatic.
Got me goin' like General Electric.
Damn, the lights are blinkin', I'm thinkin'
It's all over when go out drinkin'.
Oh makin' my mind slow,
That's why I don't fuck with the big 4–0.
Bro, I got ta maintain
'Cause a nigga like me is goin' insane.

CHORUS:
Insane in da membrane, insane in da brain!
Insane in da membrane, insane in da brain!
Insane in da membrane, insane in da brain!
Insane in da membrane, insane in da brain!

Do my shit undercover,
Now it's time for, for the blubber.
Blaba to watch dat belly get fatter.
Fat boy on a diet, don't try it.
I'll check your ass like a looter in a riot,
Much too fast, like a sumo slammin' dat ass,
Leavin' your face in the grass.
You know I don't take a chulo lightly,
Punk just jealous 'cause he can't out-write me,
So I kick that style, wicked, wild,
Happy-face nigga never seen me smile.
Rip dat mainframe,
I'll explain,
A nigga like me is goin' insane.

CHORUS

Like Louis Armstrong played the trumpet,
I'll hit dat bong and break ya off somethin' soon,
I gotta get my props.
Cops come and try to snatch my crops.
These pigs wanna blow my house down
And underground, to the next town.
They get mad when they come to raid my pad
And I'm out in the nine-deuce Cad.
Yes, I'm the pirate pilot
Of this ship if I get
Wit' the ultraviolet dream,
Hide from the red light beam.
Now do you believe in the unseen?
Look, but don't make you eyes strain.
A nigga like me is goin' insane.

CHORUS

Words and Music by The Isley Brothers,
Chris Jasper, Ice Cube, A. Goodman,
S. Robinson and H. Ray

IT WAS A GOOD DAY
RECORDED BY ICE CUBE

(Break me, shit, yo!)

Just wakin' up in the mornin', gotta thank God.
I don't know, but today seems kinda odd.
No barking from the dogs, no smog,
And Momma cooked a breakfast with no hog.
I got my grub on, but didn't pig out,
Finally got a call from a girl wanna dig out.
Hooked it up on the later as I hit the do',
Thinkin', "Will I live another twenty-fo'?"
I gotta go 'cause I got me a drop-top
And if I hit the switch, I can make the ass drop.
Had to stop at a red light;
Lookin' in my mirror, not a jacker in sight,
And everything is alright.
I got a beep from Kim, and she can fuck all night.
Called up the homies and I'm askin' y'all,
"Which court are y'all playin' basketball?"
Get me on the court and I'm in trouble.
Last week fucked around and got a triple double,
Freakin' brothers every way like M–J.
I can't believe today was a good day.

Drove to the pad and hit the showers.
Didn't even get no static from the cowards
'Cause just yesterday, them fools tried to blast me.
Saw the police and they rolled right past me.
Now flexin', didn't even look in a niggaz direction
As I ran the intersection.
Went to Short Dog's house, they was watchin' "Yo! MTV Raps!"
What's the haps on the craps?

Shake 'em up, shake 'em up, shake 'em up, shake 'em,
Roll 'em in a circle of niggaz and watch me break 'em
With the seven, seven-eleven, seven-eleven, seven.
Even back do' Joe.
I picked up the cash flow.
Then we played bones, and I'm yellin', "Domino."
And now I am yellin', "Dominos."
Plus nobody I know got killed in South Central L.A.
Today was a good day.

Left my niggaz house, paid,
Picked up a girl been tryin' to fuck since the twelfth grade.
It's ironic—I had the brew, she had the chronic.
The Lakers beat the Supersonics.
I felt on the big, fat fanny,
Pulled out the jammy, and killed the punani.
And my dick runs deep, so deep, so deep,
Put her ass to sleep.
Woke her up around one,
She didn't hesitate to call Ice Cube the top gun.
Drove her to the pad and I'm coasting,
Took another sip of the potion, hit the three-wheel motion.
I was glad everything had worked out.
Dropped her ass off, then I chirped out.
Today was like one of those fly dreams.
Didn't even see a berry flashing those high-beams.
No helicopter looking for a murder.
Two in the morning, got the fat burger.
Even saw the lights of the Goodyear Blimp
And it read, "Ice Cube's a pimp."
Drunk as hell, but no throwing up.
Half-way home and my paper still blowing up.
Today I didn't even have to use my AK.
I got to say, it was a good day.

Hey, wait, wait a minute, fool.
Stop that shit.
What the fuck am I thinkin' about?

IT'S A PARTY

Words and Music by Harvey Osten,
Trevor Smith and Rene Andrea Neufville

RECORDED BY BUSTA RHYMES

Right, right, right, right.
Right, Busta Rhymes exclusive with the Zhané,
Each and every day.
We gon' come around your way and do it our way,
Word is bond.

(It's a party, let's get it on tonight.)
Word up, hah, yeah, yeah, one time with the flow
(That's how we flow.
Gonna rock your body, we gonna do it right.
When I step up in the party, won't you move it to the left?)
Hah, hah, hah, hah, move it to the left.
(Party people move it side to side,
I'm feelin' kind of blessed.)
Ooh, hah, yeah, ooh, yes, kind of blessed, yes.
(And I'm so fly, and you're so fly.)
Oh yeah, I'm so fly, yeah, yeah, you so fly too, girl.
(Feelin' high tonight—it's a party-arty-arty-arty, ah.)
Word up, word up, uhh, hah.

Uhh! Let me get down, do my thing.
I always bring shit that always make your ass swing.
Holdin' down the fort while we keep you live all night,
Makin' moves strong while we keep rockin' on.
Now the object is survival, son, so get your hustle on.
Bust two shots while I blow up the spot.
I make it hot 'til the jam is packed to the parking lot.
Now, me and my mans feel like we astronauts
'Cause we so high from off that weed we got from new knots.
Certified stimulation got me open wide.
Before we slide to side, we grab the stash out of the ride.
We on fire tonight, and the place is lookin' steamy.
Baby girl, let me seek that gift that make your cake creamy, uhh.
Feel the heat circulatin' through your body
Every time the Flipmode click step inside the party.
Word is bond.

(It's a party, let's get it on tonight.)
Hah, right, word is bond.
(Gonna rock your body, we gonna do it right.
The stimulation circulatin' through my mind, body, and soul.)
Uhh, hah, hah, uh, hah!
(Busta Rhymes, stimuli, makin' me lose control.)
Hah, hah, hah!
(And I'm so fly, and you're so fly.)
Word is bond, yes I am.
(Feelin high tonight—it's a party-arty-arty-arty, ah.)
Ha, ha, ha.

I got my mind made up, c'mon, you can get it, girl.
Come with me if you really wit' it, girl.
Back to my dungeon shack where the party is at,
Where I can tickle your nipples and your feminine fat.
I checks for you, baby, whatchu gon' do?
There's a party at my crib designed just for me and you.
Let me let my crew know we 'bout to break out.
Flip, Star, Web, Dukwon Allah, and the Boy Scout,
My man, Black Missin, son, whylin with the shorty flippin',
Stackin' papers, sippin' bubbles, good nigga livin'.
But anyway, we 'bout to break out in my Lands,
Pursuin' our thoughts and executin' all plans.
The dope shit is that we both understand
That it's a one-night stand and you ain't even thinkin' 'bout your man.
Ooh, oh! We 'bout to turn on the heat again.
Don't you say a word until we finish partyin'.

(Don't you know that tonight is your night?)
Hah, word up, tonight is the night.
(Feelin' good when I have a peace of mind.)
Word up, a peace of mind.
(Got to set it off and just a little bit wild.)
Hah, woo, a little wild.
(It's a party-arty-arty, ah.)
Hah, it's a party, y'all.
It's a party, y'all.
It's a party, y'all.

Yo, well anyway, I'm back around my way,
Keepin' it live, you know how we do each and every day.
Rollin' through thick with my girls, Zhané
With the exclusive debut, hey, Mister DJ,
Listen to me, bay-bay.
We put somethin' together that's gon' drive you crazy.
Get from out your seat and stop actin' lazy
Or get up out my party, if you actin' shady, baby, baby.
It's a party.

(It's a party, let's get it on tonight.)
Word up, let's get it on tonight.
(Gonna rock your body, Zhané and Busta Rhymes.)
Yes, yes, uhh, Zhané and Busta Rhymes.
(It's a party, let's get it on tonight.)
Ah, woo, let's get it on, let's get it on.
(Gonna rock your body, we gonna do it right.)
Do it right, now, hah, hah.
(It's a party, let's get it on tonight.)
Throw your hands in the air!
(Gonna rock your body, Zhané and Busta Rhymes.)
Zhané and Busta Rhymes exclusive, hah.
(It's a party, let's get it on tonight.)
Hah, word is bond, let's get it on, baby girl.
(Gonna rock your body, we gonna do it right.)

Let's do it right, now, keep it movin' y'all.
Flipmode is the unit, y'all.
You can't see what we doin', y'all.
Zhané and Busta B, y'all.
Yes, we doin' the whole entire party-makin', y'all.
Woo, yeah, yeah, yeah, yeah, yeah, forever and ever and ever.

Words and Music by David Steele,
Monie Love, Stevie Wonder,
Lee Garrett and Syretta Wright

IT'S A SHAME (MY SISTER)

RECORDED BY MONIE LOVE

My sister, my sister, tell me what the trouble is.
I'll try to listen good and give the best advice that I can give.
So, what's up with you this time?
Your honey took a dive and now he's playin' with your mind?
Oh no, this cannot be accepted.
The feelings that belong to you must be protected.
Hold up, time out, I shout, get it together, sister.
Tell him to be nice or ditch the mister.

CHORUS:

It's a shame, the way you mess around with my heart.
It's a shame, the way you hurt me.
It's a shame, the way you mess around with my heart.
It's a shame, the way you hurt me.

Get back on your feet, please.
I'm beggin' you to check out all your own needs.
Don't let nobody see you in a state of grievin' over the brother.
There's another possibility,
Which is for you to work out where you went wrong.
I guarantee to you that it will not take long
For you to make your mind up if the two of you belong.
You know where honey's head at, and where he's comin' from.
Get it out your system, don't be another victim.
This took the nerve, oh boy, he really picked 'em, whad'ya know.

It's time for you to show you're not sleepin';
A progress report on the two of you, you're keepin',
Peekin' through the peephole to see if honey's sneakin'.
You estimated right that night, the other weekend.
Collectively the facts should conclude the decision.
You caught the brother in a terrible disposition.

CHORUS

That's it, pack it up, be wise my sister
'Cause the facts keep stackin' up, tell him to kiss the you-know-what.
Make sure the door is shut behind you.
I do believe the brother's out of luck and stuck,
But that's no your P–R–O–B–L–E–M.
You gotta let him go and let him know this is the end.
You've been kissed, dissed, listed as a dumb one.
I hope he likes sad songs—he's gonna hum one.
He's been a dumb-dumb, and that's the way it is forever.
There comes a time when you're at the end of your tether.
And you know, I think you went far beyond that,
So it was bound to backtrack
And smack you with an irksome vengeance as it attacks you,
Makin' sure you get the full, entire view
Of who's to blame at the end of the game.
Things will never be the same
And it's a cryin' shame.

CHORUS

Words and Music by Sean "Puffy" Combs,
Notorious B.I.G., Sean Jacobs, Jason Phillips,
David Styles, Deric Angelettie and Kim Jones

IT'S ALL ABOUT THE BENJAMINS

RECORDED BY PUFF DADDY, FEATURING JADAKISS, SHEEK, LIL' KIM, AND NOTORIOUS B.I.G.

Uhh, uh-huh, yeah.
Uhh, uh-huh, yeah.
It's all about the Benjamins, baby.
Uhh, uh-huh, yeah.
It's all about the Benjamins, baby.
Goodfellas, uhh.

[PUFF DADDY]
Now, what y'all wanna do?
Wanna be ballers? Shot callers?
Brawlers who be dippin' in the Benz wit' the spoilers
On the low from the Jake in the Taurus,
Tryin' to get my hands on some Grants like Horace.
Yeah, livin' the raw deal, three-course meals:
Spaghetti, fettuccini, and veal.
But still, everything's real in the field
And what you can't have now, leave in your will.
But don't knock me for tryin' to bury
Seven zeros over in Rio de Janier-y.
Ain't nobody's hero, but I wanna be heard
On your Hot 9–7 every day, that's my word.
Swimmin' in women wit' they own condominiums.
Five plus fives, who drive Milleniums.
It's all about the Benjamins—what?
I get a fifty-pound bag of ooh for the mutts.
Five carats on my hand wit' the cuts
And swim in European figures.
Fuck bein' a broke nigga.

[JADAKISS]
I want-a all chromed out wit' the clutch, nigga.
Drinkin' malt liquor, drivin' a Bro' Vega.
I'm wit' Mo' sippers, watched by gold-diggers, (Uhh.)
Rockin' Bejor denims wit' gold zippers. (C'mon.)
Lost your touch, we kept ours, poppin' Cristals,
Freakin' the three-quarter reptiles. (Ahahah.)
Enormous cream, forest green Benz jeep
For my team, so while you sleep, I'm-a scheme. (That's right.)
We see through, that's why nobody never gon' believe you.
You should do what we do: stack slips like Hebrews.
Don't let the melody intrigue you (Uh-huh.)
'Cause I leave you, I'm only here
for that green paper with the eagle.

[SHEEK]
I'm strictly tryin' to cop those colossal-sized Picassos
And have pappy flip coke outside Delgado's. (Whoo!)
Mienda, with cash flowin' like Sosa
And the Latin chick transportin' in the chocha.
Stampedin' over, pop Mo's, never sober,
Lex and Range Rovers, dealin' weight by Minnesota. (Uhh.)
Avoidin' narcs wit' camcorders and Chevy Novas, (Uh-huh.)
Stash in the buildin' wit' this chick named Alona (Uh-huh.)
From Daytona, when I was young I wants to bone her. (Uh-huh.)
But now I only hit chicks that win beauty pageants. (Ahahaha.)
Trickin', they takin' me skiing at the Aspens. (C'mon.)
Uhh, gangsta mental, stay poppin' Cristal,
Pack a black pistol in the Ac' Coupe that's dark brown. (Whoo!)
Pinky-ringin', gondolas wit' the man singin',
Italian music down the river wit' your chick clingin'
To my bizzalls; player, you mad false,
Actin' hard when you as pussy as Ru Paul.

[PUFF DADDY]
C'mon, c'mon, uh-huh.
It's all about the Benjamins, baby,
Uh-huh, yeah.
It's all about the Benjamins, baby,
Uh-huh, yeah.
It's all about the Benjamins, baby,
Uh-huh, yeah.
It's all about the Benjamins, baby,
Uh-huh, yeah.
It's all about the Benjamins, baby,
Now what y'all wanna do?
It's all about the Benjamins, baby,
Wanna be ballers, shot callers?
It's all about the Benjamins, baby,
Brawlers, who be dippin' in the Benz wit' the spoilers.
It's all about the Benjamins, baby,
On the low from the Jake in the Taurus.

[LIL' KIM]
Uhh, uhh, what the blood clot?
Wanna bumble wit' the Bee, hah?
Bzzzt, throw a hex on a whole family. (Yeah, yeah, yeah.)
Dressed in all black like the Oman. (Say what?)
Have your friends singin' "This is for my homie." (That's right.)
And you know me, from makin' niggaz so sick,
Floss in my six with the Lex on the wrist.
If it's Murder, you know She Wrote it, (Uh-huh.)
German Luger for your ass bitch, deep throated.
Know you wanna fill the room 'cause it's platinum-coated.
Take your pick, got a firearm you should o' toted.
Suck a dick, all that bullshit you kick,
Playa hatin' from the sideline, get your own shit.
Why you ridin' mine? (Uh-huh.)

I'm a Goodfella kinda lady,
Stash 380s and Mercedes,
Puffy, hold me down, baby!
Only female in my crew, and I kick shit
Like a nigga do, with a trigga, too, fuck you.

[NOTORIOUS B.I.G.]
Yeah, yeah, uhh, uhh, uhh!
I been had skills, Cristal spills,
Hide bills in Brazil, about a mil' to ice grill.
Make it hard to figure me, liquor be kickin' me
In my asshole, uhh, undercover, Donnie Brasco
Lent my East Coast girl the Bentley to twirl, (Uh-huh.)
My West Coast shorty, push the chrome, seven-forty.
Rockin' Redman and Naughty, all in my kitty-kat,
Half a brick of yeah, in the bra where her titties at.
And I'm livin' that, whole life, we push weight. (Uh-huh.)
Fuck the state pen, fuck hoes at Penn State. (C'mon.)
Listen close, it's Francis, the Praying Mantis,
Grip on the whip for the smooth getaway.
Playa haters get away or my lead will spray.
Squeeze off 'til I'm empty—don't tempt me.
Only, to Hell I send thee, all about the Benjis.
What?

[PUFF DADDY]
It's all about the Benjamins, baby,
Uh-huh, yeah.

Words and Music by Dante Givens,
Courtenay Henderson, Lucas Macfadden,
Mark Ali Potsic, Charles Stewart, Marc Stuart,
Jessie McDaniel and Clarence Williams

JAYOU
RECORDED BY JURASSIC 5

Yeah, testing, testing, one, two.
Uhh, one...
Press the panic button, God.

We be the crew—guess who? The Jayou.
R–A–double S, I–C,
We're in the place to be; it don't stop.
We got the rhythm that makes your fingers
Snap, crackle, pop-pop, fizz-fizz.
We're known to give a show, plus handle our biz-ness.
Stress, we'll destroy.
We're known to make noise as the original b-boys.
In the flesh; greater to the depth.
Creates the ill scenes when we manifest, yes.

I feel the vibe; I feel the vibe, too.
'Cause it's the butter from the crew.
'Cause we original.
Who wanna tussle? Flex for the muscle?
While we kick the style that busts your blood vessels
With the rhythm—the ninety-six stylism,
Pick up a pill and feel 'em kill 'em with your vocalism.

Yeah, I shoot the gift puffin' another cold spliff.
Fools are coming quicker than Anna Nicole Smith.
Malignant metaphors and ganja stay herbs.
We conjugate verbs and constipate nerds LIKE YOU.
I'm here to end the conspiracy fearlessly.
So you can really see the real MCs AT HAND.
I'm 2na Fish on the stick shift.
The eclectic hectic; desperate to set trip.

And for the niggaz who feel that they're 24-karat,
Plus the way you're livin', get your underwater baptism.
Believe it or not, it's the rugged and raw
Put a bullet in the head of four in Mount Rushmore.

Yeah, release the beast from within, baptize gin.
Keep company with friends that repel sin.
I'm out to win; ain't no pretendin'—fuck the First Amendment.
My speech was free the day my soul descended.

Earthbound, we might sound various.
Some niggaz can rhyme, but they got no character.
So we preparin' you for war; don't give up the fight.
You need to stand up for your rights.

And grab a mic and get loose; produce the juice that keeps the head-on collision
With the New World Order opposition.
Competition: none—there's only one
In the universe that know the final outcome.

We got incarcerated minds; men, women, and enzymes.
Vibin' off the rhymes
Sent from the divine essence, presence, effervescence.
Not to be contested—some miss the message: GO AHEAD AND BLESS THIS.
So don't mistake us for a crew that used to hit.
We on some underground, certified-wild-style shit.

We be the crew—guess who, and it'll be
The Jayou, '95 A.D.

We be causin' ramifications,
Physicians sendin' brothers on grammar vacations.
If they don't listen, competition bustin' shots on people basin'—
But we can delete constipation.

Jurassic 5, MCs
And we got the cure for this rap disease.
So come on, everybody, let's all get down
'Cause I'm down by law, and I know my way around.

Words and Music by Sean Combs,
Christopher Wallace, Jean Claude Olivier
and James Mtume

JUICY
RECORDED BY NOTORIOUS B.I.G.

(Fuck all you hoes.)
Get a grip, motherfucker.
Yeah, this album is dedicated
To all the teachers that told me I'd never amount to nothin';
To all the people that lived above the buildings
That I was hustlin' in front of that called the police on me
When I was just tryin' to make some money to feed my daughters
And all the niggaz in the struggle,
You know what I'm sayin'?
Uh-ha, it's all good, baby, bay-bee, uh.

It was all a dream,
I used to read *Word Up* magazine,
Salt N Pepa and Heavy D up in the limousine.
Hangin' pictures on my wall
Every Saturday, "Rap Attack," "Mr. Magic," "Marley Marl."
I let my tape rock 'til my tape popped.
Smokin' weed and bamboo, sippin' on private stock,
Way back, when I had the red and black lumberjack
With the hat to match.

Remember Rappin' Duke, duh-ha, duh-ha?
You never thought that hip-hop would take it this far.
Now I'm in the limelight 'cause I rhyme tight.
Time to get paid, blow up like the World Trade.
Born sinner, the opposite of a winner—
Remember when I used to eat sardines for dinner?
Peace to Ron G., Brucey B., Kid Capri,
Funkmaster Flex, Lovebug Starsky.
I'm blowin' up like you thought I would.
Call the crib—same number, same 'hood.
It's all good.

Uh, and if you don't know, now you know, nigga, uh.

CHORUS:

You know very well who you are.
Don't let 'em hold you down, reach for the stars.
You had a goal, but not that many
'Cause you're the only one, I'll give you good and plenty.

I made the change from a common thief,
To up close and personal with Robin Leach.
And I'm far from cheap, I smoke skunk with my peeps all day,
Spread love—it's the Brooklyn way.
The Moet and Alizé keep me pissy.
Girls used to diss me,
Now they write letters 'cause they miss me.
I never thought it could happen, this rappin' stuff.
I was too used to packin' gatts and stuff.
Now homies play me close like butter played toast,
From the Mississippi down to the East Coast.
Condos in Queens, Indo for weeks,
Sold-out seats to hear Biggie Smalls speak.
Livin' life without feat,
  Puttin' five carats in my baby girl's ears,
    Lunches, brunches, interviews by the pool.
      Considered a fool 'cause I dropped out of high school.
      Stereotypes of a black male misunderstood.
      And it's still all good.

Uh, and if you don't know, now you know, nigga.

Super Nintendo, Sega, Genesis,
When I was dead broke, man, I couldn't picture this.
Fifty-inch screen, money green, leather sofa,
Got two rides, a limousine with a chauffeur.
Phone bill about two Gs flat.
No need to worry, my accountant handles that
And my whole crew is loungin',
Celebratin' every day, no more public housin'.
Thinkin' back on my one-room shack.
Now my mom pimps a Ac' with minks on her back.
And she loves to show me off, of course.
Smiles every time my face is up in *The Source*.
We used to fuss when the landlord dissed us,
No heat, wonder why Christmas missed us?
Birthdays was the worst days,
Now we sip champagne when we thirst-ay.
Uh, damn right, I like the life I live
'Cause I went from negative to positive.
And it's all...

(It's all good.)

And if you don't know, now you know, nigga, uh.
Uh, uh, and if you don't know, now you know, nigga.
Uh, and if you don't know, now you know, nigga, uh.

Representin' B-Town in the house, Junior M.A.F.I.A., Mad Flavor, uh.
Uh, yeah, a-ight.

JUMP
RECORDED BY KRIS KROSS

Words and Music by Freddie Perren,
Alphonso Mizell, Berry Gordy, Dennis Lussier,
Jermaine Dupri, Gregory Webster, Melvin Pierce,
Norman Napier, Andrew Noland, Leroy Bonner,
Marshall Jones, Ralph Middlebrooks
and Walter Morrison

Jump, jump.
You should know, you should know that, ah,
Kris Kross is not having anything today
As we stand there totally Krossed out.
We commence to make you—

CHORUS:
Jump, jump.
The Mac Daddy will make you jump, jump.
The Daddy Mac will make you jump, jump.
Kris Kross will make you jump, jump.

Don't try to compare us to another bad little fad/
I'm the Mac and I'm bad—give you something that you never had.
I'll make ya jump, jump, wiggle, and shake your rump
'Cause I'll be kickin' the flavor that makes you wanna jump.
How high? Real high
'Cause I'm just so fly.
A young, lovable, huggable type of guy
And everything is the back with a little slack
And inside-out is wiggida-wiggida-wack.
I come stompin' with somethin' to keep you jumpin'.
R and B and bullcrap is what I'm dumpin'
And ain't somethin' about Kris Kross—we all that.
So when they ask to the rocks, they believe that.

CHORUS

I let myself knockin', knockin'.
I love it when a girl is playin' jockin', jockin'.
The D–A, double-D, Y–M–A–C,
Yeah, you know me.
I got you jumpin' and pumpin' an' movin' all around G.
In the mix, I make ya take a step back.
They try to step to the Mac, then they got jacked
To the back, you'll be sportin' the gear—that's coincidental.
And like, you know it, so don't be claimin' that it's mental.
Two lil' kids with a flow you ain't ever heard
And none fakin', you can understand every word.
As you listen to my cool school melody,
The Daddy makes you J–U–M–P.

CHORUS

Uh-huh, uh-huh.

CHORUS

Now, the formalities of this and that
Is that Kris Kross ain't comin' off wack.
And for all y'all sucks that don't know,
Check it out—

Some of them try to rhyme but they can't rhyme like this; go, go.
Some of them try to rhyme but they can't rhyme like this; go, go.
Some of them try to rhyme but they can't rhyme like this; go, go.
'Cause I'm the miggida-miggida-miggida Mac Daddy,
Miggida-miggida-miggida Mac.
'Cause I'm the miggida-miggida-miggida Mac Daddy.
I make you wanna—

CHORUS (4 TIMES)

Uh-huh, uh-huh, believe dat.

Words and Music by Marshall Mathers,
Jeffrey Bass and Mark Bass

JUST DON'T GIVE A FUCK
RECORDED BY EMINEM

INTRO:
[FROGG]
Whoa!
A-get your hands in the air, and get to clappin' 'em
And like, back and forth because
A-this is what you thought it wasn't.
It be's the brothers representin' the Dirty Dozen.
I be the F–R–O, the double G, and check out the man,
He goes by the name of er…

[EMINEM]
Slim Shady, brain dead like Jim Brady.
I'm a M-80, you Lil' like that Kim lady.
I'm buzzin', Dirty Dozen, naughty, rotten rhymer,
Cursin' at you players worse than Marty Schottenheimer.
You wacker than the motherfucker you bit your style from.
You ain't gonna sell two copies if you press a double album.
Admit it, fuck it, while we comin' out in the open,
I'm doin' acid, crack, smack, coke, and smokin' dope then.
My name is Marshal Mathers, I'm an alcoholic. (Hi, Marshall.)
I have a disease and they don't know what to call it.
Better hide your wallet 'cause I'm comin' up quick to strip your cash.
Bought a ticket to your concert just to come and whip your ass.
Bitch, I'm comin' out swingin' so fast it'll make your eyes spin.
You gettin' knocked the fuck out like Mike Tyson.
The proof is in the puddin', just ask the Shawn Holman.
It'll slit your motherfuckin' throat worse than Ron Goldman.

238

CHORUS:

So when you see me on your block with two glocks,
Screamin', "Fuck the world" like Tupac,
I just don't give a fuck!
Talkin' that shit behind my back, dirty mackin',
Tellin' your boys that I'm on crack.
I just don't give a fuck!
So put my tape back on the rack.
Go run and tell your friends my shit is wack.
I just don't give a fuck!
But see me on the street and duck
'Cause you gon' get stuck, stoned, and snuffed
'Cause I just don't give a fuck!

I'm nicer than Pete, but I'm on a search to crush a Milkbone.
I'm Everlast-ing—I melt Vanilla Ice like silicone.
I'm ill enough to just straight-up diss you for no reason.
I'm colder than snow season when it's twenty below freezin'.
Flavor with no seasonin', this is the sneak preview.
I'll diss your magazine and still won't get a weak review.
I'll make your freak leave you—smell the Folgers crystals.
This is a lyrical combat, gentlemen, hold your pistols.
But I form like Voltron and blast you with my shoulder missiles.
Slim Shady, Eminem was the old initials. (Bye-bye!)
Extortion, snortin', supportin' abortion,
Pathological liar, blowin' shit out of proportion.
The looniest, zaniest, spontaneous, sporadic,
Impulsive thinker, compulsive drinker, addict,
Half animal, half man.
Dumpin' your dead body inside of a fuckin' trash can
 With more holes than an afghan.

CHORUS

Somebody let me out this limousine. (Hey, let me out!)
I'm a caged demon, on stage screamin' like Rage Against The Machine.
I'm convinced I'm a fiend, shootin' up while this record is spinnin',
Clinically brain dead, I don't need a second opinion.
Fuck droppin' the jaw, I'm flippin' the sacred treasure.
I'll bite your motherfuckin' style, just to make it fresher.
I can't take the pressure, I'm sick of bitches,
Sick of naggin' bosses bitchin' while I'm washin' dishes.
In school I never said much, too busy havin' a head-rush.
Then I went to Jim Beam, that's when my face grayed.
Went to gym in eighth grade, raped the women's swim team.
Don't take me for a joke, I'm no comedian.
Too many mental problems got me snortin' coke and smokin' weed again.
I'm goin' up over the curb, drivin' on the median.
Finally made it home, but I don't got the key to get in.

CHORUS

Hey, fuck that!
Outsidaz, Pace One, Young Zee...

Words and Music by Jermaine Dupri,
MC Lyte and Michael Jackson

KEEP ON KEEPIN' ON
RECORDED BY MC LYTE

B-Boy, where the fuck you at?
I been lookin' for your ass since a quarter past.
Hot peas and butter, baby, come and get your supper
Before I make you suffer—that's when you had enough-a.
Can I get hot when you hit the jackpot?
Surely, I can, if you the man.
I get loose and produce large amounts of juice.
Can you get used to that or do you need a boost
Of energy to enter me and get it on?
You're gettin' warm, I can feel you gettin' closer.
Now baby, down this Mimosa.
You'd better believe it's time to give a toast to
The woman of the decade, too bad to be played.
Get vex and I'm bound to throw shade
All over your body.
Whose body? Your body.
I can rock a party like nobody.
Leavin' time to take home the loot,
Choosy about who I let knock my boots.
Now let me take sight while your lovin' Lyte.
Life ain't all that unless you're doin' it right.

CHORUS:

Keep on keepin' on
'Cause you came and you changed my world.
Your love, so brand new.
Keep on, keep kickin' on.
Doin' it right, right, right.
Ah, ah, ah.

Beware of the stare when I step into peace.
I come in peace but I got shit that need to be released.
Now who from the chosen shall I choose?
Yeah, now you wish you was in his shoes.

I found me a new nigga this year
That knows how to handle this here.
Now I look forward to goin' home at night.
Brother does me right, under candlelight.
Wax upon my back, can I handle all of that?
I guess I can.
Can I? Why not?
If I wanna guess, I can. Can I?
More honey than a bumble-bee hive,
Pullin' sixty-nine ways in my archive.
Sweet like licorice, sugar for my booga.
Juicy like Hi-C, or an Icee.
I got shit to make your ass write a bad check
'Cause, like I said, I ain't afraid of the sweat.
Beat on my drum if you feel the need to
As I proceed to open up and feed you.
I got a longing to put you where you wanna be.
When I can, I get rid of all company.

CHORUS

Many have tried strict regulation.
Lazy motherfuckers get put on probation.
Those that didn't perform well,
They get no answer when they ring-a-ring-a my bell.
You're playin' with my time,
Tryin' to jerk me, hurt me, then desert me.
You better work me
While your got the opportunity
To be in the midst of the L–Y–T–E.
Only the strong survive, only the wise excel,
Once said by my born-in-hell.
Only the lonely die slowly,
Left all alone, try to control me.
Easy does it, never ask, "How was it?"
Never speak my info, why my sheets in the streets,
'Cause that ain't cool, and that ain't cute
To talk about who knocked the boots on a video shoot.
But it's all good, though you gotta get it when you want it.
Like your prey, make your move and hop up on it.
It's natural, never be ashamed.
Fuck the fame, get the name, and kick the game.

Words and Music by
Roger Troutman and Larry Troutman

KEEP YOUR HEAD UP
RECORDED BY 2PAC

Little somethin' for my godson, Elijah, and a little girl named Corinne.

Some say the blacker the berry, the sweeter the juice.
I say the darker the flesh then the deeper the roots.
I give a holla to my sisters on welfare.
Tupac cares, and don't nobody else care.
And uhh, I know they like to beat ya down a lot
When you come around the block, brothas clown a lot.
But please don't cry, dry your eyes, never let up.
Forgive but don't forget, girl, keep your head up.
And if he can't learn to love you, you should leave him
'Cause, sista, you don't need him.
And I ain't tryin' to gas ya up, I just call 'em how I see 'em.
You know it makes me unhappy (What's that?)
When brothas make babies and leave a young mother to be a pappy.
And since we all came from a woman,
Got our name from a woman and our game from a woman,
I wonder why we take from our women,
Why we rape our women, do we hate our women?
I think it's time to kill for our women,
Time to heal our women, be real to our women.
And if we don't, we'll have a race of babies
That will hate the ladies that make the babies.
And since a man can't make one,
He has no right to tell a woman when and where to create one.
So will the real men get up?
I know you're fed up ladies, but keep your head up.

CHORUS:

Ooh, child, things are gonna get easier.
Ooh, child, things are gonna get brighter.
Ooh, child, things are gonna get easier.
Ooh, child, things are gonna get brighter.

Aiyyo, I remember Marvin Gaye used to sing to me.
He had me feelin' like black was the thing to be.
And suddenly the ghetto didn't seem so tough.
And though we had it rough, we always had enough.
I huffed and I puffed about my curfew and broke the rules,
Ran with the local crew and had a smoke or two.
And I realize Momma really paid the price.
She nearly gave her life to raise me right.
And all I had to give her was my pipe-dream
Of how I'd rock the mic and make it to the bright screen.
I'm tryin' to make a dollar out of fifteen cents.
It's hard to be legit and still pay the rent.
And in the end, it seems, I'm headin' for the pen.
I try and find my friends, but they're blowin' in the wind.
Last night my buddy lost his whole family.
It's gonna take the man in me to conquer this insanity.
It seems the rain'll never let up.
I try to keep my head up, and still keep from gettin' wet up.

You know, it's funny: when it rains, it pours.
They got money for wars but can't feed the poor.
Say there ain't no hope for the youth and the truth is
It ain't no hope for the future,
And then they wonder why we crazy.
I blame my mother for turning my brother into a crack baby.
We ain't meant to survive 'cause it's a set-up.
And even though you're fed up,
Huh, ya got to keep your head up.

CHORUS

And uhh, to all the ladies havin' babies on they own,
I know it's kinda rough and you're feelin' all alone.
Daddy's long gone, and he left you by ya lonesome.
Thank the Lord for my kids, even if nobody else want 'em
'Cause I think we can make it, in fact, I'm sure.
And if you fall, stand tall, and come back for more
'Cause ain't nuttin' worse than when your son
Wants to know why his daddy don't love him no mo'.
You can't complain you was dealt this
Hell of a hand without a man, feelin' helpless
Because there's too many things for you to deal with:
Dyin' inside, but outside you're lookin' fearless
While tears is rollin' down your cheeks,
Ya steady, hopin' things don't all down this week
'Cause if it did, you couldn't take it, and don't blame me.
I was given this world, I didn't make it,
And now my son's gettin' older and older and cold
From havin' the world on his shoulders.
While the rich kids is drivin' Benz,
I'm still tryin' to hold on to my survivin' friends.
And it's crazy—it seems it'll never let up,
But please, you got to keep your head up.

Words and Music by Keith Elam,
Angela Stone and George Spivey

KEEP YOUR WORRIES
RECORDED BY GURU, FEATURING ANGIE STONE

[ANGIE STONE]
Ooh, ooh. (Uh, mm.)
Ooh, ooh, (Uh, mm, keep your…)
Yeah, yeah, my brother, Guru
And Angie Stone. (Ooh, ooh.)
And DJ Scratch. (Yeah, mm, mm.)
Uhh, Guru, and Angie Stone.

CHORUS:
[ANGIE STONE]
Keep your feet out my shoes.
A nigga like me done paid my dues.
Keep my comb out your hair
Unless you 'bout ready to take it there.
Keep my name out your mouth
Until you got somethin' worth talkin' 'bout.
Keep your hands to yourself
'Cause I belong to someone else.

[GURU]

It's the G–U–R–U once again, settin' it off,
Lettin' it off my chest, plus bettin' it all.
Record sales, awards, accolades—I'm gettin' it all.
Mad chips right above my grip, I'm lettin' 'em fall.
Who said the G–O–D wasn't comin' to do his thing?
Who said the industry wasn't gonna bow to this king?
I paid dues, stayed true, so I made it through.
If you handle your B–I fly guy, you can make it, too.
Your potential is infinite; be wise, visualize, witness it.
Why waste your time focusin' your mind on limp shit?
Angie understands me, and Scratch got my back.
So keep away from the fire, burnin' desire, yo, we got that.

CHORUS

[GURU]

I've never been a stranger to struggle,
Gotta maintain my hustle.
Used to let the anger bubble.
These streets can bring mad danger and trouble.
And I can do bad all by myself.
Do me a favor: don't be concerned about my wealth.
If you're one of my peeps, you're gonna know that.
But if I ain't feelin' you, player, huh,
My face is gonna show that.
So keep your eyes off my pockets.
Don't be surprised if I cocked it.
Can't out-slick a can of oil—you never spoil my profits.
See how I'm flippin' this here?
Things are different this year.
Ain't got no time to listen to niggaz
That be trippin' this year.
Cause and effect, I always get applause and respect.
When I rhyme universal laws, truth, and righteousness connect.

[ANGIE STONE]
You see, the knowledge that I'm kicking's for you
And there is nothin' that another can do.
Try to stop me, but I make it through.
Recruitin' angels as a warrior, I'm true.
People need people, it's true.
True pride will sustain
In order to do what I do, I can let you live
With me inside my brain.

CHORUS

[GURU]
I've been tellin' you that there's war out here
And I've been tellin' you that there's more out here.
So stop limitin' your thoughts,
Stop reconstructin' your plots.
It's more than luck, it's an art.
No more duckin' from narcs.
Haters, stay at a distance; haters, keep away from my fam,
Haters stay in my business; haters still playin' this jam.
Mad wisdoms reflect the light of this man,
Some jealous rappers tried to pick a fight with this man.
But despite all the nonsense and false pretense, I bomb this:
Peace to those I get along with, my real nigga I'm strong with
And never get me twisted with no wack shit
And all that foolishness you was kickin', yeah.
I know you wanna take it back, kid.

CHORUS (2 TIMES)

[ANGIE STONE]
Uhh, Guru, check it.
DJ Scratch and Angie.
Uh, uh, ooh yeah, yeah.

Words and Music by
Cornell Haynes and Writer Unknown

LET ME IN NOW
RECORDED BY ST. LUNATICS

[NELLY]
Oh, baby girl, like to shake a lot more,
Drop it like over here, baby girl, uh.

CHORUS:
[NELLY]
Let me in now, there it go.
I love it when you make your knees touch your elbows.
Boom, boom.
Let me in now, there it go.
I love it when you make your knees touch your elbows.
Boom, boom.
Let me in now, there it go.
I love it when you make your knees touch your elbows.
Boom, boom.
Let me in now, there it go.
I love it when you make your knees touch your elbows.
Boom, boom.

[ALI]
Let me in, ma', so I can hit it.
Make you wanna leave wit' it, take you home and sleep wit' it.
Tell your friends that we did it in the back of the Coupe
With your back on the sunroof, hollerin' out, "Whoop-de-whoop."
You be like, "Girl, he put in work, hit it all night, he rocked my world,
Came out that skirt, soon as I hit that door, he thorough while you twerk.
So much Mo' and Cris' I hurled all on my skirt.
We still kicked it." (Let me in now.)
You ain't heard, that playa bad.
Saint Louis nigga to the end, with a fo'-fo' mag
And 'til them 'tic niggaz kick in, let a fire bag.

The party just would not begin 'til you shake that ass,
Now shake that ass.
I'm like, uh, "Whoa, hossie," and that ass ain't playin'.
I'm-a teach it to go varsity in a passin' Ram.
Marry me and divorce me and get my cash advance.
Your best bet's to deep-throat me as fast as you can.
I'm like—

CHORUS

[MURPHY LEE]
Aiyyo, I'm Murphy Lee, the ashtray, I touch butts all day.
Treat me like a toilet, you can sit on me
And let your knees touch your nostrils.
Show me that big ol' brown booty hole,
Let me record it like a studio.
You can go and get your crew, girl, like Freddy.
Huh, you Raw like Eddie, call me Murphy, if you ready.
Ready for whatever, Strictly Business, like Halle Berry,
When I'm with you like Tony Terry,
Say my name more times than Bloody Mary.
Kinda scary, gettin' more head for stones than cemeteries.
I done ran through more halls than Barry
At school, in the Hall gettin' busy like Arsenio.
I'm a rat trap like club Casino.

[KEYJUAN]
Aiyyo, it's on fo' sho', low-cut Capris so her thongs could show.
She probably got a man, but I've been wrong befo'.
All I know is that she makes her knees touch her elbows
Just to get in a show.
I'm startin' to think this how it's supposed to go.
Get blowed before we go where we supposed to go,
Workin' since ninety-fo', I'm supposed to blow.
Blow on the dice before I roll a ten-to-fo'.
Rollin' Mo-mos, Optimos—they burn slow.
Rollin' fo'-do's, sippin' Mo' with fo' hoes,

I'm a two-triple-0, U-City gigolo.
Deuce, deuce Bigalow, love a man, Joe Blow
And you should pay me, I'm Super like Nintendo.
Make your hands touch the flo', your knees don't bend, tho'.
In the Benz-o, tinted windows,
If the bounce is right, the ounce is right,
Meet me at my house tonight.

CHORUS

[NELLY]
Now, baby girl got a rump on 'er, fo'-do', and a trunk on 'er.
Low miles, no dents, title reading, "One owner."
Some are wanna be baller, baby daddies that don't want 'er,
He ain't trippin' 'til he see another nigga get on her.
But she a good girl, actin' bad when she need be.
I wish you would, girl, hit me so often she beep me
On some "Nelly, come meet me.
It's the First Lady—my President is out of the country,
I need the V–P."
I'm in the White House, butt-naked and iced-out.
Turn the lights out and I'm turnin' your wife out.
Same chick you jumped the broom with, throwin' the rice out,
Same cat shoppin' with rats, throwin' the mice out.
I like 'em clumsy, mo', just let everything hit the flo'.
Not once, not twice, three times, but fo'.
Each time, makin' her knees touchin' her elbows.
I said, each time, lookin' at me, yellin' she want mo'.
I'm like, "Oh!"

CHORUS

[NELLY]
Baby girl like to shake a lot, huh.
Baby girl like to shake a lot.
Huh, baby girl like to uh, uh, uh, uh.
Do your thizzle, Moet, hah, hah, and do your thizzle, Moet.
Hah, hah, shake it like that for, hah, yeah.
Three-one-four, fo' sho'.
S–T–L and I connect the do'.

Words and Music by Ahmir Thompson,
Tarik Collins, James Poyser and Keith Elam

LIFT YOUR FIST
RECORDED BY GURU,
FEATURING BLACK THOUGHT

[GURU]

Yeah, Guru, huh, The Roots.
Yeah, c'mon y'all, uh, lift your fist.
Uh, yeah, lift your fist, c'mon.
Uh!

CHORUS:
[BLACK THOUGHT]

To all my people, just lift your fist.
Seem like it ain't no peace, no justice.
How you want it—the bullet or the microchip?
Either way, you got to lift your fist,
We got to get it down like this.
To all my people, ball up your fist.
Seem like it ain't no peace, no justice.
How you want it—the bullet or the microchip?
Either way, you got to lift your fist.

[BLACK THOUGHT]

Yo, c'mon!
We livin' life close to the edge—don't push.
But this ain't eighty-three, and it's not the Cold Crush.
It's kids on the street strapped, huffin' that rush,
They eyein' the next cat, livin' all plush.
I guess frustration makes a brother do what he must.
What's the combination that can make a human erupt?
Team leaders gettin' mutinied up, who couldn't read the signs,
Thinkin' the day and times is nigh.

[GURU]

Indeed, we blast, refuse to kiss ass.
Quick, fast, ready to mash 'cause of a bugged-out past.

Swallow the pain, follow the mental terrain.
It takes a hell of a man nowadays to maintain.
Garments bloodstained, face bruised and battered,
Our eyes reflect the agony of dreams that were shattered.
And they love it when we wild-out and kill our own,
But the greater responsibility, yes, is still our own.

CHORUS

[GURU]
Uh, worldwide famine, ghetto people demand
That somebody do somethin' soon, and let's examine
The facts behind the violent attacks,
Behind the daily gun play, the cocaine, and the crack.
Thug season—what's the reason for the treason?
Everybody's gotta eat, some gotta resort to thievin',
Take money, money, money make money, money, money.

CHORUS

[BLACK THOUGHT]
Yo, from the time they eyes open 'til the clock strike death,
Brothers is stressed, walkin' 'round, holdin' they chest.
They got the government surveyin' they steps and can't breathe.
They dynamitin' them projects to smithereens.
Money comin', but them days too few and far between.
You tryin' to taste just what the world's offerin', ya mean?
I seen enough to make a grown man scream.
Brothers thirsty and hungry to get that thang.

[GURU]
Too many tears of pain, too many years of struggle,
Too many drops of blood, too many problems to juggle,
Too few jobs available, too few schools equipped,
Too few role models—just gangstas and pimps.
Will you succumb, will your heart grow numb?
Or will you save the world and use your mind like a gun?
I'm the one—I turn a stick-up kid to a soldier.
Me and The Roots, word up, we takin' over.

CHORUS (2 TIMES)

Words and Music by Stevie Wonder,
Jeffrey B. Atkins, Irv Gotti and Rob Mays

LIVIN' IT UP
RECORDED BY JA RULE, FEATURING CASE

Yeah, yeah, yeah.
Where all my...
Uhh, yeah, c'mon, c'mon, uhh.
To all my ladies that be givin' it up, uhh.
To all everybody that be livin' it up, we say...
To all my ladies that be givin' it up, ah.
C'mon.

Baby, this ain't your typical, everyday, one-night thing.
It's physical, I'm-a love-you-tonight thing.
Love knowin' your name, jump yo' ass in the Range,
And roll over, gettin' blown while blowin' the doja.
Bring head to a closure—that's a good chick.
Before it's all over, I'm-a meat this chick.
Probably treat this chick mo' better
'Cause if you ain't know, gangstas and hoes go together.
Poppin' my collar, partner, who in the spot?
Baby, Rule in the spot, and the mug and the watch ugly.
Half the hoes hate me, half them love me.
The ones that hate me only hate me 'cause they ain't fucked me.
And they say I'm lucky, you think I got time
To blow all these hoes and do all these shows?
Or flight in the llama-chargin', while Rolls?
Uh-oh, another episode.

CHORUS:

[CASE] Do I do…

[JA RULE] To all my everybody that be livin' it up, we say…

[CASE] What I do…

[JA RULE] To all my ladies that be givin' it up, uh.

[CASE] What you do…

[JA RULE] To all my everybody that be livin' it up, we say…

[CASE] What do I do?

[JA RULE] And all my ladies that be givin' it up.

[CASE] My love for you…

[JA RULE] C'mon.

Lady just wanna hold a name that's active,
That's why they suck dick with mo' passion than average
And I ain't mad atcha; never leave you alone
'Cause we fucks when I'm home, phone sex when I'm gone.
We both grown, both got minds of our own,
Plus I freaks off like O-Dog in "Love Jones."
Been in many zones, baby, one hoes, two hoes,
From prissy bitches to hoes that do porno.
But you know, the Rule be livin' it up
And got all these hoes givin' it up.
I like a little, "ooh, baby, how cute are you?"
With a body that rides on sexual.
I got a stick, I'll ride right next to ya.
Do a doughnut, and cut, then I'll open it up
On the freeway, hell-way, foot on the clutch.
Rule, baby, not givin' it up.

CHORUS

C'mon, we get high.
C'mon, we get right.
C'mon, we get live.
Live, yo, life.

Love, you so sexy, I just want you next to me.
Your whole vibe, like you high on exstacy,
'Cause ain't nuttin' but a E-thang, bay-bay.
I know the world is goin' cra-zay.
I wanna feel your passion, come when you askin',
Laugh when you cryin', cry when you laughin'.
But ain't nuttin' happenin', the girl got a little too high,
Turned off the light, then started cryin'.
The radio blastin', "Between Me And You."
But, you ain't on the low with the pretty thing you do.
Girl, I thought you knew (what I do), know I know (what you do)
'Cause it's ain't a good night if the head ain't right.
Like Teddy P, let's "Turn Off The Lights."
And, grind it out, takin' no times-out
'Til the sun come out.
Lemme find out.

CHORUS (2 TIMES)

C'mon, we get high.
C'mon, we get right.
C'mon, we get live.
C'mon, it's my time.

Words and Music by Mason Betha,
Chad Hugo and Pharrell Williams

LOOKIN' AT ME
RECORDED BY MASE,
FEATURING PUFF DADDY

[PUFF DADDY]
Hey yo, Mase, you know what I don't like?
(Why you over there lookin' at me?)
I don't like when, you know, I'm in a club,
(Why you over there lookin' at me?)
And I'm with my honey,
(Why you over there lookin' at me?)
You got, you know, the haters,
They wanna be tough guys all of a sudden.

CHORUS:
Why you over there lookin' at me
While my girl standin' here?
Why you over there lookin' at me
While my girl standin' here?

CHORUS

Hit you with the ice grill, you know,
Heheh, 'cause you boys ain't with you.
Little do they know, your girl roll harder than
Some of yo niggaz,
Dig?

[MASE]
Now what the hell is you lookin' for?
Can't a young man get money anymore?
Let my pants sag down to the floor.
Really, do it matter as long as I score?
Can't my car look better than yours?
Can I have a bad bitch without no flaws?
Come to see me without no drawers
In a stretch Lex with about ten doors?

How is Murder?
P. Diddy name me pretty.
Did it for the money, now can you get with me?
People wanna know, "Who is he?"
He get busy, spray so much izzy, girls get dizzy.
Niggaz on the block know Mase' motto:
One thing about Harlem World, we all got dough,
Ninety-eight Tahoe, Tommy, and a Roscoe
'Case I'm ever chased by a Donnie Brasco.

CHORUS

[MASE]
Yo, I can't get mad 'cause you look at me,
'Cause on the real, look at me.
Yo, it always be the haters that be sittin' in the rear
Dissin' every gear, but they better listen here.
You cats keepin' it real, you cats is on your own,
'Cause bein' broke and alone is somethin' I can't condone.
Plus it won't be long 'til they send me the dome.
Sit gently, while I'm on the Bentley phone.
Why you don't like me—
'Cause I'm mad and fly and icy?
And why you can't satisfy yo' wifey?
And if it wasn't for this Bad Boy exposure:
CD, TVs, really, would I know ya?
Now me and Blink float in the gold Rover,
So it's only right you get the cold shoulder.
And if you got a girl, don't be real committed
'Cause Mase will hit it; you got to deal with it.

CHORUS (2 TIMES)

Make it hot, baby; make it hot. (Come on!)
Make it hot, baby; make it hot. (Come on!)
Make it hot, baby; make it hot. (Come on!)
Make it hot, baby; make it hot. (Come on!)
We don't stop.

[MASE]
We was all at the Greek Fest, it's hot and sandy.
I rent scooters, I'm with my family.
Tank top, flip-flop, really nothing fancy,
But get approached by a girl named Tammy
Who looked good enough to be Miss Miami.
But say, since some her peeps call her Candy.
Then she starts to ask about Aaliyah and Brandy,
Tellin' me how she met Puff down at the Grammy's:
"He ain't tell you I was the one with no panties?"
Boo, you know how many he meet with no panties?
Please, tell me somethin' that I don't know,
Like, if we have sex, you don't want dough,
And if it's not a problem, you can meet me at ten.
I'll be in room 112, and bring four friends.
And if you gon' hit me, it gotta be a quickie,
And please, no hickies, 'cause wifey with me.

CHORUS

Words and Music by Albert Brown, Kyle West,
Rashad Smith and James Todd Smith

LOUNGIN'
RECORDED BY LL COOL J

It's a Queens thing, babe.
Who do you love?
Oh, oh, rock on.

How you doin', Miss? My name is L; I'm from Queens.
I heard about your man—he likes to lace you with cream.
Don't think about a Moschino with Donna jeans.
But it slipped, and threw his rock down, fiend.
He be playin' like a willy 'cause he dress ya.
Duh, never knowin' that his woman is
In need of love, you got Versace gold-link
Stomach chains with rocks, official hairstyle,
But you stuck up in the spot, makin' love,
Duke is weak, then he fallin' asleep.
You on the phone with your old peeps, dyin' to creep
'Tween my sheets; so what you got Chanel on your feet?
Hot sex on a platter makes the mission complete.

CHORUS:
Who do you love?
(I wanna lounge with you.)
Are you for sure?
(I do what I gotta do.)
Who do you love?
(I wanna lounge with you.)
Are you for sure?
(I do what I gotta do.)

Jewels and Cristal, gotta mack a phony style.
He ain't watchin' you, he rather watch his money pile.
Can't protect treasures when it's in a glass house.
Soon as he turn the corner, I'm turn this out

Full-blown, frontin' in the six wit' the chrome; yo, B
Why you leave your honey all alone with me?
Just because you blessed with cash
Doesn't mean your honey won't let me finesse this.
So, see the moral of the story is a woman need love—
The kind you so-called playas never dreamed of.
You gotta try love, can't buy love.
If you play your hand then it's bye-bye love.

CHORUS

So what you got? The cash flow and the escrow, damn.
But your honey ran away like busto-alakazam.
Man made money—money never made the man.
You still fake a tax, throwin' rocks on her hand.
See, you put your mack down,
Now you need no brown rock roller
Wit' so much ice your cap's polar.
I got them smokin' beanies, bottle in bikinis,
Pushin' ya whip on the fairway to see me.
I keep it steamy, I make it burn when it's my turn.
Teachin' shorty all the tools that you never learned.
Don't get it twisted: gettin' money ain't wrong
But she wanna make love all night long.
I'm gone.

CHORUS

LYRICS OF FURY
Words and Music by
Eric B. and Rakim
RECORDED BY ERIC B. AND RAKIM

I'm rated "R"; this is a warning, ya better 'void.
Poets are paranoid, DJs D-stroyed
'Cause I came back to attack others in spite—
Strike like lightening; it's quite frightening!
But don't be afraid in the dark, in a park.
Not a scream, or a cry, or a bark; more like a spark.
Ya tremble like a' alcoholic; muscles tighten up.
What's that? Lighten up! You see a sight, but—
Suddenly you feel like you're in a horror flick.
You grab your heart, then wish for tomorrow, quick!
Music's the clue—when I come you're warned.
Apocolypse Now—when I'm done, ya gone!
Haven't you ever heard of a' MC-murderer?
This is the death penalty, and I'm servin' a death wish.
So come on, step to this hysterical idea for a lyrical professionist!
Friday the thirteenth, walking down Elm Street,
You come in my realm—ya get beat!
This is off-limits, so your visions are blurry.
All ya see is the meters at a volume, pumpin' lyrics of fury!

It's a...fearified freestyle!

Terror in the styles, never-error-philes.
Indeed, I'm known—you're exiled!
For those that oppose to be level or next to this,
I ain't a devil and this ain't the Exorcist!
Worse than a nightmare, you don't have to sleep a wink.
The pain's a migraine every time ya think.
Flashbacks interfere; ya start to hear
The R–A–K–I–M in your ear.
Then the beat is hysterical—
That makes Eric go get an ax and chops the wack.
Soon the lyrical format is superior.
Faces of death remain:
MCs decaying 'cause they never stayed.
The scene of a crime, every night at the show,
The friend of a rhyme on the mic that you know.

It's only one capable, breaks the unbreakable,
Melodies unmakable, pattern unescapable.
A horn if want the style I possess,
I bless the child, the earth, the gods, and bomb the rest.
For those that envy a' MC, it can be
Hazardous to your health, so be friendly.
A matter of life and death, just like a' Etch-A-Sketch:
Shake 'til you're clear, make it disappear, make the next.
After the ceremony, let the rhyme rest in peace.
If not, my soul'll release!
The scene is recreated, reincarnated, updated—I'm glad you made it
'Cause you're about to see a disastrous sight:
A performance never again performed on a mic—lyrics of fury!

A fearified freestyle!

The "R" is in the house; too much tension!
Make sure the system's loud when I mention
Phrases that's fearsome.
You want to hear some sounds that not only pounds, but please your eardrums?
I sit back and observe the whole scenery,
Then nonchalantly tell you what it mean to me.
Strictly business; I'm quickly in this mood,
And I don't care if the whole crowd's a witness.
I'm-a tear you apart, but I'm-a spare you a heart.
Program into the speed of the rhyme; prepare to start.
Rhythm's out of the radius; insane as the craziest
Musical madness MC ever made.
See, it's now an emergency; open-heart surgery.
Open your mind, you will find every word'll be
Furrier than ever; I remain the future,
Battle's tempting—whatever suits ya!
For word's the sentence; there's no resemblance.
You think you're rougher, then suffer the consequences!
I'm never dying—terrifying results.
I wake ya with hundreds of thousands of volts.
Mic-to-mic resuscitation; rhythm with radiation.
Novocain ease the pain—it might save him.
If not, Eric B.'s the judge—the crowd's the jury.
How do I plead to homicide?
Lyrics of fury!

Words and Music by Will Smith, Patrice Rushen,
Fred Washington and Terry McFadden

MEN IN BLACK

RECORDED BY WILL SMITH

Here come the Men in Black.
It's the M–I–Bs, uh, here come the M–I–Bs.
Here come the Men in Black. (Men in Black.)
They won't let you remember.
Na, na, na.

The good guys dress in black, remember that,
Just in case we ever face-to-face and make contact.
The title held by me: M–I–B,
Means what you think you saw, you did not see.
So don't blink, because what was there
Is now gone, black suit with the black Ray Bans on.
Walk in the shadow, move in silence,
Guard against extra-terrestrial violence.
But yo, we ain't on no government list,
We straight don't exist, no names and no fingerprints.
Saw somethin' strange, watch your back
'Cause you never quite know where the M–I–Bs is at.
Uh, and—

Here come the Men in Black. (Men in Black.)
Galaxy defenders.
Here come the Men in Black. (Men in Black.)
They won't let you remember. (Won't let you remember.)

Uh-ah, uh-ah, now,
From the deepest of the darkest of night,
On the horizon, bright light enters sight, tight
Cameras zoom on the impending doom.
But then like, boom, black suits fill the room up
With the quickness, talk with witnesses,
Hypnotizer, neutralizer,
Vivid memories turn to fantasies.
Ain't no M–I–Bs can I please.
Do what we say, that's the way we kick it.
Ya know what I mean?
I see my noisy cricket get wicked on ya.
We're your first, last, and only line of defense against
The worst scum of the universe.
So don't fear us, cheer us.
If you ever get near us, don't jeer us, we're the fearless
M–I–Bs, freezing up all the flack.
(What' that stand for?)
Men in Black.

Uh-ah, the Men in Black.
Men in Black.

Let me see ya just bounce it with me, just bounce with me,
Just bounce it with me, come on. (Bounce with me.)
Let me see ya just slide with me, just slide with me.
Just slide with me, come on. (Slide, slide, slide, slide.)
Let me see ya take a walk with me, just walk it with me.
Take a walk with me, come on. (Walk with me.)
And make your neck work.
Now freeze!

Here come the Men in Black. (Men in Black.)
The galaxy defenders.
Right on, right on.
Here come the Men in Black. (Men in Black.)
They won't let you remember. (Oh no!)

All right, check it, let me tell you this in closing:
I know we might seem imposing,
But trust me, we never showing this section.
Believe me, it's for your own protection,
'Cause we see things that you need not see
And we be places that you need not be.
So go on with ya life, forget that Roswell crap,
Show love to the black suit, 'cause that's the Men in—
That's the Men in—

Here come the Men in Black. (Here they come.)
The galaxy defenders. (Galaxy defenders.)
Here come the Men in Black. (Oh, here they come.)
They won't let you remember. (Won't let you remember.)
Here come the Men in Black. (Oh, here they come.)
Galaxy defenders.
Here come the Men in Black.
They won't let you remember.

Words and Music by William Shelby,
Stephen Shockley, Leon Sylvers, Will Smith,
Samuel Barnes and Ryan Toby

MIAMI
RECORDED BY WILL SMITH

Yeah, yeah, yeah, yeah.
Miami, uh, uh.
South Beach, bringin' the heat, uh.
Ha, ha! Can y'all feel that?
Can y'all feel that?
Jig it out, uh.

Here I am, in the place where I come let go:
Miami, the base, and the sunset low.
Everyday like a Mardi Gras, everybody party all day,
No work, all play, okay.
So we sip a little somethin', lay the rest, the spill.
Me and Charlie at the bar, runnin' up a high bill.
Nothin' less than ill when we dress to kill.
Every time the ladies pass, they be like, ("Hi, Will.")
Can y'all feel me? All ages, all races, real sweet faces,
Every different nation: Spanish, Haitian, Indian, Jamaican,
Black, White, Cuban, Asian.
I only came for two days of playin',
But every time I come, I always wind up stayin'.
This type of town, I could spend a few days in.
Miami the city that keeps the roof blazin'.

CHORUS:
Party in the city where the heat is on.
All night on the beach 'til the break of dawn.
Welcome to Miami. (Bienvenido a Miami.)
Bouncin' in the club where the heat is on.
All night on the beach 'til the break of dawn.
I'm goin' to Miami.
Welcome to Miami.

Yo, I heard the rainstorms ain't nothin' to mess with,
But I can't feel a drip on the strip—it's a trip.
Ladies half-dressed, fully equipped,
And they be screamin' out, ("Will, we loved your last hit!")
So, I'm thinkin' I'm-a scoot me somethin' hot
In this south-sea meringue melting pot.
Hottest club in the city and it's right on the beach.
Temperature get to ya, it's about to reach
Five hundred degrees
In the Caribbean seas,
With the hot mommies screamin, ("Aii, poppy!")
Every time I come to town, they be spottin' me
In the drop Bentley, ain't no stopping me.
So, cash in your dough
And flow to this fashion show.
Pound for pound, anywhere you go,
Yo, ain't no city in the world like this.
And if you ask how I know, I gots to plead the fifth.

CHORUS

Don't get me wrong, Chi-town got it goin' on.
And New York is the city that we know don't sleep.
And we all know that L.A. and Philly stay jiggy,
But on the sneak, Miami bringin' heat for real.
Y'all don't understand,
I never seen so many Dominican women with cinnamon tans.
Ya know this is the plan—
Take a walk on the beach, draw a heart in the sand,
Gimme your hand.
Damn, you look sexy.
Let's go to my yacht in the West Keys,
Ride my jet skis, loungin' in the palm trees,
'Cause you gotta have cheese for the summer house piece on South Beach.
Water so clear, you can see to the bottom.
Hundred-thousand-dollar cars, everybody got 'em.
Ain't no surprise to see in the club, to see Sly Stallone.
Miami my second home.

CHORUS (2 TIMES)

Words and Music by Eric B. and Rakim

MICROPHONE FIEND
RECORDED BY ERIC B. AND RAKIM

I was a fiend before I became a teen.
I melted microphone instead of cones of ice cream.
Music-orientated, so when hip-hop was originated,
Fitted like pieces of puzzles complicated
'Cause I grabbed the mic and try to say, "Yes, y'all!"
They tried to take it and say that I'm too small.
Cool, 'cause I don't get upset.
I kick a hole in the speaker, pull the plug, then I jet
Back to the lab, without a mic to grab.
So then I add all the rhymes I had,
One after the other one; then I make another one.
To dis, the opposite, then ask if the brother's done.
I get a craving like I fiend for nicotine,
But I don't need a cigarette—know what I mean?
I'm ragin', rippin' up the stage.
And don't it sound amazin', 'cause every rhyme is made,
And thought of, 'cause it's sort of an addiction,
Magnetized by the mixin'—
Vocals, vocabulary, your verses; you're stuck in
The mic is a Drano; volcanoes eruptin',
Rhymes overflowin', gradually growin'.
Everything is written in the cold, so it can coincide,
My thoughts to guide, forty-eight tracks to slide.
The invincible microphone fiend, Rakim—
Spread the word, 'cause I'm in E–F–F–E–C–T.
A smooth operator operating correctly,
But back to the problem—I got a habit.
You can't solve it, silly rabbit.
The prescription is a hypertone that's thorough when
I fiend for a microphone like heroin.
Soon as the bass kicks, I need a fix.
Gimme a stage and a mic and a mix
And I'll put you in a mood—or is it a state of unawareness?

Beware: it's the re-animator!
A menace to a microphone; a lethal weapon.
An assassinator, if the people aren't steppin'.
You see a part of me that you never seen.
When I'm fiendin' for a microphone,
I'm the microphone fiend.

After twelve, I'm worse than a gremlin—
Feed me hip-hop and I start tremblin'.
The thrill of suspense is intense; you're horrified,
But this ain't the cinemas of "Tales From The Darkside."
By any means necessary, this is what has to be done.
Make way, 'cause here I come.
My DJ cuts material grand imperial.
It's a must that I bust any mic you're hand to me.
It's inherited; it's runs in the family.
I wrote the rhyme that broke the bull's back.
If that don't slow 'em up, I carry a full pack.
Now, I don't want to have to let off—you should of kept off.
You didn't keep the stage warm—step off!
Ladies and gentlemen, you're about to see
A pastime hobby about to be
Take it to the maximum; I can't relax, see,
I'm hype as a hypochondriac, 'cause the rap be one hell of an antidote;
Somethin' you can't smoke more than dope.
You're tryin' to move away, but you can't—you're broke.
More than cracked up, you should have backed up.
For those who act up, need to be more than smacked up.
Any entertainer, I got a torture chamber.
One on one and I'm the remainder!
So, close your eyes and hold your breath,
And I'm-a hit'cha wit' the blow of death.
Before you go, you'll remember you seen
The fiend of the microphone—
I'm the microphone fiend.

The microphone fiend...

Words and Music by Todd Thomas

MR. WENDAL

RECORDED BY ARRESTED DEVELOPMENT

Here, have a dollar.
In fact, no brother-man, here, have two.
Two dollars means a snack for me
But it means a big deal to you.
Be strong, serve God only.
Know that if you do, beautiful heaven awaits.
That's the poem I wrote for the first time
I saw a man with no clothes, no money, no plate.
Mr. Wendal, that's his name.
No one ever knew his name 'cause he's a no-one.
Never thought twice about spendin' on a' ol' bum
Until I had the chance to really get to know one.
Now that I know him, to give him money isn't charity.
He gives me some knowledge, I buy him some shoes.
And to think blacks spend all that money on big colleges,
Still most of y'all come out confused.

Go ahead, Mr. Wendal.
Go ahead, Mr. Wendal.

Mr. Wendal has freedom—
A free that you and I think is dumb.
Free to be without the worries of a quick-to-diss society.
For, Mr. Wendal's a bum.
His only worries are sickness
And an occasional harassment by the police and their chase.
Uncivilized, we call him,
But I just saw him eat off the food we waste.

Civilization, are we really civilized? Yes or no?
Who are we to judge,
When thousands of innocent men could be brutally enslaved.
And killed over a racist grudge?
Mr. Wendal has tried to warn us about our ways,
But we don't hear him talk.
Is it his fault, when we've gone too far
And we got too far 'cause on him we walk?
Mr. Wendal, a man, a human in flesh.
But not by law.
I feed you dignity to stand with pride.
Realize that all in all, you stand tall.

Mr. Wendal, yeah, yeah, yeah.
Lord, Mr. Wendal.

Words and Music by David Sheats,
Andre Benjamin and Antwan Patton

MS. JACKSON
RECORDED BY OUTKAST

[ANDRE 3000]
Yeah, this one right here goes out to all the babies,
Mamas, mamas,
Mamas, mamas, baby mamas, mamas.
Yeah, go like this—

CHORUS:
[Andre 3000]
I'm sorry, Ms. Jackson. (Ooh.)
I am for real.
Never meant to make your daughter cry.
I apologize a trillion times.
I'm sorry, Ms. Jackson. (Ooh.)
I am for real.
Never meant to make your daughter cry.
I apologize a trillion times.

[BIG BOI]
My baby's drama mama don't like me.
She be doin' things like havin' them boys come from her neighborhood
To the studio, tryin' to fight me.
She need to get a piece of the American Pie and take her bite out.
That's my house, I'll disconnect the cable and turn the lights out
And let her know her grandchild is a baby, and not a paycheck.
Private school, daycare shit, medical bills, I pay that.
I love your mom and everything, but see, I ain't the one who laid down.
She wanna rib you up to start a custody war, my lawyers stay down.
Shit, you never got a chance to hear my side of the story.
We was divided.
She had fish fries and cook-outs
For my child's birthday—I ain't invited.
Despite it, I show her the utmost respect when I fall through.
All you do is defend that lady when I call you, yeah.

CHORUS

[ANDRE 3000]
Me and your daughter gots this thang goin' on.
You say it's puppy love. (Arf, arf, arf!)
We say it's full-grown. (Arf, arf, woof!)
Hope that we feel this, feel this way forever.
You can plan a pretty picnic,
But you can't predict the weather, Ms. Jackson, ten times out of nine,
Now, if I'm lyin'—
Find the quickest muzzle, throw it on my mouth and I'll decline.
King meets queen, then the puppy love thing, together dream
'Bout that crib with the Goodyear swing
On the oak tree, I hope we feel like this forever.
Forever, forever, ever, forever, ever?
Forever never seems that long until you're grown
And notice that the day-by-day ruler can't be too wrong.
Ms. Jackson, my intentions were good; I wish I could
Becomes a magician to abracadabra all the sadder
Thoughts of me, thoughts of she, thoughts of he.
Askin' what happened to the feelin' that her and me
Had; I pray so much about it, need some knee-pads.
It happened for a reason, one can't be mad.
So, know this: know that everything is cool
And yes, I will be present on the first day of school
And graduation.

CHORUS

[BIG BOI]

Uh, uh, yeah.
"Look at the way he treats me."
Shit, look at the way you treat me.
You see your little nosey-ass homegirls
Done got your ass sent up the creek, G,
Without a paddle; you left to straddle
And ride this thing on out.
Now you and your girl ain't speakin' no more
'Cause my dick all in her mouth.
Know what I'm talkin' 'bout?
Jealousy, infidelity, envy,
Cheatin' to beatin', envy, and to the G, they be the same thing.
So who you placin' the blame on?
You keep singin' the same song.
Let bygones be bygones, you can go on and get the hell on.
You and your mama.

CHORUS (2 TIMES)

Words and Music by Sean "Puffy" Combs,
Notorious B.I.G., Steven Jordan
and Jason Phillips

MO' MONEY
MO' PROBLEMS
RECORDED BY NOTORIOUS B.I.G., FEATURING MASE AND PUFF DADDY

[MASE]

Now, who's hot? Who's not?
Tell me, who rock? Who sell out in the stores?
You tell me who flopped? Who copped the blue drop?
Who jewels got robbed? Who's mostly Goldie down
To the tube sock? The same ol' pimp.
Mase, you know, ain't nuttin' change but my limp.
Can't stop 'til I see my name on a blimp.
Guarantee a million sales, pullin' all the love.
You don't believe in Harlem World, nigga, double up.
We don't play around; it's a bet, lay it down.
Nigga didn't know me ninety-one, bet they know me now.
I'm the young Harlem nigga with the Goldie sound.
Can't no P–H–D niggaz hold me down,
Cooter schooled me to the game, now I know my duty.
Stay humble, stay low, blow like Hootie.
True pimp niggaz spend no dough on the booty
And then ya yell, "There goes Mase," there go your cutie.

CHORUS:

I don't know what they want from me.
It's like the more money we come across,
The more problems we see.
I don't know what they want from me.
It's like the more money we come across,
The more problems we see.

[PUFF DADDY]
Yeah, yeah, ahaha, from the D to the A, to the D–D–Y,
Know you'd rather see me die than to see me fly.
I call all the shots,
Rip all the spots, rock all the rocks, cop all the drops,
I know you thinkin' now's when all the ballin' stops,
Nigga, never; home gotta call me on the yacht.
Ten years from now we'll still be on top.
Yo, I thought I told you that we won't stop.
Now whatcha gonna do when it's cool
Bag o' money much longer than yours
And a team much stronger than yours, violate me.
This'll be your day, we don't play,
Mess around, be D.O.A., be on your way
'Cause it ain't enough time here, ain't enough lime here
For you to shine here, deal with many women
But treat dames fair,
And I'm bigger than the city lights down in Times Square.
Yeah, yeah, yeah.

CHORUS

[NOTORIOUS B.I.G.]
Uhh, uhh.
B–I–G, P–O, P–P–A,
No info for the D.E.A.
Federal agents mad 'cause I'm flagrant,
Tap my cell and phone in the basement.
My team supreme, stay clean,
Triple beam, lyrical dream, I be that
Cat you see at all events, bent.
Gatts in holsters, girls on shoulders.
Playboy, I told ya, bein' nice to me.
Bruise to much, I lose too much,
Step on stage, the girls "boo" too much.
I guess it's 'cause you run with lame dudes too much.
Me lose my touch? Never that.
If I did, ain't no problem to get the gatt.
Where the true players at?

Throw your rollies in the sky,
Wave 'em side to side, and keep your hands high
While I give your girl the eye, playa, please.
Lyrically, niggaz see, B.I.G.
Be flossin' jig on the cover of *Fortune.*
Five-double-0, here's my phone number.
Your man ain't got to know—I got to go.
Got the flow down pizat, platinum plus,
Like thizat—dangerous on trizack,
Leave your ass blizack.

CHORUS

I don't know what they want from me.
It's like the more money we come across,
The more problems we see.

What's goin' on?
What's goin' on?

CHORUS (2 TIMES)

Words and Music by Freddie Perren,
Alphonso Mizell, Berry Gordy and Deke Richards

MY BABY
RECORDED BY LIL' ROMEO

[DJ] Hotline.
[CALLER] Can I request a song?
[DJ] Sure.
[CALLER] "My Baby" by Lil' Romeo.
[DJ] You got that.

CHORUS:

[GIRL] Oh Romeo, give me a chance.
[LIL' ROMEO] Uh-uh, too young, I don't need a girlfriend.
[GIRL] Walk me home from school anyway.
[LIL' ROMEO] (Heheh) Okay.
[GIRL] Oh Romeo, the cutest boy I know.
[LIL' ROMEO] I know, I know.
[GIRL] So let me be your girlfriend.

[LIL' ROMEO]

They call me Lil' P, I represent the CP3,
Calliope, ya heard of me, straight from New Orleans.
Gotta uncle named Silkk, and a uncle named C.
I been dribblin' the ball since the age of three.
I got game like Kobe, dunk it like Poppa P.
Once I'm in the zone, ain't no stoppin' me.
You can jump-a, baby, hummer girls be jockin' me.
Them Miller boys wear No Limit gear from head to feet.

It's like that, whodi. (You got me crazy.)
It's like that, whodi. (I want to be your lady.)
It's like that, whodi. (Why won't you be my baby?)
It's like that, whodi. (Can't no girl fade me.)
Meet me at the skatin' rink.

CHORUS

[LIL' ROMEO]
Eleven years old, makin' As and Bs,
And these lil' mommies can't keep their hands off me.
When you see me in the streets, holla, "What's up, doc?"
I gotta Bugs Bunny chain wit' a matchin' watch.
I make you jump like Kris Kross, bounce like Bow.
I'm the next generation, I came to lock it down.
I'm a little boy, but live a big man's life.
I got girls passin' up, wanna be my wife.
I got grown women wanna be in my life.
By the time I reach eighteen, I'm not gon' be nothin' nice.
I'm that R–O–M–E–O, and after high school
I'm goin' straight to the pros.
Bounce, bounce.

CHORUS

[GIRL]
Soldier boy, I want you to myself.
I don't want them girls around.
You're the flyest thing up in here, boy,
And that's why it's goin' down.
I heard they call you Romeo.
Well, I'm your Juliet.
You must be playin' hide and seek
'Cause, boy, you're hard to catch.

CHORUS

(Oh, Romeo.)
Why you boys make them elbows swing?
Why you girls make them elbows swing?

Romeo gonna do dat thing,
Romeo gonna do that thing,
Romeo gonna do that thing,
Romeo gonna do that thing.

Throw 'em up, get 'em up, throw 'em up, get 'em up,
Throw 'em up, get 'em up, what?
Master P, while sayin' this is for the fly girls…
Why you boys make them elbows swing?
Why you girls make them elbows swing?

[GIRLS]
This is for the fly girls that punk them.

[BOYS]
This is for the fly boys that punk them.

[GIRLS]
This is for the fly girls, that's 'bout it, 'bout it.

[BOYS]
This is for the fly boys, that's 'bout it, 'bout it.

[TOGETHER]
Make 'em sweat, make 'em sweat.
Make 'em sweat, make 'em sweat.
Make 'em sweat, make 'em sweat.

That's all folks!

Words and Music by David Axelrod, Andre Romell Young,
Melvin Bradford, Cordozar C. Broadus and Brian Bailey

THE NEXT EPISODE
RECORDED BY DR. DRE, FEATURING SNOOP DOGG AND NATE DOGG

[SNOOP DOGG]
La-da-da-da-dah.
It's the motherfuckin' D–O, double-G. (Snoop Dogg!)
La-da-da-da-dah.
You know I'm mobbin' with the D–R–E.
(Yeah, yeah, yeah, you know who's back up in this motherfucker!)
What, what, what, what?
(Spread the weed out there!)
Blaze it up, blaze it up!
(Just blaze that shit up, nigga, yeah! 'Sup Snoop?)

Top Dogg, bit me all, nigga burn the shit up.
D–P–G–C my nigga turn that shit up.
C–P–T, L–B–C, yeah, we hookin' back up,
And when they bang this in the club, baby, you got to get up.
Thug niggaz, drug dealers, yeah, they givin' it up.
Low-life, yo' life, boy, we livin' it up.
Takin' chances while we dancin' in the party fo' sho'.
Slip my hoe a forty-fo' and she got in the back do'.
Bitches lookin' at me strange, but you know I don't care.
Step up in this motherfucker just a-swangin' my hair.
Bitch, quit talkin', crip walk if you down with the set.
Take a bullet with some dick and take this dope from this jet
Out of town, put it down for the Father of Rap.
And if yo' ass get cracked, bitch, shut yo' trap.
Come back, get back, that's the part of success.
If you believe in the X, you'll be relievin' your stress.

[SNOOP DOGG]
La-da-da-da-dah.

[DR. DRE]
It's the motherfuckin' D–R–E. (Dr. Dre, motherfucker!)

[SNOOP DOGG]
La-da-da-da-dah.

[DR. DRE]
You know I'm mobbin' with the D–O, double-G.

[DR. DRE]
Straight off the fuckin' streets of C–P–T.
King of the beats, you ride to 'em in your Fleet (Fleetwood.)
Or Coupe Deville, rollin on dubs.
How you feelin'? Whoopty-whoop, nigga, what?
Dre and Snoop chronic'd out in the 'llac
With Doc in the back, sippin' on 'gnac. (Yeah.)
Clip in the strap, dippin' through 'hoods. (What 'hoods?)
Compton, Long Beach, Inglewood,
South Central, out to the West Side. (Wesside.)
It's California Love, this California bud got a nigga gang of pub.
I'm on one, I might bail up in the Century Club
With my jeans on and my team strong.
Get my drink on, and my smoke on,
Then go home with somethin' to poke on. (Whassup, bitch?)
Loc, it's on for the two-triple-0.
Comin' real, it's the next episode.

[NATE DOGG]
Hold up, hey!
For my niggaz who be thinkin' we soft,
We don't play.
We gon' rock it 'til the wheels fall off.
Hold up, hey!
For my niggaz who be actin' too bold,
Take a seat.
Hope you ready for the next episode.
Hey!
Smoke weed every day!

Words and Music by Kandi Burruss,
Tameka Cottle and Kevin Briggs

NO PIGEONZ
RECORDED BY SPORTY THIEVZ

Nada, Franchise.
Nada, Shot-callers.
Yeah, Sporty Thievz, Sporty Thievz.
Uh-huh, nada.

A pigeon is a girl who be walkin' by.
My rimmed-up, blue, brand new, sparklin' five.
Her feet hurt so, you know, she want a ride
But she frontin' like she can't say, "Hi."
What?

CHORUS 1:

(Uh oh.) Y'all chicks ain't gettin' nada.
(Uh oh.) Your pussy ain't worth the Ramada.
(Uh oh.) Anyway, your friend looks hotter.
(Uh oh.) Game is somethin' we got a lot a.

CHORUS 2:

(Uh oh.) 'Cause I don't want no pigeons.
Them be them girls who gets no dubs from me.
Playin' the bar, dumb-broke, wit' her best friend's coat,
Tryin' to holla at me.
I don't want no pigeons.
Them be them girls who gets no dubs from me.
Playin' the bar, dumb-broke, wit' her best friend's coat,
Tryin' to holla at me.

In the front of the club I see this girl like, "Yo, love."
Thought she said, "Thug," but she called me a scrub.
Scrub? What? She must o' talk me a joke.
Broke, pigeon-head freak, you luck I spoke.
This ain't my Benz there, it's my man's, yeah.
But this ain't my car, like that ain't your hair.

(Uh oh.) Pigeon, take them fake jewels off.
(Uh oh.) Pigeon, take your friend's shoes off.
(Uh oh.) Pigeon, the hell with that crazy shit.
Y'all make me sick; go home and fuckin' babysit.
My big dogs don't love this.
King Kirk bitch, get a brush and scrub this. (Right.)

CHORUS 1

Yo, chill cousin; these birds is ill, cousin
'Cause they call me scrub like we can't even bill, cousin.
Trick Ronald's, you ain't worth the McDonald's.
Throw you on the street team, make you shit vinyls.
Hey yo, Flex, shorty tried to flash me wrong.
How she gonna wear sandals wit' nasty corns?
That be wrong.
I wonder how you get hearts
In dirty Victoria, draws with the skid marks.
Uh, yo' flat ass gets enough laughs.
Take it to the salon, pluck yo' mustache.
So next time you shotgun, and the hoe bitchin',
Hittin' you a scrub, call that bitch a pigeon.

Hey yo, I got two nuts, bitch, choose a ball.
You only walk pigeon-toed 'cause yo' shoes are small.
You don't shop, you just cruise the mall.
No dough, with Lee Press-ons.
Frontin' with yo' girlfriend dress on.
You birds wanna take over?
Get some cash and a Jenny Jones make-over.
Broke bitches, I hate pigeons.
Dirty braid pigeons, Medicaid pigeons, Section Eight pigeons.
Got me fed, burned, I tell these birds, "Shut up."
And how my left ear be double her whole get-up.
Go ahead with your lame-ass blow at night,
Throw a ripped dollar at her, tell her, "Put that on her depraved ass."

If you got more than one baby father,
Oh yes, girl, we's talkin' to you.
If you strip all week to go clubbin',
Oh, yes, girl, we's talkin' to you.
Buy a dress to front and take it back to the store.
Oh yes, girl, we's talkin' to you.
Wanna smoke wit' me, wit no money.
Oh no, I don't want no—

No pigeons.
No pigeons.

[DJ RHUDE]
Greet your highness, Queen's finest.
Gleam shine as three-clip street fighters.
Deep-dish Jeep riders.
Outlandish in they expanded Rover,
Passenger in my own whip, yeah, that's my chauffer.
I rap for ya, that's my culture.
When I holla, holla, like Ja Rule,
You in a trance from the god's jewels.
Glance at my car, drool.
Grand like the Concourse,
Wonderin', damn, how much the car cost?
Yo' just another fan, applause, encores
And when I fly through the world, tours on Concordes.
Don't need no chicken-drippin', save that for Lipton.
No scrubs here, strictly Mo' Thugs, dear.
Check the listings, no pigeons.
Flat-broke chicks out to get rich off the next bro's shit.
Instead of TLC, you give us brothers B–I–G trouble.
We're just Sporty Thievz, huddle game with the illest rebuttal.

CHORUS 1 AND 2

No pigeons.
No pigeons.
No pigeons.

NO TIME
RECORDED BY LIL' KIM, FEATURING PUFF DADDY

Words and Music by Sean "Puffy" Combs, Steven Jordan and Kim Jones

INTRO:
[PUFF DADDY]
Heh, heheheh.
I got no time for fake niggaz.
Just sip some Cristal with these real niggaz.
From East to West Coast, spread love, niggaz. (That's right.)
And while you niggaz talk shit, we count bank figures. (Say what?)

CHORUS:
[PUFF DADDY]
I got no time for fake niggaz. (Uh-uh, uh-uh.)
Just sip some Cristal with these real niggaz. (Uh-huh, uh-huh.)
From East to West Coast, spread love, niggaz. (That's right.)
And while you niggaz talk shit, we count bank figures. (He-heh.)
[NOTORIOUS B.I.G. SAMPLE]
How you figure that your team can effect my cream?
[PUFF DADDY]
I got no time for fake niggaz. (Uh-uh, uh-uh.)
Just sip some Cristal with these real niggaz. (Uh-huh, uh-huh.)
[NOTORIOUS B.I.G. SAMPLE]
I rely on Bed-Stuy to shut it down, if I gotta.
[PUFF DADDY]
From East to West Coast, spread love, niggaz. (That's right.)
And while you niggaz talk shit, we count bank figures.

Let's go—

[LIL' KIM]
Yeah, I momma, Miss Ivana.
Usually rock the Prada, sometimes Gabbana.
Stick you for your cream and your riches.
Zsa Zsa Gabor, Demi Moore, Princess Diana, and all them rich bitches.
Puff Daddy pump the Hummer for the summer.

I follow, in the E-Class with the goggles.
Ninety-six models, Bad Click on the stroll.
(Tell 'em how we roll.) Cruise control.
Nuttin' make a woman feel better
Than Berettas and Amarettos, butter-leathers, and mad cheddars.
Chillin' in a Benz with my amigos,
Tryin' to stick a nigga for his pesos.
If you say so's, then I'm the same chick
That you wanna get with, lick up in my twat,
Gotta hit the spot—if not,
Don't test the poom-poom, nanny-nanny, punani-donni, hey!

CHORUS

[PUFF DADDY]

Lil' Kim, how you like it, baby?
Uhh, from the front? Uhh, from the back?
Give that ass a smack.
Bet your man won't do it like that.
Can't work the middle, plus, his thing too little.
Let me grab your ta-tas, do the cha-cha,
Work down your ta-tas, do the cha-cha.
Make you scream, "Pa-pa!
You da best, Da-da."
Now watch, mama, go up and down dick to jaw crazy.
Uhh! Say my name, baby. (Okay.)
Before you nut, I'm-a dribble down your butt-cheeks,
Make you wiggle, then giggle just a little.
I'm drinkin' babies, then I cracks for the Mercedes
Act shady, and feel my three-eighty,
Or the raven, oohwee, I see.
Your girl ain't a Freak Like Me, or Adina.
Huh, can't fade a rhinoceros in rap. (Say what?)
Lil' Kim pussy (uhh), how preposterous is that? (Ha-hah!)

CHORUS

[LIL' KIM]
Uhh, right back atcha, the one Cleopatra. (Say what?)
Diggin' in your stash.
(Niggaz think they gonna get some ass.) No money-money,
Or licky-licky? Fuck the dicky-dicky
And the quickie, gimme your loot,
Your Mac-11, then shoot.
Your game ain't sweet, John Paul peep
Shouldn't compete, if you can't wet it, forget it,
Don't sweat it, I bet it'd
Make you cum smooth, if you let it.
Huh, you can't stop a bitch from ballin'.
Ha-ha to la-la to drive-bys, they be callin',
And you ain't know, while you be kickin'
That old shit (talk to me), we makin' hits.
Platinum and gold shit. (We don't stop.)
We stay draped in diamonds and pearls.
Beside every man is a Bad Girl.
(That's right, nine-six Bad Boy, c'mon.)

CHORUS (4 TIMES)

Words and Music by Steve Lukather,
Jay Graydon, Kim Jones and Bill Champlin

NOT TONIGHT
RECORDED BY LIL' KIM

I know a dude named Jimmy used to run up in me.
Nighttime pissy-drunk off the Henney 'n' Remy.
I didn't mind it when he fucked me from behind.
It felt fine, 'specially when he used to grind it.
He was a trick when I sucked his dick.
Used to pass me bricks, credit cards, and shit.
Suck him to sleep, I took the keys to the Jeep.
Tell him, "I'll be back," go fuck with some other cats.
Flirtin', gettin' numbers, in the summer, hoe-hop,
Raw top in my man's drop.
Then this homie, Jimmy, he's screamin', "Gimme,"
Lay me on my back, bustin' nuts all in me.
After ten times we fucked, I think I bust twice.
He was nice, kept my neck filled with ice.
Put me in Chanels, kept me out nice
Cold-suckin' his dick, rockin' the mic.
It was somethin' about this dude I couldn't understand,
Somethin' that could o' made his ass a real man.
Somethin' I wanted, but I never was pushy—
The motherfucker never ate my pussy.

CHORUS:
I don't want dick tonight,
Eat my pussy right.
Uh, uh, uh, uh, Lil' Kim, Lil' Kim,
Bring it to me now.

I know a dude named Ron Doo, push a Q,
Had a wild crew on Flatbush and Avenue U,
Had a weed spot, used to pump African black,
He used to seal his bag so his workers wouldn't cap.
I used to see him in the tunnel with fuckers at dawn,
Whisper in my ear, he wanna get his fuck on.

I dug him, so I fucked him, it wasn't nuttin'.
He wanted me to suck him, but I didn't—I ain't frontin'.
The sex was wack, a four-stroke creep.
I jumped on his dick, rode his ass to sleep.
He called next week, askin' why I ain't beep him.
"I thought your ass was still sleepin'."
He laughed, told me he bought a new Path,
Could he come over right fast and fuck my pretty ass?
I'll pass, nigga, the dick was trash.
If sex was record sales, you would be double plat.
The only way you seein' me is if you're eatin' me.
Downtown taste, my love, like Horace Brown.
Tryin' to impress me with your five-G stones,
I give you ten-Gs, nigga, if you leave me alone.
Screamin'—

CHORUS

The moral of the story is this:
You ain't lickin' this, you ain't stickin' this.
And I got witnesses—ask any nigga I been with.
They ain't hit shit 'til they stuck they tongue in this.
I ain't with that frontin' shit,
I got my own Benz, I got my own ends, immediate friends.
Me and my girls rocks worlds, some big niggaz
Fuck for car keys and double-digit figures.
Good dick I cherish, I could be blunt—
I treat it like it's precious, I ain't gonna front
For limp-dick niggaz that's frontin' like they willy,
Suck my pussy 'til they kill me—you feel me?

CHORUS

Words and Music by
Cornell Haynes and Waiel Yagham

#1
RECORDED BY NELLY

Uh, uh, uh.
I just gotta bring it to they attention, dirty, that's all.

You better watch who you talkin' 'bout,
Runnin' your mouth like you know me.
You gon' fuck around a show why they "Show Me" get called "Show Me."
Why one-on-one, you can't hold me if your last name was Haynes.
Only way you wear me out is stitch my name on your pants.
No resident of France, but you swear I'm from Paris.
Hundred-six karats, total? Naw, that's per wrist.
Tryin' to compare this—my chain to yo' chain.
I'm like Sprint or Motorola—no service, out of your range.
You out of your brains, thinkin' I'm-a shout out your name.
You gotta come up with better ways than that to catch your fame.
All the pressure you applyin', it's time to ease off
Before I hit you from the blindside, takin' your sleeves off.
As much as we's floss, still hard to please boss.
Don't be lyin', bitchin', and cryin'—suck it up as a loss
'Cause your acts is wack, your whole label is wack.
And a matter fact, eh, eh-eh, eh, a-hold that.

CHORUS:
I am number one—no matter if you like it.
Here, take it, sit down and write it.
I am number one.
Hey, hey, hey, hey, hey, hey, now let me ask you, man.
What does it take to be number one?
Two is not a winner, and three, nobody remembers. (Hey!)
What does it take to be number one?
Hey, hey, hey, hey.

[GIRL]
Do you like it when I shake it for ya, daddy?
Move it all around?
Let you get a peep before it touches the ground?

[NELLY]

Hell yeah, ma, I love a girl that's willin' to learn,
Willin' to get in the driver's seat, and willin' to turn.
And not concerned about what that he say, she say, did he say
What I think he said? Squash that—he probably got that off eBay,
Or some, Internet access, some website chat line.
Mad 'cause I got mine, oh, don't wind up on the flatline.
Oh, if my uncle could see me now,
If he could see how many rappers wanna be me now.
Straight emulatin' my style, right to the down-down.
Can't leave out the store now, better wait 'til they calm down.
I got hella shorties comin' askin', "Yo, where the party?"
Oh, Lordy, I'd like to continue to act naughty.
Mixin' Cris' and Bacardi, got me thinkin' fo' sho'.
I'm not a man of many words, but there's one thing I know, pimp.

CHORUS:

I am number one—no matter if you like it.
Here, take it, sit down and write it.
Hey, I am number one.
Hey, hey, hey, hey, hey, hey, now tell me now, dirty.
What does it take to be number one?
Two is not a winner, and three, nobody remembers.
Tell me, what does it take to be number one?
Hey, hey, hey, hey.

Check it, uhh, check, yo!
Aiyyo, I'm tired of people judgin' what's real hip-hop.
Half the time you be them niggaz who fuckin' album flop.
You know—boat done sank and it ain't left the dock.
C'mon! Mad 'cause I'm hot; he just mad 'cause he not.
You ain't gotta gimme my props, just gimme the yachts.
Gimme my rocks and keep my fans comin' in flocks.
'Til you top the Superbowl, keep your mouth on lock.
Shh. (I'm awake, ha, ha, ha!)
I'm cocky on the mic, but I'm humble in real life,
Takin' nothin' for granted, blessin' everything on my life,

Tryin' to see a new light at the top of the roof.
Baby, name not Sigel, but I speak the truth.
I heat the booth—Nelly actin' so uncouth,
Top down, shirt off in the Coupe, spreadin' the loot
With my family and friends, and my closest of kin.
And I'll do it again if it means I'm-a win.

CHORUS:

Dirty, I am, dirty, number one—no matter if you like it.
Here, take it, sit down and write it.
Hey, I am number one.
Hey, hey, hey, hey, hey, hey, hey, hey.
Dirty, what does it take to be number one? Whoo!
Two is not a winner, and three, nobody remembers.
Ey! What does it take to be number one?
Hey, hey, hey, hey, hey, hey, hey, hey.

Hey, I am number one.
I am number one.
What does it take to be number one?
Two is not a winner, and three, nobody remembers.
What does it take to be number one?
Hey, hey, hey, hey, hey, hey.

I, I am number one.
Uhh-uhh-uh, uh-uh-uhh-uh-uh.
Listen, I, I, I, I, I, I number one, yeah, yeah, yeah.
I, I, I, I number one.
The two is not a winner, and three, nobody remembers.
Number one.
'Cause two is not a winner, and three, nobody remembers.

Words and Music by Frederick Knight,
Leon Haywood and Cordozar Calvin Broadus

NUTHIN' BUT A G THANG
RECORDED BY DR. DRE
AND SNOOP DOGGY DOGG

One, two, three, and to the fo'.
Snoop Doggy Dogg and Dr. Dre are at the do',
Ready to make an entrance, so back on up.
('Cause you know we 'bout had to rip shit up.)

[SNOOP DOGGY DOGG]
Gimme the microphone first, so I can bust like a bubble.
Compton and Long Beach together, now you know you in trouble.

Ain't nothin' but a G thang, baby!
Two loc'd out Gs, so we're crazy!
Death Row is the label that pays me!
Unfadable, so please, don't try to fade this. (Hell, yeah.)

But, uh, back to the lecture at hand,
Perfection is perfected, so I'm-a let 'em understand.
From a young G's perspective
And before me dig out a bitch, I have to find a contraceptive.
You never know, she could be earnin' her man,
And learnin' her man, and at the same time, burnin' her man.
Now, you know I ain't wit' that shit, Lieutenant.
Ain't no pussy good enough to get burnt while I'm up in it.
Now, that's realer than real-deal Holyfield,
And now all you hookers and hoes know how I feel.
Well, if it's good enough to get broke off a proper chunk.
I'll take a small piece of some of that funky stuff.

It's like this and like that and like that and, uh.
It's like this and like that and like that and, uh.
It's like this and like that and like that and, uh.
Dre, creep to the mic like a phantom.

[DR. DRE]
Well, I'm peepin', and I'm creepin' and I'm creepin',
But I damn near got caught, 'cause my beeper kept beepin'.
Now it's time for me to make my impression felt,
So sit back, relax, and strap on your seatbelt.
You never been on a ride like this befo',
With a producer who can rap and control the maestro
At the same time with the dope rhyme that I kick.
You know, and I know—I flow some ol' funky shit.
To add to my collection, the selection
Symbolizes dope, take a toke, but don't choke.
If ya so, ya have no clue
O' what me and my homie, Snoop Dogg, came to do.

It's like this and like that and like that and, uh.
It's like this and like that and like that and, uh.
It's like this, and we ain't got no love for those
So jus' chill 'til the next episode.

[SNOOP DOGGY DOGG]

Fallin' back on that ass with a hellified gangsta lean,
Gettin' funky on the mic like a' old batch o' collard greens.
It's the capital S, oh yes, the fresh N, double-O–P,
D–O double-G–Y–D–O double-G, ya see.
Showin' much flex when it's time to wreck a mic,
Pimpin' hoes and clockin' a grip like my name was Dolomite.
Yeah, and it don't quit.
I think they in a mood for some muthafuckin' G shit.

So Dre, (What's up, Dogg?)
We gotta give 'em what dey want. (What's that, G?)
We gotta break 'em off somethin'. (Hell, yeah.)
And it's gotta be bumpin'. (City of Compton!)

It's where it takes place, so I'm-a ask your attention.
Mobbin' like a muthafucka, but I ain't lynchin'.
Droppin' the funky shit that's makin' the sucka-niggaz mumble.
When I'm on the mic, it's like a cookie—they all crumble.
Try to get close and your ass'll get smacked.
My muthafuckin' homie, Doggy Dogg, has my back.
Never let me slip, 'cause if I slip, then I'm slippin'.
But if I got my niña, then you know I'm straight-trippin'.
And I'm-a continue to put the rap down, put the mack down,
And if your bitches talk shit, I have ta put the smack down.
Yeah, and ya don't stop.
I told you, I'm just like a clock when I tick and I tock,
But I'm never off, always on, 'til the break of dawn.
C–O–M–P–T–O–N, and the city they call Long Beach,
Puttin' the strength together,
Like my homie, D–O–C, no one can do it better.

Like this, that, and this and, uh.
It's like that and like this and like that and, uh.
It's like this, and we ain't got no love for those
So jus' chill 'til the next episode.

Words and Music by Alphonso Mizell,
Freddie Perren, Dennis Lussier, Berry Gordy,
Anthony Criss, Keir Gist and Vincent Brown

O.P.P.
RECORDED BY NAUGHTY BY NATURE

Army with harmony.
Dave, drop a load on 'em.

O.P.P.: how can I explain it?
I'll take you frame-by-frame it.
To have y'all jumpin', shall we singin' it.
O is for "other," P is for "people," scratchin' temple.
The last P, well, that's not that simple.
It's sorta like another way to call a cat a kitten.
It's five little letters that are missin' here.
You get, on occasion, at the other party.
As a game, an' it seems I gotta start to explainin'.
Bust it.
You ever had a girl and met her on a nice hello?
You get her name and number and then you feelin' real mellow.
You get home, wait a day; she's what you wanna know about.
Then you call up and it's her girlfriend or her cousin's house.
It's not a front, F to the R, to the O, to the N, to the T.
It's just her boyfriend's at her house. (Boy, that's what is scary.)
It's O.P.P. time, other people's what you get it,
There's no room for relationship, there's just room to hit it.
How many brothers out there know just what I'm gettin' at?
Who thinks it's wrong 'cause I'm splittin' and co-hittin' at?
Well, if you do, that's O.P.P., and you're not down with it,
But if you don't, here's your membership.

CHORUS:

You down with O.P.P.? (Yeah, you know me.)
You down with O.P.P.? (Yeah, you know me.)
You down with O.P.P.? (Yeah, you know me.)
Who's down with O.P.P.? (Every last homie.)
You down with O.P.P.? (Yeah, you know me.)
You down with O.P.P.? (Yeah, you know me.)
You down with O.P.P.? (Yeah, you know me.)
Who's down with O.P.P.? (All the homies.)

As for the ladies, O.P.P. means somethin gifted.
The first two letters are the same, but the last is somethin' different.
It's the longest, loveliest, lean—I call it the leanest.
It's another five-letter word rhymin' with "cleanest and meanest."
I wont' get into that; I'll do it, ah, sorta properly.
I say the last P…hmm…stands for "property."
Now, lady, here comes a kiss—blow a kiss back to me.
Now, tell me, exactly,
Have you ever known a brother who have another, like, a girl or wife?
And you just had to stop and just, 'cause he look just as nice.
You looked at him, he looked at you, and you knew right away
That he had someone, but he was gonna be yours anyway.
You couldn't be seen with him, and honestly, you didn't care
'Cause in a room behind a door, no one but y'all are there.
When y'all finished, y'all can leave, and only y'all would know.
And then y'all could throw the skeleton bones right in the closet do'.
Now, don't be shocked, 'cause if you're done, I want your hands up high.
Say, "O.P.P." (O.P.P.), I like to say with pride.
Now when you do it, do it well, and make sure that it counts.
You're now down with a discount.

CHORUS:

You down with O.P.P.? (Yeah, you know me.)
You down with O.P.P.? (Yeah, you know me.)
You down with O.P.P.? (Yeah, you know me.)
Who's down with O.P.P.? (Every last lady.)
You down with O.P.P.? (Yeah, you know me.)
You down with O.P.P.? (Yeah, you know me.)
You down with O.P.P.? (Yeah, you know me.)
Who's down with O.P.P.? (All the ladies.)

This girl, ha, tried to O.P.P. me.
I had a girl, and she knew that, matter-of-fact, my girl was partners
That had a fall-out, disagreement, yeah, an argument, bust it.
That wasn't the thing, it must have been the way she hit the ceiling,
'Cause after that, she kept on coming back and catchin' feelings.
I said, "Let's go, my girl is coming, so you gotta leave."
She said, "Oh no, I love you, Treach."
I said, "Now, child, please, you gots to leave, come grab your coat,
Right now, you gotta go."
I said, "Now, look you to the stairs and to the stair window.
This was a thing, a little thing—you shouldn't have put your heart,
'Cause you know I was O.P.P., hell from the very start."
Come on, come on, now let me tell you what it's all bout.
When you get down, you can't go 'round, runnin' off at the mouth.
That's rule number one in this O.P.P. establishment.
You keep your mouth shut and it won't get back to her or him.
Exciting, isn't it? A special kinda business.
Many of you will catch the same sorta O.P.P.
Is you with him or her, for sure, is goin' to admit it
When O.P.P. comes, damn, skippy, I'm with it.

CHORUS:
You down with O.P.P.? (Yeah, you know me.)
You down with O.P.P.? (Yeah, you know me.)
You down with O.P.P.? (Yeah, you know me.)
Who's down with O.P.P.? (This whole party.)
You down with O.P.P.? (Yeah, you know me.)
You down with O.P.P.? (Yeah, you know me.)
You down with O.P.P.? (Yeah, you know me.)
Who's down with O.P.P.? (This whole party.)

Break it down!

Words and Music by Christopher Brian Bridges,
Melissa A. Elliott, Tim Mosley and David Pomeranz

ONE MINUTE MAN
RECORDED BY MISSY "MISDEMEANOR" ELLIOT, FEATURING LUDACRIS

CHORUS 1:
[MISSY ELLIOT]

Ooh, I don't want, I don't need, I can't stand no minute man.
I don't want no minute man.
Ooh, here's your chance, be a man, take my hand,
Understand, I don't want no minute man.
Oh…

Boy, I'm-a make you love me, make you want me.
And I'm-a give you some attention tonight.
Now, follow my intuitions, what you're wishin'.
See, I'm-a keep you all night, for a long time.
Just start countin' the ways.

CHORUS 2:

Break me off, show me what you got
 'Cause I don't want no one-minute man.
Break me off, show me what you got
 'Cause I don't want no one-minute man.
Break me off, show me what you got
 'Cause I don't want no one-minute man.
Break me off, show me what you got
 'Cause I don't want no…

Tonight, I'm-a give it to you, throw it to you.
I want you to come prepared, oh yeah. (Oh, yes.)
Boy, it's been a long time, a crazy long time
And I don't want no minute man, and that's real.
Give it to me some more.

CHORUS 2

[LUDACRIS]
Yeah, uhh, uhh.
It's time to set yo' clock back 'bout as long as you can.
I stop daylight, and Ludacris the maintenance man.
Get your oil changed, I check fluids and transmission.
You one-minute fools, you wonder why y'all missin'.
On the back of milk cartons and there's no reward,
No regards, close but no cigar.
A hard head make a soft ass, but a hard dick make the sex last.
I jump in pools and make a big splash,
Water overflowin', so get your head right.
It's all in yo' mind, punk, so keep your head tight.
Enough with the tips and advice and thangs,
I'm a big dog, havin' women seein' stripes and thangs.
They go to sleep, start snorin', countin' sheep and shit.
They so wet that they body start to leak and shit.
Just 'cause I'm an all-nighter, shoot all fire,
Ludacris balance and rotate all tires.

CHORUS 1

Break me off, show me what you got
'Cause I don't want no one-minute man.
Break me off, show me what you got
'Cause I don't want no one-minute man.
Break me off, show me what you got
'Cause I don't want no one-minute man.
Break, break me off; break, break me off.
Break me off, show me what you got.

Break me off, show me what you got.
Break me off, show me what you got.
Break me off, show me what you got.
Break me off; break, break me off.

Words and Music by Sean "Puffy" Combs,
Notorious B.I.G., Carl Thompson and Bluez Brothers

ONE MORE CHANCE (ONE MORE CHANCE/STAY WITH ME)
RECORDED BY NOTORIOUS B.I.G.

[BIGGIE'S DAUGHTER]
All you hoes callin' here for my daddy, get off his dick.
Like that, Mommy?

[ANSWERING MACHINE MESSAGE 1]
Hi, Daddy. How ya doin'? This is Tyiest.
I was thinkin' 'bout you last night.
Mmm, you actin' like you can't call me no more
'Cause you busy and all that,
But you tryin' ta tell me it wasn't good?

[ANSWERING MACHINE MESSAGE 2]
That shit is real fucked-up, what you did.
I hooked you up wit' my girl and, shit,
You fucked her eight times.
You see her, you don't say shit to her,
You know what I'm sayin'?
And all that bitch do is call me all day,
Talkin' 'bout you:
"Why the fuck do he don't want me?"

[ANSWERING MACHINE MESSAGE 3]
Yo, Big, this is Quita. Kenya told me she saw you and Shana in the mall.
And I know you ain't fuckin' her.
You fucked me last night.
That's my best friend and we don't get down like that.

[ANSWERING MACHINE MESSAGE 4]

Yeah, muthafucka, this is Stephanie.

I was waitin' outside for your ass for like a fuckin' hour.

I don't know what's goin' on, muthafuckas tryin' ta raw me.

You be disappearin' and shit,

I'm waitin' in the cold, what the fuck is goin' on?

When you get in, give me a fuckin' call, alright?

When it comes to sex, I'm similar to the thriller in Manila.

Honeys call me "Bigga, the condom filler."

Whether it's stiff tongue or stiff dick,

Biggie squeeze it to make shit fit, now check this shit.

I got the pack of Rough Riders in the back of the Pathfinder.

You know, the EP along by James Todd Smith.

I get swift with the lyrical gift.

Hit you with the dick, make your kidneys shift.

Here we go, here we go, but I'm not Domino.

I got the funk flow to make your drawers drop slow.

So recognize the dick size in these Karl Kani jeans.

I'm in thirteens, know what I mean?

I fuck around and hit you with the Hennessey dick,

Mess around and go blind, don't get to see shit.

The next batter, here to shatter your bladder,

It doesn't matter,

Skinny or fat, or white-skinned or black,

Baby, I drop these Boricua mommies screamin' "Aiy, pappy!"

I love it when they call me "Big Poppa."

I only smoke blunts if they roll propa.

Look, I gotcha caught up in the drunk flow.

Fuck Tae Kwon Do, I tote da fo'-fo'.

For niggaz gettin' mad 'cause they bitch chose me—

A big, black muthafucka with G, ya see.

All I do is separate the game from the truth.

Big bang boots from the Bronx to Bolivia,

"Gettin' Physical" like Olivia Newt.

Tricks suck my clique-dick all day with no trivia.

So gimme a hoe, a bankroll, and a bag of weed.

I'm guaranteed to fuck her 'til her nose bleed.

Even if your new man's a certified mack,

You'll get that H-town in ya; you'll want that old thing back.

Oh, Biggie, gimme one more chance.
I got that good dick, girl, ya didn't know?
Oh, Biggie, gimme one more chance.
I got that good dick, girl, ya didn't know?

In my mind, playin' tricks, like Scarface and Bushwick,
Willie D., havin' nightmares of girls killin' me.
She mad because what we had didn't last.
I'm glad because her cousin let me hit the ass.
Fuck the past, let's dwell on the five-hundred S–L,
The E and J, and ginger ale.
The way my pockets swell to the rim with Benjamins,
Another hon's in the crib—please, send her in.
I fuck nonstop, lick my lips a lot, used to lick the clits a lot.
But lickin' clits had to stop
'Cause y'all don't know how to act when the tongue go down below.
Peep the funk flow, really though,
I got the cleanest, meanest penis—ya never seen this stroke of genius.
So take off your Tim boots and your bodysuit:
I mean the spandex, and hit my man next.
Sex gettin' rougher when it come to the nut-buster,
Pussy-crusher, black, nasty motherfucker.
I don't chase 'em, I replace 'em
And if I'm caressin' 'em, I'm undressin' 'em.
Fuck whatcha heard, who's the best in New York
For fillin' fantasies without that nigga, Mr. Rourke?
Or Tattoo, I got you wrapped around my dick
And when I'm done, I got to split shit.
Back shots is my position, I gotcha wishin' for an intermission.
Fuck the kissin', lickin' down to your belly button, I ain't frontin'.
They don't call me B.I.G. for nuttin', all of a sudden.

Oh, Biggie, gimme one more chance.
I got that good dick, girl, ya didn't know?
Oh, Biggie, gimme one more chance.
I got that good dick, girl, ya didn't know?

Words and Music by Adrian Sear,
Artis Ivey Jr., Patrick Adams and Sandra Cooper

1, 2, 3, 4 (SUMPIN' NEW)
RECORDED BY COOLIO

CHORUS:

1–2–3–4,
Get your woman on the floor.
Gotta, gotta get up to get down.
Gotta, gotta get up to get down.

What up everybody, so glad you're here.
It's Coolio with the flow back in your ear.
This ain't a fantastic voyage
But I'm still on a mission
To see if I can get your attention.
Now I want drops some information;
Just a little additive to your education.
I live my life by the code of the funk.
Six-hundred-watt amp, eighteens in the trunk.
When I'm on the streets ya gotta feel my beats.
So throw your hands up if you're down with the C
Double O–L–I–O with the flow.
I'm lookin' for the party, so let a brother know.
1–2–3–4, it's like A–B–C
If hip-hop didn't pay, I'd rap for free.

Slide, slide, but that's the past
I gotta sumpin' brand new for that ass.

If ya got beef then, fool, eat a pork chop.
Once I get it goin' ya know it don't stop.
I brake like anti-locks; panties drop
From 'hood to 'hood, block to block.
Help, I need somebody to get it goin' on in the party.

Baby, you can do it, take your time, do it right.
We can drink some yak and do it all damn night.
My name ain't Wanda, but I'll rock your world.
I get more bounce than a Jheri-curl.
Too many lookie-loos be lookin' for clues.
There's a party goin' on, now whatcha gonna do?
So grab your partner, do-see-do.
If you don't know who it is, it's Coolio.

Slide, slide, but that's the past
I gotta sumpin' brand new for that ass.

CHORUS

Push, push in the bush,
But don't step on the toes, 'cause you might get smushed.
It's the brother from around the way
And what I say,
I'm in the corner on three like Doctor Dre
Comin' at 'em with a pattern
And a fresh pair a Adams.
I hope he don't trip 'cause I don't wanna have to gatt 'em.
So move your body, baby, drive the homies crazy,
Then when you shake that ass, it's always amazin'.
Ain't no party like a West Coast party
'Cause a West Coast party don't stop.
So when you see a young brother in a Chevy, hittin' switches,
Then ya gotta give a brother his props.
I got sides in my rides and a motion for your ocean.
Coolio got the potion to get the party open.

Slide, slide, but that's the past
I gotta sumpin' brand new for that ass.

CHORUS

P.I.M.P.
RECORDED BY 50 CENT

Words and Music by Denaun Porter,
Brandon Parrott and Curtis Jackson

CHORUS:

I don't know what you heard about me,
But a bitch can't get a dollar out of me.
No Cadillac, no perms, you can't see
That I'm a motherfucking P-I-M-P.

CHORUS

Now shorty, she in the club, she dancing for dollars.
She got a thing for that Gucci, that Fendi, that Prada.
That BCBG, Burberry, Dolce and Gabana.
She feed them foolish fantasies, they pay her cause they wanna.
I spit a little G man, and my game got her.
A hour later, have that ass up in the Ramada.
Them trick niggas in her ear saying they think about her.
I got the bitch by the bar trying to get a drink up out her.

She like my style, she like my smile, she like the way I talk.
She from the country, think she like me cause I'm from New York?
I ain't that nigga trying to holla cause I want some head,
I'm that nigga trying to holla cause I want some bread.
I could care less how she perform when she in the bed.
Bitch, hit that track, catch a date, and come and pay the kid.
Look, baby, this is simple, you can't see?
You fucking with me, you fucking with a P-I-M-P.

CHORUS (2 TIMES)

I'm 'bout my money you see. Girl you can holla at me.
If you fucking with me, I'm a P-I-M-P.
Not what you see on TV, no Cadillac, no greasy
Head full of hair. Bitch, I'm a P-I-M-P.
Come get money with me, if you curious to see
How it feels to be with a P-I-M-P.
Roll in the Benz with me. You could watch TV
From the backseat of my V, I'm a P-I-M-P.

Girl, we could pop the champagne and we could have a ball.
We could toast to the good life, girl. We could have it all.
We could really splurge, girl, and tear up the mall.
If ever you need someone, I'm the one you should call.
I'll be there to pick you up if ever you should fall.
If you got problems, I can solve 'em, they big or they small.
That other nigga you be with ain't 'bout shit.
I'm your friend, your father, and confidant, bitch.

CHORUS (2 TIMES)

I told you fools before, I stay with the tools.
I keep a Benz, some rims, and some jewels.
I holla at a hoe till I got a bitch confused.
She got on Payless, me, I got on gator shoes.
I'm shopping for chinchillas. In the summer they cheaper.
Man, this hoe, you can have her, when I'm done I ain't gon' keep her.
Man, bitches come and go, every nigga pimpin' know.
You saying it's secret, but you ain't gotta keep it on the low.

Bitch choose on me, I'll have you stripping in the street.
Put my other hoes down, you get your ass beat.
Now Nik, my bottom bitch, she always come up with my bread.
The last nigga she was with put stitches in her head.
Get your hoe out of pocket, I'll put a charge on a bitch.
Cause I need 4 TVs and AMGs for the six.
Hoe make a pimp rich, I ain't paying bitch.
Catch a date, suck a dick, shit, trick.

CHORUS (2 TIMES)

Yeah, in Hollywoood they say there's no business like show business.
In the hood they say there's no business like hoe business, ya know.
They say I talk a little fast. But if you listen a little faster
I ain't got to slow down for you to catch up, bitch.

Words and Music by
Christopher Martin and Lawrence Krsone Parker

"P" IS STILL FREE
RECORDED BY KRS-ONE

Awww, yeah!
All ruffneck rudebwoy hold tight.
Just a little somethin' for the Jeep.
Turn my voice up a little bit and let's get this started.
Comin' to you live and direct from the 1986 version.
Comin' up to 1993.
Of course, Premier on the beat.
Now, check it out!

CHORUS:
The girlies is FREE-EE, 'cause the crack cost money, oh yeah!
I said, the girlies is FREE-EE, 'cause the crack cost money, oh yeah!

Ridin' one day in a '92 Beemer.
After seven years, I seen Denise—she still a skeezer.
But look what she did: she went and had a kid—no dad—
And just released her ass out the rehab.
You think she'd act like she don't know
She's still a hoe, but, umm, check my man for the show.
"Hiiiii, DJ. K–R–S."
She tried to shake her butt; I rolled my window up!
She got pissed and said, "You ain't all that!"
And went and got some other girl schemin' for crack.
In my car, I couldn't hear what they spoke about.
I hit the Ac-celerator and I was out!
I never check my man, but I knew the plan:
Come to the jam, MCs in there be thinkin' they Superman.
Sure enough, the place is packed with no breeze:
Crazy girls and wall-to-wall MCs.
I'm like a cat—these MCs are Fancy Feast.
I'm thinkin' of rhymes, but I'm interrupted by Denise.

She said, "Kris, I really need a favor, honey.
My girlfriend here really needs some quick money!"
I looked at her girlfriend, and her girlfriend was fly,
But I ain't stupid—she had that LOOK in her eye.
I touched her back; she said, "Denise, has he got the crack?
Is he the one? I gotta run back and feed my son."
I said, "How old is your son?" She said, "Three months."
So she pulled out a gun and shot him in the party.
Except for the MCs, I knew everybody.
She tried to let off a shot one more time,
But got stomped so bad, she turned to wine.
No one could find Denise for several weeks.
You know the time on this '93 beat.

CHORUS

I knew a group that had a dope lead singer—
Swinger, single guy that knew his style was fly.
After the show, he was tired, sweaty, and kinda sloppy,
But, of course, a million girls are in the lobby.
He saw a group of girls hangin' out and lookin' good,
So he took one to his room because he knew he could.
Inside the room, he said, "Make love to me, and never stop."
She said, "Sure, but how's about a crack rock?"
I knew my man down the hall had it all,
So he called down the hall, but homeboy wasn't there at all.
He turned to the girl, and said, "My main ain't there."
So she let down her hair, unzipped his pants down right there.
Oral sex in effect—or rather deep throat;
But just before he came, she bit his dick and slit his throat.
As he fell back, dizzy, he began to choke.
She took his wallet and said, "You ain't broke!"

CHORUS

Oh, yeah!

Yes, Premier, you know you rule hip-hop, an'
Yes, Ced Gee, you know you run hip-hop, an'
Yes, Kenny Bwoy, you run hip-hop, an'
But KRS-One'll rock it non-stop!
When I'm in Brooklyn, we rulin' HIP-HOP!
When I'm in Jersey, we runnin' hip-hop.
Over in Brazil, yes, we rulin' HIP-HOP!
Over in Germany, we rulin' hip-hop.
But in New York, we rulin' y'all tonight, badda-bye-bye-bye.
In New York, we rulin' y'all to-NIGHT!
We come to rock you whether you black or you white,
'Cause KRS-One, you know I'm never frank—come catch the style.

CHORUS

Boogie Down Productions!

Words and Music by
Ice-T and Afrika Islam

PEEL THEIR CAPS BACK

RECORDED BY ICE-T

Coolin' in my crib, cold video dubbin',
F.B.I. wanted? Huh, don't mean nuttin'.
They call that shit a crime? Yo, that shit's a joke.
Hit record on my dope remote.
I heard my phone ringin', I wonder, "Who could it be?"
It was the E, the V, yes, the I–L–E.
He said, "We got static—word, I just got out.
Punks tried to move at the club, and we shot out.
Bullets everywhere." Okay, what's the prob?
"Ink got popped; he's dead as a doorknob."
You bullshittin'! "I ain't fuckin' around.
The posse's rollin' tonight, nigga, are you down?"
I grabbed my AK, my 16, and my baby Mac,
Strapped on my vest and threw the nine in the small of my back.
I said, "Chill—don't let nobody move without me.
Say, you know where they are?"
He said, "I know where they be."
Let's peel their caps back.
Let's peel their caps back.

Twelve o'clock midnight, posse was airtight.
Twenty-five cars under the streetlights.
Some people talked while others cried.
Ink was a brother who shouldn't have died.
Then the silence broke—Ice, what's it gonna be?
Thirty-eight hard brothers stood and stared at me.
There were only two words that I had to say:
P–A–Y B–A–C–K.

The car's loaded with a silence that could rape the dead.
Pistols clipped as the chamber's loaded full of lead.
Everyone in the crew knew what I said
Would mean by morning: somebody else soon would be dead.
Let's peel their caps back.

The car's at the corner like a long, black snake
Night-prowlin' for a life to take.
Ya see, down in the ghetto, it's an eye for an eye.
That's the answer to the question, "Why?"
In my throat there's a lump, then I swallow it—I ain't no chump.
Face of Death, then I cocked my pump.
I'm a nigga on the trigger, madder than a pit bull,
Just layin' for a reason to pull
On you, any duck-motherfucker that gets in my way.
I'm insane and my homeboy's death made me this way.
But then we spot him, Evil-E shot him
Dead in the face, made sure that he got him.
Others ran, but no mercy to the posse's wrath.
Automatic-Uzi-Motherfuckin' bloodbath.
Let's peel their caps back.
Let's peel their caps back.
Let's peel their caps back.

Then all of a sudden, a bullet came through my eye.
My dome exploded and I felt my other brothers die.
I drink my blood as I fell like shit into the street.
My corpse stunk like a burnt-out, rotten piece of meat.
Ten brothers died in this stupid homicidal binge
'Cause whenever someone dies, nobody wins.
But this drama, you'll never hear a word of
'Cause all the paper's gonna read is "a gang murder."
Gang murder.

Words and Music by Todd Thomas

PEOPLE EVERYDAY

RECORDED BY ARRESTED DEVELOPMENT

See, I was resting at the park, minding my own
Business, as I kick up the treble tone
On my radio tape player box, right?
Just loud enough so folks could hear its hype, see?
Outta nowhere comes the woman I'm dating,
Investigating—maybe she was demonstrating.
But nevertheless, I was pleased.
My day was going great and my soul was at ease
Until a group of brothers started bugging out,
Drinking the forty ounce, going the nigga route,
Disrespecting my black queen,
Holding their crotches and being obscene.
At first I ignored them 'cause, see, I know their type.
They got drunk and got guns and they wanna fight.
And they see a young couple having a time that's good
And their egos wanna test a brother's manhood.
So they came to test Speech 'cause of my hairdo,
And the loud, bright colors that I wear. (Boo!)
I was a target 'cause I'm a fashion misfit,
And the outfit that I'm wearin, brother's dissin' it.
Well, I stay calm and pray the niggaz leave me be,
But they're squeezin' parts of my date's anatomy.
Why, Lord, do brothers have to drill me?
'Cause if I start to hit this man, they'll have to kill me.

CHORUS:
I am everyday people.
I am everyday people.

I told the niggaz, "Please let us pass, friend."
I said, "Please, 'cause I don't like killin' Africans."
But he wouldn't stop, and I ain't Ice Cube,
But I had to take the brother out for being rude.
And, like I said before, I was mad by then.
It took three or four cops to pull me off of him.
But that's the story, y'all, of a black man
Actin' like a nigga and get stomped by an African.

CHORUS

Words and Music by Christopher Wallace, Kimberly Jones, James Lloyd,
Rodolfo Franklin, Harvey Fuqua and Lottie Wiggins

PLAYER'S ANTHEM
RECORDED BY JUNIOR M.A.F.I.A., FEATURING NOTORIOUS B.I.G.

[NOTORIOUS B.I.G.]
Niggaz, bitches.
Uh.

CHORUS:
[NOTORIOUS B.I.G.]
(Niggaz.) Grab your dick if you love hip-hop.
(Bitches.) Rub your titties if you love Big Poppa.
Gotcha, open off the words I say because

[SLICK RICK]
This type of shit, it happens every day.

[LIL' CAESAR]
Check it out, uhh.
Now who smoke more blunts than a little bit?
What are you, a idiot?
Listen to the lyrics I spit like M-1s.
Got mad guns up in the cabin,
'Cause Caese ain't the one for the dibbin' and dabbin' shit.
I make it happen, you got your ass caught.
All you saw was fire from the Honda Passport,
Or the M.P., what if you see, then I miss ya?
I blow up spots like little sisters.
G' on, grit yo' teeth; g' on, bite yo' nails to the cuticles
Like Murray, my killings be the most beautiful.
Junior M.A.F.I.A., click, thick like Luke dancers.
Niggaz grab your gatts; bitches take a glance at
The little one, pullin' over in the Land Rover,
Playin' Big Willy-style with a chauffer, ya know wha' I mean?
Stack the green, read all between the lines.
A nigga act up, make the bastard hard to find.

CHORUS (2 TIMES)

[NOTORIOUS B.I.G.]
(How ya livin', Biggie Smalls?) I'm surrounded by criminals.
Heavy rollers, even the shysty individuals.
Smokin' skunk and mad Phillies,
Beatin' down Billy Badasses, cracks in stacks and masses.
If robbery's a class, bet I pass it.
Shit get drastic, I'm buryin' ya bastards.
Big Poppa never softenin'.
Take you to the church, rob the preacher for the offerin',
Leave the fucker coughin' up blood and his pockets like rabbit ears,
Covered with wife, Kleenex for the kids' tears.
Versace wear, Moschino on my bitches.
She whippin' my ride, countin' my ones, thinkin' I'm richest.
Just the way players play, all day, every day,
I don't know what else to say.
I've been robbin' niggaz since Run and them was singin', "Here We Go,"
Snatchin' ropes at the Roxie, homeboy, you didn't know
My flow detrimental to your health.
Usually roll for self, I have son ridin' shotgun.
My mind's my nine, my pen's my Mac-10.
My target: all you wack niggaz who started rappin'.
Junior M.A.F.I.A., steel-o, niggaz know the half.
Caviar for breakfast, champagne bubble baths.
Runnin' up in pretty bitches constantly,
The Smalls, bitch, who the fuck was it supposed to be?

CHORUS (3 TIMES)

[LIL' KIM]
I used to pack Macs in Cadillacs.
Now I pimp gatts in the Acs, watch my niggaz backs.
Nines in the stores, glocks in the bags,
Maxin' mini-markets, gettin' money with the Arabs.
No question, confession, yes, it's the lyrical.
Bitches squeeze your tits, niggaz grab your genitals.
Proteins and minerals, excuse subliminals,
Big Momma shoots the game to all you willies and criminals.

I kick the rollie with my peeps all day,
Three-twenty-fives roll by with the windows down half-way.
DKNY, oh my, I'm jiggy.
It's all about the Smalls and my fuckin' nigga, Biggie.
Bitches love the way I bust a rhyme
'Cause they all in line, screamin', "One more time."
Niggaz, grab your dicks if you love hip-hop.
Bitches, rub-a-dub in the back of the club, straight up.

Words and Music by Stevie Wonder, Peter Nash,
Michael Berrin, John Dajani, John Gamble,
Dante Ross and Peter Gabriel

POP GOES THE WEASEL
RECORDED BY 3RD BASS

Antoine, Antoine's got somethin' here, re-roll that window.
We have to turn around because I want to shoot you.
Park the limousine in front of the swamp,
Then I want to shoot you dancin' on the limousines
With the swamp in the background.
It looks like you're in the jungle, okay?

Let's all sing, "Pop Goes the Weasel!"

[PETE NICE]
Pop goes the, pop goes the windin' of the weasel.
I see the empty pocket needs a refill.

[MC SERCH]
I got a squad with a list of complainers.
I should have started R.A.P.E: Rappers Against Phony Entertainers.
So we can make it known that we won't get swayed.
It's ninety-one, son, so something's gotta change.

[PETE NICE]
Gettin' paid to peddle sneakers and soda pop. (Pop, pop, pop.)
Pop goes the weasel as drawers drop. (Drop, drop, drop.)
Why not take your Top-Ten pop hit,
Fix the music and make senseless rhymes fit.

[MC SERCH]
I guess it's the fact that you can't be artistic.
Intricate raps becomin' so simplistic.
I gotta strong mind—it doesn't have to be spoon-fed,
And I can read what doesn't have to be read.

[PETE NICE]
So, some stay illiterate and feeble, legally licked.
You got the ways of the weasel. (The weasel.)

CHORUS:
[3RD BASS]
Pop goes the weasel, the weasel.
Pop goes the weasel, the weasel.
Pop goes the weasel, the weasel.
Pop goes the weasel 'cause the weasel goes pop.

[MC SERCH]
Hip-hop got turned into hit-pop
The second a record was Number One on the pop charts.
For those that get on heart, that gotta in the ghetto,
Let no one forget about the hard part.
Now in ninety-one, we got a new brand, a new band.
Lookin' like the same old Klan,
Same old thieves that skeeze, so we gotta make sure
That real rap has got to endure.

[PETE NICE]
Why score all my points in one period?
Appearin' in complex structures like a pyramid.
The paper for the media presence,
Ya learn lesson from the face of false legend.
Stop vexin' on the skills, ya ain't originate.
The thin ice you skate upon will break and set ya straight.
Ate up on the plate, now who's diesel?
Not the weasel, not the weasel.
Pop goes the weasel.

CHORUS

[MC SERCH]
Ya stole somebody's record, then ya looped it, ya looped it.

[PETE NICE]
Ya boosted the record, then ya looped it, ya looped it.

[MC SERCH]

Aiyyo, I came from Cali, and they hooped it, they hooped it.

[PETE NICE]

But now you're gettin' sued—kinda stupid.

[MC SERCH]

Boosted tracks get slaps, ya got no haps
To reach all four corners of the map.
For kids in Kansas, to those who speak Spanish,
Doin' crazy damage so the wack gets banished.
Can't manage the truth until you buy a way.
Ya ain't quick so ya switch off the exit from my highway.
To rest but a crook, had to take a second look.
Ever heard of a chef who can't cook?
But the Minister Prime can lay laws.
Hey, yo, Pete Nice, rip the mic and go for yours.

[PETE NICE]

Goes for mine, I goes for mine.
Find the Prime won't eat the green eggs and swine.
Online like the Serch, in the 'hoody with the woody.
Get a disc or tape at Sam Goody.
Why'd ya run through the doors—some left open?
Ropin' off the scenes of the crime, smokin'.
I got pub and I'm-a nut like a SCUD, see?
Blowin' up like I'm throwin' up a beef patty.
Sell-outs run about like the measles.
No cures 'cause pop goes the weasel.

CHORUS (2 TIMES)

Words and Music by Marshall Mathers, Jeff Bass, Von Carlisle,
De Shaun Holton, Rufus Johnson, Ondre Moore and Denaun Porter

PURPLE PILLS
RECORDED BY EMINEM

CHORUS 1:

I take a couple uppers,
I down a couple downers,
But nothin' compares to these blue and yellow purple pills.
I been up mushroom mountain
Once or twice, but who's countin'?
But nothin' compares to these blue and yellow purple pills.

[EMINEM]

Cool, calm, just like my mom
With a couple of Valium inside her palm.
It's Mister Mischief with a trick up his sleeve.
Crawl up on you like Christopher Reeve.
I can't describe it, the vibe I get
When I drive by six people and five I hit—ah, shit.
I started a mosh pit, squashed a bitch
And stomped the foster kids.
These 'shrooms make me hallucinate,
Then I sweat 'til I start losing weight,
'Til I see dumb shit start happenin'—
dumber than Vanilla Ice tryin' to rap again.
So bounce, bounce, c'mon, bounce.
Everybody in the house with a half an ounce.
Not weed—I meant coke, dumb-ass, sit down.
We don't bullshit—better ask around.
D12 throws the bomb to gas your town.
Bizarre, your mom is passing out.
Get her ass on the couch while she passes out.

[KON ARTIST AND KUNIVA]

Fuck that, someone help Denaun
Who's upstairs naked with a weapon drawn.
Hey, Von, you see me steppin' on these leprechauns?

It's gonna be acid 'cause the X is gone.
Yeah, I took 'em all down with some Parmesan
And I think my arm is gone—it's probably numb.
Young, dumb, and full o' cum,
And I think he's 'bout to swallow his tongue.
You, scary ass, it was false alarm.
You think I'm 'bout to die when I just gon on?
So stop actin' stupid; you so high
That you might wake up with a guy.
On some new shit; I think I did too much.
This substance equals cuffs.
Red pills, blue pills, and green.
Big pills (that's ill), Mescaline.

CHORUS 1

CHORUS 2:
[EMINEM]
Dirty Dozen—eighty of us
Shady brothers; ladies love us.
That's why our baby mothers
Love us, but they hate each other.
They probably wanna take each other out
And date each other.
Some-, somethin', somethin', somethin',
Somethin', somethin', somethin', somethin'.

[PROOF]
Pop pills, pills I pop.
Pop two pills, on stilts I walk.
Snort two lines that were filled with chalk.
Thought I was incredible and killed the Hulk.
I wanna roll away like a Rollerblade
Until my eyes roll back in my skull for days.
And when I'm old and gray, look for coke to smoke.
No? Okee-doke—I pack up my nose with coke.
Am I supposed to choke?
Had an accident when the Trojan broke.
Ah, poor baby born by whore lady.
Now I got a straight-born infant. (You're crazy!)

[SWIFTY]
I pop four Es, one at a time,
And I don't need water when I'm swallowin' mine.
You got any 'shrooms?
Does Bizarre smoke crack?
We can't get jobs 'cause our arms show tracks.
Why the hell you niggaz think I rap?
I do it just to get your company hijacked.
If you like smack, then I might, too.
(Swift chill.) I just wanna stay high like you.
And I don't give a damn if they're white or blue,
Chew 'shrooms, down the Valium,
Even smoke weed outta vacuums.
I just got some and I'm goin' back soon.

CHORUS 1

[BIZARRE]
I'm at rave, lookin' like a slave,
High off chronic, gin, and tonic—demonic.
Body smelt like vomit,
Pussy poppin', acid droppin', dope-headed guy.
Heroline, Mescaline, pencil legs, wanna try?
Blue pills, golden seals got Bizarre actin' ill.
Drugs kill. (Yeah, right.)
Bitch, I'm for real.
Shut your mouth, you dirty slut.
You know you want it in your butt.
I'll bleed in your cunt—let Bizarre nut!

CHORUS 1 AND 2

Words and Music by
Ray Davies and Herby Azor

PUSH IT
RECORDED BY
SALT N PEPA

Ah, push it.
Ah, push it.

Ooh, baby, baby.
Baby, baby.
Ooh, baby, baby.
Baby, baby.

Get up on this!
Ow! Baby!
Salt and Pepa's here!

Now wait a minute, y'all.
This dance ain't for everybody—only the sexy people.
So all of you fly mothers get on out there and dance!
Dance, I said!

Salt and Pepa's here and we're in effect.
Want you to push it, babe.
Coolin' by day then at night, working up a sweat.
C'mon, girls, let's go show the guys that we know
How to become Number One in a hot party show.
Now push it.

Ah, push it—push it good.
Ah, push it—push it real good.
Ah, push it—push it good.
Ah, push it—p-push it real good.

Hey! Ow!
Push it good!

Ooh, baby, baby.
Baby, baby.
Ooh, baby, baby.
Baby, baby.

Push it good.
Push it real good.
Ah, push it.
Ah, push it.

Yo, yo, yo, yo, baby-pop.
Yeah, you come here, gimme a kiss.
Better make it fast or else I'm gonna get pissed.
Can't you hear the music pumpin' hard,
Like I wish you would?
Now push it.

Push it good.
Push it real good.
Push it good.
P-Push it real good.

Ah, push it.
Get up on this!

Boy, you really got me goin'.
You got me so I don't know what I'm doin'.

Ah, push it.

Words and Music by Irving Lorenzo,
Jeffery Atkins, Paul Walcott and Thiheem Crocker

PUT IT ON ME
RECORDED BY JA RULE, FEATURING VITA

(Where would I be without you, baby?)
So if you need me,
If you want me to put it on you.
Because I love ya. (Ya.)
And don't you forget it.
Whenever you need me,
If you want me to put it on you. (Come on!)

[JA RULE]
Where would I be without my baby?
The thought alone might break me.
And I don't wanna go crazy,
But every thug needs a lady.

Girl, it feels like you and I been mournin' together.
Inseparable, we chose pain over pleasure.
For that, you'll forever be a part of me.
Mind, body, and soul, ain't no I in we, baby.
When you cry, who wipes your tears?
When you scared, who's telling you there's nothing to fear?
Girl, I'll always be there when you need a shoulder to lean on.
Never hesitate knowing you can call on
Your soulmate, and vice versa.
That's why I be the first to
See Jacob and frost your wrist up.
Now you owe me.
I know you're tired of bein' lonely.
So, baby girl, put it on me.

CHORUS:

Where would I be without you? (Uh.)
I only think about you. (Yeah.)
I know you're tired of bein' lonely. (Lonely.)
So, baby girl, put it on me. (Put it on me.)
Where would I be without you? (Uh.)
I only think about you. (Yeah.)
And what you're sayin' is true. (Yeah.)
I know you're tired of bein' lonely. (Lonely.)
So, baby girl, put it on me. (Put it on me.)

[VITA]

Yo, and I appreciate the rocks and gifts that you got me, baby,
And that house on the hill when you drop like eighty
On a down payment, thinkin', "Damn, ain't life gravy?"
And ever since, for my honey, I been twice the lady,
What would I do without the nights that you kept me warm
When this cold world had a girl caught in a storm?
And I accept when you riff, when you caught in a roam.
And I respect when you flip 'cause our love is strong.
And when you hit the block, I watch for ten-four.
And when my pop's asleep, you snuck in the back door.
Baby boy, we been down since junior high,
So when life get hot in July, it's the world against you and I.
B-ballin', tied together and never,
Heart from the heart, knew that it would last forever.
When you told me you would never leave me lonely.
So, baby boy, put it on me.

CHORUS

[JA RULE]
Since we met, it's been you and I.
A tear for a tear, baby, eye for an eye.
And you know that my heart gon' cry
If you leave me lonely
'Cause you not just my love, you my homie.
Who's gonna console me, my love?
I'm outta control—hold me, my love,
'Cause I'm yours.
And I don't wanna do nothin' to hurt my baby girl.
If this was our world, it'd be all yours, baby.
The thought alone might break me,
And I don't ever wanna go crazy
'Cause every thug need a lady. (Yeah, yeah.)
I feel you, baby, 'cause them eyes ain't lyin'.
Wash away all the tears—there be no more cryin'. (Baby.)
And you complete me, and I would die if you ain't wit' me.
So, baby girl, put it on me.

CHORUS

Words and Music by
Jimmy Seals and T. Smith

PUT YOUR HANDS
WHERE MY EYES CAN SEE
RECORDED BY BUSTA RHYMES

Ah, yeah…Flipmode.
Here we come, 'bout to bust and explode.

Flipmode…Busta Bus. (Huh, what?)
Nine-seven. (C'mon, what?)
Hot shit! (Hah, hah!)
Check it out.

Hit you with no delayin', so what you sayin', yo? (Uh.)
Silly with my nine milli', what the deal-i-o, yo? (What?)
When I be on the mic, yes, I do my duty, yo.
Wild up in the club, like we wild in the studio. (Uh.)
You don't wanna violate, nigga, really and truly, yo. (Uh.)
My main thug nigga named Julio—he moody, yo. (What?)
Type of nigga that'll slap you with the tool-io. (Blaow!)
Bitch nigga scared to death, act fruity, yo. (Uh.)
Fuck that! Look at shorty—she a little cutie, yo. (Yeah.)
The way she shake it make me wanna get all in the booty, yo. (Whoo!)
Top miss, just hit the bangin' bitches in videos. (Huh?)
Whylin' with my freak like we up in the freak shows. (Damn.)
Hit you with the shit make you feel it all in your toes. (Yeah.)
Hot shit got all you niggaz in wet clothes. (Take it off.)
Stylin' my metaphors when I formulate my flows. (Uh.)
If you don't know, you fuckin' with lyrical player pros. (Like that.)

CHORUS:

Do you really wanna party with me?
Let me see just what you got for me.
Put all your hands where my eyes can see.
Straight buck-whylin' in the place to be.
If you really wanna party with me,
Let me see just what you got for me.
Put all your hands where my eyes can see.
Straight buck-whylin' in the place to be.

If you really wanna party with me—In God We Trust. (What?)
Yo, it's a must that you heard of us, yo, we murderous. (Uh!)
A lot of niggaz is wonderin' and they furious. (What?)
How me and my niggaz do it; it's so mysterious. (That's true.)
Furious, all of my niggaz is serious. (Huh!)
Shook niggaz be walkin' around fearin' us. (What?)
Front nigga, like you don't wanna be hearin' us. (No!)
Gotta listen to hot radio, yo, be playin' us. (Ah.)
Thirty times a day, shit'll make you delirious. (What?)
Damaging everything all up in your areas.
Yo, it's funny how all the chickens be always servin' us.
All up in between they ass where they wanna carry us. (What?)
Hit ya good, then I hit 'em off with the alias. (What?)
Various chickens, they wanna marry us. (Hah!)
Yo, it's Flipmode, my nigga, you know we 'bout to bust.
Seven-figure money, the label preparin' us.
Bit the dust, instead of you makin' a fuss. (What?)
Niggaz know better 'cause there ain't no comparin' us. (Nope.)
Mad at us, niggaz is never—we fabulous. (Yup!)
Hit my people off with the flow that be marvelous. (Hah!)
Hoe shit, my whole chick victorious. (Yup!)
Takin' no prisoners, niggaz is straight-up warriors. (What?)
While you feelin' that, I know you be feelin' so glorious. (Uh.)
Then I blitz and reminisce on my nigga Notorious.

Like that, like that-tha-that-that.
That, that, that, tha-that-that-that.
Like that.

CHORUS

Words and Music by Richard Cedric Hailey,
Anthony Banks, Earl T. Stevens and Todd Anthony

RAPPER'S BALL
RECORDED BY E-40,
FEATURING TOO SHORT AND K-CI

Where them naked hoes at?
E-Freezey!
Too Scheezy!
We off the heezy fo' sheezy, baby.
Off the heezy, I thought you theezy!
Niggaz ain't havin' no cheesy like us, man!
They ain't havin' no raveez!
Shit, ha-ha, you know us.
Where the K-Ceezy at, man! Tell him sing that shit.
Lace dem fools or somethin'.
Beotch!

CHORUS:
[K-CI]
Say that you got it all,
Love the way you players ball.
Every day, you're at the mall.
Tell me, is it true or false?
Say that you got it all,
Love the way you players ball.
Claimin' that your mall is tall.
Tell me, is it true or false?

[E-40 AND TOO SHORT]
I put my mack-hand down, ain't never been around.
I was havin' B–R–E–A–D way before this rap-game nigga been town.
Thought you theezy, for sheezy, niggaz 'member
Earl, Brat, and Denell: dem boys from Vallel.
At every light, it's automatic—burn rubber.

See my folkers in the traffic—Whassup, Erb?
Follow that cab, it got dope in it, uhh.
My partna, Short, got hoes in it.

I'm always hearin' rappers big-ballin' on they songs.
I do that shit for real, and you'll never say I'm wrong.
S-500 straight, sittin' on twenties.
TV in the dash, pimpin' hoes, gettin' money.
I'm Too Short, baby, been down since the eighties.
For the last eight years, rode around in a Mercedes,
Lexus, trucks, drop-'vette, Caddy.
Bitches don't call me by many name, they call me, "Daddy."

CHORUS

[E-40 AND TOO SHORT]
K-Ci, Short, E-40, Fonzarelli.
I'll probably never have long money like Ross Perelli.
But, shit, we just want a hip, don't want the whole plate.
Don't put the two on the ten, don't ever perpetrate
Like a lot of these fools I see on TV,
With the Armani, Chanel versus Versace.
Why motherfuckers can't be broke sometimes?
Sometimes it's cool to floss,
But don't buy an eighty-five-thousand dollar car
Before you buy a house.

They always said I couldn't rap—I just say, "Bitch."
I guess the bitch made me rich.
And now you wanna call me hardcore
While I be steppin' out the shower on a marble floor.
I paid the I.R.S. taxes, send FedEx and taxes.
This industry is like fuckin' fat bitches.
All work and no play—I do it everyday,
Anyway, 'cause I gotta stay paid, Forty.

CHORUS

[E-40 AND TOO SHORT]
We throw parties on big-ass boats; niggaz wrap they paper.
Ultrafied, all-inclusive trips—Montego, Jamaica.
Front-row seats at the Ultimate Fights; shamrock and severin'.
Long, expensive f-flights up der in the heavens.
Fat-ass royalty checks, fat-ass cribs,
Smokin' blunts and drinkin' brew on the balcony, barbecuin' ribs.
The more scrilla, the merrier.
I represent the Ya area.

I walk from Foothill and Paperscourt to Sixty-Seven MacArthur,
To Freddie B house to make tapes with my partna.
Hit Arroyo Park; we had tapes for sale.
Got a paper bag full of that—can't you tell?
It's funky; everybody nod they head like this.
I said, "Bitch," and everybody read my lips.
I got rich suckin' up the game from the O
And even though a lot of rappers got the same kind of flow,
I survived 'cause I got mo' game than them.
It came straight from the prostitutes, playas, and pimps.
It was my destiny; I came the same every time.
So don't question me; I transfer the game in rhymes.
I'm not a freestyler, don't rap for free, man.
It's Paystyle on mine 'cause I love money, man.
Land Rovers and Toyota, Lexuses,
Six-hundred-feet-twelve, with them big-ass motor Mercedes.
We don't be savin' hoes; bitches be savin' us.
Bitch disrespect me in my car, bitch best to catch the bus.
I keep a briefcase full of game while y'all be ear-hustlin'.
Ain't no paperback-pimpin' nigga; we ain't strugglin'.

CHORUS

[TOO SHORT]
I'm Shorty the Pimp, I come funky
Again and again, they say, "When will it end?"
Maybe never, 'cause I can still spit it.
But I ain't rappin' for cheese—I want meal tickets.
Gotta start somewhere, and I'm past that.
For the right scratch, I be the last mack.
So stick ya'self, Pretty Tony.
You tryin' ta make a hit, but your shit sounds phony—
Not like AT&T, but like ET.
You can't be me, so would you please see
If you can't keep my name out your mouth
'Cause you don't really know what the game's all about,
It's 'bout feedin' the family, not freakin' in the Benz.
Instead of rentin', pay for that roof on your head.
And stop pimpin' in your mind, knowin' you a trick.
Put your hustle down, playa; go an' hit you a lick.
Bitch!

(That's writ, Too Scheezy, Ant Banks, Forty Fonzarelli, K-Ci.)
Damn, is that right?
(That's right!)

By Nile Rodgers and Bernard Edwards

RAPPER'S DELIGHT
RECORDED BY SUGARHILL GANG

[WONDER MIKE]

I said-a hip-hop.

Hippie to the hippie,

The hip, hip-a-hop, and you don't stop-a rock it.

To the bang-bang boogies, say, "Up jump the boogie."

To the rhythm of the boogie, the beat.

Now, what you hear is not a test—I'm rappin' to the beat

And me, the groove, and my friends are gonna try to move your feet.

See, I am Wonder Mike, and I'd like to say, "Hello"

To the black, to the white, the red, and the brown,

The purple and yellow; but first, I gotta

Bang-bang the boogie to the boogie.

Say, "Up jump the boogie to the bang-bang boogie."

Let's rock, you don't stop.

Rock the rhythm that'll make your body rock.

Well, so far, you've heard my voice, but I brought two friends along.

And the next on the mic is my man, Hank.

C'mon, Hank, sing that song!

[HANK]

Check it out, I'm the C–A–S–A, the N–O–V–A

And the rest is F–L–Y.

You see, I go by the code of the doctor of the mix

And these reasons, I'll tell you why.

You see, I'm six-foot-one, and I'm tons of fun

When I dress to a tee,

You see, I got more clothes than Muhammad Ali

And I dress so viciously.

I got bodyguards, I got two big cars

That definitely ain't the wack—

I got a Lincoln Continental and a sun-roofed Cadillac.

So after school, I take a dip in the pool,

Which is really on the wall.

I got a color TV, so I can see the Knicks play basketball.

Hear me talk about checkbooks, credit cards, mo' money

Than a sucker could ever spend.

But I wouldn't give a sucker or a bum from the Rucker.

Not a dime 'til I made it again.

Everybody go, "Hotel, motel, whatcha gonna do today?" (Say what?)

'Cause I'm-a get fly girl,

gonna get some spank 'n' drive off in a def O.J.

Everybody go, "Hotel, motel, Holiday Inn."

Say, if your girl starts actin' up, then you take her friends.

Master Gee! My mellow!

It's on to you, so whatcha gonna do?

[MASTER GEE]

Well, it's on 'n' on 'n' on 'n' on 'n' on,

The beat don't stop until the break of dawn.

I said, M–A–S, T–E–R, a G with a double E.

I said, I go by the unforgettable name

Of the man they call the Master Gee.

Well, my name is known all over the world

By all the foxy ladies and the pretty girls.

I'm goin' down in history

As the baddest rapper there ever could be.

Now, I'm feelin' the highs and you're feelin' the lows.

The beat starts gettin' into your toes.

You start poppin' your fingers and stompin' your feet

And movin' your body while you're sittin' in your seat.

And then, damn! Ya start doin' the Freak,

I said, damn! Right outta your seat.

Then ya throw your hands high in the air.

Ya rockin' to the rhythm, shake your derriere.

Ya rockin' to the beat without a care

With the sure-shot MCs for the affair.

Now, I'm not as tall as the rest of the gang,

But I rap to the beat, just the same.

I got a little face and a pair of brown eyes.

All I'm here to do, ladies, is hypnotize.

Singin', on 'n' on 'n' on 'n' on 'n' on,

The beat don't stop until the break of dawn.

Singin', on 'n' on 'n' on 'n' on 'n' on,

Like a hot-buttered pop-da-pop-da-pop dibbie-dibbie.

Pop-da-pop-pop, don't you dare stop.

Come alive, y'all, gimme whatcha got.

I guess by now you can take a hunch
And find that I am the baby of the bunch.
But that's okay, I still keep in stride,
'Cause all I'm here to do is just wiggle your behind.
Singin', on 'n' on 'n' on 'n' on 'n' on,
The beat don't stop until the break of dawn.
Singin', on 'n' on 'n' on 'n' on 'n' on,
Rock, rock, y'all, throw it on the floor.
I'm gonna freak you here, I'm gonna freak you there,
I'm gonna move you outta this atmosphere
'Cause I'm one of a kind, and I'll shock your mind.
I'll put TNT in your behind.
I said, one, two, three, four, come on, girls, get on the floor.
A-come alive, y'all, a-gimme whatcha got
'Cause I'm guaranteed to make you rock.
I said, one, two, three, four, tell me, Wonder Mike,
What are you waitin' for?

[WONDER MIKE]

I said, a-hip-hop,
The hippie to the hippie,
The hip, hip-a-hop, and you don't stop-a rock it
To the bang-bang boogie, say, "Up jump the boogie."
To the rhythm of the boogie, the beat.
A-skiddle-ee-be-bop, we rock, scooby-doo.
And guess what, America, we love you
'Cause you rocked and a-rolled with so much soul,
You could rock 'til a hundred-and-one-years old.
I don't mean to brag; I don't mean to boast,
But we like hot butter on our breakfast toast.
Rock it up, baby bubba!
Baby bubba to the boogie, da-bang-bang-da-boogie.
To the beat, beat, it's unique.
Come on, everybody, and dance to the beat!

A hip-hop,
The hippie to the hippie,
The hip, hip-a-hop, and you don't stop, rock it.
Rock it out, baby bubba, to the boogie-da-bang-bang,
The boogie, to the boogie, the beat.
I said I can't wait 'til the end of the week.

When I'm rappin' to the rhythm of a groovy beat
And I attempt to raise your body heat,
Just blow your mind, so you can't speak,
And do a thing but a-rock and shuffle your feet,
And let it change up to a dance called the Freak.
And when you finally do come into your rhythmic beat,
Rest a little while so you don't get weak.
I know a man named Hank:
He has more rhymes than a serious bank.
So come on, Hank, sing that song
To the rhythm of the boogie, the bang-bang-da-bong!

[HANK]

Well, I'm imp the dimp, the ladies' pimp.
The women fight for my delight
But I'm the grandmaster with the three MCs
That shock the house for the young ladies,
And when you come inside, into the front,
You do the Freak, spank, and do the Bump.
And when the sucker MC try to prove a point,
We're a treacherous trio; we're the serious joint.
A-from sun to sun, and from time to time,
I sit down and write a brand new rhyme
Because they say that miracles never cease.
I've created a devastating masterpiece.
I'm gonna rock the mic 'til you can't resist.
Everybody, I say, it goes like this:
Well, I was walkin' home late one afternoon.
A reporter stopped me for an interview.
She said she's heard stories and she's heard fables
That I'm vicious on the mic and the turntable.
This young reporter I did adore,
So I rocked some vicious rhymes like I never did before.
She said, "Damn, fly guy, I'm in love with you.
The Casanova legend must have been true."
I said, "By the way, baby, what's your name?"
Said, "I go by the name of Lois Lane.
And you could be my boyfriend, you surely can.
Just let me quit my boyfriend called Superman."
I said, "He's a fairy, I do suppose,
Flyin' through the air in pantyhose.

He may be very sexy, or even cute,
But he looks like a sucker in a blue and red suit."
I said, "You need a man-man, who's got finesse,
And his whole name across his chest.
He may be able to fly all through the night,
But can he rock a party 'til the early light?
He can't satisfy you with his little worm,
But I can bust you out with my super sperm!"
I go do it, I go do it, I go do it, do it, do it.
An' I'm here an' I'm there, I'm Big Bad hank, I'm everywhere.
Just throw your hands up in the air
And party hardy like you just don't care.
Let's do it, don't stop, y'all, a-tick-tock, y'all, you don't stop!
Go, "Hotel, motel, whatcha gonna do today?" (Say what?)
I'm gonna get a fly girl, gonna get some spank, drive off in a def O.J.
Everybody go, "Hotel, motel, Holiday Inn."
You say if your girl starts actin' up, then you take her friend.
I say, "Skip, dive, what can I say?"
I can't fit 'em all inside my O.J.
So I just take half, and bust 'em out,
I give the rest to Master Gee, so he can shock the house.
It was twelve o'clock on Friday night,
I was rockin' to the beat and feelin' all right.
Everybody was dancin' on the floor,
Doin' all the things they never did before.
And then this fly girl with a sexy lean,
She came into the bar, she came into the scene.
She traveled deeper inside the room.
All the fellas checker out her white Sassoons.
She came up to the table, looked into my eyes,
Then she turned around and shook her behind.
So, I said to myself, "It's time for me to release
My vicious rhyme I call my masterpiece."
And now people in the house, this is just for you:
A little rap to make you boogaloo.
Now the group you hear is called Phase Two,
And let me tell you somethin', we're a helluva crew.
Once a week, we're on the street
Just to cut in the jams and look at your feet.
For you to party, you gotta have the moves,
So, we'll get right down and get you a groove.

For you to dance, you got to be hot,
So we'll get right down and make you rock.
Now the system's on and the girls are there,
You definitely have a rockin' affair.
But let me tell you somethin', there's a-still one fact,
And to have a party, you got to have a rap.
So when the party's over, you're makin' it home,
And tryin' to sleep before the break of dawn.
And while you're sleepin', you start to dream
And thinkin' how you danced on the disco scene.
My name appears in your mind.
Yeah, a name, you know, that was right on time.
It was Phase Two, just doin' a do.
Rockin' you down 'cause you knew we could
To the rhythm of the beat that makes you freak,
Come alive, girls, get on your feet.
To the rhythm of the beat, to the beat of the beat,
To the double beat-beat that makes you Freak,
To the rhythm of the beat that says, "You go on."
On 'n' on, into the break of dawn.
Now, I got a man comin' on right now,
He's guaranteed to throw down.
He goes by the name of Wonder Mike.
Come on, Wonder Mike, do what you like!

[WONDER MIKE]

I say a can of beer that's sweeter than honey,
Like a millionaire that has no money,
Like a rainy day that is no wet,
Like a gamblin' fiend that does not bet,
Like Dracula without his fangs,
Like the boogie to the boogie without the boogie-bang,
Like collard greens that don't taste good,
Like a tree that's not made out of wood,
Like goin' up, and not comin' down,
It's just like the beat without the sound—no sound.
To the beat-beat, you do the Freak.
Everybody just rock and dance to the beat.
Have you ever went over a friend's house to eat
And the food just ain't no good?
The macaroni's soggy, the peas are mushed,

And the chicken tastes like wood.
So you try to play it off, like you think you can,
By sayin' that you're full
And then your friend says, "Mama, he's just bein' polite.
He ain't finished, uh-uh, that's bull!"
So your heart starts pumpin', and you think of a lie
And you say that you already ate,
And your friends says, "Man, there's plenty of food."
So you pile some more on your plate
While the stinky food's steamin', your mind starts to dreamin'
Of the moment that it's time to leave
And then you look at your plate and your chicken's slowly rottin'
Into somethin' that looks like cheese.
Oh, so you say, "That's it, I gotta leave this place.
I don't care what these people think,
I'm just sittin' here makin' myself nauseous
With this ugly food that stinks."
So you bust out the door while it's still closed,
Still sick from the food you ate
And then your run to the store for quick relief
From a bottle of Kaopectate.
And then you call your friend two weeks later,
To see how he has been
And he says, "I understand about the food,
Baby bubba, but we're still friends."
With a hip-hop, the hippie to the hippie,
To the hip, hip-a-hop, a-you don't stop the rockin'.
To the bang-bang boogie,
Say, "Up jump the boogie."
To the rhythm of the boogie, the beat.
I say, "Hank, can ya rock?
Can ya rock to the rhythm that just don't stop?
Can ya hip me to the shoobie-doo?"
I said, Come on, Hank, make the people move!"

[HANK]
I go to the balls and then ring the bell
Because I am the man with the clientele.
And if ya ask me why I rock so well,
A big bang, I got clientele.
And from the time I was only six years old,

I never forgot what I was told.
It was the best advice I ever had.
It came from my wise, dear, old dad.
He said, "Sit down, punk, I wanna talk to you,
And don't say a word until I'm through.
Now there's a time to laugh, and a time to cry,
A time to live, and a time to die.
A time to break, and a time to chill.
To act civilized or act real ill.
But whatever you do in your lifetime,
You never let an MC steal your rhyme."
So from six to six 'til this very day,
I'll always remember what he had to say.
So when the sucker MCs try to chump my style,
I let them know that I'm versatile.
I got style, finesse, and a little black book
That's filled with rhymes and I know you wanna look.
But the thing that separates you from me,
And that is called originality.
Because my rhymes are on from what you heard,
I didn't even bite, not a god damned word.
And I say a little more, later on tonight,
So the sucker MCs can bite all night.
A-tick-a-tock, y'all, a beat-beat, y'all,
A-let's rock, y'all, you don't stop.
Ya go, "Hotel, motel, whatcha gonna do today?" (Say what?)
Ya say, "I'm gonna get a fly girl, gonna get some spank, and drive off in a def O.J."
Everybody go, "Hotel, motel, Holiday Inn."
Ya say, if your girl starts actin' up, then you take her friends.
A-like that, y'all, to the beat, y'all.
Beat-beat, y'all, ya don't stop!
A-Master Gee, my mellow.
It's on to you, so whatcha gonna do?

[MASTER GEE]
Well, like Johnny Carson on the Late Show,
A-like Frankie Crocker in stereo,
Well, like the Barkays singin' "Holy Ghost,"
The sounds to throw down, they're played the most.
It's like my man, Captain Sky
Whose name he earned with his super sperm.

We rock and we don't stop.
Get off, y'all, I'm here to give you whatcha got.
To the beat that it makes you Freak
And come alive, girl, get on your feet.
A-like a-Perry Mason without a case,
Like Farrah Fawcett without her face,
Like the Barkays on the mic,
Like gettin' down right for you tonight,
Like movin' your body so you don't know how,
Right to the rhythm and throw down.
Like comin' alive to the Master Gee,
The brother who rocks so viciously.
I said, the age of one, my life begun.
At the age of two, I was doin' the do.
At the age of three, it was you and me,
Rockin' to the sounds of the Master Gee.
At the age of four, I was on the floor,
Givin' all the freaks what they bargained for.
At the age of five, I didn't take no jive
With the Master Gee, it's all the way, live.
At the age of six, I was a-pickin' up sticks,
Rappin' to the beat, my stick was fixed.
At the age of seven, I was rockin' in heaven,
Don't ya know, I went off?
I gotta run on down to the beat, you see.
Gettin' right on down, makin' all the girls.
Just take off their clothes to the beat, the beat,
To the double beat-beat that makes you Freak.
At the age of eight, I was really great
'Cause every night, you see, I had a date.
At the age of nine, I was right on time
'Cause every night I had a party rhyme.
Goin', on 'n' on 'n' on 'n' on 'n' on,
The beat don't stop until the break of dawn.
A-sayin', on 'n' on 'n' on 'n' on 'n' on,
Like-a hot-buttered de-pop-pop-de-popcorn.

Words and Music by Marshall Mathers,
Andre Young, Tommy Coster and Mike Elizondo

THE REAL SLIM SHADY
RECORDED BY EMINEM

May I have your attention, please?
May I have your attention, please?
Will the real Slim Shady please stand up?
I repeat: will the real Slim Shady please stand up?
We're gonna have a problem here.

Y'all act like you never seen a white person before.
Jaws all on the floor like Pam, like Tommy just burst in the door
And started whoopin' her ass worse than before.
They first were divorce, throwin' her over furniture. (Ahh!)
It the return of the—
(Ah, wait, no way, you're kidding; he didn't just say what I think he did, did he?)
And Dr. Dre said…nothing, you idiots.
Dr. Dre's dead; he's locked in my basement! (Ha-ha!)
Feminist women love Eminem. (Chigga, chigga, chigga.)
(Slim Shady—I'm sick of him.
Look at him,
Walkin' around, grabbin' his you-know-what,
Flippin' the you-know-who.)
(Yeah, but he's so cute, though!)
Yeah, I probably got a couple of screws up in my head loose.
But no worse than what's goin' on in your parents' bedrooms.
Sometimes I wanna get on TV and just let loose,
But can't; but it's cool for Tom Greene to hump a dead moose.
(My bum is on your lips; my bum is on your lips.)
And if I'm lucky, you might just give it a little kiss.
And that's the message that we deliver to little kids
And expect them not to know what a woman's clitoris is.
Of course, they gonna know what intercourse is
By the time they hit fourth grade.
The got the Discovery Channel, don't they?
(We ain't nothin' but mammals.)
Well, some of us cannibals
Who cut other people open like cantaloupes. (Slurp.)
But if we can hump dead animals and antelopes

Then there's no reason that a man and another man can't elope. (Eww!)
But if you feel like I feel, I got the antidote.
Women, wave your pantyhose;
Sing the chorus, and it goes—

CHORUS:
I'm Slim Shady, yes, I'm the real Shady.
All you other Slim Shadys are just imitating.
So won't the real Slim Shady please stand up,
Please stand up, please stand up?
I'm Slim Shady, yes, I'm the real Shady.
All you other Slim Shadys are just imitating.
So won't the real Slim Shady please stand up,
Please stand up, please stand up?

Will Smith don't gotta cuss in his raps to sell his records.
Well, I do—so fuck him and fuck you, too!
You think I give a damn about a Grammy?
Half of you critics can't even stomach me, let alone stand me.
(But Slim, what if you win; wouldn't it be weird?)
Why? So you guys could just lie to get me here?
So you can sit me here, next to Britney Spears?
Shit, Christina Aguilera better switch me chairs
So I can sit next to Carson Daly and Fred Durst
And hear 'em argue over who she gave head to first.
You little bitch, put me on, blast on MTV.
(Yeah, he's cute, but I think he's married to Kim, he-he!)
I should download her audio on MP3
And show the whole world how you gave Eminem V.D. (Ahh!)
I'm sick of you little-girl and –boy groups—all you do is annoy me.

So I have been sent here to destroy you; (*Bzzzt.*)
And there's a million of us just like me,
Who cuss like me; who just don't give a fuck like me;
Who dress like me; walk, talk, and act like me;
And just might be the next best thing, but not quite me!

CHORUS

I'm like a head-trip to listen to 'cause I'm only givin' you
Things you joke about with your friends inside your living room.
The only difference is I got the balls to say it
In front of y'all, and I don't gotta be false or sugar-coated at all—
I just get on the mic and spit it.
And whether you like to admit it,
Er, I just shit it
Better than ninety percent of you rappers out there can.
Then you wonder, "How can kids eat up these albums like Valiums?"
It's funny 'cause at the rate I'm goin', when I'm thirty
I'll be the only person in the nursing home flirtin',
Pinchin' nurses' asses when I'm jacking-off with Jergens,
And I'm jerkin', but this whole bag of Viagra isn't workin',
And every single person is a Slim Shady, lurkin'.
He could be workin' at Burger King,
Spittin' on your onion rings, (*Hach.*)
Or in the parking lot, circling,
Screamin', "I don't give a fuck!"
With his windows down and his system up.
So, will the real Slim Shady please stand up
And put one of those fingers on each hand up?
And be proud to be outta your mind and outta control,
And one more time, loud as you can—how does it go?

CHORUS (2 TIMES)

Ha-ha!
Guess there's a Slim Shady in all of us.
Fuck it—let's all stand up.

Words and Music by
Ishmael Butler and Mary Ann Vieira

REBIRTH OF SLICK (COOL LIKE DAT)
RECORDED BY DIGABLE PLANETS

[BUTTERFLY]

We like the breeze flow straight out of our lids.
Them, they got moved by these hard rock Brooklyn kids.
Us flow a rush when the DJs boomin' classics.
You dig the crew on the fattest hip-hop records.
He touch the kinks and sinks into the sounds.
She frequents the fatter joints called "undergrounds."
Our funk zooms like you hit the Mary Jane.
They flock to booms, man, boogie had to change.
Who freaks the clips with mad amount percussion,
Where kinky hair goes to unthought-of dimensions?
Why's it so fly? 'Cause hip-hop kept some drama.
When Butterfly rocked his light blue suede Pumas.
What by the cut we push it off the corner.
How was the buzz entire hip-hip era?
Was fresh and fat since they started sayin' "Audi"
'Cause funk's made fat from right beneath my 'hoody.
The poo-bah of the styles like miles and shit,
Like sixties funky worms with waves and perms.
Just sendin' chunky rhythms right down yo' block.
We be to rap what key be to lock.
But I'm cool like dat.
I'm cool like dat.
I'm cool like dat.
I'm cool like dat.
I'm cool like dat.
I'm cool like dat.
I'm cool like dat.
I'm cool; I'm cool.

[LADYBUG]
We be the chocolate taps on my raps.
Innovates at the sweeter catnaps.
He at the funk club with the vibrate,
Them, they be crazy, down with the five plate.
It can kick a plan, then a crowd bursts.
Me, I be diggin' it with a bump verse.
Us, we be freakin' 'til dawn blinks an eye.
He gives the strangest smile, so I say "Hi." (Wassup?)
Who understood, yeah, understood the plan?
Him heard a beat and put it to his hands.
What I just flip, let borders get loose.
How to consume or they'll be just like juice.
If it's the shit, we'll lift it off the plastic.
The babes'll go spastic.
Hip-hop gains a classic.
Pimp playin' shock, it don't matter, I'm fatter.
Ask Butta' how I zone. (Man, Cleopatra Jones.)
And I'm chill like dat.
I'm chill like dat.
I'm chill like dat.
I'm chill like dat.
I'm chill like dat.
I'm chill like dat.
I'm chill like dat.
I'm chill; I'm chill.

[ALL]
Blink, blink, blink, blink, blink, blink, blink.
Think, think, think, think, think, think, think.

[DOODLEBUG]
We got ya free 'cause the clips be fat, boss.
Them, they're the jams and commence to goin' off.
She sweats the beat and ask me 'cause she puffed it.
Me, I got crew kids, seven and a crescent.
Us cause a buzz when the nickel bags are dealt.
Him, that's my man, with the asteroid belt.
They catch a fizz from the Mister Doodlebug.
He rocks a tee from the Crooklyn non-pips.

The rebirth of slick like my gangsta stroll,
The lyrics just like loot: come in stacks and rolls.
You used to find a bug in a box with fade.
Now he boogies up your stage, plaits, twist, or braids.
And I'm peace like dat.
I'm peace like dat.
I'm peace like dat.
I'm peace like dat.
I'm peace like dat.
I'm peace like dat.
I'm peace like dat.
I'm peace.

[BUTTERFLY]
Check it out, man, I groove like dat.
I'm smooth like dat.
I jive like dat.
I roll like dat.

[LADYBUG]
Yeah, I'm thick like dat.
I stack like dat.
I'm down like dat.
I'm black like dat.

[DOODLEBUG]
Well yo, I funk like dat.
I'm fat like dat.
I'm in like dat
'Cause I swing like dat.

[BUTTERFLY]
We jazz like dat.
We freak like dat.
We zoom like dat.
We out, we out.

Words and Music by Jerry Leiber, Mike Stoller,
Nathaniel Hall and Warren Griffith

REGULATE
RECORDED BY NATE DOGG
AND WARREN G

[WARREN G]

Regulators—
We regulate any stealing of his property,
And we're damn good, too.
But you can't be any geek off the street.
Gotta be handy with the steel,
If you know what I mean—earn your keep!
Regulators! Mount up!

It was a clear, black night; a clear, white moon.
Warren G was on the streets tryin' to consume
Some skirts for the eve, so I can get some funk.
Just rollin' in my ride; chillin' all alone.

[NATE DOGG]

Just hit the East Side of the L.B.C.
On a mission, tryin' to find Mister Warren G.
Seen a car full of girls; ain't no need to tweak
All you skirts know what's up with 213.

[WARREN G]

So I hooks a left on the Twenty-one and Lewis.
Some brothas shootin' dice, so I said, "Let's do this."
I jumped out the ride and said, "What's up?"
Some brothas pulled some gatts, so I said, "I'm stuck."

[NATE DOGG]

Since these girls peepin' me, I'm-a glide and swerve.
These hookers lookin' so hard, they straight hit the curb.
Won'tcha think of better things than some horny tricks?
I see my homie and some suckers all in his mix.

[WARREN G]

I'm gettin' jacked; I'm breakin' myself.
I can't believe they takin' Warren's wealth.
They took my rings; they took my Rolex.
I looked at the brotha and said, "Damn, what's next?"

[NATE DOGG]

They got my homie hemmed up and they all around.
Ain't none of them seein' if they goin' straight pound-for-pound.
I gotta come up real quick before they start to clown.
I best pull out my strap and lay them busters down.

[WARREN G]

They got guns to my head; I think I'm goin' down.
I can't believe this happenin' in my own town.
If I had wings, I could fly; let me contemplate.
I glanced in the cut and I see my homie, Nate.

[NATE DOGG]

Sixteen in the clip and one in the hole.
Nate Dogg is about to make some bodies turn cold.
Now they droppin' and yellin'—it's a tad bit late.
Nate Dogg and Warren G had to regulate.
I laid all them busters down; I let my gatt explode.
Now I'm switchin' my mind back into freak mode.
If you want skirts, sit back and observe.
I just left a gang of those over there on the curb.

[WARREN G]

Now Nate got the freaks and that's a known fact.
Before I got jacked I was on the same track.
Backup, backup, 'cause it's on N–A–T–E and me:
The Warren to the G.

[NATE DOGG]

Just like I thought:
They were in the same spot,
In need of some desperate help.
The Nate Dogg and the G-child were in need of somethin' else.
One of them dames was sexy as hell.

I said, "Ooh, I like your size."
She said, "My car's broke down and you seem real nice;
Would ya let me ride?"
I got a car full of girls and it's goin' real swell.
The next stop is the East Side Motel.

[WARREN G]

I'm tweaking into a whole new era.
G-Funk, step to this, I dare ya.
Funk on a whole new level.

[NATE DOGG]

The rhythm is the bass and the bass is the treble.

[WARREN G]

Chords, strings, we brings melody.
G-Funk: where rhythm is life and life is rhythm.

[NATE DOGG]

If you know like I know, you don't wanna step to this.
It's the G-Funk era—funked out with a gangsta twist.
If you smoke like I smoke, then you high, like, every day,
And if your ass is a buster, 213 will regulate.

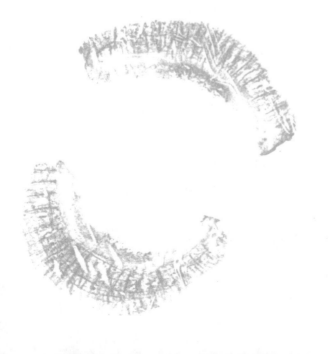

Words and Music by James Harris III,
Terry Lewis, Terrance Cocheeks Kelly,
Garfield Duncan and Dexter Archer

RENEE
RECORDED BY LOST BOYZ

Here's a tune about this honey named Renee
That I met one day on my way back from John Jay.
I'm peepin' shorty as she walkin' to the train.
I tap her on her shoulders,
"Excuse me, Miss, but can I get your name?"
She said, "My name is Renee."
I said, "I got a whole lot to say,
So may I walk you to your subway?"
She said, "If you want."
So yo, we started talking.
I bought two franks and two drinks, and we began walking.
I had to see where that head was at
Because the gear was mad phat.
So we must chat about this and that.
She told me what she was in school for.
She wants to be a lawyer.
In other words, shorty studies law.
I'm tellin' shorty I'm a writer.
And as she's lookin' for the token,
She drops a pack of EZ-widers,
Covers her mouth with her name ring.
I said, "Yo, don't sweat the technique,
Shorty rocks, I do the same thing."
But yet, I use Philly Blunts.
She said, "I never dealt with Philly Blunts
Because I heard that's for silly stunts."
I said, "Nah, they burn slower.
Right now, I really don't know ya,
But maybe later on I can get to show ya."

CHORUS:

A ghetto love is the law that we live by.
Day by day, I wonder why my shorty had to die.
I reminisce over my ghetto princess every day.
Give it up for my shorty, shorty.
A ghetto love is the law that we live by.
Day by day, I wonder why my shorty had to die.
I reminisce over my ghetto princess every day.
Give it up for my shorty, shorty.

So now, we sittin' on the train.
Besides the fingernails,
Now, shorty got the hairdo of pain.
Now I understand, she got flava.
A tough leather jacket with some jeans
And a chain that her moms gave her.
Got off the train about six thirty-four.
She wasn't sure she had grub for the dog,
So we hit the store.
Went to the crib and turned the lights on.
A mad magazine stand—from *Essence* to *Right On*.
A leather couch, stereo system with crazy CDs.
Understand? 'Cause she got cheese.
She said, "Cheeks, do what you want."
She said, "I'm gonna feed the dog."
I said, "Alright, well, I'm gonna roll this blunt."
She came back with stretch pants and a ponytail, a t-shirt.

Aiyyo, Fam, I got a tenderoni girl.
We're sittin' on the couch, chattin'.
We're smokin' blunts off the balcony.
We're staring at Manhattan now;
She started feelin' on my chest.
I started feelin' on the breasts—
And there's no need for me to stress the rest.
And yo, I got myself a winner.
We sparked a blunt before we ate,
And a blunt after we ate dinner.
She had a tattoo she only wanted Boo to see.
But first, dim the lights and turn up the Jodeci.
I'm like, whatever, shorty rock, we can swing it like that.
'Cause on the real, this is where it's at.

CHORUS (2 TIMES)

I woke up the next day on the waterbed.
A letter's on the pillow,
Eh, and this is what it said.
It said, "Cheeks, I'll be home around two.
You was deep in your sleep,
So I didn't want to bother you."
I left my number for shorty to call me later,
Got dressed, smoked a blunt,
And then I bounced towards the elevator.
I got a beep around three.
I'm asking shorty, "What's up with you?"
She's asking what's up with me?
And now we been together for weeks.
Candlelight dinner with my shorty,
Crack a forty with my naughty freaks.
Hey man, I never been in love,
But every time I'm burstin' in and outta state,
It's shorty that I'm thinkin' of.
I'm hangin' out with my crew.

I get a beep from Renee because Renee uses code, too.
But yet, I'm chattin' with her mom dukes.
She said, "Renee has been shot,
So Cheeks, meet me at Saint Luke's."
I jumps on the Van Wyck—
I just gotta make it there quick.
Aiyyo, this shit is gettin' mad thick.
Not even thinkin' about the po-nine.
I'm doin' a buck—who gives a fuck.
I'm smokin' boom and the whole nine.
I gotta see what's goin' on,
But by the time I reach the hospital,
They tell me, "Cheeks, Renee is gone."
I'm pourin' beer out for my shorty who ain't here.
I'm from the ghetto, so listen—
This is how I shed my tears.

CHORUS (2 TIMES)

Words and Music by
Tony Cottrell and Dante Smith

RESPIRATION
RECORDED BY BLACK STAR, FEATURING COMMON

"What did you do last night?"
"We did, um, two whole cars.
It was me, Dez, and Main Three, right?
And on the first car, in small letters, it said,
'All you see is…' and then, you know,
Big, big, you know, some block silver letters
That said, '…crime in the city,' right?"
"It just took up the whole car?"
"Yeah, yeah; it was a whole car and shit."

[WOMAN]
Escuchela…la ciudad respirando.*
Escuchela…la ciudad respirando.
Escuchela…la ciudad respirando.
Escuchela…la ciudad respirando.

[MOS DEF]
The new moon rode high in the crown of the metropolis,
Shinin', like, who on top of this?
People was tusslin', arguin', and bustlin'.
Gangstaz of Gotham, hardcore hustlin'.
I'm wrestlin'
With words and ideas.
My ears is picky, seekin' what will transmit.
The scribes can apply to transcript, yo.
This ain't no time where the usual is suitable.
Tonight, alive, let's describe the inscrutable,
The indisputable.
We New York—the narcotic,
Strength in metal and fiber optics;
Where mercenaries is paid to trade hot stock tips,

*Translation: Listen to it…the city is breathing.

For profits, thirsty criminals take pockets,
Hard knuckles on the second-hands of workin'-class watches,
Skyscrapers is colossus,
The cost of living is preposterous;
Stay alive, you play or die—no options.
No Batman and Robin;
Can't tell between the cops and the robbers—
They both partners; they all heartless
With no conscience; back streets stay darkened,
Where unbeliever hearts stay hardened.
My eagle talons stay sharpened, like city lights stay throbbin'.
You either make a way or stay sobbin';
The Shiny Apple is bruised but sweet,
And if you choose to eat you could lose your teeth.
Many crews retreat; nightly news repeat
Who got shot down and locked down.
Spotlight to savages, NASDAQ averages.
My narrative
Rose to explain this existence
Amidst the harbor lights which remain in the distance.
So much is on my mind that I can't recline.
Blastin' holes in the night 'til she bled sunshine.
Breathe in—inhale vapors from bright stars that shine.
Breathe out—weed smoke retrace the skyline.
Heard the bass ride out like an ancient mating call.
I can't take it, y'all—I can feel the city breathin'.
Chest heavin' against the flesh of the evenin'.
Sigh before we die like the last train leavin'.

[TALIB KWELI]
Breathin' in deep city breaths, sittin' on shitty steps.
We stoop to new lows; hell froze the night the city slept.
The beast crept through concrete jungles,
Communicatin' with one another,
And ghetto birds where waters fall from the hydrants to the gutters.
The beast walk the beats, but the beats we be makin'.
You on the wrong side of the track, lookin' visibly shaken.
Takin' them plungers,
Plungin' to death that's painted by the numbers.
With crime, unapplied pressure, cats is playin' God

But havin' children by a lesser baby mother—but fuck it.
We played against each other like puppets,
Swearin' you got pull
When the only pull you got is the wool over your eyes.
Gettin' knowledge in jail, like a blessin' in disguise.
Look in the skies for God;
What you see, besides the smog
Is broken dreams flyin' away on the wings of the obscene
Thoughts that people put in the air.
Places where you could get murdered over a glare.
But everything is fair.
It's a paradox we call reality.
So keepin' it real will make you casualty
Of abnormal normality.
Killers Born Naturally, like Mickey and Mallory,
Not knowing the ways'll get you capped like an N.B.A. salary.
Some cats be MC'ing to illustrate what we be seein'.
Hard to be a spiritual being when shit is shakin'
What you believe in.
For trees to grow in Brooklyn, seeds need to be planted.
I'm askin' if y'all feel me and the crowd left me stranded.
My blood pressure boiled and rose
'Cause New York niggaz actin' spoiled at shows.
To the winners the spoils go.
I take the L, transfer to the 2, head to the gates.
New York life type trife the Roman Empire state.

[MOS DEF AND CREW]
So much on my mind, I just can't recline.
Blastin' holes in the night 'til she bled sunshine.
Breathe in—inhale vapors from bright stars that shine.
Breathe out—weed smoke retrace the skyline.
Yo, don't the bass ride out like an ancient mating call?
I can't take it, y'all—I can feel the city breathin',
Chest heavin' against the flesh of the evenin'.
Sigh before we die like the last train leavin'.

[WOMAN]
Escuchela…respirando?

[COMMON]

Yo, on the Amen corner I stood lookin' at my former 'hood.
Felt the spirit in the wind; knew my friend was gone for good.
Threw dirt on the casket; the hurt, I couldn't mask it.
Mixin' down emotions, struggle I hadn't mastered.
I choreograph seven steps to heaven
And hell; waiting to exhale and to make the bread leavened.
Veteran of a Cold War, it's Chica-I-go
For what I know, or what's known.
So, some day I take the bus home, just to touch home.
From the crib I spend months gone.
Sat by the window with a clutched dome,
Listenin' to shorties cuss long.
Young girls with weak minds, but they butt strong.
Tried to call or, at least, beep the Lord,
But he didn't have touch-tone.
It's a dog-eat-dog world; you gotta mush on.
Some of this land I must own
Outta the city—they want us gone.
Tearin' down the 'jects; creatin' plush homes.
My circumstance is between Cabrini and Love Jones.
Surrounded by hate, yet I love home.
Ask my God how He thought travelin' the world sound.
Found it hard to imagine He hadn't been past downtown.
It's deep; I heard the city breathe in its sleep
Of reality; I touch, but for me, it's hard to keep
Deep; I heard my man breathe in his sleep
Of reality; I touch, but for me, it's hard to keep.

[MOS DEF AND CREW]

So much on my mind, I just can't recline.
Blastin' holes in the night 'til she bled sunshine.
Breathe in—inhale vapors from bright stars that shine.
Breathe out—weed smoke retrace the skyline.
Yo, how the bass ride out like an ancient mating call.
I can't take it, y'all—I can feel the city breathin',
Chest heavin' against the flesh of the evenin'.
Kiss the Ides goodbye; I'm on the last train leavin'.

Words and Music by Ahmir K. Thompson,
Malik Smart, Tarik Collins and Kenyatta Saunders

RESPOND REACT
RECORDED BY THE ROOTS

It's jazzy, hip-hop hangin' in my head heavy.
Malik said, "Riq, you know the planet ain't ready for the half."
Boy, we comin' with the action pack
On some Dundee shit, representin' the outback.
(Yo, we do it like this.)
All the way, live from 2–1–5.
(You witnessin' the fifth dynasty family clique.)
All the way, live from 2–1–5.
(Across the map—one time for your…)
All the way, live from 2–1–5.
(It's time to react, to respond, to react, to respond.)
All the way, live from 2–1–5.

CHORUS:
We setting it from Southside, pushing this up north,
From Illadelphian reps to fly points across the map.
Bring it back to respond/react,
To bring it back to respond/react to this.

[BAD LIEUTENANT AND M-ILL-ITANT]
The attractive assassin blastin' the devil trespassin'.
Master gettin' cash in an orderly fashion.
Message to the fake nigga, flashin':
Slow up, OC, before you get dropped and closed like a caption.
Fractional kids don't know the time for action.
Style's got the rhythm—that of an Anglo-Saxon.
Round of applause, then avalanche o' clappin'.
"Plow," that's what happen; now, what's your reaction?
We heavyweight traction, pro-pornographin'.
Specialize in science and math and original black man,
Bustin' thoughts that pierce your mental defense;
Rippin' your sacks and vocal, toe-to-toe, impeccable,

Splittin' your backs, son, simple as addition and subtraction.
Black Thought—the infinite relaxed one.
Shorties say they love it with a passion.
Bring the international charm.
See a squad, I harass.
React—you best adapt when I sling this rap.
Another chapter
Before, when I have to trap ya.
Map your whole path out.
Go get your crowd, so we can clap out.
I drive down streets and take back-route positionin'.
When I'm in your system—like glycerin.
Fans listenin' from Michigan to Switzerland.
Malik B blitzed again, on the station with the discipline.
Solicitin', sometimes illicit or explicit, with it then.
From the deep end where the hills are steep,
Nobody cares to speak—a land where life is cheap.
The street mentality mixed with the intellect,
Personality; hell, where I dwell, is well.
Niggaz rebellious,
Bodies are found down in the cellars.
My man caught a shot to the stomach—now who wants it?
Confronted by these dusty-blunted cats
Who act like they don't know that the fact is that
They're being hunted—a process of elimination.
Activate your mind with the stimulation.
Enter your zone with penetration.
I've seen more horror than Bram Stoker.
Strip your broad, a-play poker, then drink mocha.
The sometimes socializer,
The joke despiser.
You woke the wiser,
Dealin' with the Roots vocalizer.
Up in your flesh from South Philly to West,
I stamped your style.
I'll compile the bless.

CHORUS (2 TIMES)

[BLACK THOUGHT AND MALIK B]
Hey yo, I'm just a lyricist,
A chemist of the hemp,
The beat pimp,
The ill Philly resident
That's far from hesitant;
Corrupt like a president;
Never benevolent,
But politically prevalent;
Cooler than peppermint;
The lieutenant for niggaz talkin' 'bout represent.
No doubt, it's obviously evident—I get bent.
Far from temporary, son, I'm very permanent.
Hittin' MCs like an intoxicant.
Sent to prevent.
Monopoly is my intent.
The means is what I invent.
This mental murder pay the rent.
Lyrically, I'm the dominant ingredient,
The swift extravagant,
Smooth lubricant,
Down with the M-the-Ill-itant.
(Ch-ch-ch...) That's the sound of the dynasty chant.
We surround your camp
Assumin' the war stance,
And bring it from the chest.
Now let's dance.
M-ILL-ITANT.
Feel the fifth Gorilla chant.
Y'all talk about bodies
But you would not kill a' ant.
My skill is amp.
Would peel a nigga like a stamp.
Caliber is of Excalibur; now you be damp
When I operate a crop or copulate my game.
I make a womb populate and 2–1–5th is the stock of hate.

Peep the logistics,
Slump your squad of misfits;
They all get they wrists slit.
Blast your ass if you insist it.
Leave no trace so there's no trace for ballistics.
Turn your soul and body to statistics.
In particular, I've got that extracurricular
Squad in the stash who could be stickin' ya.
Slip, and they vicking ya.
Harass your police commissioner.
Don't like chicks with weaves talkin' 'bout, "I need conditioner."
That shit's deader than niggaz with a morticianer.
A gymnanza
Up in your flesh like plasma,
Take away your last breath when you got asthma,
Then meet Bad Lieu down at the plaza.
Hip-hop extravaganza.
Tell your man I slump him with a stanza.
Now, who's the boss? Not Tony Danza.
My force not green, but the force is obscene.
P.O. took a piss test—it came out not clean.
Brody with my man, Miz-Moose and Hakim.
My squad from deuce-four up the West Oak Lane
All the way to Takahwana and Frankfurt—they know the name.
It's like that…M-Ill-itant.

CHORUS

Words and Music by Thomas Derrick Mc Elroy,
Denzil Foster, Jay A. King, Garrick Husband,
Jerold Ellis, Anthony Douglas Gilmour and Dig

RIDE
RECORDED BY C-MURDER, FEATURING SAM AND D.I.G.

CHORUS:

We gon' die thuggin' 'cause that's just the life we lead.
We gon' die thuggin', bustin' at our enemies.
We gon' die thuggin' 'cause that's just the life we lead.
We gon' die thuggin', bustin' at our enemies.

[SAM]

Bustin' at our foes, for the sake of bein' riders.
'Til the casket close, thug shit be inside us.
We try to survive it 'cause all we got is the projects
On the camouflage sets, in the bricks, niggaz die wet.
'Til the death for the street glory, it's infinite beef,
though it's most of the reasons lotta niggaz six deep.
With heat, when we ride, we 'posed to roll that way,
To keep a soul that way, with forty-fours that spray.
The key to the city, it comes in bricks or them birds.
Thug niggaz, drug dealers makin', flippin' that third.
Born to my work, deserve what's supposed to be mine.
If it's what the fuck we need,
Then, D, we 'posed to be ride.
Try to separate us, but it's survival of a thug
While you try to play us, now you gotta watch my slugs.
Ride wit' us, die wit' us, follow us to the war.
We got five on the weed and we blowin' inside of the car.

CHORUS

[D.I.G.]

Y'all niggaz better, I'm-a die for this shit that I need.
I've been committed too long for me not to succeed.
I been in greed my whole life,
And caught up in the weed,
Hustlin' with thugs and every day, go to sleep,
Keepin' the guns cocked,

Surroundin' the block, opening up shop
With a bundle of rocks in my socks.
Niggaz wan' beef,
If it come to that, dog, I'm down with it.
Stank a lick for the 'fetti,
Get the cash and clown with it.
Hennessey and weed when I'm comin'.
Throw your guns up, let me see
If you bitch-ass niggaz gon' make some noise, bro.
Follow me now, 'cause I'm comin' up.
And ain't that cold, I got too many bitches runnin' up
And niggaz wanted to blast me, police harass me.
If I slip in the street,
I really think them niggaz'll snatch me.
Like I'm fakin' the game
But takin' the pain, lettin' them niggaz know
How I'm shakin' the game with nothin' to explain.

CHORUS

[C-MURDER]
We gon' die thuggin', we ride or die, stay muggin'
And bustin', and floodin' many bullets in your cousin.
Survive or not, any block I hit is hot.
Ask them warlocks shit, them hard knocks give me props.
Like them Melphomine boys,
I got them toys that'll split ya,
With enough ammo for every nigga that's with ya.
I hit ya, sun up or sundown—it don't matter,
As long as my muthafuckin' pockets get fatter.
Bitch-ass niggaz on the edge, they 'bout to fall.
You wanna brawl? I make a muthafuckin' call
And kill y'all shit, that's what I said and I meant it.
That was your last dollar and you spent it, ya heard me.
You forty-five-cent-ass nigga, I make mils.
Your bet's to chill before you get your shit spilled.
Lil' daddy, I hope you make the right decision.
I know some that'll have your ass missin'.

CHORUS (2 TIMES)

Words and Music by Rene Moore, Angela Winbush, Lamar Johnson,
Victor Merritt, Gerald Baillergeau and William Warner

ROMEO & JULIET
RECORDED BY SYLK-E FYNE

CHORUS:

It's like Romeo and Juliet—
Hot sex on a platter just to get you wet.
You's about to get in somethin' you will never regret
And it's gonna be the bomb—this is what I bet.
Yep!
It's like Romeo and Juliet—
Hot sex on a platter just to get you wet.
You's about to get in somethin' you will never regret
And it's gonna be the bomb—this is what I bet.
Yep!

Since the first time I saw ya,
I knew I was attracted.
Reacted to the fact
On how ya make me act.
Shy, but sexy at the same time,
Always on my mind was a little bump and grind.

Usually, I don't play it that close.
You gots ta kick it wit' me
Before I serve you up
With an overdose
Of that bomb-ass punani.
Make you my man.
I ain't got no love
For nobody else but you.

'Cause you's my boo.
I prove to you
My love is true.
So do you know where you goin' to?
Through thick and thin, baby,
You all in, time will reveal
That my love for you will never end.

My heart keep tickin',
No time for trickin'.
You who I'm pickin'.
So lay me down,
Just give it a good lickin'.
I'll treat you like my king
'Cause you royal
And only give my love to you
Because I'm loyal.
Escape with me.

Come over to my place.
I'll teach you a few things in love-makin'.
Now, I can't wait, I won't wait.
So take me by my arms and rock me, baby,
'Cause I'm-a always and forever be yo' lady.

CHORUS

After our first night,
You discovered who's the bombast mommy,
L.A.'s finest, with my top dogs all around me.
Down to ride, harder than Bonnie and Clyde.
We're sexual healers—do ya feel this?
Baby, check my vibe.

They'll never be a love like me
That got your back in this industry,
That got your back in these streets.
So don't you have to worry 'bout me
On the creep,
And I don't want you ever to try to
Play me cheap.

'Cause I don't sleep around
because it's sleazy.
Good lesson taught by my big homie, E–Z.
I got to compliment you on how you please me,
Touch me, but don't tease me.
Now put it in nice and easy.

And rub my body down—I'm feelin' wheezy.
And cuddle up to me
'Cause now I'm gettin' sleepy.
But I'm-a be dedicated
To this relation.
So stay away from all them cowboys
So we cannot be playa-hated.

'Cause if you wit' me, boo, then keep it real
And if I catch you sleepin' around,
Then I'm gon' have to chill.
When ya find good love,
You best to keep it.
I'm puttin' all my sista's up on game,
So why ain't ya peep it?

CHORUS

RUFF NECK
RECORDED BY MC LYTE

Words and Music by Aqil Davidson,
Markell Riley and Walter Scott

CHORUS:

Gotta what? Yo.
Gotta get a ruffneck.
Gotta what? Yo.
Gotta get a ruffneck.
Gotta what? Yo.
Gotta get a ruffneck.

I need a ruffneck.
I need a dude with attitude
Who only needs his fingers with his food.
Karl Kani saggin', Timbos draggin',
Frontin' in his ride with his homeboys braggin'.
Lyin' 'bout the Lyte—how he knocked boots last night.
But he's a ruffneck, so that's alright.
Triple-0 baldie under the hood,
Makin' noise with the boys, up to no good.
C-low on the down, low cops come around,
So ruffneck front like he gotta go.
Evil grin with a mouth full of gold teeth,
Startin' beef is how he spells "relief."
Actin' like he don't care
When all I gotta do is beep him 911 and he'll be there,
Right by my side with his ruffneck tactics,
Ruffneck attitude; the ruffneck bastard.

CHORUS (2 TIMES)

I need a ruffneck.
I need a man that's quick and swift
To put out the spliff and get stiff.
Boxer shorts and everything is fittin' large,
But he don't gotta be large to be in charge.
Pumpin' in and out and out and in and here we go.
He knows exactly how I want my flow—and that's slow.

Never questioning, can he get buck wild?
He's got smack it, lick it, swallow it up style.
Drinkin' a beer, sittin' his chair,
Hands in his pants, fiddlin' with his dick hairs.
He's a rudeboy, a rag-a-muff,
Ready to bag another brother that he ranks ruff enough
'Cause if it ain't ruff, it ain't right.
And if he ain't ruff, well then, he's all wrong for the Lyte.
I love my ruffneck and ain't nothin' goin' down
Or goin' up if my ruffneck ain't in town.

CHORUS (2 TIMES)

I need a ruffneck.
I need a man that don't stitch like a bitch.
She's tears or switch,
Doin' whatever it takes to make ends meet,
But never meetin' the end 'cause he knows the street.
Eat, sleep, shit, fuck, eat, sleep, shit,
Then it's back to the streets to make a buck, quick.
Quick to beg even though gimme got 'em here.
Hit 'em wit' a bit o' skins then he's out of there.
On the avenue, girls are passin' through.
Too much of ruffneck, so they ain't havin' you.
Hard boppin', always grabbin' his jock
And braggin' about his Tec.
That's the rep; he'll pull the plug on the tour.
Pissin' in corners,
Doin' eighty by funeral mourners,
Showin' little respect—
Now that's a ruffneck.

CHORUS (6 TIMES)

Words and Music by Eldra DeBarge, William DeBarge,
Etterlene Jordan, Aqil Davidson, Anton Lamont Hollins,
Teddy Riley, Markell Riley, David Wynn and Pharrell Williams

RUMP SHAKER
RECORDED BY WRECKX-N-EFFECT

All I wanna do is zoom-a-zoom-zoom-zoom,
And a-poom-poom, just shake ya rump!

CHORUS 1:
All I wanna do is zoom-a-zoom-zoom-zoom,
And a-poom-poom, just shake ya rump! (Rump shaker!)
All I wanna do is zoom-a-zoom-zoom-zoom,
And a-poom-poom, just shake ya rump! (Rump shaker!)
All I wanna do is zoom-a-zoom-zoom-zoom,
And a-poom-poom, just shake ya rump! (Rump shaker!)
All I wanna do is zoom-a-zoom-zoom-zoom,
And a-poom-poom, just shake ya rump! (Rump shaker!)

CHORUS 2:
Check, baby, check, baby, one, two, three, four.
Check, baby, check, baby, one, two, three.
Check, baby, check, baby, one, two.
Check, baby, check, baby, one.

[A-PLUS]
It's called the "rump shaker," the beats is like, sweeter than candy.
I'm feelin' manly and your shaker's comin' in handy.
Slide 'em across, from New York, down by your Virginia,
Ticklin' you around Delaware before I enter.
Turn to seduction from face, hips, to feet,
A-wiggle and a-jiggle can make the night complete.
Now, since you got the body of the year, come and get the award.
Here's a hint—it's like a long, sharp sword.
Flip tail, so let me see you shake it up like dice.
The way you shake your rump is turnin' mighty men to mice.
But A-Plus got a surprise that's a back-breaker.
Now let me see you shake your rump like a rump shaker.

CHORUS 1

CHORUS 2

[TEDDY RILEY]
Yup, yup, it's Teddy, ready with the one-two checker.
Wreckx-N-Effect is in effects but I'm the wrecker
Of the track, 'bout the honey-shakin' rumps and they backs in
Booties of the cuties, steady shakin', but relaxin'.
The action is packed in a jam like a closet.
Beats bound to get you up, cold-flowin' like a faucet.
Not mean to make you sit, not mean to make you jump,
But, yep, make the hotties in the party shake your rump.
I like the way you comb your hair. (Uh!)
I like the stylish clothes you wear. (Uh!)
It's just the little things you do (Uh!)
That makes me wanna get with you. (Uh!)

CHORUS 1

[MARKELL RILEY]
Shake it, shake it, shake it, now shake it!
She can spend every birthday butt-naked!
Body is soft, makin' me wanna squish her.
More than just a game, a rumper like sub-woofer.
Shake it to the left (shake it), shake it the right.
I don't mind stickin' it to her every single night.
Come on, pass the poom-poom, send it to poppa.
Shake it, baby, shake it, baby, shake it, don't stop-a.
Let me see you do the booty hop (Hop.)
And now make the booty stop.
Now drop and do the booty wop (Ooh.)
The way you shakin' your reals, will appeal,
Is makin' mils of a whole lotta bills.
But I ain't into trickin', just to treatin'
And I ain't into treatin' every trick that I'm meetin'.
(Nah, nah, nah, nah, nah, nah, nah.)
Yeah, shake it, baby, shake it, now shake it like that.

CHORUS 1

CHORUS 2 (2 TIMES)

CHORUS 1

CHORUS 2 (2 TIMES)

All I wanna do is zoom-a-zoom-zoom-zoom,
And a-poom-poom, just shake ya rump! (Rump shaker!)
All I wanna do is zoom-a-zoom-zoom-zoom,
And a-poom-poom, just shake ya rump! (Rump shaker!)

All I wanna do is zoom-a-zoom.
All I wanna do is zoom-a-zoom—just shake ya rump!
All I wanna do is zoom-a-zoom-zoom-zoom,
And a-poom-poom, just shake ya rump! (Rump shaker!)
Break it down.
Uhh, yeah, just shake ya rump.
W–N–E, uhh, yeah.
Is in effect, uhh, yeah.
Peace, peace.
And we out.

Words and Music by Sean "Puffy" Combs, Roger Greene, Kelly Price, R. Kelly,
Jeff Walker, Jay King, Denzil Foster and Thomas McElroy

SATISFY YOU
RECORDED BY PUFF DADDY, FEATURING R. KELLY

[PUFF DADDY]

All I want is somebody who's gonna love me for me—
Somebody I can love for them.
All this money don't mean shit
If you ain't got nobody to share it wit'.
Love rules the world; you feel me?

CHORUS:
[R. KELLY]

He don't understand you like I do.
No, he'll never make love to you like I do.
So, give it to me
'Cause I can show you 'bout a real love
And I can promise: anything that I do
Is just to satisfy you.

[PUFF DADDY]

When it hurt, I ease the pain, girl,
Caress your frame, get them worries off your brain, girl.
I'm in your corner; do what you want, it's your thing, girl.
Opposites attract, but we one in the same, girl.
It ain't a game, so I can't play with you.
I wanna lay with you, stay with you, pray with you,
Grow old and gray with you.
In good and bad times, we'll always make it through
'Cause what we got is true.
No matter what they say to you,
I can straight-lace you, not just appearance;
Stimulate your mind, strengthen your spirits,

Be the voice of reason when you ain't tryin' to hear it.
You want it, but you fear it; but you love it when you near it.
Sit here on the sofa, get a little closer.
Touch it right, do it like a man's suppose to.
Knew you was the one; that's why I chose ya,
'Cause you get down for yours and ride like a soldier.

CHORUS

Your soul ain't a toy; you ain't dealin' with a boy.
Feel emptiness inside? I can fill that void.
When you spend time with your woman and listen,
It shines more than any baguette diamond can glisten.
I can't impress you with the cars and the wealth
'Cause any woman with will and drive can get it herself.
I'd rather show you it's heartfelt; make your heart melt,
And prove to you you're more important than anything else,
Worthwhile, special like my first child.
When I see your face, it's always like the first time
Our eyes met—I knew we'd be together and they tried, yet
I wanna give you things that I didn't buy yet,
Hold you, mold you, drink no liquor, show you
Ain't no tellin' what we could grow to.
Let it be known, I told you
And I'm-a be there for whatever you go through.
My love's true.

CHORUS

[R. KELLY]
Don't let him sing you a sad song. (No, baby.)
Waiting for love like this too long.
(You don't have to wait; you don't have to wait on him, baby.)
All that you need, I can give you.
(You don't have to wait; you don't have to wait on.)
I do satisfy you.
(You don't have to wait on him.)

[PUFF DADDY]
I'm the light when you can't see.
I'm the air when you can't breathe.
I'm that feeling when you can't leave.
Some doubt, some believe, some lie, some cheat and deceive.
So it's only you and me.
When you weak, I'll make you strong; here's where you belong.
I ain't perfect, but I promise I won't do you wrong.
Keep away from harm, my love is protected.
I'll wrap you in my arms so you'll never feel neglected.
I'll just make you aware of what we have is rare.
In the moment of despair, I'm the courage when you're scared.
Loyal, down for you soon as I saw you.
Wanted to be there 'cause I could hold it down for you,
Be around for you, plant seeds in the soil,
Make love all night, bending bed coils.
You're a queen, therefore I treat you royal.
This is all for you 'cause I simply adore you.

CHORUS

[PUFF DADDY]
This one right here goes out to all my sisters.

Words and Music by Pharrell Williams,
Chad Hugo and Mike Tyler

SHAKE YA ASS
RECORDED BY MYSTIKAL

Mmm! Mmm, mmm, mmm.
Ooh-OOH!

Shake ya ass, but watch yourself.
Shake ya ass; show me what you workin' with.
Shake ya ass, but watch yourself.
Shake ya ass; show me what you workin' with.

I came here with my dick in my hand.
Don't make me leave here with my foot in yo' ass.
Be cool
And don't worry 'bout how I'm rippin' this shit
When I'm flippin' what I'm kickin', nigga,
That's just what I do.
I'm effervescent and I'm off that crescent.
Nastier than a full-grown German Shepherd.
Motherfucker, keep steppin'.
They don't fuck with me, and they don't.
Y'all bitches can't catch me, and you won't.
Pay ya fare, fix ya hair, throw that pussy.
Got Prada for my boo-nopolist and Debussy.
You think I'm trickin', bitch? I ain't trippin'.
I'm buyin' if you got nice curves for your iceberg.
Drinkin' Henn and actin' like it do somethin' to me.
Hope this indecent proposal make you do somethin' with me.
Fuck a dollar, girl, pick up fifty
And fuck that coward; you need a real nigga.
Off top knickerbockers hurtin' shit.
Bend over, hoe; show me what you workin' with!

Shake ya ass, but watch yourself.
Shake ya ass; show me what you workin' with.
Shake ya ass, but watch yourself.
Shake ya ass; show me what you workin' with.

CHORUS:

Attention all y'all players and pimps:
Right now, in the place to be, (Shake ya ass.)
I thought I told y'all niggaz before,
Y'all niggaz can't fuck with me. (Watch yourself.)
Now, this ain't for no small booties.
No sir, 'cause that won't pass. (Show me whatcha workin' with.)
But if you feel you got the biggest one,
Then, mama, come shake ya ass.

Shake ya ass, but watch yourself.
Shake ya ass; show me what you workin' with.
Shake ya ass, but watch yourself.
Shake ya ass; show me what you workin' with.

I like my women fire, like cayenne!
Chocolate and bowlegged, when I'm runnin' up behind her.
Go 'head, get ya pop-a-lock, let the cock out.
For, girl, don't lie; you know you wanna go back to my house.
"The Man Right Chea" wanna get under that dress right there.
You spicy Cajun, we gon' a good time over there.
You better suck the head on them there crawfish
And you gotta bend all the way over to dance off this.
Handle yo' business, but I know you do it way better;
You dead wrong.
So if you talkin' 'bout how niggaz make noise when you pass by,
Get yo' fine ass on the floor, girl, this yo' fuckin' song!
Do yo' thang; don't be scared, 'cause you gon' get served.
You get mine, then you gon' get yours.
'Bout to make yo' ass love it.
Raise it up, show the G-string; hustlin', hustlin'.

CHORUS

Shake ya ass, but watch yourself.
Shake ya ass; show me what you workin' with.
Shake ya ass, but watch yourself.
Shake ya ass; show me what you workin' with.

Stop yo' cryin', heifer; I don't need all that.
I got a job for you; the braided up pimp is back.
Break them handcuffs; fuck you, nigga, move somethin',
And if they ask you what you doin' say, "Oh, nuttin'!"
And we been doin' for the past two somethin',
And I've been beatin' that pussy up—now it's smooth fuckin'.
You can bet ya bottom dollar: if that pussy fire,
You gon' holla, "Michael Tyler!"
So don't act like you don't be backin' that stuff up,
Girl, in the club 'cause that's what you got ass for.
Wobble, wobble—I'm infatuated.
Bitch ride a dick like she makin a baby.
And I see that we gon' have to go to a quiet corner for just us two an'
Don't worry about who's lookin; just keep on doin' what you doin'.
'Cause a nigga like me gon' get to work before I know the girl.
Bitch, what's happenin'? Let 'em see, show the world!

CHORUS

Shake ya ass, but watch yourself.
Shake ya ass; show me what you workin' with.
Shake ya ass, but watch yourself.
Shake ya ass; show me what you workin' with.

Uhh! Ooh-wee! Good Lawd!
Damn!

Words and Music by
Kejuan Muchita and Albert Johnson

SHOOK ONES PT. 1
RECORDED BY MOBB DEEP

[PRODIGY]

The most violent of the violentest crimes, we give life to
If these Queens Bridge kids don't like you.
We bring drama of the worst kind of enemies.
Your first time would be your last earth memories.
It's only your own fault—
I gave you fair warning: beware
Of killa kids who don't care.
Unaware fools who be dealt with in time.
It ain't a mystery.
Hop on the words and rhyme.
In nineteen hundred and ninety square,
All shook niggaz is supposed to have fear,
Tryin' to get a piece of this pie we don't share.
Prepare for the worst 'cause I been there.
Try to keep a positive mind and walk a straight line don't work,
So niggaz is forced to do dirt.
And God made...so this jerk wouldn't hurt.

If I listen to the lessons and the rules I learnt
On the streets for nineteen years, and not leaving;
My first priority is to reach twenty-one, breathing.
Forever beef; nobody would ever be even.
So I grab the heat before breathing.
Lost in this foul mind-state, I can't keep straight-thinkin',
But I keep my eyes on the earth without blinking.
It's hard to be a man in this land of the venom.
Any man try to front, he gets slugs in him,

Because he ain't a crook, son; son, he just shook one, shook one.

CHORUS:
[PRODIGY]
We live the life: that of diamonds and guns
And numerous ways that we choose to earn funds, earn funds.
Some niggaz get shot, locked down, and turned nuns.
Cowardly hearts send straight up shook ones, shook ones.
He ain't a crook, son; he just a shook one, shook one.

[HAVOC]
For every rhyme I write,
Is twenty-five to life.
To all my peoples in the Bridge
Know what I'm talkin' 'bout, right?
Ain't no time for hesitation—
That only leads to incarceration.
You don't know me, there's no relation.

'Cause Queens niggaz don't play,
I don't got time for the "he say, she say,"
I'm bigga than dat.
Claimin' that you packin' gatts,
But you scared to get locked
Once you get upon the Island.
Change your ways and stop.
Thirteen years in the projects—my hard-times of living.
Wake up in the morning, thank God I'm still living.
Sometimes I wonder, do I deserve to live?
Or am I going to hell for all the shit I did?
No time to dwell on that
'Cause my brain reacts.
Front if you want to, nigga.
Lay on ya back.
I don't fake jacks.
Kid, you know I bring it to ya live.
Stay in a child's place, kid, you outta line.
Criminal mind, thirsty for recognition mission.
I'm strictly sippin' E&J, like, got my mind flippin'.
I'm buggin', diggin', over hustlin'.
Get that loot, kid—you know my motherfuckin' function.
'Cause as long as I'm alive, I'm-a live illegal.
And once I get it, I'm-a put it on my people.
React quick to lyrics, like Macs, I hit
Your dome up when I roll up—don't get caught sleepin',
'Cause I'm creepin'.

You just shook one.

CHORUS (2 TIMES)

Yeah.

Words and Music by Sean "Puffy" Combs,
Notorious B.I.G., Clark Kent, Bobby Caldwell,
Hubert Eaves and James Williams

SKY'S THE LIMIT
RECORDED BY NOTORIOUS B.I.G., FEATURING 112

[NOTORIOUS B.I.G.]

Good evenin', ladies and gentlemen,
How's everybody doin' tonight?
I'd like to welcome to the stage, the lyrically acclaimed, ha!
I like this young man, because, when he came out,
He came out wit' the phrase; he went from ashy to classy.
Ha! I like that.
So everybody in the house give a warm round of applause for
The Notorious B.I.G.
The Notorious B.I.G., ladies and gentlemen—give it up for him, y'all.

Uhh!
A nigga never been as broke as me, I like that
When I was young, I had two pair of Lees, besides that
The pinstripes and the gray, (Uh-huh.)
The one I wore on Mondays and Wednesdays.
While niggas flirt, I'm sewing tigers on my shirt
And alligators.
Ya wanna see the inside—huh, I see ya later.
Here come the drama—oh, that's that nigga wit' the fake, blaow!
Why you punch me in my face?
Stay in ya place,
Play ya position—here come my intuition.
Go in this nigga pocket,
Rob him while his friends watchin'.
That hoes clockin', here comes respect.
His crew's your crew, or they might be next.
Look at they man eye, B.I.G. man they never try.
So we roll wit' 'em, stole wit' 'em.
I mean loyalty—niggas bought me milks at lunch.
The milks was chocolate; the cookies, buttercrunch.
In gear—Oshkosh with blue and white ducks.
Pass the blunt.

CHORUS:

[112]

Sky is the limit, and you know that you keep on,
Just keep on pressin' on.
Sky is the limit, and you know that you can have
What you want, pressin' what you want.
Sky is the limit, and you know that you keep on,
Just keep on pressin' on.
Sky is the limit, and you know that you can have
What you want,
Be what you want,
Have what you want,
Be what you want.

[NOTORIOUS B.I.G.]

Uh-huh.
I was a shame; my crew was lame.
I have enough heart for most of 'em,
Long as I got stuff from most of 'em.
It's on, even when I was wrong I got my point across.
They depicted me the boss, of course.
My orange box-cutter make the world go 'round.
Plus I'm fuckin' bitches ain't my homegirls now.
Start stackin', dabbled in crack, gun packin',
Nickname Medina, make the seniors tote my ninas
From gym class to Englass, pass off a global.
The only nigga wit' a mobile, Can't You See like Total,
Gettin' larger in waist and taste.
Ain't no tellin' where this felon is headin', just in case—
Keep a shell at the tip of ya melon, clear da space.
Ya brain was a terrible thing ta waste.
Eighty-eight long gates, snatch initial nameplates,
Smokin' spliffs wit' niggas, real life beginner killers,
Prayin' God forgive us for bein' sinners—help us out.

CHORUS

[NOTORIOUS B.I.G.]

After realizin', to master enterprisin',
I ain't have ta be in school by ten—I was in.
Began to encounter wit' my counterparts
On how ta burn the block apart, break it down into section.

Drugs by the selection,
Some use pipes, others use injections.
Syringe sold separately, Frank the deputy
Quick to grab my Smith and Wesson, like my dick was missin'.
To protect my position, my corner, my layer
While we out here, say the hustla's prayer.
If the game shakes me or breaks me,
I hope it makes me a better man,
Take a better stand,
Put money in my mom's hand,
Get my daughter this college plan, so she don't need no man.
Stay far from timid,
Only make moves when ya heart's in it,
And live the phrase, "sky's the limit."
Motherfucker—see you chumps on top.

[112]

Sky is the limit, and you know that you keep on,
Just keep on pressin' on.
Sky is the limit, and you know that you can have
What you want, be what you want.
Sky is the limit, and you know that you keep on,
Just keep on pressin' on.
Sky is the limit, and you know that you can have
What you want, pressin' what you want.
Sky is the limit, and you know that you keep on,
Just keep on pressin' on.
Sky is the limit, and you know that you can have
What you want, be what you want.
Sky is the limit, and you know that you keep on,
Just keep on pressin' on.
Sky is the limit, and you know that you can have
What you want, be what you want.

Sky is the limit, and you know that you keep on,
Just keep on pressin' on.
Sky is the limit, and you know that you can have
What you want, be what you want.

Words and Music by Chylow Parker,
Fredo Scruggs, Kirk Jones,
Tyrone Taylor and Jason Mizell

SLAM
RECORDED BY ONYX

CHORUS:
SLAM! Duh-duh-duh, duh-duh-duh, let the boys be boys!
SLAM! Duh-duh-duh, duh-duh-duh, let the boys be boys!

Well, here's another one. (What?!)
In the gutter one. (What?!)
Getting running up.
Troublesome, extra, double-double,
I come to feed them.
The feed 'em then I shreed 'em.
So what if that I'm cheating?
Now everybody wanna sound (yeah) grimy. (Yeah!)
I'm gonna show you how come on. (All and together now!)
Yeah, oh yeah!
Yeah!
That's how we gotta be,
So stop tryin' to beat loud as me
'Cause you can't do that.
Think about the pay-offer,
So left with an automatic rifle
For last against the lightning,
Last bullets, first on line.
Toughest step and a rep and a run rep and a run wreck and a swine.
Peace to the brothers on Riker's Isle
Pumping up a trumple and didn't like his criminal

Lickin' buck my eye.
Oh my God, I'm so high.
Just they say a Rodney, say you like a criminum, what?
Just they say to make get,
Making milliangh, children slam! SLAM!

CHORUS (2 TIMES)

I'm the mean, nasty grease smashing ever slow, gashing. (Ooh.)
Sticky swift blast of the basty,
Of the basty-basty-bast bashing. (Ahh.)
Then I provide, I provide the you was cheat.
Beside the ghetto five,
Make me feel like Jekyl and Hyde, of course,
I come across with no fear.
For sure!
Unadulterated, unconfirmed,
Disgusted, busted—you wanna touch it.
Too hot! You forgot; you're not ready.
You're head could get ruptured.
Hit between the eye.
I planned the plan alive.
I'm the plonic-sonic.
Uh, rule with the bad guys.
The villain, crooks, hot Midas, in confide us.
See the big jerk put you look inside us.
My mind—it's graphic, expresstic graphic.
So kill the cop because it's kept all mastic.
Directin' it when y'all least expected it
And thought it was safe—
Onyx hit you in the face.
So—

CHORUS (2 TIMES)

I'm a b-boy
Standin' in my b-boy stance.
Hurry up and give me the microphone before I bust in my pants.
The mad author of anguish,
My language: polluted.
Onyx is heavyweight. (And still undisputed!)
He took the words right out of my mouth and walked a mile in my shoes.
I've paid so many dues; I feel used and abused,
And I'm so confused.
Umm, excuse me, for example,
I'm the inspiration for a whole generation.
And unless you got ten Sssssssssticky Fingaz,
It's straight imitation;
A figment of your imagination.
But, but, but, but wait—it gets worse!
I'm not watered down, so I'm dyin' of thirst.
Comin' through wit' a scam, a foolproof plan,
B-boys make some noise and just, just SLAM!

CHORUS (4 TIMES)

SLAM! Duh-duh-duh, duh-duh-duh, let the boys be boys!
SLAM!

Words and Music by Shawntae Harris, Melissa Elliott,
Tim Mosley, William Hart and Thom Bell

SOCK IT 2 ME
RECORDED BY MISSY "MISDEMEANOR" ELLIOT, FEATURING DA BRAT

Do it, do it, do it, do it, do it, no!

[MISSY ELLIOT]
I was lookin' for affection,
So I decided to go swing that dick in my direction.
I'll be out of control.
Let's take it to perfection.
Just you and me.
Let's see if you can bring the, bring the, bring the nasty out of me.
Now, now, now, now sock it.

CHORUS:
[MISSY ELLIOT]
Ooh, ahh, sock it to me like you want to.
I can take it like a pro, and you'll know.
Do it long, bro, with a backstroke.
My hormones are jumpin' like a disco.
I be poppin' mats like some Crisco,
And all you gotta say is that, "Missy go."
And when you say it, though, I want it moved slow.

[MISSY ELLIOT]

I'm at your house around midnight.
Don't fall asleep.
It'll just be me, me, me on a late night creep.
I'm-a show you thangs that you can't believe.
Jump in this B–E–beat.
And won't you sock it to me?

CHORUS (3 TIMES)

[DA BRAT]

Uh, why Missy be sockin' it to niggaz like Ree-Ree?
The baddest industry bitches of the century
Hit hard like penitentiary, did finally admitted
That we the shit combination on this lethal-poppin' patron
In the 600 with no see-through
Hundred with no see-through
'Cept for the repercussion fuckin' with shit.
Like this, we parlay, puffin', constantly makin' niggaz suffer
The consequences—gotta get these ends, bitch:
House on the Chi with a Caddy in Atlanta with a Benz.
Niggaz been huffin' and puffin', but ain't try shit.
Got cream, motherfuckers, steady ride quick.
Besides, kid wanna but bust you shouldn't forget ends when you fuckin'
With me; you jealous 'cause I live more flushed.
Me and Missy been livin' with the harass, been ruckused, plus
When I'm sellin', never gon' stop it, sockin' it to niggaz
And rockin' it, droppin' 'em on the spot, heat up and glock
And wreck a shot, knockin' you off of your socks.
Guaranteed platinum, watch two of the coldest bitches get hot.
I be da B–R–A–T, her be Missy
And we some bad bitches who be fuckin' it up.
I'm the B–R–A–T, her be Missy
And we some bad bitches who be fuckin' it up.

Words and Music by
Christopher Bridges and Pharrell Williams

SOUTHERN HOSPITALITY
RECORDED BY LUDACRIS

Uh, Cadillac grills, Cadillac mills.
Check out the oil on my Cadillac spills.
Matter fact, candy paint Cadillacs kill,
So check out the hoes my Cadillac fills.
Twenty-inch wide, twenty-inch high.
Oh, don't you like my twenty-inch ride?
Twenty-inch thighs make twenty-inch eyes.
Hopin' for American twenty-inch Pies.
Pretty-ass clothes, pretty-ass toes.
Oh, how I love these pretty-ass hoes.
Pretty-ass, high-class—anything goes.
Catch 'em in the club throwing pretty-ass bows.
Long john jaw, long john stalls.
Any stank puss make my long john pause.
Women on they cells makin' long-time calls.
And if they like to juggle, give 'em long john's balls.

CHORUS:
All my players in the house that can buy the bar,
And the ballin'-ass niggaz wit' the candy cars,
If you a pimp and you know you don't love them hoes,
When you get on the flo', nigga, throw them bows.
All my women in the house: if you chasin' cash,
And if you got some big titties wit' a matchin' ass,
Wit' ya fly-ass boots or ya open toes,
When ya get on the flo', nigga, throw them bows.

Dirty south mind blowin' dirty south bread.
Catfish fried up dirty south fed.
Sleep in a cot pickin' dirty south bed.
Dirty south gulls give me dirty south head.
Hand-me-down flip-flops, hand-me-down socks,
Hand-me-down drug dealers, hand-me-down rocks.

Hand me down a 50-pack Swisher Sweets box
And goodfella rich niggaz hand me down stocks.
Mouth full of platinum, mouth full of gold,
Forty glock cal' keep your mouth on hold.
Lie through your teeth, you could find your mouth cold.
Rip out ya tongue 'cause of what ya mouth told.
Sweat for the lemonade, sweat for the tea,
Sweat from the hot sauce, sweat from the D.
And you can sweat from a burn in the third degree,
And if you sweat in your sleep, then you sweat from me.

CHORUS

Hit by stars, hit by cars,
Drunk off the liquor, getting hit by bars.
Keep your girl close 'cause she's hit, by far.
Hit by the Neptunes, hit by guitars.
Afro picks, Afro chicks.
I let my soul glow from my Afro dick.
Rabbit out the hat, pullin' Afro tricks.
Afro-American, Afro thick.
Overall country, overall jeans,
Over all Georgia we overall clean.
Southern hospitality—we overall mean.
Overall triple-overall-beams.
Thugged-out niggaz wear thugged-out chains.
Thugged-out blocks playin' thugged-out games.
All black-tinted up thugged-out range.
DTP stay doin' thugged out thangs.

CHORUS (2 TIMES)

(Nigga, throw them bows.)
(Nigga, throw them bows.)
(Nigga, throw them bows.)
(Nigga, throw them bows.)

STILL D.R.E.
RECORDED BY DR. DRE, FEATURING SNOOP DOGG

Words and Music by Shawn C. Carter,
Andre Romell Young, Melvin Bradford
and Scott Spencer

[SNOOP DOGG]
Yeah, nigga, we still fuckin' wit' ya.
Still water runs deep.
Still Snoop Dogg and D–R–E. (Guess who's back?)
Still, still doin' that shit, oh, for sure.

[DR. DRE]
Oh, for sho', check me out.
It's still Dre Day, nigga, AK, nigga.
Before I chrome the lot, can't keep it home a lot
'Cause when I frequent the spots that I'm known to rock
You hear the bass from the trunk when I'm on the block.
Ladies, they pay homage, but haters say Dre fell off.
How, nigga? My last album was *The Chronic*.
They want to know if he still got it.
They say rap's changed; they want to know how I feel about it.

[SNOOP DOG]
If you ain't up on thangs.

[DR. DRE]
Dr. Dre is the name, I'm ahead of my game.
Still puffin' my leafs, still fuck with the beats.
Still not lovin' police. (Uh-huh.)
Still rock my khakis with a cuff and crease.
Still got love for the streets, reppin' 213.
Still the beat bangs, still doin' my thang.
Since I left, ain't too much changed.
Still—

CHORUS:
[SNOOP DOGG]
I'm representin' for them gangstas all across the world,
Still hittin' them corners in them low lows, girl.
[DR. DRE]
Still takin' my time to perfect the beat,
And I still got love for the streets.
It's the D–R–E.
[SNOOP DOGG]
I'm representin' for them gangstas all across the world,
Still hittin' them corners in them low lows, girl.
[DR. DRE]
Still takin' my time to perfect the beat,
And I still got love for the streets.
It's the D–R–E.

[DR. DRE]
Since the last time you heard from me, I lost a friend.
Well, hell, me and Snoop, we dippin' again.
Kept my ear to the streets, signed Eminem.
He's triple-platinum, doin' fifty a week.
Still, I stay close to the heat
And even when I was close to defeat,
I rose to my feet.
My life is like a soundtrack I wrote to the beat.
Treat my rap like Cali weed; I smoke 'til I sleep.
Wake up in the A.M., compose a beat.
I bring the fire 'til you're soakin' in your seat.
It's not a fluke—it's been tried; I'm the troop.
It's "Turn Out The Lights" from the World Class Wreckin' Crew.
I'm still at it, aftermathematic
In the home of drive-bys and AK-matics.
Swap meets, sticky green, and bad traffic,
I dip through, then I get skin, D–R–E.

CHORUS

[DR. DRE]
I ain't nothin' but more hot shit.
Another classic CD for y'all to vibe with.
Whether you're coolin' on a corner with your fly bitch,
Laid back in the shack, play this track.
I'm representin' for the gangstas all across the world.
(Still hittin' them corners in them low lows, girl.)
I'll break your neck; damn near put your face in your lap.
Try to be the king, but the ace is back.

[SNOOP DOGG]
So, if you ain't up on thangs.

[DR. DRE]
Dr. Dre is the name, still runnin' the game,
Still got it wrapped like a mummy,
Still ain't trippin'; love to see young blacks get money;
Spend time out the 'hood, take they moms out the 'hood.
Hit my boys off with jobs; no more livin' hard—
Barbeques every day, driving fancy cars.
Still gon' get mine, regardless.

CHORUS (2 TIMES)

[SNOOP DOGG]
Right back up in ya motherfuckin' ass,
Ninety-five plus four pennies.
Add that shit up, D–R–E right back on top of thangs.
Smoke some with your dog.
No stress, no seeds, no stims, no sticks!
Some of that real sticky-icky.
A little weed, put it in the air
For you's a fool, D.R.

STREET DREAMS
RECORDED BY NAS

Words and Music by Annie Lennox,
Dave Stewart, Jean Claude Olivier,
Nasir Jones and Samuel Barnes

Uhh, what, what, uhh.

CHORUS:
Street dreams are made of these.
Niggaz push Beemers and three-hundred Es.
A drug dealer's destiny is reachin' a key.
Everybody's lookin' for somethin'.
Street dreams are made of these.
Shorties on they knees, for niggaz with big Gs.
Who am I to disagree?
Everybody's lookin' for somethin'.

My man put me up for the share—one-fourth of a square.
Headed for Delaware with one change of gear.
Nothin' on my mind but the dime-sack we blazed
With the glaze in my eye, that we find when we crave
Dollars and cents, a fugitive with two attempts.
Jakes had no trace of the face, now they drew a print,
Though I'm innocent 'til proven guilty.
I'm-a try to filthy-purchase a club and start up realty,
For real, G, I'm-a fulfill my dream.
If I conceal my scheme, then precisely, I'll build my cream,
The first trip without the clique.
Sent the bitch with the quarter brick, this is it.
Fresh face, New York plates got a Crooked-I for the Jakes.
I want it all, Armor All, Benz, and endless papes.
God sake, what nigga got to do to make a half-million
Without the F.B.I. catchin' feelings?

CHORUS

From fat cat to pappy, niggaz see the cat.
Twenty-five to flat, push a thousand feet back,
Holdin' gatts wasn't makin' me fat, snitches on my back,
Livin' with moms, gettin' it on, flushin' crack down the toilet,

Two sips from bein' alcoholic,
    Nine hundred, ninety-nine thou from bein' rich, but now I'm all for it,
        My man saw it, like Dionne Warwick.
           A wiser team, for a wiser dream, we could all score with
              The cartel, Argentina coke with the niña
              Up in the hotel, smokin' on sessamina.
              Trina got the fish scale between her.
              The way the bitch shook her ass, yo, the dogs never seen her.
              She got me back livin' sweeter, fresh Caesar,
              Guess, David Robinson's, Wallé moccasins.
              Bitches blow me while hoppin' in the drop-top B–M.
              Word is bond, son, I had that bitch down on my shit like this.

CHORUS

    Growin' up project-struck, lookin' for luck, dreamin',
Scopin' the large niggaz beamin', check what I'm seein':
Cars, ghetto stars pushin' ill Europeans,
G'n heard about them old timers O.D.'n.
Young, early eighties, throwin' rocks at the crazy lady,
Worshippin' every word them rope-rockin' niggaz gave me.
The street raised me up, givin' a fuck.
I thought Jordans and a gold chain was livin' it up.
        I knew the dopes, the pushers, the addicts—everybody.
          Cut out of class just to smoke blunts and drink naughty.
          Ain't that funny? Gettin' put on to crack money,
            With all the gunplay, paintin' the kettle black, hungry,
            A case of beers in the staircase, I wasted years.
            Some niggaz went for theirs, flippin' coke as they career.
            But I'm a rebel, stressin' to pull out of the heat, no doubt,
          With Jeeps tinted out, spendin', never holdin' out.

CHORUS (2 TIMES)

Words and Music by Mark Makonie, Gary Brown,
Arnaz Blount, Henry Thomas and Lamon Turner

SUMMERTIME IN THE LBC
RECORDED BY DOVE SHACK

INTRO:

[C KNIGHT]

Yeah, this is C Knight from the Dove Shack,
Gettin' those here out,
Kickin' it a King's Park wit' all the homies.
Heh, and you know what I'm sayin',
So why don't you, uh, check out my homie, Bo to the Roc.

[BO ROC]

I ride wit' the,
I slide wit' the
Locs and dogs from the L.B.C.
All of the hoes wanna kick it wit' me
'Cause I run wit' Warren G.
Braid your weaves, bustas and Gs.
Water balloon fighters,
Low riders, and East Siders (East Siders.)
All come around (Come around.)
To hear the Dove Shack, G-funk sound.
All come around (Come around.)
To kick it in my town.
Yeah.

CHORUS:

Let me hear you say, "Ooh, aah,
Summertime in the L.B.C.
Ooh, aah,
Summertime in the L.B.C."

[ARNITA PORTER]

Now, me and my girls are deep
In a '94 Wrangler Jeep,
Flow so long through Long Beach.
Daisy Dukes get props,
Hair and nails fresh from the shop,
And we're at the bombast spot
Called "The Shack."

[2-SCOOP]

Three months of pleasure,
How can I measure
The relaxation,
All the fun I'm facin'?
My homies got green.
That's them, for show 'do,
Hit the sto' 'do,
So I can get a forty.
My lil' cousin rushin' to the park too much,
Standin' in line to get a free lunch.
Why do we do what we do when we do what we do?
Hangin' out late wit' no curfew.

CHORUS

[C KNIGHT]

Damn, it's hot than a mutha.
I'm smotherin' ribs wit' barbecue sauce.
Fools get tossed if they reach across my barbecue grill,
So continue to chill
At King's Park in the L.B.C.
That's where y'all find me,
Hangin' wit' my homies and my friends.
We got the coke in hand,
We got da Five Footaz and the Twinz,
We got Warren G and the D–O–G,
All come around
To hear the Dove Shack G-funk sound.

CHORUS

SWING MY WAY

Words and Music by
Michael O. Johnson Jr. and Javalyn N. Hall

RECORDED BY K.P. & ENVYI

Oh, yeah, oh.

CHORUS:
Shorty, swing my way.
You sure look good to me.
Now would you please swing my way.
Shorty, swing my way.

I stopped off in a club on a Friday night,
Lookin' for a man that would do me right.
First move that I made was on the dance floor,
But got down one time, then I went down for mo'.
Physical action was happenin', loud,
Saw this young playa dip through the crowd,
Looked over to my left and told my girl, "Hey."
If I see him again, I'm-a have to say,
And I'm-a have to say—

CHORUS

Swing it over here, shorty.

CHORUS

I got off the floor, tryin' to find this man,
Lookin' all around, doin' all I can.
Damn, he sure look (fine).
By the end of the night, he's gonna be (mine).
I thought to myself, he couldn't have gone far,
Then I saw him again, standing by the bar.
So far, everything is going my way,
Now that I found him, I'm-a have to say—

CHORUS

Swing it over here, shorty.

CHORUS

Got to get up the nerve to get my swerve on,
Gotta do it fast, or he'll be gone
'Cause it'll be just my luck
That somebody else will scoop him up.
Can't have that—
Wanna be the girl that
Find herself a perfect match,
Didn't wanna come off as bein' too fly.
Got contact, eye to eye,
Then I walked over to him slowly,
Said, "This might be my only shot at
A tenderoni."
He told me that "we can do this
'Cause a girl like you I can't resist."
Got straight to the point, no time to play,
Didn't need no game, just had to say—

CHORUS

Swing it over here, shorty.

CHORUS (2 TIMES)

I'll hold you tight all through the night.
Anything that you want, I'll keep it chrump.
Boy, you're gonna see how good it can be.
Just come to me.
I'll hold you tight all through the night.
Anything that you want, I'll keep it chrump.
Boy, you're gonna see how good it can be.
Just come to me.

CHORUS

Swing it over here, shorty.

CHORUS

You're lookin' good, shorty, good, sure 'nough, good enough for me.
You're lookin' good, shorty, good, sure 'nough, good enough for me.
You're lookin' good, shorty, good, sure 'nough, good enough for me.
You're lookin' good, shorty, good, sure 'nough, good enough for me.
You're lookin' good, shorty, good, sure 'nough, good enough for me.
You're lookin' good, shorty, good, sure 'nough, good enough for me.
You're lookin' good, shorty, good, sure 'nough, good enough for me.
You're lookin' good, shorty, so swing it over to me.

CHORUS

Swing it over here, shorty.

CHORUS

I've been watchin' you from across the room.
I wanna know your name.
Would ya swing my way?
Shorty, come my way, swing my way.
Oh, swing my way, swing my way.
Swing my way, shorty, oh yeah.

Words and Music by Chanelle Jones,
Reggie Noble, Erick Sermon,
Clifford Smith and Parrish Smith

SYMPHONY 2000
RECORDED BY EPMD, FEATURING LADY LUCK, METHOD MAN, AND REDMAN

[PMD]
Yeah, Erick Sermon, EPMD, check it.

[ERICK SERMON (E-DUB)]
Redman, Method Man, Lady Luck, Def Jam.

[PMD]
Erick and Parrish Millennium Ducats.
Hold me down, hold me down.
Uhh, yo!
I grab the mic and grip it hard like it's my last time to shine.
I want the chrome and the cream, so I put it down for mine.
Ill cat, slick talk, slang New York,
To break it down to straight English, what the fuck you want?
Remember me? You punk, faggot, crab MC.
Get your shit broke in half for fuckin' around with P.
Aiyyo, strike two, my style: Brooklyn like the Zoo.
Hey you, look, nigga, one more strike, you through.
Word is b-id-ond, rock Esco, FUBU, and Phat F-id-arm.
Every time I get my spit on, no doubt, I spark the gridiron.
I step up and bless the track and spit a jewel.
We keep cool, no need for static, I strap tools.
Next up!

[ERICK SERMON (E-DUB)]
Yo, I believe that's me.

[PMD]
Yo, get on the mic and rock the Symphony.

[ERICK SERMON (E-DUB)]
Yo, P!
Time to rock, the sound I got, it reigns hot.
Makin' necks snap back, like a slingshot.
E hustle, and muscle my way in
Then tussle for days in, on my own with guns blazin'.
Not for the fun of it, just for those who want me to run it,
Then leave them like—who done it?
Sucka duck, I do what I feel right now,
When I spit the illest shit, cats be like, "Wow!"
Yo! I get looks when I'm in the place.
That's that nigga, makin' you "Smile" with Scarface.
Uhh, "It Ain't My Fault," that my stile Silkk enough to Shock ya,
Hit you with the fifth, block-a, block-a.
If I get caught, you can bet I'll blow trial.
Be "Downtown Swingin'," M.O.P. style.
Next up!

[REDMAN]
Yo, yo, it's Funk D–O–C.

[ERICK SERMON (E-DUB)]
Yo, you're on the mic to rock the Symphony.

[REDMAN]
Hehah! Yo! Yo!
Did you ever think you would catch a cap?
Yo, did you ever think you would get a slap?
Yo, did you ever think you would get robbed
At gunpoint, stripped, and thrown out the car?

It's Funk Doc, you know my name, hoe.
My style, dirty, underground, or Ukraine po'.
When it hits you, pain pumps Kool-Aid through the vein and shit.
Snatch the trap, then I "Dash" like Damon did.
Doc, walk "Thin Red Lines" to shell shock,
Hair-lock with fuckin' broads in nail shops.
Hydro? Got more bags than bellhops,
Two thousand Benz on my eight-by-ten picture.
Papichu slayin' crews in I.C.U.,
Battlin', usin' hockey riles
For Keith Murray, Doc gon' cock these tools.
Rollin' down like dice in Yahtzee, fool!
I "Just Do It" like Nike, outta 'Bama
With ten kids with hammers, hooked to a camper!
Yo! Next up!

[METHOD MAN]
It's the G–O–D.

[REDMAN]
Yo, yo, get on the mic for the Symphony.

[METHOD MAN]
Youth on the move, payin' them dues, nuttin' to lose.
Huh, street kids, broken and bruised, eyein' yo' jewels.
Huh, bad news, barin' they souls through rhythm 'n' blues.
"Hardcore," to make them brothers act, fool,
Hands on the steel, flip you heads over heel.
Smell the daffodils from the lyric overkill,
Feelin' like the mack inside a Cadillac Seville.
Too ill, on cuts, the *Barber of Seville*, *Figaro*.
The sky is fallin, Geronimo!
I feel my high comin' down—look out below!
Aiyyo! Dead that roach clip and spark another.
Chicken hawks playin' themselves like Parker Brothers.
I rock for the low-class, from low cash,
The broke-assed, even rock for the trailer park trash.

Yeah, yeah, the God on your block like Godzilla.
Yeah, yeah, she gave away my pussy, I'm-a kill her.
John-John phenomenon, in Japan they call me Ichiban.
Wu-Tang Clan, number one!
In the whole none, I hold mine.
Keep playin' with it, kid, you might go blind—jerk off!
Fuck them A.K.A.—for now it's just Meth.
That's it, that's all, solo, single no more or less.

[ALL]
Next up!

[LADY LUCK]
I believe that's me.

[ALL]
Bastard!

[PMD]
Get on the mic and rock the Symphony.

[LADY LUCK]
Missus Stop, Drop, and Roll, rocks top the told,
Hot, even though dames is froze.
Pop close range at foes, and blaze them hoes.
Leave 'em with they brains exposed and stains on clothes.
Y'all better change your flows, hear how Luck spittin'?
Stay drunk-pissed in the S-type, stay whippin'.
When the guns spittin', duck or get hittin'.
It's written, we in the game, but ball different.
Point game like Jordan, y'all play the role of Pippen.
Stay switchin', like tight-ass after stickin'.
Man, listen, stop your cryin' and your bitchin'.
Like E and P's last CD, you're out of business.

Words and Music by
Todd Thomas and Tarre Jones

TENNESSEE

RECORDED BY ARRESTED DEVELOPMENT

Lord, I've really been real stressed,
Down and out, losin' ground.
Although I am black and proud,
Problems got me pessimistic.
Brothers and sisters keep messin' up.
Why does it have to be so damn tough?
I don't know where I can go
To let these ghosts out of my skull.
My grandma's passed, my brother's gone.
I never at once felt so alone.
I know you're supposed to be my steering wheel,
Not just my spare tire. (Home.)
But Lord, I ask you (Home.)
To be my guiding force and truth. (Home.)
For some strange reason, it had to be. (Home.)
He guided me to Tennessee. (Home.)

CHORUS:
Take me to another place.
Take me to another land.
Make me forget all that hurts me.
Let me understand your plan.

Lord, it's obvious we got a relationship,
Talkin' to each other every night and day.
Although you're superior over me,
We talk to each other in a friendship way.

Then outta nowhere, you tell me to break
Outta the country and into more country,
Past Dyesburg, into Ripley,
Where the ghost of childhood haunts me.
Walk the roads my forefathers walked,
Climbed the trees my forefathers hung from.
Ask those trees for all their wisdom.
They tell me my ears are so young. (Home.)
Go back to from whence you came. (Home.)
My family tree, my family name. (Home.)
For some strange reason, it had to be. (Home.)
He guided me to Tennessee. (Home.)

CHORUS

Now I see the importance of history,
Why people be in the mess that they be.
Many journeys to freedom made in vain
By brothers on the corner playin' ghetto games.
I ask you, Lord, why you enlightened me
Without the enlightenment of all my folks.
He said 'cause I set myself on a quest for truth
And He was there to quench my thirst.
But I am still thirsty—
The Lord allowed me to drink some more.
He said what I am searchin' for are
The answers to all which are in front of me;
The ultimate truth started to get blurry.
For some strange reason, it had to be.
It was all a dream about Tennessee.

CHORUS

Words and Music by O'Kelly Isley, Ronald Isley,
Rudolph Isley, Ernie Isley, Marvin Isley,
Chris Jasper, Bone, DJ U-Neek and Tony C

THA CROSSROADS
RECORDED BY
BONE THUGS-N-HARMONY

Bone, Bone, Bone, Bone, Bone, Bone, Bone, Bone, Bone.
Now tell me whatcha gonna do (Now tell me what.)
When there ain't nowhere to run,
When judgment comes for you,
When judgment comes for you?
Now tell me whatcha gonna do (Now tell me what.)
When there ain't nowhere to hide,
When judgment comes for you?
'Cause it's gonna come for you.

Head south, this song's for Wally, Eazy, C's uncle Charlie, Little Boo.
God's got 'em, and I'm gonna miss everybody I done roll with.
Flow's my game; looked at him while he lay.
When playin' with destiny, play too deep for me to say.
Little Layzie came to me, told me,
If he should decease, well then, please bury
Me by my gran-gran and when you can; come follow me.

[LAYZIE BONE]
God bless you; workin' on a plan to heaven,
Follow the Lord all twenty-four-seven
Days; God is who we praise,
Even though the devil's all up in my face.
But He's keepin' me safe and in my place.
Say grace to engage the race
Without a chance to face the Judge,
Sayin' again my soul won't budge.
Grudge because there's no mercy for thugs.
Oh, what can I do? It's all about a family and how we roll.
Can I get a witness? Let it unfold.
Livin' our lives to eternal our souls, a-oh, a-oh.

[KRAYZIE BONE]

Hey, and we pray, and we pray, and we pray, and we pray
Every day, every day, every day, every day.
And we pray, and we pray, and we pray, and we pray.
Still we lay.

Now follow me, roll, stroll.
Whether it's hell or it's heaven, come, let us go
Take a visit to the people that's long gone—they rest.
Wally, Eazy, Terry, Boo.
It's steady creepin' up on my family.
Exactly how many days we got lastin'?
While you laughin', we're passin', passin' away.
Now y'all rest, y'all souls,
'Cause I know I'm-a meet you up at Tha Crossroad.
Y'all know ya forever got love from them Bone Thugs, baby.

[WISH BONE]

Little Eazy's long gone.
Really wish he could come home,
But when it's time to die, gotta go bye-bye.
All a little thug could do is cry, cry.
Why's they kill my dog?
Damn, man, I miss my Uncle Charles, y'all.
And he shouldn't be gone in front of his home.
What they did to Boo was wrong,
Oh, so wrong—killin' so wrong.
Gotta hold on, gotta stay strong.
When the day comes, better believe
Bone got a shoulder you can lean on.

Hey, and we pray, and we pray, and we pray, and we pray
Every day, every day, every day, every day.
And we pray, and we pray, and we pray, and we pray
Every day, every day, every day, every day.

See you at Tha Crossroads. (Crossroads, Crossroads, Crossroads.)
So you won't be lonely.
See you at Tha Crossroads. (Crossroads, Crossroads, Crossroads.)
So you won't be lonely.

See you at Tha Crossroads. (Crossroads, Crossroads, Crossroads.)
So you won't be lonely.
See you at Tha Crossroads. (Crossroads, Crossroads, Crossroads.)
So you won't be lonely.

[BIZZY BONE]
And I'm gonna miss everybody.
And I'm gonna miss everybody. (Long gone, long gone.)
And I'm gonna miss everybody.
And I'm gonna miss everybody.
And I'm gonna miss everybody. (Long gone, long gone.)
And I'm gonna miss everybody.

[LAYZIE BONE]
Livin' in a hateful world.
Send me straight to heaven; that's how we roll.
Livin' in a hateful world.
Send me straight to heaven; that's how we roll.
Livin' in a hateful world.
Send me straight to heaven; that's how we roll.
And I'm askin' the good Lord, "Why?" and sigh.
He told me we lived to die.

[KRAYZIE BONE]
What's up with that murder, y'all?
See my little cousin was hung; somebody really wrong.
Everybody want to test this dog,
And Miz Sleazy set up Eazy to fall.
You know why we sinnin'?
And Krayzie intendin' on endin' it when it ends.
Murder come again, again, and again.
Now tell me, whatcha gonna do?

[WISH BONE]
Can somebody, anybody, tell me why, hey?
Can somebody, anybody, tell me why we die, we die?
I don't wanna die.
Oh, so wrong, oh, wrong.

See you at Tha Crossroads. (Crossroads, Crossroads, Crossroads.)
So you won't be lonely.

Words and Music by
Andre Weston and Willie Hines

THEY WANT EFX
RECORDED BY DAS EFX

Bum-stiggidy, bum-stiggidy-bum, hon.
I got the old pa-rum-pum-pum-pum.
But I can fe-fi-fo-fum, diddly-bum—here I come.
So Peter Piper, I'm hyper than Pinocchio's nose.
I'm Supercalifragilistic, tic-tac pro.
I gave my oopsy-daisy, now you've got the crazy.
Crazy with the books, googley-goo, where's the gravy?
So one, two, unbuckle my, um, shoe.
Yabba-doo, hippity-hoo, crack a brew.
So trick or treat, smell my feet; yup, I drippedy-dropped a hit.
So books, get on your make and spark that old censorship.
Drats and double-drats, I smiggidy-smacked some whiz kids.
The boogidy-woogidly Brooklyn boy's about to get his dig.
My waist bone's connected to my hip bone.
My hip bone's connected to my thigh bone.
My thigh bone's connected to my knee bone.
My knee bone's connected to my hardy-har-har-har.
The jibbidy-jabber jaw ja-jabbing at your funny bone,
Um, skip the Ovaltine, I'd rather have a Honeycomb.
Or preferably the sesame; let's spriggidy-spark the blunts.
Um, dun-dun-dun-dun-dun, dun-dun.

CHORUS:
They want EFX, some live EFX.
They want EFX, some live EFX.
They want EFX, some live EFX.
Snap a neck for some live EFX.

Well, I'll be darned, shiver me timbers, yo, head for the hills.
I picked a weeping willow and a daffodil.
So back up, bucko, or I'll pulverize McGruff
'Cause this little piggy gets busy and stuff.
Arrivederci, heavens to mercy, honky-tonk, I get swift.
I caught a snuffalupagus and smoked a boogaloo spliff.

I got the nooks, the crannies, the nitty-gritty, fodey-do.
All aboard, cast away, hey, where's my boogaloo?
Oh, I'm streaming agony.
Why's everybody always picking on me?
They call me Puddin' Tane, and rap's my game.
You ask me again and I'll t-tell you the same
'Cause I'm the vulgar vegemintarian, so stick 'em up—freeze!
So no Park sausages, Mom, please.
A blitz shoots the breeze, twiddly-dee shoots his lip.
Crazy-dazy, shot the sheriff; yup, and I got the gift.
And that's pretty sneaky, sis; oh yep.
I got my socks off, my rocks off, my Nestle's cup of cocoa.
Holly Hobby tried to slob me, tried to rob me—silly stunt.
Diggidy-dun-dun-dun-dun-dun, dun-dun.

CHORUS

Yahoo, hidee-ho, yup, I'm comin' around the stretch.
So here, Fido boy; fetch, boy, fetch.
I got the rope-a-dope, a slippery choker; look at me get raw
And I'm the hickory-dickory, top-of-the-morning, boogaloo big jaw
With the yippidy-zippidy, Winnie the Pooh, bad boy blue.
Yo, crazy got the gusto; what up? I swing that, too.
So nincompoop, give a hoot, and stomp a troop without a strain
Like Roscoe B. Coltrane.
I spriggidy-spark a spliff and give a twist like Chubby Checker.
I take my Froot Loops with two scoops—make it a double-decker.
Oh Vince, the baby come to Papa Duke.
A babaloo, ooh, a babaloo boogidy-boo.
I went from Gucci to Stussy, to fliggidy-flam, a groupie,
To Zsa Zsa, to yibbidy-yabba-dabba-hoochie-koochie.
Tally ho, I-I'll take my Stove Top instead of potatoes, so—
Maybe I'll shoot 'em now; nope, maybe I'll shoot 'em later, yep.
I used to have a dog and Bingo was his name-o, so uh,
B–I–N–G–O, oh.
You do the hokey-pokey and your turn yourself around, hon, so uh,
Dun-dun-dun-dun-dun, dun-dun.

CHORUS

Words and Music by Nile Rodgers, Andrew Hale,
Leroy Osbourne, Stuart Matthewman, Bernard Edwards,
Lawrence Parker and Joey Longo

13 AND GOOD
RECORDED BY
BOOGIE DOWN PRODUCTIONS

I walked in the place—very big space.
Every kind of race dancin' and niggaz made chase.
A very pretty face; feel the bass.
Basses kick, flygirl jumps on my tip.
The drink that I sip implies this is it.
She looked to be about twenty-six; I ain't dizzy.
It's time to get busy!
Welcome female is in my arms,
Overwhelmed by my playboy charms.
We jumped in the ride; rushed to the crib.
I ain't gotta explain what we did.
Built to last, I simply waxed that.
Aks the question, no need for guessin'.
Hey, baby, how old are you—
Twenty-one, twenty-four, maybe twenty-two?
I'm twenty-five.
She shucked and kinda neeghed
And said, "Hee, hee, hee, I'm only thirteen."
Thirteen! I need a quick escape.
That's statutory rape.
But she was GOOD!

CHORUS:
GOOD!
(You should' been there—she was.)
GOOD!
(Man, that jail term won't be.)
GOOD!
(But she looked—)
GOOD!
(Man, her brothers will beat you.)
GOOD!
(Even if I get beat down, it was still—)
GOOD!

The story gets better: this girl is kinda clever.
She said, "I wanna be with you forever."
I said, "Forget it; I need to get my life in order.
You could almost be my daughter."
She started sighin' and her sighin' turns to cryin'.
Her cryin' turns into her replyin':
"Where's the phone? I think it's time that I went home."
She called her pops and said, "Come get me, I'm all alone.
I'm sorry, Daddy, I slept with an older man."
He said, "Don't worry; the 45 is in my hand.
I'll be there before you count to four."
One, two, three, four—
He's at my door.
She said, "See what you did? You caused me all this grief.
You're goin' to jail—my daddy's a police chief.
If I can't have you, no one will.
And I ain't even on the pill."
But you was—

CHORUS (6 TIMES)

Daddy walked in, and the whole scene kinda changed.
He grabbed his daughter, and he almost beat the girl insane.
She's cryin' down the hall, and now goin' home.
He closed the door and said, "I'm happy we're alone.
Jump on the bed and look me straight into my eyes.
I think you're kinda cute—don't make me use my 45."
Daddy's lookin' for a lubricant;
He pulled out a little piece of gum and started chewin' it.
He said, "For a year I've been lookin' for a big, strong man.
I've got an apartment out in Brooklyn;
Only my daughter and I live there.
You can see my daughter anytime, anywhere,
But it's you that I want to be mine.
The price tag is your behind.
Don't worry; it'll be—

CHORUS

GOOD!

The moral of this story?
There is no moral; you finish the story for me.
When you're livin' your life every day in the 'hood,
Wakin' up in the mornin' should feel—

GOOD!

Words and Music by Chylow Parker,
Fredo Scruggs, Kirk Jones and Tyrone Taylor

THROW YA GUNZ
RECORDED BY ONYX

Take 'em out, take 'em out, bring 'em out dead.
Shine 'em up, shine 'em up, shine the bald head.
One gun, two gun, three gun, four.
You're mine; it's all about crime.
Onyx!

It's time to get live, live, live like a wire.
I set a whole choir on fire. (Uhh!)
Well-done on the grill, shot skills kills and no frills.
They try to diss me? They gettin' crispy.
Ha, ha, hah, hah, and we do it like this.
In fact, mack Mack and jack Jack
'Cause they can burn in hell shit for all that I care.
Beware the bald head, the dread said is they fear.
Stick-up's assassin, traction, new reaction.
These fuckin' niggaz shoulda made the All-Madden.
Onyx is wreckin' shit, slip, slide, step quick.
Infinite that gets crashed like a rented.
The shit they write is black and white; well, mine's got mad color.
Ain't that right, my blood brother?
Word up, raise it up!
We do it with the crew that don't give a fuck.

So throw ya gunz in the air, throw ya gunz in the air.
Buck, buck like you don't care.

Uh-oh! Heads up, 'cause we're droppin' some shit
On your now-shot skills; Onyx Tec-9 for awhile.
Keep your eyes open in the fight—I'm-a swell 'em.
The hardcore style, rowdy an' wild; hits, I'm-a sell 'em. (Sell 'em.)
To all competition, slide back, then listen.
I'm kickin' all that shit to the doormat,
Claimin' this domain, cause mad pains,
Blood stains; long range—got gatts!
Crazy clips, I sink ships, cuttin' faces like a pirate.

I've never caught a flood for the mad shit that I did.
Heard you got the word, so observe.
I shatter and splatter bodies that blows and bust nerds open!
I always leave my barrel smokin'.

CHORUS:

Throw ya gunz in the air
And buck, buck like you just don't care.
Just throw ya gunz in the air
And buck, buck like you just don't care.
Just throw ya gunz in the air
And buck, buck like you just don't care.
Just throw ya gunz in the air
And buck, buck like you just don't care.

Ah, I hate your fuckin' guts and I hope that you die.
Sticky Fingaz the name, and my life is a lie
'Cause I'm havin' a bad day, so stay out of my way.
And what the pistol-packin' people say, you better obey.
Just in the nick of time, I commit the perfect crime.
Rip my heart from my chest, put it right into a rhyme. (Yeah!)
I don't feel pain 'cause it's all in the mind,
And what's mine is mine's and yours is mine.
Don't fuckin' blink or I'm-a rob yo' ass blind.
Onyx is rippin' shit, I got the Tec-9.
So what the plumber got, boy, buck, buck, buck, buck.
It's like a catastrophe, fuckin' with me, G.
I'm a bald head with a knife.
I want your money or your life.
So, so, so, so?

CHORUS

We the motherfuckin' Onyx!
And we don't give a flying, motherfuckin' fuck.
Aiyyo, DS, man, we gonna come get you out of jail, man.
Fuck that, yo, DS, we comin' man; we got the bail.
We got the bail; we gonna break you out, man.
Fuck that, yeah!
We the fuck up out of this place.

Words and Music by Jermaine Dupri,
Betty Wright, Willie Clarke, Keith Harrison, Tyrone Crum,
Ralph Aikens, Roger Parker, Robert Neal and Clarence Satchell

TONITE'S THA NIGHT

RECORDED BY KRIS KROSS

Shhhhhhhhhh.
Kris Kross, nine to five.
Yeah.
Who gotcha open, scopin' out tha track?
It's no other than the sounds of the Daddy Mac,
Still slackin', back-packin' up my turf
'Cause after me was a factor real worse at the worst:
Stompin', jumpin' wanna-bes.
But ever, however, there's only one M–A–C. (Say what?)
Me and Daddy for the big picture.
Ways of gettin' richer, mister quick to hit your sister.

I'm rollin' in the Green County, all chrome.
I sling brothers on the deck on my cellular phone.
I'm just loungin', leather, sound all around
And a dip on the other and wanna put me down.
Now, no hesitation, I hops to it.
See, it ain't easy bein' a Mac but somebody gotta do it.
True, it's usually not represented right,
But I'm the M–A–C–D–A–double-D–Y, and tonight's tha night.

CHORUS:
Please, my whole crew makes Gs.
Tonight's tha night, baby, so blow up on these.
Tonight, tonight's tha night.
Please, my whole crew makes Gs.
Tonight's tha night, baby, so blow up on these.
Tonight, tonight's tha night.

Tonight's tha night I call up all the girls
I used to go to school with, fool with,
And all the niggaz that I'm cool with.
Let 'em all know that my mom is gone
And it will be tomorrow before she comes back home.

Ding-dong, it's on; Nigga, say no more.
I'm with a truck full of women, so just open the door,
'Cause, yo, we came here to party.
Gitty crunk, get drunk, and leave your house with somebody.
True that some homies don't bring your main misses
'Cause it's real deal mackin' when it comes to the Chris's.
And this could be your very last time seein' her.
One look at me and you better believe that I be ge'in her.

So come along or don't come at all. (Why?)
'Cause it's real big pimpin' at this playa's ball.
True, it's usually not represented right,
But with me it's all to the G, and tonight's tha night.

CHORUS (2 TIMES)

Words and Music by Kirk Burrell, Louis Burrell,
James Earley, Michael Kelly and Felton Pilate

TOO LEGIT TO QUIT
RECORDED BY MC HAMMER

Too legit (ba ba), too legit to quit.
Too legit (ba ba), too legit to quit.
Too legit (ba ba), too legit to quit.

Sweat runnin' all over my chest (chest).
I don't quit, no I just press harder (yeah)
Than I ever did before.
Goin' for the dreams that I have in store,
In my mind (mind).
Then I know that I'm makin' it.
I gotta get mine and nobody's takin' it away (no)
'Cause Hammer don't play that.
You tryin' to get mine, boy, you'd better step back.
Freeze (freeze)
'Cause you don't want none.
I hustle for my muscle and you look weak to me, yeah.
I'm goin' for all that I can get,
Takin' it to the top
'Cause I'm too legit to quit.
Say—

CHORUS:
Too legit, too legit to quit (hey, hey).
Too legit, too legit to quit (hey, hey).
Too legit, too legit to quit (too legit).
Too legit, too legit to quit.

When I feel hot force, don't you play me close.
A day comes back, I'll get you back
And now I hit you with a dose of old-town power
And charge you by the hour.
I'm shakin', like-a quakin', punks gettin' devoured.
I choose to abuse it, to use and confuse.
Competitors who'll think that they're makin' up all the rules.
Fools in the game, lame and insane.
It's a shame I gotta do it, but I remain the same.
Unchanged, gettin' better, never known as a sweater,
Bein' on top because I got myself together.
So roll with a guy who's physical and fit, knows the times
And too legit to quit.

CHORUS (2 TIMES)

Step to the rhythm of a sure-enough woman,
When I've been here before, yo, I ain't no beginner.
Well, I've been new, tried and true,
Survival ought to finish you.
It brought me through.
My crew talk, we're ready to strike.
Trained for the music,
So believe the hype and sweat it (sweat it)
'Cause you're gonna regret it:
The day that you dissed her
She'll wish you never met her.
You remind me of a real short story:
One hit record (one record) and you start to bore me.
Get ready, 'cause this is it.
Your crew is through and we're too legit to quit.

CHORUS (2 TIMES)

Keep on, keep on,
Keep on, keep on, keep on.
Keep on, keep on,
Keep on, keep on, keep on.
Keep on, keep on,
Keep on, keep on, keep on.
Keep on, keep on,
Keep on, keep on, keep on.

My ego, we don't know the beat.
We crush the strong and percolate the weak.
Daily (every day) we make our move to improve our groove
'Cause we love to rule, but we play, yo (yo), lock of play.
We started at the bottom, now we'll lead the way
And yey (yey), I'm havin' a fit,
Kickin' at the top 'cause I'm too legit to quit.
Say, hey, hey—

CHORUS

Words and Music by Rick James,
Alonzo Miller and MC Hammer

U CAN'T TOUCH THIS
RECORDED BY MC HAMMER

You can't touch this.
You can't touch this.
You can't touch this.
You can't touch this.
You can't touch this.

My, my, my music hits me so hard,
Makes me say, "Oh, my Lord,
Thank you for blessing me
With a mind to rhyme and two hype feet."
It feels good, when you know you're down.
A super-dope homeboy from the Oaktown.
And I'm known as such,
And this is a beat, uh, you can't touch.

I told you, homeboy (you can't touch this).
Yeah, that's how we living and you know (you can't touch this).
Look at my eyes, man, (you can't touch this).
Yo, let me bust the funky lyrics. (You can't touch this.)

Fresh new kicks, advance,
You gotta like that, now you know you wanna dance.
So move, outta your seat
And get a fly girl and catch this beat
While it's rolling, hold on,
Pump a little bit and let 'em know it's going on,
Like that, like that.
Cold on a mission, so fall them back,
Let 'em know that you're too much
And this is a beat, uh, you can't touch.

Yo, I told you (you can't touch this).
Why you standing there, man? (You can't touch this.)
Yo, sound the bell, school is in, sucka. (You can't touch this.)

Give me a song, or rhythm.
Make 'em sweat, that's what I'm giving 'em.
Now they know,
You talking about the Hammer, you talking about a show
That's hype, and tight.
Singers are sweating, so pass them a wipe
Or a tape to learn
What's it gonna take in the nineties to burn
The charts? Legit.
Either work hard or you might as well quit.
That's the word because you know—

You can't touch this.
You can't touch this.
You can't touch this.

Break it down!
Stop, Hammer time!

Go with the funk, it is said
That you can't groove to this, then you probably are dead.
So wave your hands in the air,
Bust a few moves, run your fingers through your hair.
This is it, for a winner,
Dance to this and you're gonna get thinner.
Move, slide your rump
Just for a minute, let's all do the bump, bump, bump.

Yeah, (You can't touch this.)
Look, man. (You can't touch this.)
You better get hype, boy, because you know (you can't touch this).
Ring the bell, school's back in. (You can't touch this.)

Break it down!
Stop, Hammer time!

You can't touch this.
You can't touch this.
You can't touch this.
You can't touch this.

Break it down!
Stop, Hammer time!

Every time you see me,
The Hammer's just so hype.
I'm dope on the floor and I'm magic on the mic.
Now why would I ever stop doin' this
With others makin' records that just don't hit?
I've toured around the world, from London to the Bay.
It's "Hammer, go Hammer, MC Hammer, yo, Hammer!"
And the rest can go and play.

You can't touch this.
You can't touch this.
You can't touch this.
You can't touch this.
You can't touch this.
You can't touch this.
You can't touch this.
You can't touch this.

VICTORY
RECORDED BY PUFF DADDY, FEATURING NOTORIOUS B.I.G. AND BUSTA RHYMES

Words and Music by Sean "Puffy" Combs,
Notorious B.I.G., Jason Phillips,
Bill Conti and Steven Jordan

[NOTORIOUS B.I.G.]
One, one, two.
Check me out, right here, yo.

[PUFF DADDY] Yo, the sun don't shine forever.
[B.I.G.] You can turn the track up a little bit for me.
[PUFF] But as long as it's here, then we might as well shine together.
[B.I.G.] All up in my ears.
[PUFF] Better now than never, business before pleasure.
[B.I.G.] The mic is loud, but the beats isn't loud.
[PUFF] P. Diddy and the Fam, who you know do it better?
Yeah, right, no matter what, we airtight.
[B.I.G.] Yeah!
[PUFF] So when you hear somethin', make sure you hear it right.
Don't make a' ass outta yourself by assumin'.
[B.I.G.] Yeah! Now the mic is lower; turn the mics up.
[PUFF] Our music keeps you movin'; what are you provin'?
[B.I.G.] Turn that shit all the way up, yeah!
[PUFF] You know that I'm two levels above you, baby.
[B.I.G.] Music's gettin' louder.
[PUFF] Hug me, baby; I'm-a make you love me, baby.
[B.I.G.] This shit is hot!
[PUFF] Talkin' crazy ain't gonna get you nuthin' but choked.
[B.I.G.] Uh-huh, uh-huh, uh-huh.
[PUFF] And that jealousy is only gonna leave you broke.
So, the only thing left now is God for these cats.
And, Big, you know, you too hard for these cats.
I'm-a win 'cause I'm too smart for these cats.
While they makin' up facts (uhh), you rakin' up plats.

[NOTORIOUS B.I.G.]

In the Commission, you ask for permission to hit 'em.

He don't like me; him and wild wifey was wit' 'em.

You heard of us: the murderers most shady.

Been on the low lately, the feds hate me.

The son of Satan, they say my killing's too blatant.

You hesitatin', I'm in your mama crib, waitin'.

Duct tapin', your Fam destiny lays in my hands; gatt lays in my waist.

Francis, M to the iz–H phenomenal.

Gun rest under your vest by the abdominal.

Rhyme a few bars so I can buy a few cars

And I kick a few flows so I can pimp a few hoes.

Excellence is my presence, never tense,

Never hesitant; leave a nigga bent real quick.

Real sick, brawl nights, I perform like Mike.

Anyone—Tyson, Jordan, Jackson,

Action, pack guns; ridiculous.

And I'm quick to bust if my ends you touch.

Kids or girl you touch, in this world I clutch

Two auto-matoes; used to call me fatso,

Now you call me Castro; my rap flows

Militant, y'all faggots ain't killin shit.

Oops, Cristal keep spillin'; shit, you overdid it, homes.

You in the danger zone—you shouldn't be alone.

Hold hands and say it like me,

The most shady, Frankie baby, fantastic,

Graphic, tryin' to make dough like Jurassic

Park did quick to spark kids who start shit.

See me, only me;

The underboss of this holocaust.

Truly yours, Frank White.

CHORUS:
[BUSTA RHYMES]
We got the real, live shit from front to back.
To my people in the world—where the fuck you at?
Where my niggaz at?
Where my niggaz at?
Where the fuck my bitches at?
Where my bitches at?
We got the real, live shit from front to back.
To my people in the world—where the fuck you at?
Where my niggaz at?
Where my niggaz at?
Where the fuck my bitches at?
Where my bitches at?

[PUFF DADDY]
Put your money on the table and get your math on.
Break it down, split it up, get your laugh on.
See you later, dog, I'm-a get my stash on.
There's a bed full of money that I get my ass on.
I never lose the passion to go platinum.
Said, I'd live it up 'til all the cash gone.
Ain't that funny? Only use plastic, craft it
To make classics hotter than acid.
P–D rollin' on your tape or CD.
The girl-boy killa, no team illa.
The Fam-o, ammo, is every channel.
We been hot for a long time, burnin' like a candle.
What you can do is check your distribution.
My songs bump in Houston like Scarface produced 'em.
You ain't gotta like me; you just mad
'Cause I tell it how it is, and you tell it how it might be.

[NOTORIOUS B.I.G.]

We got the shit, Mac tight, brass knuckles and flashlights.

The heaters in the two-seaters with two Midas,

Señoritas kiss rings when you meet us.

P. Diddy run the city, show no pity.

I'm the witty one, Frank's the crook from the Brook'.

Matty broke the neck of your coke connect.

No respect, squeeze off 'til all y'all diminish.

Shootouts for twenty minutes—until we finish.

Venice took the loot, escaped in the Coupe.

Break bread with the Kiss, Peniro, Sheek Louch.

Black Rob joined the mob; it ain't no replacin' him.

Niggaz step up, with just Mase and 'em

Placin' them in funerals, criminals turned aroused.

The Brick City, nobody came off like P. Diddy.

Business-wise, I play men,

Hide money on the Island Cayman, y'all; just betray men.

You screamin', I position competition.

'Nother day in the live of the Commission.

CHORUS (2 TIMES)

[PUFF DADDY]

Aiyyo, can you hear me out there?

Aiyyo, turn me up, nobody can hear me out there.

That's good; it's all fucked-up now.

Y'all know it's all fucked-up now, right?

What the fuck I'm-a do now?

What I'm-a do now?

Can y'all hear me out there?

Can y'all hear me out there?

Fuck y'all niggaz wanna do?

It's all fucked-up now.

What I'm-a do now, huh?

What I'm-a do now?

It's all fucked-up now.

Words and Music by
Steven Tyler and Joe Perry

WALK THIS WAY
RECORDED BY RUN-DMC, FEATURING AEROSMITH

[RUN-DMC]

Now there's a backseat/lover
That's always under/cover,
And I talk 'til my daddy say:
Said, you ain't seen/nothin'
'Til you're down on her/muffin,
And there's sure to be a change in ways.
Now there's a cheer/leader
That's a real big/pleaser
As far as I can remi/nisce.
But the best thing/love it.
Was her sister and her/cousin
And it started with a little kiss, like this—

She starts/swingin'
With the boys in/tune
And her feet just fly up in the air.
Singin', "Hey, diddle-diddle" with a kitty in the middle
And they swingin' like it just don't care.
So I took a big/chance
At the high school/dance
With a lady who was ready to play.
It wasn't me she was/foolin'
'Cause she knew what she was/doin'
When she told me how to walk this way.

CHORUS:
[RUN-DMC AND AEROSMITH]
She told me to—
Walk this way! Talk this way!
She told me to—
Walk this way! Talk this way!
She told me to—
Walk this way! Talk this way!
She told me to—
Walk this way! Talk this way!
Well, just gimme a kiss/some head!
Ooh, a-like this—

[RUN-DMC]
School girl/sleazy
With a/classy kind of sassy,
Little skirt hangin' way up her knee.
It was three young ladies
In the school gym/locker
And they find they were lookin' at D.
I was a high school/loser,
Never made it with a/lady
'Til a boy told me somethin' I missed:
That my next-door/neighbor
Had a daughter/had a favor
And I gave the girl just a little kiss, like this—

[AEROSMITH]
She starts swingin' with the boys in the school
With her feet flyin' way up in the air.
Singin' "Hey, diddle-diddle" with a kitty in the middle.
I was swingin' like I didn't care.
So, I took a big chance at the high school dance
With a miss who was ready to play.
Wasn't me she was foolin' 'cause she knew what she was doin'
When she told me how to walk this way.

CHORUS

WANKSTA
RECORDED BY 50 CENT

Words by Curtis Jackson and Michael J. Clervoix
Music by John Freeman

It's 50, a.k.a. Ferrari F-50.
Break it down,
I gotta lotta livin' to do before I die
And I ain't got time to waste.
Let's make it.

You said you a gangsta, but you never pop nuttin'.
You said you a wanksta and you need to stop frontin'.

You ain't a friend of mine. (Huh.)
You ain't no kin of mine. (Nah.)
What makes you think that I'm-a run up on you with the nine?
We do this all the time, right now we on the grind.
So hurry up and copy and go sellin' nicks and dimes.
Shorty, she's so fine, I gotta make her mine.
An ass like that gotta be one of a kind.
I crush 'em every time, punch 'em with every line.
I'm fuckin' with they mind.
I make 'em press rewind.
They know they can't shine if I'm around the rhyme.
Been on parole since '94 'cause I commit the crime.
I send ya my line, I did it three to nine.
If the Ds ran up in my crib, you know who droppin' dimes.

CHORUS:

You said you a gangsta,
But you never pop nuttin'.
You said you a wanksta,
And you need to stop frontin'.
You go to the dealership,
But you don't never cop nuttin'.
You been hustlin' a long time
And you ain't got nuttin'.

CHORUS

Damn, homie, in high school you was the man, homey.
The fuck happened to you?
I got the sickest vendetta when it comes to the cheddah.
And if you play with my paper, you gotta meet my berretta.
Now, shorty think I'm-a sweat her, sippin' Amaretto.
I'm livin' once than deader, I know I can do better.
She look good, but I know she after my cheddah
She tryin' get to my pockets, homie, and I ain't gon' let her
Be easy, stop the bullshit, you get your whole crew wet.
We in the club doin' the same ol' two-step.
Gorilla unit 'cause they say we bugged out
'Cause we don't go nowhere without toast—we thugged out.

CHORUS (2 TIMES)

Me, I'm no mobsta.
Me, I'm no gangsta.
Me, I'm no hit man.
Me, I'm just me, me.
Me, I'm no wanksta.
Me, I'm no actor.
But it's me you see on your TV
'Cause I hustle, baby; this rap shit is so easy.
I'm getting' what you get for a brick to talk greasy.
By any means, partner, I got to eat on these streets.
If you play me close, for sure I'm gon' pop my heat.
Niggas sayin' they gonna murder 50—how?
We ridin' 'round with guns the size of Lil' Bow Wow.
What you know about AKs and AR-15s?
Equipped with night vision, shell catchers, and them things, huh.

CHORUS (2 TIMES)

Words and Music by Jermaine Dupri

WARM IT UP
RECORDED BY KRIS KROSS

Uh, well, this is how nice and smooth it is.
Hey, uh, listen to them.

Warm it up, Kris, I'm about to
Warm it up, Kris, 'cause that's what I was born to do.
Warm it up, Kris, I'm about to
Warm it up, Kris, 'cause that's what I was born to do.

So many times, I heard you rhyme, but you can't touch this.
I'm kickin' the type of flow that makes you say, "You're too much, Kris."
So feel the fire of the one they call the Mac Dad,
The fire's what I pack and what I pack is real bad.
I'd like to grab ahold of your soul and never let go,
Never 'til they jump, 'til they say, "Hoo!"
Now that's the state of mind I'm in, huh,
With rhyme after rhyme, I win.

The Mac, the Mac,
'Nough for breakin' 'em off somethin',
They layin' in the back and front,
Keepin' the speakers pumpin'.
The miggida-miggida-miggida-Mac came to get a-warm,
And my pants to the back, that's my everyday uniform.
You little cream puff, Mac-Daddy wannabe,
Keep dreamin' 'cause the Mac you will never be.
So all y'all with the Dr. Seuss riddles,
You can get the finger—the middle.

Warm it up, Kris, I'm about to
Warm it up, Kris, 'cause that's what I was born to do.
Warm it up, Kris, I'm about to
Warm it up, Kris.

Hey, yo, Kris, kick it first.
You know, it's sto', it's sto',
Peepin' at my rhymes, it's dope, it's dope.
And for you, there's now, call my name, what?
The Daddy Mac, baby, totally Krossed out.
Catchin' all the ladies,
The age I be I should be playin' with toys.
Instead, I put my hand into, make you make noise.
That's how I kick it, that's my everyday life and
I rehearse to keep it sharp as a knife, man.

I'm the wrong brother that sucks to be messin' with
'Cause when I put the mic in my hand, I start wreckin' it.
They call me the D–A, double-D, Y–M–A–C,
And there ain't another brother bad as me.
When I let go,
Somethin' from the ghetto.
Word, a little brother kickin' rhymes like you never, ever heard.
Daddy of them all, shootin' to kill like a gun,
Showin' suckas how it's done.

Warm it up, Kris, I'm about to
Warm it up, Kris, 'cause that's what I was born to do.
Warm it up, Kris, I'm about to
Warm it up, Kris, 'cause that's what I was born to do.
Warm it up, Kris, I'm about to
Warm it up, Kris, 'cause that's what I was born to do.

Yeah, now you all know,
What's up?
And the Mac to all that.
Yeah, we gonna kick one more verse for you all.

So many times, I heard you rhyme, but you can't touch this.
I'm kickin' the type of flow that makes you say, "You're too much, Kris."
So feel the fire of the one they call the Mac Dad,
The fire's what I pack and what I pack is real bad.
I'd like to grab ahold of your soul and never let go,
Never 'til they jump, 'til they say, "Hoo!"
Now that's the state of mind I'm in, huh,
With rhyme after rhyme, I win.

I'm the wrong brother that sucks to be messin' with
'Cause when I put the mic in my hand, I start wreckin' it.
They call me the D–A, double-D, Y–M–A–C,
And there ain't another brother bad as me.
When I let go,
Somethin' from the ghetto.
Word, a little brother kickin' rhymes like you never, ever heard.
Daddy of them all, shootin' to kill like a gun,
Showin' suckas how it's done.

Warm it up, Kris, I'm about to
Warm it up, Kris, 'cause that's what I was born to do.

Warm it up, Kris.

Words and Music by David Crawford

WHAT A MAN

RECORDED BY SALT N PEPA

Yeah, yeah. (Ooh.)
Uh, hey, hey.
All right, yeah.
Ooh.

CHORUS:

What a man, what a man, what a man.
What a mighty good man.
What a man, what a man, what a man.
What a mighty good man.
What a man, what a man, what a man.
What a mighty good man.
What a man, what a man, what a man.
What a mighty good man.

I wanna take a minute or two and give much respect due
To the man that's made a difference in my world.
And although most men are hoes, he flows on the down-low
'Cause I never heard about him with another girl.
But I don't sweat it, because it's just pathetic
To let it get me involved in that "he said, she said" crowd.
I know that ain't nobody perfect; I give props to those who deserve it.
And believe me, y'all, he's worth it.
So here's to the future, 'cause we got through the past.
I finally found somebody that can make me laugh. (Ha, ha, ha!)
You so crazy; I think I wanna have your baby.

CHORUS

My man is smooth like Barry, and his voice got bass;
A body like Arnold with a Denzel face.
He's smart like a doctor with a real good rep
And when he comes home, he's relaxed and Pep,
He always got a gift for me every time I see him.
A lot of snot-nosed ex-flames couldn't be him.
He never ran a corny line once to me yet,
So I give him stuff that he'll never forget.
He keeps me on Cloud Nine, just like the Temps.
He's not a fake wanna-be tryin' to be a pimp.
He dresses like a dapper-don, but even in jeans
He's a God-sent original—the man of my dreams.

Yes, my man says he loves me; never says he loves me not,
Tryin' to rush me good and touch me in the right spot.
See other guys that I've had; they tried to play all that mack shit,
But every time they tried, I said, "That's not it."
But not this man; he's got the right potion.
Baby, rub it down and make it smooth like lotion.
Yeah, the ritual, highway to heaven,
From seven to seven, he's got me open like Seven-Eleven.
And yes, it's me that he's always choosin'.
With him, I'm never losin' and he knows that my name is not Susan.
He always has heavy conversation for the mind,
Which means a lot to me 'cause good men are hard to find.

CHORUS

My man gives real loving, that's why I call him killer.
He's not a wham-bam-thank-you-ma'am; he's a thriller.
He takes his time and does everything right,
Knocks me out with one shot for the rest of the night.
He's a real smooth brother; never in a rush,
And he gives me goose-pimples with every single touch.
Spends quality time with his kids when he can.
Secure in his manhood 'cause he's a real man.
A lover and a fighter and he'll knock a knucker out.
Don't take him for a sucker 'cause that's not what he's about.
Every time I need him, he always got my back.
Never disrespectful 'cause his mama taught him that.

CHORUS

Words and Music by Shawntae Harris,
Jermaine Dupri, Joerg Evers and Juergen Korduletsch

WHAT 'CHU LIKE
RECORDED BY DA BRAT, FEATURING TYRESE

[DA BRAT] Oh, look out! Oh, uh, come on.
What'chu like? A whole lot of us, what?
[TYRESE] Yeah.
[DA BRAT] What'chu like? Me on a what?
[TYRESE] What'cha like, what'cha like?
[DA BRAT] What'chu like?
[TYRESE] Can you tell me, baby?
[DA BRAT] Why? How? All night long?
[TYRESE] All night long.

[DA BRAT]
I like 'em brown, yellow, Puerto Rican, or Haitian
With good conversation, plenty of big faces.
It's a must I stay luxurious.
Jewelry cut precision like I bust.
Been winnin' since "Funkdafied" blew up.
It's evident, shit, I can't be touched.
Niggaz say I'm too much; I trust it's true.
Why lie? See for yourself when I slide through.
Drive by, your bitch say, "Don't look." You do.
Shine so bright in the wet U2.
You wish boo-boo could ride with you tonight.
Ain't nothin' in the world that Brat can't do.
She attractive to them, him, her, and you shit.
Frostbit, December unrestricted.
Drop dead—the cost is priceless.
Due to the content I suggest you'll like this.

CHORUS:
[TYRESE]
What do you like?
A whole lot of foreplay right before you get it started.
What do you like?
Me on top, you on the bottom, tight body.
What do you like?
Somebody that can make you say,
"Wow, oh wow," all night long,
All night long, tell me.

[DA BRAT]
Whassup? The setting, a hot-ass club
And you still be sweatin' me.
I don't see nothin' wrong with givin' a little love,
But, nigga, just let me breathe.
Damn, you cute as hell, so let's switch the digits.
Then I got to leave
And you can buy me a couple of drinks.
But I'm-a go socialize and smoke my weed
And I like it when you keep your eyes on me.
And I like it when you touch my privacy.
And I like it sex and ecstasy
When the belt buckle loosen up, undress me.
Already juiced up—that come naturally.
Wax on and off so romantically.
No woman can slow dance or throw down like I can.
Ask, if you curious, to know what I like, man.

CHORUS
[DA BRAT]
Let me tell you something—
Well, I start at the top of the list:
With my pretty eyes, a cute nose, and these fat-ass lips.
My medallion sit in the middle of my tits.
It's hit after hit; shit sweet every sip,
Down to the last drip-drop; watch the hips rock.
Color me bad, tick-tock, you don't stop
'Til the thick thighs; dick rise when I skip by.
I ain't surprised I'm what'chu like, nigga.

CHORUS

Words and Music by
Robby Pardlo and Ryan Toby

WHAT WOULD YOU DO?
RECORDED BY CITY HIGH

Boys and girls, wanna hear a true story?
Saturday night, was at this real wild party.
They had the liquor overflowin' the cup,
About five to six strippers tryin' to work for a buck.
Then I took one girl outside wit' me.
Her name was Lonnie; she went to junior high wit' me.
I said, "Why you up in there, dancin' for cash?
I guess a whole lots changed since I seen you last."
She said—

CHORUS:
"What would you do if your son was at home,
Cryin' all alone on the bedroom floor
'Cause he's hungry, and the only way to feed him is to sleep
Wit' a man for a little bit of money.
And his daddy's gone,
Somewhere smokin' rock now,
In and out of lock-down.
I ain't got a job, now.
So for you this is just a good time,
But for me this is what I call life."

Girl, you ain't the only one wit' a baby.
That's no excuse to be livin' all crazy.
Then she looked at me right square in the eye
And said, "Every day I wake up hopin' to die."
And she said, "Nigga, I know about pain 'cause
Me and my sister ran away so my daddy couldn't rape us.
Before I was a teenager, I done been through more sh-shit
You can't even relate to.

CHORUS

Hold up! What would you do?
Get up on my feet, let go of every excuse.
What would you do?
'Cause I wouldn't want my baby to go through what I went through.
(Come on.) What would you do?
Get up on my feet and stop makin' tired excuses.
What would you do?
Girl, I know, if my mother can do it, baby, you can do it.
Ooh, ooh, ooh.

CHORUS (3 TIMES)

Words and Music by Sean Combs, Mason Betha,
Keisha Spivey, Nasheim Myrick
and Curtis Mayfield

WHAT YOU WANT
RECORDED BY MASE, FEATURING TOTAL

[TOTAL]

Tell me what you want.

Tell me what you want.

Just tell me what you want.

Tell me what you want.

Tell me what you want.

Tell me what you want.

CHORUS:
[TOTAL]

Tell me what you want for me.

Take a look at what you see.

Let me know if this right here

Is something you can have for years.

Tell me what you want for me.

Take a look at what you see.

Let me know if this right here

Is something you can have for years.

[MASE]

Now, Mase be the man wanna see you doin' good.

I don't wanna get rich, leave you in the 'hood.

Girl, in my eyes you the baddest.

The reason why I love you: you don't like me 'cause my status.

I don't wanna see you with a carriage, living average.

I wanna do my thing so we be established.

And I don't want you rock in them fabrics.

Girl, I will give you karats 'til you feel like a rabbit.

Anything in your path you want, you can have.

Walk through the mall—if you like it, you can grab.

Total it all up and put it on my tab

And then tell your friends all the fun you had.

CHORUS

[MASE]
Hey Mama, won't you come here to Papa?
You don't like the way your ta-tas lookin' at Shada?
In a 600, ain't no smokin' cigada.
Come over here; I think I see your baby faddah.
Here ya go; the number to my casa.
If you in a rush, you call me mañana.
Whatever your need, girlfriend, I got the whole enchilada,
Just the way you like it; Mase gon' do you propa.
Girl, I can tell you was meant for me.
I can tell by the way you was sent to me.
While I'm on tour tryin' to make them centuries
And they ask who your man—you better mention me.
If you don't, you know you got a problem.
Said, you want no beef, girlfriend? Don't start none.
And it just so happens that I'm seein' cash
'Cause you messed up a lot just tryin' to be fast.
And I ain't gonna ask who smashed the E-Class:
Pull up to the crib with the whole front crashed.
Now you wanna laugh; good thing that's the past.
If you ever lie again, girl, that will be your last.

CHORUS

[MASE]

Now the more you treat me royal, I adore you.
That's why I don't mind doin' these things for you.
You did things for me I wouldn't believe you did.
That's why I always want to keep you here.
In a year or two, girl, I could see you with my kids.
Girl, you make a thug want to get a legal gig.
It's only right we spend our lonely nights
Gettin' crazy biz til we awake the kids.
Don't get too loud, got respect for you, honey.
To keep it all real, you come second to my money.
And can you be my ghetto love prophecy?
Everybody love you, girl; not just me.
And I know that you really care a lot for me.
Wanna to see you happy even if it's not with me.

CHORUS

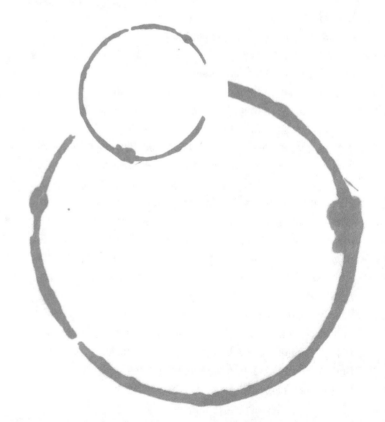

Words and Music by Kevin McKenzie,
Roderick Roachford, Joseph Jones,
Lennox Maturine and Shaquille O'Neal

WHAT'S UP DOC (CAN WE ROCK?)
RECORDED BY FU-SCHNICKENS, FEATURING SHAQUILLE O'NEAL

CHORUS:
Can we rock?
Yeah, what's up, doc?
Can we rock?
What's up, doc?

[MOC]
Cha, cha, cha, cha, cha.
What's up, pa, yo, who poop?
Your Ma Dukes or Pa Dukes?
There's two scoops o' raisin in the sun.
Brothers try to rally up, then dilly-dally for some room.
Bird-peckin', double-deckin', rubber-neckin' in my tomb.
Check it out, yo, I smile like Groucho Marx.
I make a joke, hokey-pokey, and slide by like egg yolk.
Play me like a punk, like Penguin and the Joker,
Snoopin' in my biz like Tom and Roxie Roker.
So bust the freaky, freaky, freaky ways.
The brothers with the Asian guise, makin' Gs
And now we're sellin' records overseas.
Holy smokes, oops, your whole plan goofed up.
Now you get kicks, 'nough licks, plus cuffed up
'Cause you can catch a quick drop for tryin' to take the Schnicks' props.
So tick-tock around the clock, and shock while we lick shots.
(Boom!) For goodness sakes, the stakes are high.
I'm out. (You out?)
A–B–C ya, bye!

CHORUS

[CHIP]

I thought I saw a putty cat, I did.
I did the humpty-dumpty, bashful-grumpy, Quaker, Nabisco, Crisco, kid
'Cause my style's *Figaro, Figaro, Figaro, Figaro* like Pinocchio's.
Big Digital Underground, humpy-dumpty, camel-hump nose,
So play dosey-do, sufferin' succotash, my mistletoe is gone.
Snow White is after my seven dwarves, my styles, and after me Lucky Charms.
So leapin' leprechauns, be glad I'm pushin' my pedal to the metal.
I'm rugged and rough for Cocoa Puffs, and yes, I love my Fruity Pebbles.
So howdy, my partner, I starts to get meaner,
So ask Bob for Hope, nope, not Mr. Bob Dole-a-lina.
Oh, where has my mic gone? Tell me, have you seen her?
I stretch like a condom and gets plump like a wiener
Or sausage, but of course, it's time for Chip to wreck it.
But before my intro, I gots to check it.
So who is the nicest in your neighborhood?
Lyrics are merry, merry, quite contrary, and Captain Crunch berry good.
So, rah, rah, sis-boom-bah,
Chip Fu is comin' again, give thanks and praises to Jah.
My lyrics are smooth like the head on Telly Savalas,
My tongue starts to quicken like Speedy Gonzales.

Take up your pen, your pad, your lyrical bag, and run, go whole, afresh.
Touché, pussy cat, put down that mic 'cause you can't rap,
'Cause I'm dip-dip-divin', so socializin'.
Clean out your ears, yes, and open up your eyes and
I kick like Bruce Lee and Jean-Claude Van Damme.
So dunna, nana, nana, nana, nana, nana, Batman!
I hip-hop, hop-hop,
Don't-don't, stop-stop.
I'm harder than a Flintstone and much bigger than a Club Rock.
Our types of lyrical styles? Yes, the Schnickens can pick 'em.
I burp, stick 'em, ha, ha, ha, stick 'em.

CHORUS

[POC]

Rippin' the program, slow man, hot damn.
I grand slam, swingin' things again and again. (Whoo!)
Golly ha-chooey, macho like Roscoe.

Randy Savage Manwich, swingin' the ding-a-ling with damage.
Pauish not Antoinish nor Montego
Spanish like "que" for the nine-two lingo.
Next, a new hex, commentators stand aside.
Stringin' MCs like a bikini or panty line. (Ha, ha!)
Nut you might bust, but you can't even come right,
Spite the strokin' or hopin' or pullin' a peace pipe.
Huff and puff, so what the fuck is happening?
On the lyrical, miracle, spiritual,
But everybody's rockin'.
Flip a new hit, catch wreck to the nine ship
Equipped, never slip with tongue twister.
All my styles that's Buckwild,
No fake rap, I push pounds.
I flip made scripts and hips I hit,
So bring the Goya, oh boy-a, as I say, "Hasta Mañana."
Soft and chewy, Hong Kong fooey, reggae not Rasta tough stuff.
Can I rock?

CHORUS

[SHAQ]
I'm the hooper, the hyper,
Protected by Viper.
When I rock the hoop, yo, you'd better decipher.
In other words, you'd better make a funky decision, (Whoo!)
'Cause I'm-a be a Shaq-knife and cut you with precision.
Forget Tony Danza, I'm the boss.
When it comes to money, I'm like Dick Butkus.
Now, who's the first pick? Me, word is born and
Not a Christian Laettner, not Alonzo Mourning.
That's okay, not being bragadocious,
Supercalifragilistic, Shaq is alidocious.
Peace, I gotta go, I ain't no joke.
Now I slam it (what?), jam it (uhh),
And make sure it's broke.

CHORUS

WHO DAT
RECORDED BY JT MONEY, FEATURING SOLÉ

Words and Music by Diandre Davis,
Tonya Johnston, Thabiso Nkhereanye,
Christopher Stewart and Jeffrey Thompkins

[JT MONEY]
Jack, jack, yeah!
Put 'em up! Put 'em up!
Yo, yo, JT Money!
Throw 'em up! Throw 'em up!
JT Money!

Aiy-ya-ya-ya-ya-ya-ya. (Go nutty; who dat?)
Aiy-ya-ya-ya-ya-ya-ya (Who dat? Huh?)
Who dat, who dat, who dat, who dat, who dat, who dat, who?
(Who dat, who dat, who dat, who dat?)
Who dat, who dat, who dat tryin' to get up my crew?
(Huh? Yeah!)

Yo, who dat off-brand nigga tryin' to hang wit' the clique?
Flossin' like you came wit' the clique.
But would you bang wit' the clique if it was thick,
Or do you just ride dick?
Cause, playa, I don't know you, nigga, tell me who you wit'!
If you hang wit' the Squad, you bound to get scarred.
Sucker boys run they mouth; real niggaz run the yard.
'Round here we blow trees, don't fuck with the O.B.s.
You dick-ride niggaz might be the police; ahh-iight?

Aiy-ya-ya-ya-ya-ya-ya. (Aiy-ya, NIG-GA!)
Aiy-ya-ya-ya-ya-ya-ya (Yeah.)
Who dat, who dat, who dat, who dat, who dat, who dat, who?
(Who dat, who dat, huh?)
Who dat, who dat, who dat tryin' to get up my crew?
(Tryin' to…in my…it's you!)

Aiy-ya-ya-ya-ya-ya-ya. (Aiy-ya-ya.)
Aiy-ya-ya-ya-ya-ya-ya (Ya-ya-ya-ya-ya.)
Who dat, who dat, who dat, who dat, who dat, who dat, who?
(Who dat, who dat, who dat?)
Who dat, who dat, who dat tryin' to get up my crew?
(Who dat tryin' to get up in my…)

[SOLÉ]
Uhh, me an my girls rollin' deep, represent the Solé.
Bunch of fly-ass bitches; when we ride, it's on.
See them niggaz all pause, droppin' digital phones,
Askin' me, "Where you from?" 'Cause they wantin' to clone.
Niggaz, them lines, they split; they want my shit.
But game be wack; I turn my back
Then hear that you're lickin', stickin' it,
Tell all your friends that you're dickin' it.
Swingin' on them?
Hi-Fi shit, nigga, get sick with this.
Say, "Who dey? Who dat?" No chance—blew that
When you said that you wrote this.
Have Red Zone niggaz on blow for this bitch.
Don't deny it, nigga, don't even try it, nigga.
You makin' claims that you laid wit' the fly nigga.
Don't know your name; it still remains
That you would say you fucked Solé.
Every time they turn a back, burn tracks,
Niggaz wanna say they've earned stacks.
Dick be jack, picture that.
Say my name, I'm the one; who the fuck is dat?
Why?

[JT MONEY]
Aiy-ya-ya-ya-ya-ya-ya. (Aiy-ya-ya.)
Aiy-ya-ya-ya-ya-ya-ya (Ya-ya-ya-ya-ya.)
Who dat, who dat, who dat, who dat, who dat, who dat, who?
(Who dat, who dat, who dat? Huh?)
Who dat, who dat, who dat tryin' to get up my crew?
(Who dat tryin' to get up in my crew?)

Aiy-ya-ya-ya-ya-ya-ya. (Aiy-ya-ya.)
Aiy-ya-ya-ya-ya-ya-ya (Ya-ya-ya-ya-ya.)
Who dat, who dat, who dat, who dat, who dat, who dat, who?
(Who dat, who dat, who dat? Huh?)
Who dat, who dat, who dat tryin' to get up my crew?

I been said a legendary up in this motherfucker.
Veteran in this game and still bringin' ruckus.
Never had no time for tricks or no bustas.
I only fuck wit' dat real, I got no love for suckers.
All these tiny-ass niggaz be wanna wear my shoes.
Ain't got the slightest of clues or either paid your dues.
Then these hoes goin' crazy 'bout J baby!
The way you show me your love is by the way you pay me.
The game room been closed, so stay up out of mine.
Just know I keep niggaz up and crunk like battle lines.
Motherfuckers be all up in a nigga biz,
Tryin' to question my shit just like a pop quiz.
Nigga, what this is? Aaaa-ight?

Aiy-ya-ya-ya-ya-ya-ya. (Aiy-ya-ya.)
Aiy-ya-ya-ya-ya-ya-ya (Ya-ya-ya-ya-ya.)
Who dat, who dat, who dat, who dat, who dat, who dat, who?
(Who dat, who dat, who dat? Huh?)
Who dat, who dat, who dat tryin' to get up my crew?
(Who dat tryin' to…in my…it's you!)

Aiy-ya-ya-ya-ya-ya-ya. (Aiy-ya-ya.)
Aiy-ya-ya-ya-ya-ya-ya (Ya-ya-ya-ya-ya.)
Who dat, who dat, who dat, who dat, who dat, who dat, who?
(Who dat, who dat, who dat? Huh?)
Who dat, who dat, who dat tryin' to get up my crew?
(Who dat tryin' to get up in my crew?)

(We out to change, nigga!)
Aiy-ya-ya-ya-ya-ya-ya.
(We runnin' game, nigga! You wanna bang, nigga?)
Aiy-ya-ya-ya-ya-ya-ya.
(It ain't no thang, nigga! We out to change, nigga!)
Who dat, who dat, who dat, who dat, who dat, who dat, who?
(We runnin' game, nigga! You wanna bang, nigga?)
Who dat, who dat, who dat tryin' to get up in my crew?
(It ain't no thang, nigga! Aaaa-ight!)

Aiy-ya-ya-ya-ya-ya-ya. (Aiy-ya-ya.)
Aiy-ya-ya-ya-ya-ya-ya (Ya-ya-ya-ya-ya.)
Who dat, who dat, who dat, who dat, who dat, who dat, who?
(Who dat, who dat, who dat? Huh?)
Who dat, who dat, who dat tryin' to get up my crew?
(Who dat tryin' to…in my…it's you!)

Who dat, who dat, who dat, who dat, who dat, who dat, who?
Who dat, who dat, who dat, who dat, who dat, who dat, who?
Who dat, who dat, who dat, who dat, who dat, who dat, who?
(Who dat, who dat, who dat? Huh?)
Who dat, who dat, who dat tryin' to get up in my crew?
(Who dat tryin' to get up in my crew?)

Yeah!

WHOA!
RECORDED BY BLACK ROB

Words and Music by
Anthony Best and Roberto Ross

Yo, I'm gettin' ready to put y'all up on somethin', man. (What's goin' on? Yo.)
Yo, when you see somethin' ill. (Uh-huh.)
Know what I mean?
That shit is whoa. (That's what whoa means.)
Anything ill you see is whoa. (Uh-huh.)
Nigga have a big six at the curb, that's whoa. (Okay?)
Especially if he got the fully equipped kit on it; it's whoa.
Like, you know what I mean? Like yo—

I had this bad bitch Uptown—she was whoa!
Had me fucked-up in the head; I mean, whoa!
Bought the bitch diamonds and pearls; I mean, whoa!
Shoulda seen them shits shinin' on her wrist; whoa!
Now money ain't a problem; see my dough is like, whoa!
Pulled out my bankroll on y'all niggaz like, whoa!
Floss the blue shrimp from two-tenth, like, whoa!
Faggot wanna peep my blueprints; I'm like, whoa!
Had to hit the brakes on y'all niggaz, like, whoa!
Niggaz gettin' pulled on my block, like, whoa!
Comin' home within a half an hour, like, whoa!
Frontin' like they had the manpower, like, whoa!
More or less, more or so; I'll rip your torso.
I live the fast life, come through in the Porsche slow, like, whoa!
My niggaz like dough, light 'dro,
Nitro, might flow, nice clothes, like, whoa!

Ease pain with cocaine, like, whoa!
Now I'm in Doc Strange in the Range, like, whoa! (They don't know me.)
Hundred miles an hour, switchin' lanes, like, whoa!
Plus I'm gettin' brain from this chick, like, whoa!
Finger near a nigga asshole, like, whoa!
Scene floss riches and bitches, like, whoa!
Nine-nine Jag, Benz, Coupe, like, whoa!
Keep them cheese lines on you blocks, like, whoa!
Grenade through your window, bitch, like, whoa!
Love to see me do this shit, like, whoa!
Niggaz put me through this shit, like, whoa!
So, I'm-a go toe to toe, blow for blow, like, whoa!
And rip your torso.
Live the fast life, come through in the Porsche slow, like, whoa!
My niggaz like dough, light 'dro,
Nitro, might flow, nice clothes, like, whoa!

We bag it, then flip it, like, whoa!
Cars we jack it, then strip it, like, whoa!
Fully equip it, front to back, like, whoa!
Spittin' on fiends that come for crack, like, whoa!
Askin' for shorts and shit, nigga, like, whoa!
Half on his crunk, now nigga, that's whoa!
Flow so properly, you'll see I'm whoa!
Ain't no stoppin' me, I'm deep, like, whoa!
Guns be poppin' B, we creep, like, whoa!
Hear my name in these streets; it's like, whoa!
Must I pound the concrete, like, whoa?
Fill his bitch ass, head to feet, like, whoa!
Your man ain't whoa; this judge ain't whoa;
C.O.s ain't whoa; P.O.s ain't whoa.
Play y'all-self; I get the G.I. Joe.
D–I–C–K riders ain't whoa!
I'll rip your torso.
Live the fast life, come through in the Porsche slow, like, whoa!
My niggaz like dough, light 'dro,
Nitro, might flow, nice clothes, like, whoa!

Niggaz gettin' money in the V.A. is whoa!
Honeys lookin' right in A.T.L. is whoa!
Niggaz pimpin' hoes in Chi-Town is whoa!
Bitches takin' paper in L.A. is whoa!
Niggaz stackin' dough in D.C. is whoa!
P.R. D.R., hold me down, like, whoa!
Ballers in Detroit, hold me down, like, whoa!
Niggaz in New Orleans, hold me down, like, whoa!
Boston and Jersey muthafuckas is whoa!
Florida niggaz and Philly niggaz is whoa!
Tampa and Texas, Cleveland is whoa!
Memphis and Lil' Rock, my niggaz is whoa!
Panama niggaz, they hold me down, like, whoa!
My New York peoples, they hold me down, like, whoa!
Bad Boy nigga, word is bond, we whoa!
Alumni bitches, word is bond, we whoa!
N.C, S.C. muthafuckas is whoa!
My nigga Buckwild, word is bond, he whoa!
Uhh, and that's just how the story go.

And whoever I forgot on this shit, is whoa!
Aw, man, whoa!
Eighth Street, Life Stories. (Whoa!)
P.D.P.R., that nigga…
The beat I got from big Buckwild is whoa!
That nigga Black Rob on the mic is whoa!
My whole fuckin' flow on the mic is whoa!

Words and Music by Marvin Young,
Matt Dike and Anthony Smith

WILD THING
RECORDED BY TONE LOC

Let's do it.

Workin' all week, nine-to-five for my money.
So when the weekend comes, I go get live with the honey.
Rollin' down the street, I saw this girl, and she was pumpin'.
I winked my eye, she got into the ride, went to a club, was jumpin'.
Introduced myself as Loc; she said, "You're a liar."
I said, "I got it goin' on, baby doll, and I'm on fire."
Took her to the hotel; she said, "You're the king."
I said, "Be my queen, if you know what I mean, and let's do the wild thing."

Wild thing.
Wild thing.

Shoppin' at the mall, lookin' for some gear to buy.
I saw this girl, she cool-rocked my world and I had to adjust my fly.
She looked at me and smiled, and she said, "You have plans for the night?"
I said, "Hopefully, if things go well, I'll be with you tonight?"
So we journeyed to her house; one thing led to another.
I keyed the door; we cold-hit the floor, looked up and it was her mother.
I didn't know what to say; I was hanging by a string.
She said, "Hey, you two, I was once like you, and I liked to do the wild thing."

Wild thing.
She loved to do the wild thing.
Wild thing.
Please, baby, baby, please.

Posse in effect, hangin' out is always hype.
And when me and the crew leave the shindig, I want a girl who's just my type.
Saw this luscious, little frame—I ain't lyin', fellas, she was fine.
The sweet young miss go gave me a kiss, and I knew that she was mine.
Took her to the limousine still parked outside.
I tipped the chauffeur when it was over, and I gave her my own ride.
Couldn't get her off my jack; she was like static cling.
But that's what happens when bodies start slappin' from doin' the wild thing.

Wild thing.
She wanna do the wild thing.
Please, baby, baby, please.
Wild thing.

Doin' a little show at the local discotheque.
This fine young chick was on my jack, so I say what the heck.
She want to come on stage and do her little dance.
So I said, "Chill for now, but maybe later you'll get your chance."
So when the show was finished, I took her around the way.
And what do you know, she was good to go without a word to say.
We was all alone, and she said, "Tone, let me tell you one thing:
I need fifty dollars to make you holler—I get paid to do the wild thing."

Say what?
Yo, love, you must be kidding.
You're walkin', babe.
Just break out of here.
Hasta la vista, baby.

Wild thing.

Words and Music by Stevie Wonder,
Will Smith and Mohandas Dewese

WILD WILD WEST

RECORDED BY
WILL SMITH

Wicki-wicki-wild, wicki-wicki-wild.
Wicki-wild, wicki-wild, Wild, Wild West.
Jim West, desperado,
Rough rider; no you don't want nada.
None of this six-gunnin' this; brother runnin' this
Buffalo soldier; look it's like I told ya—
Any damsel that's in distress
Be outta that dress when she meet Jim West.
Roughneck, so go check the law and abide.
Watch your step or flex and get a hole in your side.
Swallow your pride; don't let your lip react.
You don't wanna see my hand where my hip be at.
With Artemis from the start of this, runnin' the game,
James West, tamin' the West; so remember the name.
I know who ya gonna call—not the G.B.s.
Now who ya gonna call?
G–double-A–G.
If you ever riff with either one of us,
Break out before you get bum-rushed

At the Wild, Wild West. (When I roll into the…)
The Wild, Wild West. (When I stroll into the…)
The Wild, Wild West. (When I bounce into the…)
The Wild, Wild West. (Sisqo, Sisqo.)
The Wild, Wild West. (We're goin' straight to…)
The Wild, Wild West. (The Wild, Wild West.)
The Wild, Wild West. (We're goin' straight to the Wild, Wild, c'mon!)

Now, now, now,
Now once upon a time in the West,
Mad man lost his damn mind in the West.
Loveless, kidnap a dame, nuttin' less.
Now I must put his behind to the test. (Can you feel me?)
Then through the shadows, in the saddle, ready for battle,
Bring all your boys in; here comes the poison.
Behind my back, all that riffin' ya did?
Front and center, now where your lip at, kid? (Lookin' at me?)
Who dat is? A mean brother, bad for your health.
Lookin' damn good, though, if I could say it myself.
Told me Loveless is a mad man, but I don't fear that.
He got mad weapons, too? Ain't tryin' to hear that.
Tryin' to bring down me, the champion?
When y'all clowns gon' see that it can't be done?
Understand me, son; I'm the slickest they is.
I'm the quickest they is. (Yeah.)
Did I say I'm the slickest they is?
So if you barkin' up the wrong tree, we comin'.
Don't be startin' nuttin'; me and my partner gonna test your chest, Loveless.
Can't stand the heat? Then get out of the Wild, Wild West.
The Wild, the Wild—

CHORUS:

The Wild, Wild West. (We're goin' straight to…)
When I'm rollin' to the…
The Wild, Wild West. (The Wild, Wild West.)
When I'm strollin' to the…
The Wild, Wild West. (We're goin' straight to…)
When I'm bouncin' to the…
The Wild, Wild West. (The Wild, Wild.)

We're goin' straight (straight) to (to)
The Wild, Wild West. (The Wild, Wild West.)
The Wild, Wild West.
We're goin' straight (straight) to (to)
The Wild, Wild West. (The Wild, Wild West.)
The Wild, Wild West.

Breakdown.

Yeah, can you feel it? C'mon, c'mon.
Yeah, keep it movin'! Keep it movin'!
Ooh, yeah.

To any outlaw tryin' to draw, thinkin' you're bad:
Any drawn on West, best with a pen and a pad.
Don't even think about it, six-gun, weighin' a ton.
Ten paces and turn (one...two...three...) just for fun, son.
Up 'til sundown, rollin' around,
See where the bad guys are to be found, and make 'em lay down.
The defenders of the West,
Crushin' all pretenders in the West.
Don't mess with us 'cause we in the—

CHORUS (2 TIMES)

The Wild, Wild West.

I done, done it again, y'all.
Done, done it again.
Ha, ha, ha, ha.
Big Will, Dru Hill, uh.
Bringin' the heat, bringin' the heat.
Can't stop the bum-rush.

WILL 2K
RECORDED BY WILL SMITH, FEATURING K-CI

Words and Music by Joe Strummer, Mick Jones, Topper Headon, Will Smith, Bobby Robinson, Lennie Bennett and Cedric Hailey

[WILL SMITH]

Here it comes: the party of a lifetime.
Thirty-first of December.
Man, I remember when the ball dropped for ninety.
Now it's nine-nine; ten years behind me.
What's gonna happen?
Don't nobody know.
We'll see when the clock gets to twelve-0-0.
Chaos, the cops gonna block the street.
Man, who the hell cares?
Just don't stop the beat.
No time to sleep; yo, it's on tonight.
K–C, you feelin' me right? (Yeah.)
2–0–0–0, the Will 2–K.
The new millennium; yo, excuse me—Willennium. (Yeah.)
It can't get thicker than this. (Big Will.)
Slick like Rick, I can't miss.
(And we gonna party like it's nineteen...)
Hold up—it is.

CHORUS:
[K-CI]

Here it comes: another year.
Come on, everyone, new millennium.
Here it comes: another year.
Everyone; new millennium.

[WILL SMITH]

There's a party tonight,
Everybody was drinking,
The house was screamin,
And the bass was shaking.

And it won't be long
'Til everybody knowing
That twelve o'clock the roof will be blowing.
Drinks on me; up the cups, and
Midnight coming at full-thrust, and
Dick Clark holding it down, and
The second-hand rolling around. (Na, na, na, na.)
Hundred-thousands deep, worldwide press,
Hate to be the man that gotta clean this mess.
Same resolution: get the money.
Ain't ready to hum "Auld Lang Syne"
'Cause a person that know the words is hard to find.
First soul train line of the year.
Four, three, two, one.

[K-CI]
It's here and I like it.
Gonna pack the dance floor;
Rock the dance floor.

CHORUS

[K-CI]
Yeah, yeah.
Say, yeah, yeah.
Say, yeah, yeah.
Say, yeah, yeah.
Say, yeah, yeah.
Say, yeah, yeah.
Say, yeah, yeah.
Say, yeah, yeah.

[WILL SMITH]
I remember trying to count how old I'd be
When the clock struck twelve in the year 2–G.
Media noche, finally near,
This will be that anthem amongst the cheers.
Just the man to usher it in:
Big Will bringing the heat,
K-Ci bringing the plan.

Ringing it in, waiting for the ball to drop.
That 2000 vault—we breaking the lock.
Let hip-hop keep blazing the charts.
May the past keep a warm spot in your heart.
May the future hold more joy than pain.
Hands in the air, waiting for confetti to rain.

[K-CI]
It's here, and I like it.
Gonna pack the dance floor;
Rock the dance floor.

CHORUS

[WILL SMITH]
There's a party tonight,
Everybody was drinking,
The house was screaming,
And the bass was shaking.
And it won't be long
'Til everybody knowing
At twelve o'clock, at twelve o'clock;
Say what? Say what? Say what? What?

CHORUS

True dat, true dat, true dat,
Yo, London, uh, come on.
Yo, Bangkok, come on, come on.
L.A., ha, ha.
The N–Y–C.
Come on, say what? Say what?
Yo, Philly, come on, hey.
Hey, Tokyo, come on.
Everybody say, "What" now.
Come on, come on, come on.

Words and Music by Jeffrey Bass, Kevin Bell,
Anne Dudley, Trevor Horn, Marshall Mathers
and Malcolm McLaren

WITHOUT ME
RECORDED BY EMINEM

[OBIE TRICE]
Obie Trice…real name…no gimmicks.

[EMINEM]
Two trailer park girls go 'round the outside,
'Round the outside, 'round the outside.
Two trailer park girls go 'round the outside,
'Round the outside, 'round the outside.

[FEMALE]
Ooh!

[EMINEM]
Guess who's back, back again?
Shady's back; tell a friend.
Guess who's back, guess who's back?
Guess who's back, guess who's back?
Guess who's back, guess who's back?
Guess who's back?

I've created a monsta 'cause nobody wants to
See Marshall no more—they want Shady.
I'm chopped liver.
We'll if you want Shady, this is what I'll give ya:
A little bit of weed mixed with some hard liquor,
Some vodka that will jumpstart my heart quicker,
Then a shock when I get shocked at the hospital
By the doctor, when I'm not cooperating,
When I'm rockin' the table while he's operating, hey!
You waited this long to stop debating
'Cause I'm back, I'm on the rag, and ovulating.
I know that you got a job, Ms. Cheney,
But your husband's heart problem is complicating.

So the FCC won't let me be,
Or let me be; so let me see;
They tried to shut me down on MTV,
But it feels so empty without me.
So come on, dip, bum on your lips.
Fuck that—cum on your lips and some on your tits,
And get ready 'cause this shit's about to get heavy.
I just settled all my lawsuits—fuck you, Debbie!

CHORUS:

Now this looks like a job for me,
So everybody, just follow me,
'Cause we need a little controversy
'Cause it feels so empty without me.
I said, this looks like a job for me,
So everybody, just follow me
'Cause we need a little controversy
'Cause it feels so empty without me.

Little hellions, kids feelin' rebellious;
Embarrassed—their parents still listen to Elvis.
They start feelin' like prisoners, helpless
'Til someone comes along on a mission and yells, "Bitch!"
A visionary, vision is scary; could start a revolution,
Pollutin' the airwaves.
A rebel,
So let me just revel and bask
In the fact that I got everyone kissin' my ass.
And it's a disaster; such a catastrophe
For you to see so damn much of my ass—you ask for me?
Well, I'm back. (Na, na, na, na, na, na, na, na, na, na.)
Fix your bent antenna,
Tune it in and then I'm gonna enter
Into the front of your skin like a splinter.
The center of attention, back for the winter.
I'm interesting—the best thing since wrestling.
Infesting your kids' ears and nesting.
"Testing: Attention, please!"
Feel the tension soon as someone mentions me.
Here's my ten cents, my two cents is free.
A nuisance; who sent, who sent for me?

CHORUS

A-tisk-it, a-task-it,
I go tit for tat with anybody who's talkin' this shit,
That shit.
Chris Kirkpatrick, you can get your ass kicked
Worse than them little Limp Bizkit bastards.
And Moby, you can get stoned by Obie.
You thirty-six-year-old, bald-headed fag, blow me.
You don't know me; you're too old.
Let go, it's over; nobody listens to techno.
Now, let's go; just give me the signal.
I'll be there with a whole list full of new insults.
I been dope, suspenseful with a pencil
Ever since Prince turned himself into a symbol.
But sometimes that shit just seems
Everybody only wants to discuss me.
So this must mean I'm disgusting,
But it's just me, I'm just obscene,
Though I'm not the first king of controversy.
I am the worst thing since Elvis Presley
To do black music so selfishly
And use it to get myself wealthy. (Hey!)
There's a concept that works:
Twenty million other white rappers emerge,
But no matter how many fish in the sea,
It'll be so empty without me.

CHORUS

Chem-hie-la-la-la, la-la-la-la-la.
La-la-la-la-la, la-la-la-la.
Chem-hie-la-la-la, la-la-la-la-la.
La-la-la-la-la, la-la-la-la.

Kids!

470

Words and Music by
Jay-Z and Vyshon Miller

YOU KNOW WHAT WE 'BOUT

RECORDED BY SILKK THE SHOCKER, FEATURING MASTER P AND JAY-Z

[MASTER P] Yo, Silkk.
[SILKK] What up?
[MASTER P] Tell Jigga we need four apples,
Two bananas, and five oranges.
[SILKK] You sure?
[MASTER P] Nigga, he know what I'm talkin' 'bout.
[SILKK] Aight, I'll get him on the phone.
[MASTER P] From my block to yo' block, nigga,
The world belongs to who?

[SILKK THE SHOCKER]
The world belongs to us.
You can do what you wanna do.
What you gon' do? Huh? What?
The streets belong to us.
You can do what you wanna do.
What you gon' do? Huh? What?

Yo, from the South to the East, nigga, from the streets to the 'burbs,
I fuck wit' that when they talk, the speech just be slurred.
You know me, Mister Got-Dough, Mister Got-Flow.
Couldn't figure out which one wanted both of 'em, so
Mister Got-Both: if you hate me stop, if you jealous,
Silkk the Shock, Jigga, No Limit, Master P, Roc-A-Fella
Used to cop bricks for thirty.
Now I do nothin' but sit back and drop hits; ya heard me?
I ain't nothin' but a thug that got rich; ya heard me.
Drop the top when it's hot.
If not, call Jay and tell him, "Blow the mall up
And come and shop in Jersey."

You know what I did? You know how I come?
You wouldn't even think about testin' me, dog, if you know what I done.
Didn't change a bit; I'm still thuggish, still thuggin'.
Niggaz ask how much money I got, do math.
You know how to add? I'm P little brother.
Shit, I can't tell y'all nothin', I gotta show y'all
Real in this; I'm as real as it gets; I told y'all.
Yo, I sleep through the rain, sleep through the pain.
Would have knew about me, but you don't
'Cause, know why? 'Cause you was sleep when I came.
But I'm here now, y'all suckas, fear now.
Look, plan on bein' on top, don't stop, plan on bein' hot year 'round.
I don't do it for no love, I do it for the thugs.
Do it for my block, do it for the V.I.P. spots in the club.
It's hard to stop this life, like it's hard to call cocked dice.
We ain't nothin' but some 'bout it, 'bout it, niggaz
That live the "Hard-Knock Life."

CHORUS:

From my block to yo' block, it's a sho' shot.
We out the door, out the most, and the flow don't stop.
You know what we do, you know what we 'bout.
You know what we do, you know what we 'bout.
From my block to yo' block, it's a sho' shot.
We out the door, out the most, and the flow don't stop.
From the ghetto to the suburbs, from Marcy to the Third.
You know what we do when we come through, ya heard?

[JAY-Z]

In the South, nigga,
Deep in the four-door, watchin' that old dog,
Or in the club, nigga, shakin' them hoes off,
Poppin' my foes off, ain't nothin' changed.
Or catch me on the block with thugs, knockin' the Os off,
Baggin' that 'dro, nigga, stackin' that dough.
Clappin' at foes and I'm laughin at hoes.
Holdin' them dice and I'm breakin' yo' bank.
You see the shit Roc-A-Fella make wit' The Tank?
Even without airplay, platinum off of heresy.
It's your year, Jay; get off my dick.
Been my year; you talkin' to a winner here.
Iceberg winter's wear, linen chair.
My style, in fact, money ain't come from rap,
And we can take it back if it comes to that.
Block or *Billboard*, you gotta feel, dog.
I stay real, y'all; that's how I kill y'all.

CHORUS

[MASTER P]

I used to rap, now b-ball's my life.
Move that house on the lake for the kids and wife.
Check that bank account—it's seven figures.
Who that Rolls in the video for? It's mines, nigga.
I got game; ask the players in the pros.
Who got shot? It ain't my fault.
(Oh, it ain't my fault.) He owed me dough.
Independent, black-owned, my world, my country.
No Limit and Roc-A-Fella run this like drug money
So I can get a huh, huh? A what, what?
Pass the weed, 'cause soldiers like to puff, puff
From the South the to East, baby, baby.

A couple of "Unggh"s, now they gotta pay me
And flip bricks with ghetto chicks with no dicks,
And nines with no clips, and sides with no chips.
Come fast or slow, from cheddar to dough.
Master P, Silkk the Shocker, Jay-Z:
The rowdiest niggaz you know.

CHORUS

[SILKK THE SHOCKER]
Get ya money, dog.
Get ya money, y'all.
Get ya money, dog.
Get ya money, y'all.
Get ya money, dog.
Get ya money, y'all.
Get ya, get ya money, do.
Get ya, get ya...

From the South to the Midwest,
To the East, to the West, whatever
Y'all get, y'all money, y'all.
From my block to yo' block,
It just don't stop.

Words and Music by Pharrell Williams,
Chad Hugo and John Jackson

YOUNG'N
RECORDED BY FABOLOUS

Brooklyn, uh, uh, uh, uh.
Huh, huh, uh-huh, do it , yeah.
Uh, uh, do it, huh, huh, what y'all want, huh?

Rollin' gold two-seater,
Stash in the dash,
Hole through the heaters,
Blockahhhhh put holes through beaters.
Ghetto Fab stroll through cheetahs,
Ballin', Brooklyn dawn,
Addicted to Cris', hooked on Dom.
Fifteen Gs, hookers on.
Ma, I wanna see how you look in thongs.
Hustlin', guys that send pos
'Cause I chop rocks the size of Mentos.
Blame me, I tried to hint those.
Look at the hurt in your eyes—they squint closed.
Pimpin' here's a new way to flirt.
Ya listen to the two-way alert.
It goes…
Let's go V.I.P.; boo, raise your skirt.

CHORUS:
Holla back, young'n. (Hoo, hoo!)
Holla back. (Hoo, hoo!)
Holla back, young'n. (Hoo, hoo!)
Holla back. (Hoo, hoo!)
Holla back, young'n. (Hoo, hoo!)
Holla back. (Hoo, hoo!)
Holla back, young'n. (Hoo, hoo!)
Holla back. (Hoo, hoo!)

I'm gangsta.
Y'all just wanna-bes.
Federal Agents on their Ps.
Thirty grand, twenty-eight on the keys.
Got a good lawyer; I'm gonna squeeze.
Thuggin' jeans and Timbs,
Fitted to the front, lean the brim.
Ride but never on teenage rims
And I keep a chick's face between my limbs.
Stylin', y'all heard about my kick game.
I'm on the park where you see me at the Knick game.
Probably seen this tatted on your chick frame:
F–A–B–O–L–O–U–S.
Ridin', y'all know as well I do,
That's the way you can tell I'm blue.
So I got a deal, I sell pot, too,
'Cause before I hit the pens; I'm gettin' bailed by Clue.

CHORUS

Cruisin' top on the Caddies, low.
Turn this up when you hear this on the radio.
Blastin' with the nineteen-eighty flow.
Make the necks on the ladies go (woo-woop)!
Holla, that's what a pretty thug will do.
Hit Branson, get a fifty-jug or two.
Y'all throwin' on them gritty mugs for who?
Like y'all don't know what fifty slugs will do.
Hatin', I just bought the booze.
I put y'all in the front page articles.

I got 'em lookin' at the *Billboard* charts, confused
And I still freestyle just to start the Clue's
Rappin'; I'm that kid about the dough,
I done copped coke and started droughts before.
Shit platinum out the door,
Now I drop the top down just to shout to hoes.

Holla back, young'n. (Hoo, hoo!)
Holla back. (Hoo, hoo!)
Holla back, young'n. (Hoo, hoo!)
Holla back. (Hoo, hoo!)
Holla back, young'n. (Hoo, hoo!)
Holla back. (Hoo, hoo!)
Holla back, young'n. (Hoo, hoo!)

Holla back, back, back, back. (Hoo, hoo!)

Big Poppa
Words and Music by Notorious B.I.G.
© 1983, 1994 EMI APRIL MUSIC INC, JUSTIN COMBS PUBLISHING COMPANY, INC.,
    BIG POPPA MUSIC and BOVINA MUSIC
All Rights Controlled and Administered by EMI APRIL MUSIC INC.
All Rights Reserved   International Copyright Secured   Used by Permission
This song contains portions of "Between the Sheets" by Ronald Isley, O'Kelly Isley, Ernie Isley,
    Marvin Isley and Chris Jasper

Breakadawn
Words and Music by Stevie Wonder, Susaye Greene-Brown, William Robinson Jr., Rose Ella Jones,
    Kelvin Mercer, Vincent Lamont Mason and David J. Jolicoeur
© 1993 JOBETE MUSIC CO., INC., BLACK BULL MUSIC, BERTAM MUSIC COMPANY,
    DOLLFACE MUSIC INTERNATIONAL and DAISY AGE MUSIC
All Rights for BERTAM MUSIC COMPANY Controlled and Administered by EMI APRIL MUSIC INC.
JOBETE MUSIC CO., INC. and BLACK BULL MUSIC c/o EMI APRIL MUSIC INC.
All Rights Reserved   International Copyright Secured   Used by Permission
-contains elements of "I Can't Help It" (Wonder/Greene-Brown) © 1979 Black Bull Music,
    Jobete Music Co., Inc. and Dollface Music International
-Also contains elements of "Quiet Storm" (Robinson/Jones) © 1975 Jobete Music Co., Inc. o/b/o
    Bertam Music Company

Bust a Move
Words and Music by Marvin Young and Matt Dike
Copyright © 1989 Varry White Music, Inc., Young Man Moving, Inc. and EX VW Music
All Rights for Varry White Music, Inc. and Young Man Moving, Inc. Administered by
    Spirit Two Music, Inc. (ASCAP)
International Copyright Secured   All Rights Reserved

C.R.E.A.M. (Cash Rules Everything Around Me)
Words and Music by Gary Grice, Clifford Smith, Cory Woods, Dennis Coles, Jason Hunter,
    Lamont Hawkins, Robert F. Diggs Jr., Russell Jones, Isaac Hayes and David Porter
Copyright © 1993 by BMG Songs, Inc., Careers-BMG Music Publishing, Inc.,
    Wu-Tang Publishing and Irving Music, Inc.
All Rights for Wu-Tang Publishing Administered by Careers-BMG Music Publishing, Inc.
International Copyright Secured   All Rights Reserved

California Love (Remix)
Words and Music by Larry Troutman, Roger Troutman, Woody Cunningham, Norman Durham,
    Ronnie Hudson and Mikel Hooks
Copyright © 1996 Sony/ATV Tunes LLC, H & R Lastrada Music, Saja Music, Embassy Music Corp.,
    Stonsee Music and Songs Of Lastrada
All Rights on behalf of Sony/ATV Tunes LLC and H & R Lastrada Music Administered by
    Sony/ATV Music Publishing, 8 Music Square West, Nashville, TN 37203
International Copyright Secured   All Rights Reserved
-contains elements of "So Ruff, So Tuff" and "Intimate Connection"

Can I Get A...
Words and Music by Shawn Carter, Irving Lorenzo, Jeffrey Atkins and Rob Mays
© 1998 EMI BLACKWOOD MUSIC INC., LIL LULU PUBLISHING, DJ IRV PUBLISHING,
    6 MO SHOTS MUSIC and JA MUSIC
All Rights for LIL LULU PUBLISHING Controlled and Administered by EMI BLACKWOOD MUSIC INC.
All Rights for DJ IRV PUBLISHING and 6 MO SHOTS MUSIC Administered by ENSIGN MUSIC CORPORATION
All Rights Reserved   International Copyright Secured   Used by Permission

Can't Nobody Hold Me Down
Words and Music by C. Chase, E. Fletcher, Greg Prestopino, Mashion Myriak, Mason Betha,
    Matthew Wilder, S. Robinson, Steve Jordan, M. Glover and Sean Combs
© 1997 BUCHU MUSIC (ASCAP)/Administered by BUG MUSIC, NO EARS MUSIC,
    WILDER KINGDOM MUSIC and SUGAR HILL MUSIC
All Rights Reserved   Used by Permission

Cantaloop (Flip Fantasia)
Words and Music by Mel Simpson, Geoff Wilkinson, Rahsaan Kelly and Herbie Hancock
© 1991 EMI BLACKWOOD MUSIC INC., US-3 MUSIC and HERBIE HANCOCK MUSIC
All Rights for US-3 MUSIC Controlled and Administered by EMI BLACKWOOD MUSIC INC.
All Rights Reserved   International Copyright Secured   Used by Permission

Funkdafied
Words and Music by Jermaine Dupri, Shawntae Harris, O'Kelly Isley, Ronald Isley, Rudolph Isley,
    Ernie Isley, Marvin Isley and Chris Jasper
© 1994 EMI APRIL MUSIC INC., SO SO DEF MUSIC, BOVINA MUSIC INC., AIR CONTROL MUSIC and
    THOWIN' TANTRUMS MUSIC
All Rights Controlled and Administered by EMI APRIL MUSIC INC.
All Rights Reserved   International Copyright Secured   Used by Permission
-contains elements of "Between the Sheets"

Funky Cold Medina
Words and Music by Matt Dike, Marvin Young and Michael Ross
Copyright © 1989 Varry White Music, Inc., EX VW Music and Loc'd Out Music
All Rights for Varry White Music, Inc. Administered by Spirit Two Music, Inc. (ASCAP)
International Copyright Secured   All Rights Reserved

G'd Up
Words and Music by Cordozar C. Broadus, Tracy La Marr Davis, Keiwan Dashawn Spillman and
    Danny Elliott Means
© 2000 EMI BLACKWOOD MUSIC INC., EMI APRIL MUSIC INC., MY OWN CHIT MUSIC,
    BLACK FOUNTAIN PUBLISHING, SHOW YOU HOW DADDY BALL MUSIC, TRAY TRAY'S MUSIC,
    GOLD L'S MUSIC and MEAN FAMILY PUBLISHING
All Rights for MY OWN CHIT MUSIC Controlled and Administered by EMI BLACKWOOD MUSIC INC.
All Rights for BLACK FOUNTAIN PUBLISHING and SHOW YOU HOW DADDY BALL MUSIC Controlled and
    Administered by EMI APRIL MUSIC INC.
All Rights Reserved   International Copyright Secured   Used by Permission

Gangsta's Paradise
Words and Music by Stevie Wonder, Doug Rasheed, Artis Ivey and Larry Sanders
© 1995 JOBETE MUSIC CO., INC., BLACK BULL MUSIC, UNIVERSAL - SONGS OF POLYGRAM
    INTERNATIONAL, INC., MADCASTLE MUZIC, T-BOY MUSIC PUBLISHING, INC.,
    BOO-DADDY MUSIC, 2 FARGONE MUSIC and LARGE VARIETY MUSIC
All Rights Reserved   International Copyright Secured   Used by Permission
- contains elements of "Pastime Paradise" by Stevie Wonder/Jobete Music Co., Inc. and
    Black Bull Music c/o EMI April Music Inc.

Get Money
Words and Music by Christopher Wallace, Kimberly Jones, Roy Ayers, Sylvia Striplin and B. Bedford
© 1995 EMI APRIL MUSIC INC., JUSTIN COMBS PUBLISHING, BIG POPPA MUSIC,
    UNDEAS MUSIC INC. and CHRYSALIS MUSIC
All Rights for JUSTIN COMBS PUBLISHING and BIG POPPA MUSIC Controlled and Administered by
    EMI APRIL MUSIC INC.
All Rights Reserved   International Copyright Secured   Used by Permission
-contains elements of "You Can't Turn Me Away"

Gettin' Jiggy wit It
Words and Music by Nile Rodgers, Bernard Edwards, Will Smith, Samuel J. Barnes and J. Robinson
Copyright © 1997 Sony/ATV Songs LLC, Warner-Tamerlane Publishing Corp., Bernard's Other Music,
    Treyball Music, Slam U Well Music and Jelly's Jams, L.L.C.
All Rights on behalf of Sony/ATV Songs LLC Administered by Sony/ATV Music Publishing,
    8 Music Square West, Nashville, TN 37203
International Copyright Secured   All Rights Reserved
-contains a sample of "He's the Greatest Dancer" written by Nile Rodgers and Bernard Edwards.
    Copyright © 1978 Sony/ATV Songs LLC, Warner-Tamerlane Publishing Corp. and
    Bernard's Other Music

Ghetto Heaven
Words and Music by Peter Lord, Sandra Kay St. Victor and Jeffrey Vernon Smith
© 1990 EMI APRIL MUSIC INC., LEOSUN MUSIC, MAANAMI MUSIC, EMI BLACKWOOD MUSIC INC.
    and VERMAL MUSIC
All Rights for LEOSUN MUSIC and MAANAMI MUSIC Controlled and Administered by
    EMI APRIL MUSIC INC.
All Rights for VERMAL MUSIC Controlled and Administered by EMI BLACKWOOD MUSIC INC.
All Rights Reserved   International Copyright Secured   Used by Permission

Ghetto Is a Struggle
Words and Music by Albert Joseph Brown III and Kyle Albert West
© 1999 EMI APRIL MUSIC INC. and ACROSS 110TH ST. PUBLISHING
All Rights Controlled and Administered by EMI APRIL MUSIC INC.
All Rights Reserved   International Copyright Secured   Used by Permission

Ghetto Love
Words and Music by Shawntae Harris, Eldra DeBarge, Betty Wright, Carlton Ridenhour and Hank Schocklee
© 1996 EMI APRIL MUSIC INC., AIR CONTROL MUSIC, THOWIN' TANTRUMS MUSIC,
    JOBETE MUSIC CO., INC. and SONGS OF UNIVERSAL, INC.
All Rights for AIR CONTROL MUSIC, THOWIN' TANTRUMS MUSIC and JOBETE MUSIC CO., INC.
    Controlled and Administered by EMI APRIL MUSIC INC.
All Rights Reserved   International Copyright Secured   Used by Permission

Ghetto Supastar (That Is What You Are)
Words and Music by Barry Alan Gibb, Maurice Ernest Gibb, Robin Hugh Gibb, James Brown,
    Russell Jones, Ronald Lenhoff, Samuel Michel, Nel Jean and Bobby Byrd
Copyright © 1998 by Gibb Brothers Music, Unichappell Music Inc., TCF Music Publishing, Inc.,
    Warner-Tamerlane Publishing Corp., Sony/ATV Tunes LLC, Tete San Ko Publishing,
    Huss-Zwingli Publishing, Inc., Wu-Tang Publishing and Crited Music
All Rights for Gibb Brothers Music Administered by Careers-BMG Music Publishing, Inc.
All Rights for Sony/ATV Tunes LLC, Tete San Ko Publishing and Huss-Zwingli Publishing, Inc.
    Administered by Sony/ATV Music Publishing, 8 Music Square West, Nashville, TN 37203
International Copyright Secured   All Rights Reserved

Gin and Juice
Words and Music by Harry Wayne Casey, Richard Finch, Cordozar Broadus, Andre Young,
    Steve Arrington, Steve Washington, Raymond Turner, Daniel Webster and Mark Adams
© 1992 EMI LONGITUDE MUSIC, WB MUSIC CORP., SUGE PUBLISHING, HARRICK MUSIC,
    WARNER-TAMERLANE PUBLISHING CORP., COTILLION MUSIC and SONY/ATV TUNES LLC.
All Rights on behalf of SONY/ATV TUNES LLC Administered by SONY/ATV MUSIC PUBLISHING,
    8 Music Square West, Nashville, TN 37203
All Rights Reserved   International Copyright Secured   Used by Permission

Girls Ain't Nothing but Trouble
Words and Music by Hugh Montenegro, Buddy Kaye, Williard C. Smith and Jeffrey Townes
© 1986, 1987 COLGEMS-EMI MUSIC INC., ZOMBA ENTERPRISES INC. and
    JAZZY JEFF & THE FRESH PRINCE
All Rights Reserved   International Copyright Secured   Used by Permission
-contains elements of "Jeannie" by Hugo Montenegro and Buddy Kaye

Give It 2 Ya
Words and Music by Jermaine Dupri and Chris Kelly
© 1994 EMI APRIL MUSIC INC., SO SO DEF MUSIC and MY WORLD MUSIC
All Rights for SO SO DEF MUSIC Controlled and Administered by EMI APRIL MUSIC INC.
All Rights Reserved   International Copyright Secured   Used by Permission

Going Back to Cali
Words and Music by Christopher Wallace, Osten Harvey and Roger Troutman
© 1997 EMI APRIL MUSIC INC., JUSTIN COMBS PUBLISHING COMPANY, INC.,
    BIG POPPA MUSIC, BEE MO EASY MUSIC, UNIVERSAL - SONGS OF POLYGRAM
    INTERNATIONAL, INC. and SAJA MUSIC CO.
All Rights for JUSTIN COMBS PUBLISHING COMPANY, INC., BIG POPPA MUSIC and
    BEE MO EASY MUSIC Controlled and Administered by EMI APRIL MUSIC INC.
All Rights Reserved   International Copyright Secured   Used by Permission
-contains elements of "More Bounce to the Ounce"

Gone Till November
Words and Music by Wyclef Jean
Copyright © 1997 Sony/ATV Tunes LLC and Tete San Ko Publishing
All Rights Administered by Sony/ATV Music Publishing, 8 Music Square West, Nashville, TN 37203
International Copyright Secured   All Rights Reserved

Got Me Waiting
Words and Music by Dwight Myers, Luther Vandross and Peter Phillips
© 1994 EMI APRIL MUSIC INC., E-Z-DUZ-IT PUBLISHING, UNCLE RONNIE'S MUSIC and
    PETE ROCK PUBLISHING
All Rights for E-Z-DUZ-IT PUBLISHING and UNCLE RONNIE'S MUSIC Controlled and
    Administered by EMI APRIL MUSIC INC.
All Rights Reserved   International Copyright Secured   Used by Permission

Hot in Herre
Words and Music by Pharrell L. Williams, Cornelius Haynes and Charles L. Brown
© 2002 EMI BLACKWOOD MUSIC INC., WATERS OF NAZARETH, BMG SONGS, INC.,
    JACKIE FROST MUSIC, SWING T PUBLISHING, ASCENT MUSIC INC. and
    NOUVEAU MUSIC COMPANY
All Rights for WATERS OF NAZARETH Controlled and Administered by EMI BLACKWOOD MUSIC INC.
All Rights for JACKIE FROST MUSIC Administered by BMG SONGS, INC.
All Rights Reserved   International Copyright Secured   Used by Permission

Hot Shit (Country Grammar Hot Shit)
Words and Music by Cornell Haynes and Jason Epperson
Copyright © 2000 by BMG Songs, Inc., Jackie Frost Music, Universal Music Corp., Jay E's Basement
    and D2 Pro Publishing
All Rights for Jackie Frost Music Administered by BMG Songs, Inc.
All Rights for Jay E's Basement and D2 Pro Publishing Controlled and Administered by
    Universal Music Corp.
International Copyright Secured   All Rights Reserved

How Do U Want It
Words and Music by Bruce Fisher, Leon Ware, Stanley Richardson, Quincy Jones, Tupac Shakur and
    Johnny Jackson
Copyright © 1998 ALMO MUSIC CORP., QUICKSAND MUSIC CO., SONGS OF UNIVERSAL, INC.,
    JOSHUA'S DREAM MUSIC, BMG SONGS, INC. and BLACK-HISPANIC MUSIC
All Rights for QUICKSAND MUSIC CO. Controlled and Administered by ALMO MUSIC CORP.
All Rights Reserved   Used by Permission

How High
Words and Music by Reggie Noble, Erick Sermon and Clifford Smith
Copyright © 1995 by Famous Music Corporation, Funky Noble Productions,
    Careers-BMG Music Publishing, Inc., Wu-Tang Publishing, Zomba Enterprises Inc. and
    Erick Sermon Enterprises Inc.
All Rights for Funky Noble Productions Administered by Famous Music Corporation
All Rights for Wu-Tang Publishing Administered by Careers-BMG Music Publishing, Inc.
International Copyright Secured   All Rights Reserved

Hypnotize
Words and Music by Sean "Puffy" Combs, Notorious B.I.G., Deric Angelettie, Ronald Anthony Lawrence,
    Ron Badazz and Andy Armer
© 1997 EMI APRIL MUSIC INC., JUSTIN COMBS PUBLISHING COMPANY, INC., BIG POPPA MUSIC,
    EMI BLACKWOOD MUSIC INC., DERIC ANGELETTIE MUSIC, MYSTERY SYSTEM MUSIC,
    CAREERS-BMG MUSIC PUBLISHING, INC., AUSAR MUSIC, ALMO MUSIC CORP. and
    BADAZZ MUSIC CO.
All Rights for JUSTIN COMBS PUBLISHING COMPANY, INC. and BIG POPPA MUSIC Controlled and
    Administered by EMI APRIL MUSIC INC.
All Rights for DERIC ANGELETTIE MUSIC Controlled and Administered by EMI BLACKWOOD MUSIC INC.
All Rights for AUSAR MUSIC Administered by CAREERS-BMG MUSIC PUBLISHING, INC.
All Rights for BADAZZ MUSIC CO. Controlled and Administered by ALMO MUSIC CORP.
All Rights Reserved   International Copyright Secured   Used by Permission
-contains elements of "Rise." Also contains elements of "La Di Da Di" by Slick Rick/Danica Music

I Cry
Words and Music by Jeffrey Atkins, Kenneth Gamble, Irving Lorenzo, Cynthia Loving and Robert Mays
Copyright © 2000 by Ensign Music Corporation, DJ Irv Publishing, 6 Mo Shots Music,
    Warner-Tamerlane Publishing Corp. and Mo Loving Music
All Rights for DJ Irv Publishing and 6 Mo Shots Music Administered by Ensign Music Corporation
International Copyright Secured   All Rights Reserved

I Get Around
Words and Music by Roger Troutman, Larry Troutman, Shirley Murdock, Ron Brooks, Tupac Shakur and
    Gregory Jacobs
Copyright © 1995 Sony/ATV Songs LLC, Songs Of Lastrada, Saja Music, Styleetron Music,
    Songs Of Universal, Inc., Joshua's Dream, Zomba Enterprises Inc. and GLG II Music
All Rights on behalf of Sony/ATV Songs LLC and Songs Of Lastrada Administered by
    Sony/ATV Music Publishing, 8 Music Square West, Nashville, TN 37203
International Copyright Secured   All Rights Reserved
-contains elements of "Computer Love"